THE MYTH OF POWER AND THE SELF

•

ESSAYS ON

FRANZ KAFKA

Kritik: German Literary Theory and Cultural Studies

Liliane Weissberg, Editor

A complete listing of the books in this series can be found at the back of this volume.

THE MYTH OF POWER AND THE SELF

•

ESSAYS ON FRANZ KAFKA

WALTER H. SOKEL

Wayne State University Press
DETROIT

Library of Congress Control Number 2001135957

ISBN 0-8143-2608-0 (alk. paper)

CONTENTS

ACKNOWLEDGMENTS

My special thanks go out to Professor Liliane Weissberg for her enthusiastic reception of the idea of this volume, her invaluable advice, and her indefatigable prodding of a sometimes quite dilatory author in the furtherance of a shared goal; and to Arthur B. Evans, director and editor of Wayne State University Press, for his highly appreciated helpfulness, care, and at times needful voice of conscience in hastening to bring this volume into existence. I likewise wish to express deeply felt gratitude to Professor Ernst Behler, whose tragically early passing our whole profession mourns, and to Professor James Rolleston for their heartening encouragement of the publication of this volume. I want to acknowledge my special gratitude to Dr. Jennifer Geddes for her invaluable assistance in preparing the index. My wife, Jacqueline, has been a constant and essential support, a provider of the free time that has made this work possible as well as a vitally important, untiring, and critical listener to and first reader of each of the essays assembled here. Last but not least, I wish to thank the students of the Kafka seminars I gave at Stanford University and the University of Virginia from whose papers and dialogues I received stimulating insights without which the readings of Kafka gathered here would not have received the form in which they appear. To them I dedicate this book.

Grateful acknowledgments for permissions to republish essays in this volume are due to: Columbia University Press for *Franz Kafka: Essays on Modern Writers; Modern Austrian Literature* for "Kafka's Poetics of the Inner Self"; *The German Quarterly* for "Language and Truth in the Two Worlds of Franz Kafka"; Holt, Rinehart and Winston for "Freud and the Magic of Kafka's Writing" from *The World of Franz Kafka,* ed. J. P. Stern; Indiana University Press for "Kafka's Beginnings," from *Kafka and the Contemporary Critical Performance,* ed. Alan Udoff; Gordian

Press for "Perspectives and Truth in 'The Judgment'," from *The Problem of the Judgment: Eleven Approaches to Kafka's Story,* ed. Angel Flores; Barnes and Noble for "The Program of K.'s Court: Oedipal and Existential Meanings of *The Trial,*" from *On Kafka: Semi-Centenary Perspectives,* ed. Franz Kuna; Gordian Press for "The Three Endings of Josef K. and the Role of Art in *The Trial,*" from *The Kafka Debate: New Perspectives for Our Time,* ed. Angel Flores; *South Atlantic Review* for "Between Gnosticism and Jehovah: The Dilemma in Kafka's Religious Attitude."

THE MYTH OF POWER AND THE SELF

An Autobiographical Account of Reading Kafka

THIS VOLUME unites my essays on Franz Kafka written over a period of thirty-one years, from 1966 to 1997, following the publication in 1964 of my book *Tragik und Ironie* (*Tragedy and Irony*). These essays represent clarifications, elaborations, and modifications of the readings of Kafka expressed in *Tragedy and Irony* and trace the development that my thoughts on Kafka underwent in light of currents in literary criticism and cultural theory that emerged after the book was written. Because the book forms the frame of reference for these essays and provides the bond that connects them, it is useful in introducing this volume to outline the approach to Kafka that informs *Tragedy and Irony* and demonstrate in what respects my work since then has, while building on it, gone beyond it. However, *Tragedy and Irony* evolved from still earlier responses to and understandings of Kafka, long antedating its inception and reaching back to a New York summer afternoon in my twenty-fourth year, when one of Kafka's texts determined the course my future professional life was to take.

TOWARD THE MYTH

Fantastic Mimesis

The work that opened my access to Kafka was "The Metamorphosis." As I have learned since then, it is the text by Kafka that has opened his world to many other readers as well. Its impact on me was overwhelming, changing my life and determining my choice of profession. I embarked upon the study of literature, and German literature in particular, to get to know the secret of Kafka's power and for the opportunity to preoccupy myself with his writings. Through the study of the literature to which he—at least linguistically—belonged, I hoped to acquire a key to the enigma of his work.

The enormous effect that "The Metamorphosis" had on me was first of all based on identification with its main character's situation. The text literally captivated me in the sense that it kept me emotionally glued to the deplorable position of its protagonist. I suffered and agonized in Gregor's place. Suppose, I asked myself, an analogous fate should happen to me? Empirically it was inconceivable, but the persuasive magic of Kafka's story made it appear by no means certain that something like it could not happen to me or, for that matter, to anyone. Even if I would not turn literally into a bug, could I not get into the same kind of absolute isolation, turn into an object of horrendous disgust beneath even the contempt reserved for human beings? World War II was raging. Couldn't I be transformed by mutilation into a thing like Gregor? And, if not by war, by some accident or the disfiguring effects of disease? And even if the cause of quarantining might not be physical, could it not be some mental or moral lapse, or any stroke of outrageous fortune, that might make me exactly like Gregor? Horrifying uniqueness was not limited to individuals. The horror of it was its being potentially a universal condition with, for those unfortunate enough to fall victim, the sting of absolute aloneness. And was it not the fate of each one of us eventually to find her or himself cut off forever from all fellowship in the transition from life to death? Tolstoy's *The Death of Ivan Ilyich* seemed to me to be the only other narrative that came close to producing something comparable to Kafka's metamorphosis effect.

Like *The Death of Ivan Ilyich*, "The Metamorphosis" also achieved, through the reader's identification with a single victim, an enormous enlargement of the scope of empathetic sensitivity toward all human beings. Going beyond *Ivan Ilyich*, however, Kafka's text had the effect upon me of extending sympathy and solidarity in suffering to life beyond the human species. A human being had been changed into a specimen of vermin. Might not the huge cockroach I chanced upon in an upper Manhattan bathroom be a creature with some feeling, some sensibility? Might it not by some inexplicable fluke be sheltering another traveling salesman or former clerk, another Gregor Samsa? Or at least a being not totally unlike myself? Kafka's fiction gave such horrendously persuasive testimony to the possibility that it took me quite a while after the reading to gather enough insensitivity to get rid of cockroaches again.

For Northrop Frye, as I was to learn not long thereafter, identification with a fictional character was the distinguishing sign of the effect of mimesis in literature. For Aristotle, mimesis was the essence of art. Teaching

Aristotle's *Poetics* several years after my first soul-shaking encounter with Kafka's story made me better understand that experience and place it in a cultural context. Kafka's tale seemed to me a prime example of mimetic art, and it produced the effect of tragedy. More than any other story, it was the text that had made me identify with the abysmal suffering depicted in it, and it engendered in me the emotions of fear and pity ascribed by Aristotle to tragedy—pity for poor, lonely Gregor and fear for myself if somehow his fate should also become mine. Despite the grotesque singularity of this fate, there radiated a deeply disquieting universality from the life that Kafka portrayed. What went on in his work concerned me with terrifying urgency, and I felt that it would equally concern anyone else who allowed himself to be opened by and drawn into its magnetic power.

Kafka's tale seemed to encompass the whole spectrum of mimesis, combining what Northrop Frye was to distinguish as high and low mimesis. It was mimesis at its highest because it moved on a level of identification that Aristotle understood as tragic, and it was low mimesis because it presented tragedy in a modern petty-bourgeois milieu peopled by banal characters. Its hero one could pity, but not admire, and the supporting cast of characters aroused one's indignation by their callous and brutal self-centeredness in the face of their family member's unimaginable plight. Yet their behavior was quite understandable if one's expectations of human beings was correspondingly low.

Yet, while "The Metamorphosis" was the consummation of mimetic art, it was also mimetic art's opposite. Its plot derived from and was predicated on an utterly improbable, indeed a fantastic, event. Tzvetan Todorov employs "The Metamorphosis" as his prototypal instance of fantastic literature, distinguishing it from the marvelous. The marvelous, the realm of fairytale and mythology, is set completely apart from everyday empirical reality and consistently deviates from its rules. The fantastic, by contrast, presents the penetration of empirical reality by an enigmatic event that remains unexplained but might eventually find either a natural or a supernatural explanation. A text remains fantastic as long as the case remains undecided and the explanation is withheld. That, I felt, was precisely the case in "The Metamorphosis." The text began with an eruption of the fantastic—Todorov's definition of the term was, of course, unknown to me at the time—into an everyday world, and the mysterious event remained unexplained in the story and continued to puzzle and haunt the reader forever. Todorov speaks of a naturalization of the fantastic in Kafka's story as the realistic representation of the hero's psyche, through which the behavior of the other characters makes us tend to lose sight of the fantastic nature of the whole. But that never happened in my reading. I could not cease to be perplexed, to wonder, and to speculate on the possible causes of Gregor's miraculous transformation and never, while reading, gave up entirely the hope that an explanation might be forthcoming. Whatever it might be, it would with enlightenment bring consolation and, in a sense, redemption. Enlightenment, of course, never came. The story remains, in our ordinary as well as in Todorov's sense of the term, fantastic. I saw, however, that it was not the fantastic event as such but the response of the characters to it, their total failure to ask the questions and marshal the emotions appropriate to the mystery that had entered their lives; it was their refusal to venture mentally beyond the "natural" world. In other words, it was the naturalistic, the mimetic element of the story that left the reader with that overwhelming sadness, that feeling of irredeemable loss and final defeat of life that we call tragic. By contrast, the fantastic, even though it sets the sad fate in motion, provides a glimmer of unrealized hope. It invites the hope for a countermetamorphosis, for a repeal of the disastrous eruption, or at least for an insight into the enigma. The fantastic provides the constant incentive, so strangely absent from the narrative scene itself, to continue the search, to question, to wonder, and to reflect. The fantastic activates. It functions as a countereffect to the mimetic aspect, a utopian—in the original sense of not appearing in any actual place—alternative to the saddening and depressing reality that the story depicts.

The uplifting effect of the fantastic showed itself in my initial response to the beginning of the story. It was neither terror nor commiseration but humorous amusement. I subsequently realized that the humor in Gregor's initial situation derives from the reader's still looking at him from outside or above, as he or she follows with amused detachment Gregor's bravely absurd attempts to adjust to his altered shape and go on with his life, trying to minimize what has happened to him, to "naturalize" the transnatural. The initially humorous effect of the fantastic expresses the superiority of writing to its subject, the elevated perspective writing automatically assumes toward what it writes. This enables the reader to smile at the character. In Northrop Frye's terminology, it produces irony, a mode opposed to mimesis. Instead of making him identify with the world represented in the work, irony enables the reader to feel superior to it. This humorous effect vanishes, the smile is wiped off the face, as Kafka's text turns radically mimetic, immersing the reader into the internal perspective of the narrative, the protagonist's consciousness. This effect of "freezing the laughter" by abruptly ending the reader's detachment was, I later found, also characteristic of *The Trial.* Yet, by continuing to keep alive the urge to understand, to search for the illuminating answer, the fantastic in Kafka's work continues to counterbalance the tragic effect of mimetic identification. It represents the tonic nature of the writing process, creation as distinct from its content.

I became consciously aware of the liberating function of Kafka's fantastic mode when, inspired by my discovery of "The Metamorphosis," I voraciously read all the works of Kafka on which I could lay my hands. The very short pieces especially acted upon me as a transfiguring experience, expanding, to an incredible degree, my emotional and mental horizons, pushing out of sight the boundaries of literature that had hitherto confined me to mimetic representation. The usual response of Kafka's readers—not too many at that time—who found him depressing baffled me. Yes, to be sure, sad and horrific events occurred in his stories, frustrating, defeating, and destroying his characters. Yet the effect of the whole was tonic, as exciting and invigorating as the discovery of new worlds.

I found Kafka liberating because he seemed to free us from the shackles of mimesis, the dictate that bound art to the portrayal of nature. Kafka's writing opened for me another dimension of reality in which the rules of waking life were overthrown without, however, letting us escape into the wish-fulfilling conventions of daydreams and fairytale. Kafka simply pushed back the walls that had imprisoned experience transmitted in and through literature. In Kafka, banal everyday bourgeois reality and the miraculous interpenetrated and formed a unity that mystified and gave rise to incessant emotional and mental activity. As Kafka himself had noted after having written the text of his "breakthrough," "The Judgment," his writing expanded immeasurably the scope of what was sayable, and thus significant. For that reason, Kafka appeared to be a revolutionary force of the greatest potency.

My discovery of Kafka led me to, and subsequently coalesced with, my discovery of Surrealism, Expressionism, and avant-garde art in general. Kafka thus appeared in the context of a revolution of the most encompassing ambitions, ranging from the aesthetic to the psychological, social and even political realm, and collapsing their traditional distinctions. It was a revolt against human submission to any established reality. Even though it had failed in historical actuality and been superseded by worldwide reaction and the relapse into bourgeois "normality," or even worse, had to see its aspirations perverted into the "antibourgeois" tyrannies of Fascism, Nazism, and Stalinism, it nonetheless retained for me, its sadly belated convert, the promise of a resurrection and rebirth. The attempt to explore and to understand Kafka, and the avant-garde Expressionism in which I saw him situated, formed for me an access to this promise.

Kafka's initial effect on my life was activating in a twofold way. He acted upon me as a writer as well as a reader. Under Kafka's immediate spell, I produced a flood of short stories and novellas, each based on a dream of the preceding night. I jotted them down rapidly and spontaneously, writing without plan and outline, as Kafka himself had written "The Judgment," as he reports in his diary, in one uninterrupted sitting. I, too, used my few spare hours of late evenings and nights to write these stories and entitled the volume they eventually formed "Out of the World Night," alluding with it to their source in my dreams, to the nocturnal hours of their composition, and the nightmarish look history had assumed at the time—the middle of the Second World War—when the fate of civilization hung in the balance. Contemporary reality seemed bent on imitating Kafka in a gruesome way.

Kafka's effect on me as a reader was more lasting in my life, however, since the compulsive need of seeking to understand him led to my choice of profession—one that would give me the opportunity to pursue this need. In my interpretive quest, the dreamlike or oneiric element in his writing provided my point of departure.

Oneiric Functionalism

As a native of the city of Freud, I found it natural to use the author of the classic text of dream interpretation as the first guide in my quest to understand and interpret Kafka's work that fascinated me on account of its dreamlike quality. Kafka himself, as I read in his diary, had found thinking of Freud quite "natural" when composing the work of his "breakthrough." Thus Freud offered himself as the first key in trying to unlock the "secret doors" to Kafka's texts. They seemed to me structured according to principles analogous to dreams as analyzed by Freud. I saw the manifest text as a disguised expression or projection of the protagonist's feelings, tendencies, and desires that were never admitted to the consciousness presented in the text. As in dreams, events appeared to occur in the external world, even though they were the dreamer's own projections. Thus they seemed bewildering and mystifying to the reader, who remained dependent on the explicit consciousness of the narrative that, like a dream, kept the forces that produced and moved the action concealed.

This view of Kafka's writing seemed to receive strong support from Friedrich Beissner's theory of the "unimental" ("einsinnige") perspective, which he saw characteristic of Kafka's narrative art. "Unimental perspective" implies that the entire content of a narrative—all events, actions, characters, and scenes represented in it—are perceived by a single consciousness, that of the protagonist. There is no omniscient narrator who allows the reader to enter the mind of any other character or who intrudes with information and opinions of his own.[1] It is through the protagonist's consciousness alone that the reader gains access to the story. As Beissner points out, the unimental perspective is also the perspective of the dreaming mind.

Beissner's notion of the unimental perspective of Kafka's works seemed to me an ideal corroboration of the dreamlike or oneiric principle that I saw structuring Kafka's fiction. In dreams, too, a single mind, the dreamer's, perceives and produces all the events and scenes that appear. All that happens is the projection of one mind, yet it appears to be occurring in a world external to that mind. Something closely analogous seemed to me to occur in Kafka's narratives. The fantastic and distorting element in them indicated that the narrated events were expressions of movements and forces in the protagonist's psyche. Yet, as in dreams, the narrative consciousness was never allowed to become explicitly aware of that. Like dreams, Kafka's narratives signified the self-alienation of the human mind. The oneiric analogy accounted for the weird distortions and fantastic happenings in Kafka's stories that mingled with and penetrated their mimetic and realistic aspects.

Kafka's narrative creations appeared to share with the oneiric text, as interpreted by Freud, a fundamental feature of all works of literary art as approached by the work-immanent school of the New Critics, then, in the 1950s, at the height of their influence. I should like to term that common element "textual functionalism," by which I understand a view of textual creations that sees the meaning of a text emerging from its structure as the interplay and interconnectedness of all its elements. The Freudian method of interpreting dreams and the work-immanent approach of the New Critics together led me back to Aristotle's *Poetics,* which sees the meaning of an epic or drama to lie in its mythos, in the entire action, and not in any individual part, such as the speeches of characters, considered in isolation. No matter how great the general significance of their content might appear to be, only the role they play in the action as a whole decides their meaning. Thus I began to look at Kafka as the creator of narrative textures whose meaning would have to be looked for in the functions of their details.

The critic who helped me most in this task was Theodor Adorno, with his pioneering essay on Kafka published in his *Prismen* (*Prisms*). Adorno turned against the religious allegorizing of Kafka that, initiated by Max Brod, had been the principal approach to Kafka until then. It equated overarching figures of his works—such as the father in "The Judgment," the Court in *The Trial,* the Castle bureaucracy in *The Castle*—with divinity. This view of Kafka had always disappointed me. I felt that its facile subordinating of Kafka to traditionally received patterns of thinking cheated us of the fascinating novelty and strange power of his work. Adorno rejected this cultural "domestication" of Kafka that reduced the unknown to the known. He rejected it on grounds that seemed to me related to the work-immanent approach to literature. Adorno held that the basic mistake of

Brod's school in its search for the meaning of Kafka's works lay in the arbitrary equation of a part of the work—for example, the Court or the Castle—with a work-external idea such as God that gets no mention in the text. Kafka's reader, he maintained, should not rush to look for the "meaning" of overarching images by translating them into cultural concepts ready at hand but external to the text. The web between Leni's fingers in *The Trial,* or the land surveyor's inability in *The Castle* to distinguish between his two "assistants," might prove much more important to the understanding of these novels than the question of the meaning of Court and Castle that offers itself to the reader right away. For Adorno meaning was not be found in a referentiality to something outside the text. Meaning could be looked for only in the interconnectedness of all the details that together formed the narrative. With that, Adorno appeared to point toward the only promising approach to understanding Kafka.

The functionalist approach to which Freud's theory of dreams, the Aristotelian New Critics, and Adorno had led me was to receive the most powerful confirmation from Kafka himself. In trying to interpret "The Judgment" for Felice, Kafka explains the figure of the protagonist's friend in Russia not as an independent, three-dimensional, mimetically conceived character, but as a function in the protagonist's relationship with his father. The friend, Kafka says, is what father and son have in common. He goes on to say that the whole story is a "tour" ("Rundgang") around this relationship. Kafka's own reading of his work thus seems to endorse a functionalist and oneiric approach, which sees characters and scenes not as mimetic representations, but as functions in the dreamlike narrative, which in turn is the projection into apparently external scenes and characters of forces and problems in the protagonist's existence.

Thus Kafka's own reading of his work tends to support an "intrinsic" against the religious school's "extrinsic" interpretation. The intrinsic approach does not look for what a narrative text "means," but for what it tells and does. It looks for its mythos, that is, for the entire thread of represented actions, scenes, events. I understood mythos not as a synopsis that can be abstracted from the work and recounted as its "gist," but as the structure that forms a work and makes it cohere, as the entity that all textual details together produce by implicitly referring to each other. What was to be considered in seeking to understand a text was the part each textual element—character, event, scene, gesture, image, spatial and temporal reference, simile and metaphor, etc.—played in relation to all other elements that together made the texture as that by which a text manifests itself. That was for me the "intrinsic meaning" of a work.

In my first publication on Kafka, "Kafka's *Metamorphosis:* Rebellion and Punishment" (1956), I inquired into the function of Gregor's transformation in the narrative. I examined its relationship to a textual detail, Gregor's narrated monologue near the beginning of the story, that conveyed his feelings toward his job and its connection with his father's debt to Gregor's firm. I concluded that Gregor's metamorphosis functions as the accommodation and union of two contradictory impulses in a single event and image—rebellion and simultaneous punishment for it. Through the investigation of the narrative function of a central detail of the text, the representation of ambivalence emerged for me as a basic meaning of Kafka's writing that also accounted for its dreamlike effect.

Kafka's works shared with dreams, as Freud had taught us to see them, a dual nature. Like dreams they had a liberating function—they gave expression to socially forbidden feelings and thoughts. However, again like dreams, they also had a censoring, concealing, and thus repressive side that made the rebellion they tried to express unrecognizable to consciousness. By the same expressive activity by which they sought to give shape to revolt against patriarchal authority, they sought to cancel this revolt, camouflaging its meaning and compromising rebellious impulse with the gesture of submission. By the same signifying act with which Kafka's writing assaulted and provoked authority, it reinstated it and restored it to its ruling place. The very nature of the fantastic in Kafka that before, in the context of the avant-garde cultural revolution, I had seen only as emancipating, I now recognized as consisting, to an equal degree, of self-censoring repression. Self-subjection to patriarchal power would become an extremely important factor in my further reflections on Kafka.

Kafka's life-documents, his diaries, and especially his "Letter to His Father" contained the most profound ambivalence toward authority in general and paternal authority in particular. They also gave voice to the most severe self-doubts and the most bitter self-accusations and -condemnations, rarely rivaled in the literature of autobiography. Worship of his father, the prototypal authority figure of his life, alternated with a deeply rebellious and ironically, and even satirically, critical stance. Kafka appeared to me to be understandable only if these two opposite sides were equally taken into account. Thus years later, I could not agree with Deleuze's influential reading of Kafka that, in the spirit of the late 1960s, extols Kafka as a master of rebellious subversion, while ignoring or downplaying the self-punishing and worshipfully submissive aspect of his life as well as his art. Omitting that side of his work could not, I felt, do justice to its fundamental complexity.

Oneiric functionalism and close attention to ambivalence and ambiguity—especially toward the patriarchal power figure that, as the antagonistic force in it, dominates Kafka's work—guided me through the writing of *Tragik und Ironie* (*Tragedy and Irony*) (1964).

THE MYTH

Tragedy and Irony emerged from an inquiry into the narrative function of women in Kafka's total oeuvre. What brought me to it was the crucial role I saw women play in Kafka's life-documents—his diaries and letters. His letters to two women, Felice and Milena, fill volumes that rank among the most remarkable epistolary literature of all time. That is only one example attesting to the decided importance of woman in Kafka's world.

With the question of the function of Kafka's fictional women in mind, I proceeded to investigate all relevant fictional texts, comparing them with each other. In the course of this undertaking I came to realize the amazing degree of inner unity, interconnectedness, and dense cross-referentiality of all his works. They seemed to form a kind of mega- or meta-text that I began to see as a kind of myth, or rather a mythos or supernarrative, with numerous fascinating variations and a decided development. Kafka's myth appeared as a developing unity in rich diversity.

The content of Kafka's myth coincided with the title of his earliest extensive narrative, "Description of a Struggle." I saw the myth describing or enacting a threefold conflict—a combat within the self, the protagonist-persona of Kafka's fiction, and a struggle of each half of the divided self with the supreme antagonist of Kafka's myth, a patriarchal power figure.

In my realization of the fundamental oneness of Kafka's work, in which its character as a myth resided, Wilhelm Emrich's monumental *Franz Kafka* (1958) inspired me. I found the basic thesis of Emrich's work freighted with the baggage of German Idealism and much too abstractly philosophical to be relevant to Kafka. Emrich's metaphysical preoccupation completely ignored the biographical and psychological roots of Kafka's work as well as, in the broadest sense, its political dimension, given the essential part power and power struggles played in it. Emrich ignored the close relation of Kafka's work to, on the one hand, everyday existence and, on the other, the realm of the unconscious and the dream. Emrich's Kafka was too theoretical, in a German Idealist way, to be recognizable in the author I had experienced. Kafka's life-documents told a story that had nothing to do with Emrich's construction of him as the hidden prophet of Hegel's Universal that was fragmented and lost in a modern world, aware only of the particular. The complete omission of the text Kafka considered his most important, "The Judgment," from Emrich's discussion of Kafka's opus appeared to me symptomatic of his tendency to miss what was essential in Kafka. Emrich seemed to me to substitute the Idea of German Idealism for God that Brod's school had, albeit with considerably greater justification, interpolated into Kafka's fictional universe.

Emrich, however, was extremely helpful in making a mythos appear the unifier of Kafka's bewildering work. He superbly showed the interconnectedness of Kafka's texts and the need to approach his opus intertextually within its own parameters. He succeeded in attuning Kafka's reader to the teeming and often extremely subtle cross-references among Kafka's texts that made them into a meta-text. The links among the texts are objects, characters, actions, gestures, spatial references, images occurring in them that function not like allegories or symbols pointing to text-extrinsic domains, but as allusive signs with special meanings largely restricted to Kafka's work.[2] They make for a coherence of Kafka's total opus that is both structural and thematic.

Through the examination of the narrative function of women figures in Kafka's works, the fundamental conflicts that I have mentioned came into view as the theme of Kafka's myth. The struggle between the ascetic bachelor and the worldly self appears, in its earliest version, "Description of a Struggle," initially at least, between two independent characters. However, by the oddness and fantastic nature of their behavior and discourse, the text soon hints at their actually emanating from a single self divided within itself. In this earliest phase of the struggle, the ascetic bachelor self is the I-narrator of the story. For that reason, I called this prototype of an ever-recurring figure in Kafka's myth the "pure self," with the dual meaning of "pure" in mind as signifying both the chastity and the fundamental authenticity of that aspect of the self. The action shows the pure self's effort to undermine the self-confidence of the worldly, "engaged" self and win him over to his own withdrawn and solitary way of life. He finally drives the other to an act of symbolic self-destruction.[3]

In the text of what Kafka called his "breakthrough," "The Judgment," the paternal power figure enters the struggle of the selves. The power figure is here literally the father of the—likewise literally—engaged self, the son as the father's ostensibly successful rival and successor, about to marry and found a household of his own. In this second phase of the struggle between the pure and the engaged self, described by Kafka's myth, the role of protagonist and perceiving consciousness of the story has shifted from the pure-self figure to the engaged self. The latter has entered a second struggle that it wages against the paternal power figure. The protagonist, in the literal sense of the hero fighting in an agon of wills, seeks to take the father's place in a conflict that has the features of a classical Freudian Oedipal struggle. In it, the pure-self figure, Georg Bendemann's estranged childhood friend who has exiled himself to Russia, functions as the father's ally against the hero—according to the father's version of events, which is the only one the reader gets. With the friend's help, the father defeats the worldly self and drives it to self-destruction.

In "The Judgment," the bachelor self still seems to be an independent, apparently mimetically conceived character. Upon close reading, however, it appears to embody a repressed aspect of the protagonist.[4] The combined attack of father and pure-self figure functions as the projection of an internal conflict in the protagonist's self, a self-repudiation of the self's engagement and adulthood. This actual nature of the conflict, however, never becomes explicit and articulated. It reveals itself only in the strange dreamlike sequence of actions and events. The father's surprising and puzzling verbal assault on his son triggers only apparently the latter's self-liquidation. It is the hero himself who indirectly, by action, gesture, and subtext of his discourse, asks for the father's judgment of his engagement, which represents his maturing and emancipation. And in the end, it is the self alone that carries out its "punishment."

This internalization of the three-cornered battle between worldly self, paternal power figure, and pure self is complete in the two tales of punishment following "The Judgment"—"The Metamorphosis" and *The Trial.* In these texts the struggle between the two selves appears totally interiorized. It is a ferocious battle within a single character between self-assertion and humiliating self-destruction, the latter winning out over the former.[5]

In the destruction of the self-assertive hero in Kafka's tales of punishment, the repressed truth of the hero plays the decisive role. There is in the protagonist a hidden longing to be rid of the adult self, to return to a childlike "innocence," to surrender to and be reunited with the power figure as the self's origin. As that is impossible, nonbeing is preferable to being. Because this tendency, which in *Tragedy and Irony* I called the "true self," operates so powerfully on the deepest level of the protagonist's being, never acknowledged by his consciousness, his apparently worldly self so readily cooperates and brings about, or helps in bringing about, its own destruction. The deepest, long-repressed but ultimately effective wish of the protagonists of Kafka's tales of direct and indirect self-destruction is, even as in Nietzsche's view of Dionysian tragedy, the repeal of the individuated self.[6]

This deepest and "true," i.e., ultimately effective and prevailing, tendency in the protagonist remains excluded from articulated acknowledgment. It erupts, as a "return of the repressed," against the protagonist's consciousness, which it subverts and destroys. Since these texts are structured on a unimental perspective, namely the protagonist's consciousness, the reader has no other possibility but to identify with it. Thus the turn of events perplexes and dumbfounds the reader who shares in the protagonist's defeat. The seemingly groundless, unjust, and irrational attack upon and final destruction of the protagonist also assault, shake, and utterly bewilder the reader's rationality and assail its self-confidence. In that way, the text undermines and subverts the principle of reason, consciousness, and selfhood as such in the reader as well as in the character.

There exists a subtle but very important difference between the truth of the self, which aims to undo and dissolve the self, and the ascetic or pure-self figure of Kafka's work. For the latter embodies self-assertion greater even than that of the worldly self. A way toward understanding that difference is offered by the poetics as sketched in Kafka's "Letter to His Father." There Kafka gives two mutually contradictory accounts of the motivations underlying his writing. On the one side, writing is all about his father. It is the paltry substitute for his father's presence, for the closeness that has been denied to the son. In writing, Kafka avers, he voices the lament that he is not permitted to confide at his father's breast. Writing functions as a substitute for living. It gives voice to absence, to the gap left by the vanishing of what the heart craves. Writing is mourning of a loss; it is a veiled appeal for a restitution that will never come, expressing the longing for the impossible return of parental grace. As implied in this poetics, the writer's adult self will always be the obstacle to that reunion. However, as the writer's adult self blocks the return, writing as an activity and a process may at least indicate the direction where an unblocking might occur. Writing acts as a symbolic substitution for the dissolution of the obstacle that is the self.[7] My reading of "The Judgment," the text in which Kafka considered that his "breakthrough" to his most authentic form of writing had occurred, sees it as the enactment of the poetics contained in this passage of Kafka's "Letter to His Father." Writing, in this sense, is the locus of what I had called the "true self."

According to another passage in the same document, however, writing for Kafka has a purpose exactly opposite to the one just described. Writing, Kafka maintains here, is his flight from his father, the refuge and sole hiding place on earth where his father's power cannot reach. In the writer as one fleeing from the patriarchal sphere, I saw the prototype of what I called the ascetic or pure-self figure of Kafka's myth, most strikingly exemplified by Georg Bendemann's childhood "friend" who had "virtually fled" their common place of origin to a bachelor's existence in distant Russia. As the father figure becomes broadened and universalized in Kafka's work into patriarchal authority in general, and finally collectivized as family, community, people, species, and ultimately procreative life, nature, and indeed physical reality as a whole, the pure-self figure's flight from paternal power turns into a flight from life, nature, and empirical reality.

Flight, too, is a kind of self-assertion as it seeks to save the self from the reach of paternal power. In this self-preserving movement, the self discovers a power of its own, totally different, to be sure, from the nature-given power of the father figure, and potentially superior to it. In the poetics of flight, writing is not a mourning over absence and loss, but the base for a defiant self-aggrandizement.

Self-elevation and -aggrandizement mark the pure-self figure of Kafka's myth from the Ego's exercise of magical capabilities in "Description of a Struggle" to the "singing" mouse Josefine's insistence on her special status, which should exempt her from the communal duties all members of the people have to assume. Unlike the worldly self, the pure self does not seek to supplant the father figure in its own domain. Instead it asserts its apartness, its absolute uniqueness, its difference from and superiority to that domain. Thus an arena of enormous conflict opens up, the combat of the absolute self against the power of natural and collective life.

However, this struggle involves no violence, since, unlike the worldly self, the pure self does not aim at displacing the power figure. In consequence there is in this combat no destruction of the self. The pure self is frustrated and denied in its ambition, but it is not killed. Irony replaces tragedy in the later phase of Kafka's work. The pure-self protagonists of Kafka's late fiction are not internally divided. They are fanatically unified, merged with the quest they single-mindedly and doggedly pursue. (One of their number is indeed a canine investigator.) Their identity is one with the claim they tenaciously uphold.

This claim or demand might have as its content recognition for a unique achievement or an extraordinary talent such as indefinite fasting ("A Hunger Artist") or producing music in a species in which such a capacity is deemed unique ("Josefine"). Or it might consist of a professional call for doing some special work (*The Castle*). Or it might be a unique distinction supposedly conferred upon one ("Investigations of a Dog"). It might be the possession of the correct interpretation of a societal procedure (*In the Penal Colony*) or a "right" one believes is his ("Before the Law"). The claim sets the pure self apart and pits it against the world that surrounds it, and, in that sense, the pure-self protagonists of Kafka's myth resemble, or rather caricature, the "absolute individual" of Kierkegaard's *Fear and Trembling*. They are Quixotic versions of Kierkegaard's Abraham. The demand of the pure-self figures usually relates to some form of "art," as in "A Hunger Artist" and "Josefine," or to a mission based on a skill and a calling, as in the case of the land surveyor of *The Castle,* or to some magical power with which the protagonist believes himself endowed, as in "Description of a Struggle" and "Investigations of a Dog." These very special "abilities" claimed by Kafka's protagonists point to their function as metaphoric significations of Kafka's self-image as a writer with very special powers and consequently very special requirements, which his *Letters to Felice* as well as his diaries make vividly clear.[8] The pure-self figures also share with the image of their author, as represented in his life-documents, a certain "fussiness," a compulsive concern with dietary "purity," as in "Jackals and Arabs," or unending fasting, as in "A Hunger Artist" and "Investigations of a Dog." The striking parallels between Kafka's self-representation as a very special kind of writer, fanatically devoted to and consisting of nothing but literature, and the pure-self figures' claimed or demonstrated extrahuman achievements and magical powers, which make them creatures *sui generis,* reveal the close kinship of the protagonists of Kafka's late works to their creator.[9]

The pure-self figure's claim receives no validation. The power figure, which comes to coincide with the fictional reality prevailing in Kafka's texts, persists in denying or ignoring the self's claim. The claimant stays forever cheated of fulfillment. Sharing the pure-self figure's perspective, the reader, at least initially, also shares the protagonist's feeling of being wronged. She or he sympathizes with the claimant when his strenuous attempts to have his claim recognized fail. The reader does not at first experience the irony of the situation, but only its pathos, inhering in the subject's view. The protagonist appears a victim of injustice. That, at least, was my own first response upon reading these works, and I found it confirmed by most other readers. With Kafka's protagonists we too felt aggrieved and driven to protest a flagrantly unfair social and world order. However, upon continued close rereadings, the irony in the claim, albeit unacknowledged by the protagonist, became apparent. The claim turned out to be invalid. It was founded on false premisses, on wrong assumptions and deceptions, which either remained unconscious, i.e., unarticulated in the text, or so fleetingly mentioned that the reader tends to stay unaware of them.[10] If the reader detects this deception, she or he does so in spite of the narrative perspective.

The irony of Kafka's late texts resides in the discrepancy between the ostensible and the actual. Ostensibly the protagonist's claim appears to be justified, but actually it is absurd, or, at any rate, at sharp variance with the fictional reality represented in the text. Beneath this irony, however, lurks another, deeper irony, the contradiction between a claim that expresses an absolute subjectivity of inner conviction and its need to have an external agency confirm it. The contradiction between the subjective arrogance of the claim and the desperate appeal for its "objective" validation constitutes the fundamental irony permeating the last phase of Kafka's writing. Now the struggle enacted in Kafka's myth is the self's insistent appeal to the power figure for recognition and confirmation of its unique status and special being summed up in its claim. The self seeks to impose itself upon the power figure—which might extend to include the community, the species, or the world—that blocks its cause. Insistence upon admission into a specific space, seat, and domain of the power figure ("Before the Law," *The Castle*), most aptly expresses the self's demand.

The irony in Kafka's myth ultimately inheres in the nature of self-assertion that paradoxically is forever in need of an Other's recognition and acquiescence to attain its triumphant fulfillment. The appeal to have the self's specialness validated ironically reconfirms the Other's power as the force that, by bestowing or withholding recognition, decides the subject's fate. In the very quest to realize itself, selfhood reveals its utter dependence on the Other. Kafka's writing describes a project that pursues a self-contradictory and thus unrealizable goal—the creation of the absolutely sovereign self through the administration of external power.

This self-contradiction in the pure self's quest continues the self-division of the protagonists of Kafka's earlier narratives of self-destruction. Now, however, the division does not lie in the repression of one part of the self by another, leading eventually to a "return of the repressed" that erupts and explodes the self. Now it lies in the self's embodiment of a conceptual self-contradiction.

This difference entails a markedly different narrative structure.[11] In the tales of punishment where the hero's destruction was built into the narrative from the beginning, the action moves with a more or less dramatic momentum toward the fatal ending. The end inheres in the narrative as its *telos*. In composing *The Trial,* for instance, Kafka wrote the last scene of the novel, Josef K.'s execution, soon after the opening chapter, which describes his arrest. In the later works, where the self's refutation proceeds by ironizing rather than destroying the self, this change of narrative objective requires a new form. Now the text does not enact a drama, but demonstrates an object lesson on the problematic nature of the self. Narrative becomes parabolic exposition and requires no conclusion. These late narratives are either fragments, such as *The Castle,* or the ending is an arbitrary cutoff point, the hero's death from natural causes terminating a condition that could go on indefinitely ("Before the Law," "A Hunger Artist," "Josefine"). Only in the transitional text, *In the Penal Colony,* the violent end of the Officer is intrinsic to the plot, since here claim and self-destruction coincide.

Apart from a very small group of texts, foremost among them "A Report to an Academy," in which the ego becomes an at least partially positive force,[12] Kafka's myth appears, in *Tragedy and Irony,* as a severe critique and refutation of selfhood—first in a violent and tragic, then in an ironic and parabolic mode. I saw the ultimate "truth" of Kafka's narratives, resting in the power figure of his work, become coextensive with collective life and reality itself. I did not see Kafka worshiping power uncritically. Far from it—a great portion of the satirizing irony of his texts I saw aimed at the authority figures in them, from the fathers in his projected volume *Sons* to Josef K.'s Court, K.'s Castle bureaucracy, and the empire of China. Yet, in the main, the power figure serves as the catalyst that reveals the falsity and nullity of the self. The refutation of self-assertion formed for me the unifying theme of the myth told by Kafka's works.

Since I saw this myth developing in two principal phases or modes—one tragic, the other ironic—I chose, emphasizing this development, *Tragedy and Irony* to be the title of my book. If the unity of Kafka's myth had been my overriding concern, the title would have been *The Myth of Power and the Self*. That the present collection of essays bears this title now highlights the continuity between the two books.

BEYOND TRAGEDY AND IRONY

The present volume relates to *Tragedy and Irony* in three ways. It makes explicit some subjects only implied in the earlier book; it complements it and enlarges its scope; and it modifies some of the former volume's positions. These changes have been influenced by developments in literary criticism and theory and in the general intellectual and cultural climate since the time—the early 1960s—when *Tragedy and Irony* was written. In rereading and in teaching Kafka again and again, my thoughts on him have been particularly stimulated and enriched by poststructuralist thinking, by intertextuality and the attention to contextual subtexts in works of literature, by cultural studies with their emphasis on the historical and cultural-political synchronicity of literary texts, and by reader theory. Yet, I have always sought to integrate these influences into close readings of Kafka's texts. The text-immanent approach has, in this respect, remained dominant. In these essays, I have always started with Kafka's texts and always returned to them.

Poetics

Poststructuralism directed me toward the overarching role of poetics, explicit and implied, in Kafka. It led me to see the attack upon the self, which Kafka's myth describes, as enacted by the process and activity of writing. The tragic dissolution or ironic refutation of the self is thus not purely a thematic occurrence in the content of Kafka's narratives. It is enacted in and through Kafka's writing. The "truth of the self" of Kafka's myth can be equated with the writing process. The conflict between writing as an activity and the writer as a person, as an ego, underlies and forms the contrast between the truth of the self and the pure-self figures in Kafka's myth. Writing, not merely as thematic representation but as narrative process, undoes selfhood, not only in the story but in the activity that makes the story.[13]

In *Tragedy and Irony* the dissolution or refutation of the self appeared in negative terms, as the negation of the self, the longing for its disappearance in reunion with its origin, as analogous to Freud's death instinct. Writing would thus have a purely negating function. It was to serve the undoing of the ego, of individuated being. However, rereading Kafka, particularly his diaries, has shown me an affirmative mission of writing. It came with the discovery of the enormous significance that his dreamlike, visionary inner world possessed for Kafka. He viewed the lifting of this haunting inner world to the light of day as the mission of his writing. Writing as giving expression to the pressing multitudes of oneiric visions of the mind was thus quite literally an evocation of the truth of the self. This truth I came to see as the source of Kafka's art. This inner world of dreams and visions was precisely the world forever beyond the reach of the paternal power figure. It was the realm of escape where the inner self could hold sway as truth. Kafka's writing served this truth. Its truthfulness, however, depended on immediacy, on the abolition of the writer's ego as medium of the writing. The ultimate impossibility of such immediacy doomed the writer to self-despair.[14]

Since both self and power figure manifest themselves in and as language, the consideration of Kafka's thinking on language made both acquire a new aspect. Since language is a realm shared by both contestants of Kafka's myth, their contest appears as one of competing notions of language. However, since language is what both antagonists have in common, can it also provide the ground on which power and self could be reunited?[15]

Attention to language as the medium of Kafka's art also made me aware of the superpersonal character of the oneiric. Dreams are metaphors that, as linguistic formations, partake of the sociocultural realm. Thus, taking up a suggestion made by Günther Anders in the 1930s, I extended consideration of the oneiric structure of Kafka's writing to an examination of the part played in it by the metaphors buried in language.[16]

Poststructuralist and deconstructionist emphasis on the self-reflexivity of writing made me see Kafka's fiction as the arena of conflicting and alternative poetologies implied in it.[17]

In *Tragedy and Irony,* I had fully accepted Friedrich Beissner's theory of the protagonists' unimental perspective as the sole narrative perspective of Kafka's works. I failed to look into the problem posed by the contradiction between a strictly unimental perspective and the overwhelming evidence of irony in Kafka's writing. For irony is not possible without at least a duality of points of view. I felt that the coexistence of irony and singleness of narrative perspective had to be addressed. By examining the relationship of narrative perspective to narrated action in works of Kafka's middle period, I was able to put the distinction between what I had seen as the tragically dramatic and the ironically expository form of Kafka's writing into terms of narrative point of view. In the dramatic subgenre, the bearer of the point of view is identical with the subject of the narrative action. The ironically and parabolically expository texts by contrast distance the bearer of the narrative point of view from the action that the narrative represents. The introduction of an observer figure at some distance from the action, who assumes the reader's role within the text, accomplishes this shift. Thus while the unimental perspective is preserved, it moves from the agonist of the struggle to a detached character who, within the text, represents the reader called upon to interpret and judge what he perceives. The narrated action thus assumes the character of a staged event capable of being reflected upon. This distancing of narrative perspective from narrated action lays the structural foundation for the possibility of irony.[18]

However, subsequent reexamination of a text of the tragically dramatic type, *The Trial,* caused me to realize that even in what I had termed the "tragic" phase of Kafka's writing, the very presence of a narrating voice distinct from the agent of the narrative action makes for a duality of perspectives, and, with it, irony.[19] Irony emerged as ubiquitous in Kafka's oeuvre. Thus I have been led not only to modify the strict polarity between a tragic and ironic phase in the development of Kafka's work, but also to qualify the notion of the unimental perspective as applying to Kafka's total work. The notion of the unimental perspective is valid, to be sure, in regard to the absence of an omniscient narrator in Kafka's work. It is not valid, however, if it implies the lack of a narrative point of view that markedly differs from and, with subtle irony, undermines the protagonist's point of view. In that sense, all of Kafka's works are based on a duality of perspectives, and irony is one of the foundations not only of Kafka's late works, but of his entire output.[20]

Contexts

In *Tragedy and Irony,* I had, despite heavy reliance on Freudian psychoanalytic concepts and on Nietzsche's *Birth of Tragedy* and his attack upon ascetic values, mainly resorted to intertextuality within Kafka's works. From close text-immanent examination of Kafka's texts and the numerous interconnections and cross-references between them, which included his life-documents, I had gained the idea of Kafka's myth as the description of a number of intertangled struggles—within the self, and between the self and variants of patriarchal power.

Stimulated by critical developments in intertextuality and the placement of literature in interdisciplinary cultural studies, I began to reread Kafka's texts in the light of other texts from literary, intellectual, social, and cultural history. Some of the essays in this volume are the result of such rereadings. I have continued to rely on close textual reading but have also allowed contexts to help cast additional light on Kafka's texts. I have not been primarily interested in a study of "influences," but in analogies widening the horizons of the reading of Kafka's texts. Analogies and relationships were to help me to place Kafka's myth in a broader framework of significance and historical-cultural relevance, transcending biographical and psychological referentiality. Intertextuality has aided me in discovering added dimensions of individual texts as well as Kafka's myth as a whole.

To begin with, I went beyond using Freud merely as an explanatory model in the thematic analysis of Kafka's works and investigated through close intertextual readings the structural parallelism between Freudian thinking and Kafka's way of writing.[21] I also tried to make specific Freudian concepts, such as narcissism and the Ego, as well as particular case studies shed light on individual texts by Kafka.[22]

Paying attention to the metonymic relationship between bourgeois patriarchal family and capitalist business hierarchy in "The Metamorphosis" led me to see striking analogies between Kafka's representation of human self-alienation and corresponding notions crucial to Marxist theory.[23] Those analogies do not by any means imply that Kafka was influenced by Marxism. They are rather to highlight the historical and sociocultural relevance of the struggle between patriarchal power and the self depicted in Kafka's story. Bringing out the anthropological implications of Kafka's myth enabled me to show how the bourgeois nuclear family, depicted in "The Judgment" and "The Metamorphosis," contains the seeds of the cultic community of *In the Penal Colony* and the bureaucratic feudalism of *The Castle*.[24] It also showed how Kafka's representation of the son figure in the patriarchal bourgeois family tends to make the latter the locus of prominent myths in Frazer's anthropological classic, *The Golden Bough*.

The contextual approach to Kafka also endowed the individual players in Kafka's myth with broader significance. Connecting Kafka's aphorisms of the Zürau period, with their copious comments on the Book of Genesis, to both Gnosticism and the Hebrew Bible, the pure-self figure's conflict with patriarchal power acquired aspects of the historic struggle between two great strains of Western religious traditions.[25] The split self of Kafka's tales of punishment gains an important additional dimension when associated with Kafka's role in the conflict between Jewish assimilation and the search for roots in Jewish traditions and the Yiddish language.

The contexts built into Kafka's texts do not merely enrich the understanding of the latters' sociohistorical significance, but are also essential to the grasp of their structure and content. Analogies between notions of existential thought and Kafka's K.-novels enable us to see the nature of K.'s "call" to be the land surveyor of the Castle[26] and Josef K.'s "trial" as a challenge to define and project himself as what he chooses to be. Self-creation appears as a hermeneutical choice between competing interpretations of and responses to his "arrest."[27]

Aspects of Kafka's texts neglected or ignored in previous readings came into prominent view through their contexts, and conversely previously neglected parts of Kafka's texts revealed new contexts for them. In *Tragedy and Irony,* I had read Kafka's story of the humanization of an ape, "A Report to an Academy," to use an example, by exclusively focusing on the problems faced by the simian narrator and the solutions found by him. Read in that light, "A Report" appeared in Freudian terms as the account of the formation of an Ego through adaptation to and partial identification with violently Oedipal father figures. Dwelling, in rereading, upon the richly described human environment of the ape and the crucial role played by it in his transformation, the narrative came to reveal, in addition, an extremely significant cultural-historical and political referentiality. Kafka's short text emerged as an important contribution to the "grand narrative" of the twentieth century, the Westernization of the globe from its colonialist-imperialist to its "postmodern" phase.[28]

It became clear to me, however, that a single context could never do justice to the complexity of any text by Kafka. Each context can illuminate only one of the numerous aspects and positions that the struggles described in Kafka's mythos present. The richness of Kafka's texts demands that each context receive complementations by very different contexts. For instance, in the text of "The Metamorphosis," the context of Marxist notions of human self-alienation and reification shifts to the anthropological-cultic context of the scapegoat-savior myth.[29] However, even two such widely differing contexts do not contain the spectrum of Kafka's story. Following the example of Marthe Robert's reading of *The Castle* as a kind of history or compendium of the subgenres of the European novel, I found a rich variety and sequence of discourses, each of central import to Kafka's and our century, forming together the contextual referentiality of the story of Gregor Samsa's transformation.[30]

"The Metamorphosis" begins with a comic discourse describing Gregor Samsa's initial reaction to his transformation. One can easily read this opening scene in terms of Henri Bergson's view of the comic as a human being's inappropriately routinized, automatonlike behavior. However, as the reader gets absorbed into the point of view of the protagonist, experiencing the latter's fate from within the character's consciousness, the comic discourse gives way to a quasi-Marxist and quasi-Freudian discourse that presents human self-alienation as the individual's victimization by the hierarchical orders of capitalist business and patriarchal family.[31] This discourse of human self-reification, familiar from Georg Lukacs's *History and Class Consciousness,* goes over into a protoexistential discourse in which self-alienation results from the individual's "bad faith," the lack of courage to make authentic decisions in shaping one's life—a discourse subsequently made familiar by Martin Heidegger and Jean-Paul Sartre. In the concluding parts of Kafka's text, this existential view of Gregor's mode of being gives way to a discourse with echoes from Kierkegaard's *Fear and Trembling,* in which the "absolute individual," which Gregor has literally turned into because of his totally unique, unprecedented form of being that transcends all species, is thrown beyond the confines of speech into an inability to be understood by others because an utterly unique fate eludes the generalizing nature of language. Here speechlessness hints at a realm of transcendence alluded to through music—his sister's violin playing and its effect upon Gregor. Finally this discourse in turn cedes place to the discourse of myth—the myth of the scapegoat-hero, the rain king sacrificed to the survival of the group, a discourse prominent in turn-of-the-century anthropology.[32] "The Metamorphosis" thus can serve as an example illustrating Kafka's writing as the scene in which prominent discourses of the late nineteenth century and the twentieth century converge. In the at times strikingly anticipatory relationship of Kafka's text to subsequently emerging discourses lies what has often been felt as the "prophetic" power of Kafka's writing.

Not any single one of these discourses illuminates the whole text. Only their sequence and interplay provides something approximating a "meaning" of the tale.[33]

As he confessed to his publisher, Kurt Wolff, Kafka felt very attuned to the "embarrassing" nature of his age, which he found again in his work. The conflicts represented in his work—to a degree that his writings and life-documents would not let one suspect at first—strangely and markedly converge with the conflicts that formed the twentieth century. However, his writing corresponds to the age on a level far below explicit articulation. It relates to the age as dreams do to waking life. The latter permeates them in a manner not conceptualized and articulated, but allusive and concealing. In the same estranging and mystifying way, Kafka's mythos alludes to and expresses historical reality.

Emancipation, Myth, and the Reader

In *Tragedy and Irony*, a divided or self-contradicting protagonist confronted a triumphantly monolithic power figure. Subsequent rereadings of "Urban World," a protoversion of "The Judgment," "A Report to an Academy," and the short parables of the Emperor and China complex caused me to look at Kafka's power figure in a new light. The power figure, too, appeared divided—into two aspects: one hostile and oppressively menacing, the other benign but unattainable. While the former conforms to the Oedipal violator and aggressor, the latter embodies the origin and source of being to which the self longs to return.[34] In "A Report to an Academy," the two aspects of the power figure appear distributed over two species—simian and human, corresponding to the two identities of the protagonist who evolves from ape to man.[35] This division between two aspects or two ways of being of the power figure extends through Kafka's entire work.[36] It finds its historical-religious context in the division within the divinity as envisioned by the Gnostics.[37]

In the late phase of his writing, however, Kafka deconstructs this split. It is not the power figure that is divided into two aspects or two natures. Both are projections of the self's dependence. Power does not exist and rule by itself. It exists only as the hold it has on the subject. It is the embodiment of the subject's self-enslavement.[38] This adds a new dimension to the notion of guilt so pervasive in Kafka's work. The self is guilty not only toward its truth, which aims to dissolve it, and not only toward an "objective" reality, which its subjective claim misses and contradicts. It bears guilt also toward itself for not developing the independence that would make it an adult autonomous self. It is guilty of an obsessive fixation on the power figure that allows the latter to judge and rule it.[39] Thus a critical and emancipatory view of the self emerges that complements the self-punishing and self-ironizing view I had emphasized in *Tragedy and Irony.*

Yet, even in Kafka's most critical stance toward the power figure, the primary target is still the self for allowing power to obsess and dominate it. Kafka remains a self-reflexive author, differing from the unambiguously subversive producer of "Minor Literature" whom Deleuze, in the wake of the revolt of 1968, has made so widely fashionable.

However, as over against the Kafka image of *Tragedy and Irony,* the present volume takes an important step toward bringing Kafka closer to emancipatory literature. I no longer see Kafka, as I had tended to do in *Tragedy and Irony,* identifying "truth" with the power figure. Beyond the voice of power, which I had seen swaying Kafka's work, I now hear the voice of the victimized self protesting it.[40] "Truth"—in the sense of a final, "official," evaluative judgment or "message"—I now find quite unavailable in Kafka's world. No single player in the contests that are his myth possesses it. No single position provides a longed-for resting point, an ultimate, satisfying closure, for the reader. That is also the reason why no single context is able to cope with any of Kafka's texts. Kafka does not put forward a particular world view in his works. He does not advocate any one of the positions he presents. He merely describes ever-varied, ever-shifting conflicts of competing points of view. He does not present a thesis, but he represents a mythos. A mythos shows, but does not judge. None of its phases, aspects, and forms that Kafka's individual texts enact can be reduced to and equated with a single position represented in it. Therefore, there cannot be one single context that could "explain" a Kafka text.

In Kafka's telling of the myth of Prometheus, the narrator views myth as a doomed attempt to explain the inexplicable, to master the irreducible strangeness and groundlessness of fact.[41] Applied to Kafka's own myth, the irreducible fact around which his myth weaves its circles is ambivalence that finds no possibility of a definitive and closing answer to a never-ending, ever-open contest.

Throughout Kafka's work, we encounter the fateful interlocking of two mutually exclusive perspectives in a combat without end. One is condemnatory toward selfhood and the assertiveness to which it has to resort. The other critiques the opposite—the self's dependence on and subjection to the power figure. The unresolvable contradiction between these two perspectives underlies and permeates all of Kafka's work, spawning an irony that is directed at all combatants of the struggles his myth relates. A final evaluative meaning, expressing a definite and definable intentionality in his work, is thus impossible. The fundamental ambiguity of Kafka's writing precludes an ultimate judgment that could be called an "explanation."

Yet, Kafka's myth is the ever-renewed attempt to push toward such an explanation. It harbors a profound need to interpret and to "understand" that profoundly infects the reader.[42] Constantly redramatizing and reenacting the ways that lead to the impasse, the myth presses toward, without ever getting to, its eventual "understanding." This gives enormous prominence to the role of reading in Kafka's writing.[43]

As he confided in his diary, Kafka wrote to lift his inner world, the dreamlike visions that crowded in on and haunted him, into the light of day. That he considered to be his mission.[44] Writing was to enact the transformation of his chaotic inner world into a world that could be read, interpreted, and thus possibly, eventually, understood. In that way, writing served as the means of transforming the visionary writer into a reader. As a letter to Felice that accompanied a copy of his recently composed story "The Judgment" makes clear, Kafka sought to understand his writing. He turned into a reader, trying to interpret and make sense of his texts.

However, he had to turn to a second reader, Felice, asking whether she could find any sense in his story. For he himself could find none. This request to his reader, quite astonishing for an author to make, shows that Kafka's writing received its meaning from reading, and not, as we would traditionally expect, the other way around. Kafka, in writing, does not seem to have a preconceived meaning, a fixed intention, in his mind. Writing is merely the means of bringing his inner world to the light of day, into readable form, which perhaps makes attainable that further light that is understanding. Reading is to provide what writing by itself cannot give. When the writer fails in his task as a reader, he turns to another reader. Thus the reader is to continue the writer's work of bringing his visionary inner world closer to the light of understanding. Even though, according to Kafka's view of myth, a full "explanation" will, because of the groundless nature of being, never be possible, portions of the way toward understanding can become progressively clearer through the process of interpretive reading. It is my hope that the essays gathered here can serve as a road map on that—the reader's—way.

NOTES

Citations in these notes refer to chapters in this volume, unless otherwise indicated.

1. "Franz Kafka," chap. 2.
2. "Symbol, Allegory, Existential Sign," chap. 5.
3. "Franz Kafka," chap. 2, and esp. "Kafka's Beginnings," chap. 8.
4. "Franz Kafka," chap. 2, "Perspectives and Truth in 'The Judgment,'" chap. 9.
5. "Franz Kafka," chap. 2
6. "Franz Kafka," chap. 2; "Perspectives and Truth in 'The Judgment'," chap. 9; "The Program of K's Court," chap. 11; "The Three Endings of Josef K. and the Role of Art in *The Trial,*" chap. 12.
7. "Kafka's Poetics of the Inner Self," chap. 3.
8. Ibid.
9. Ibid.
10. "Franz Kafka," chap. 2
11. Ibid.
12. "Identity and the Individual, or Past and Present," chap. 13.
13. "Kafka's Poetics of the Inner Self," chap. 3, and "Kafka's Beginnings," chap. 8. See also Walter H. Sokel, "Frozen Sea and River of Narration: The Poetics behind Kafka's 'Breakthrough'," *New Literary History* 17(2) (Winter 1986): 351–63.
14. "Kafka's Poetics of the Inner Self," chap. 3.
15. "Language and Truth in the Two Worlds of Franz Kafka," chap. 4.
16. "Franz Kafka," chap. 2

17. "The Three Endings of Josef K. and the Role of Art in *The Trial*," chap. 12.

18. "The Relationship of Narrative Perspective to Narrative Action and Meaning in 'Before the Law,' 'Jackals and Arabs,' and *The Trial*," chap. 6.

19. Walter H. Sokel, "Franz Kafka: *Der Prozess* (1925): Ironie, Deutungszwang, Scham und Spiel," in *Deutsche Romane des 20. Jahrhunderts: Neue Interpretionen.* Ed. Paul Michael Lützeler. Königstein/Ts.: Athenäum, 1983, 110–27.

20. Ibid.

21. "Freud and the Magic of Kafka's Writing," chap. 7.

22. "Kafka's Beginnings," chap. 8, and "Identity and the Individual, or Past and Present," chap. 13. See also Walter H. Sokel, "The Wolfman and the Castle," *Journal of the Kafka Society of America* 1–2 (1988): 64–68.

23. "From Marx to Myth," chap. 10.

24. "Franz Kafka," chap. 2

25. "Between Gnosticism and Jehovah," chap. 14.

26. "Franz Kafka," chap. 2.

27. "The Program of K.'s Court," chap. 11.

28. "Identity and the Individual, or Past and Present," chap. 13.

29. "From Marx to Myth," chap. 10.

30. Walter H. Sokel, "Kafka and the Twentieth Century: Its Discourses in His Work," *Journal of the Kafka Society of America* 19(1–2) (1997): 4–8.

31. "From Marx to Myth," chap. 10, and "Freud and the Magic of Kafka's Writing," chap. 7.

32. "From Marx to Myth," chap. 10.

33. Sokel, "Kafka and the Twentieth Century."

34. "Identity and the Individual, or Past and Present," chap. 13, and "Freedom and Authority in the Fiction of Franz Kafka," chap. 15.

35. "Identity and the Individual, or Past and Present," chap. 13.

36. "Freedom and Authority in the Fiction of Franz Kafka," chap. 15.

37. "Between Gnosticism and Jehovah," chap. 14.

38. "Freedom and Authority in the Fiction of Franz Kafka," chap. 15.

39. Walter H. Sokel, "Schuldig oder subversiv? Zur Schuldproblematik bei Kafka," in *Das Schuldproblem bei Franz Kafka.* Kafka Symposium 1993. Klosterneuburg. Eds. Wolfgang Kraus and Norbert Winkler. Schriftenreihe der Franz-Kafka-Gesellschaft. Vienna-Cologne-Weimar: Böhlau Verlag, 1995, 1–11.

40. "Perspectives and Truth in 'The Judgment'," chap. 9

41. Walter H. Sokel, "Kafka and Modernism," in *Approaches to Teaching Kafka's Short Fiction.* Ed. Richard T. Gray. New York: Modern Language Association of America, 1995, 20–34.

42. "The Program of K.'s Court," chap. 11. See also Sokel, "Franz Kafka: *Der Prozess.*"

43. See note 42 above.

44. "Kafka's Poetics of the Inner Self," chap. 3.

2

FRANZ KAFKA

FRANZ KAFKA was born on July 3, 1883, the only surviving son of Hermann Kafka, a self-made businessman and prosperous shopkeeper in the heart of the "Old Town" of Prague. The figure of his father loomed enormous in the emotional life of the son. Kafka saw in his vigorous father the example of life "dans le vrai," Flaubert's phrase that Kafka applied to a way of life from which his own nature excluded him.

The works published by Kafka during his life do not comprise more than a single volume in the six-volume edition of his works, edited and published posthumously by his close friend Max Brod. These six volumes consist of three major novels, two volumes of stories, and a volume of miscellaneous pieces, including his very significant aphorisms. Kafka's diaries (1910–1923), his letters published by Max Brod, and the letters to Milena Jesenská-Pollak, his Czech woman friend and translator, published by Willy Haas, form three additional volumes. It is important to realize that Kafka himself neither completed nor edited the bulk of his writings, including his three great novels, *Amerika, The Trial,* and *The Castle,* all of which are fragments. The only narratives of normal story length that he completed were those published during his life. These must consequently occupy a privileged position in any critical concern with Kafka's work.

Kafka's work can be called a spiritual autobiography clothed in metaphoric disguise. In a diary entry of August 6, 1914, Kafka noted that his sense for the presentation of his "dreamlike inner life" had stunted all his other interests and talents and had become the only quality that could afford him full satisfaction. Indeed, the oneiric character of Kafka's

From *Franz Kafka,* by Walter H. Sokel, ed. William York Tindall, writings strikes every reader. Their enigmatic suggestiveness is their most pronounced feature. They are like dreams in that they compel interpretation but seem to withhold the key. Sometimes his stories did grow out of dreams, and the dreams Kafka frequently relates in his diaries show a striking resemblance to his stories. Yet his writings differ profoundly from those of the surrealists who jotted down their dreams in automatic writing. Unlike theirs, Kafka's narratives are thoroughly disciplined. They are by no means simple copies of dreams; rather they are structured analogous to dreams in some essential respects.

One of these characteristics is the peculiar relationship of Kafka's narratives to metaphor. His stories tend to present enactments of metaphors buried in language, not only in the German language in which he wrote but also in the universal symbolism of prerational thought. Basic metaphors by which prescientific language expresses experiences, attitudes, and relationships become event in Kafka's tales. He reinstates, or recreates, the pictorial expressiveness that the original metaphor, frozen in a cliché or idiom, once conveyed. Thus Kafka's writing conforms to or repeats the activity of the dreaming mind. As Freud has shown in his *Interpretation of Dreams,* a work with which Kafka was familiar, dreams speak in the pictorial language speech once was. They take the metaphors hidden in speech literally and act them out as visualized events.

A few examples might help to clarify the preceding remarks. A decisive and profound experience is said to "leave a mark"; a lasting memory is "engraved" on one. Kafka's *In the Penal Colony* depicts both metaphors as physical happenings. The penal machine slowly kills the condemned prisoner by literally engraving (German: *einkerben*) on his flesh the law he transgressed. He dies, in fact, of his remembering this lesson; "the mark left" by the law kills him. German usage applies the term *Ungeziefer* (vermin) to persons considered low and contemptible, even as our usage of "cockroach" describes a person deemed a spineless and miserable character. The traveling salesman Gregor Samsa, in Kafka's "The Metamorphosis," is "like a cockroach" because of his spineless and abject behavior and parasitic wishes. However, Kafka drops the word "like" and has the metaphor become reality when Gregor Samsa wakes up finding himself turned into a giant vermin. With this metamorphosis, Kafka reverses the original act of metamorphosis carried out by thought when it forms metaphor; for metaphor is always "metamorphosis." Kafka transforms metaphor back into his fictional reality, and this countermetamorphosis becomes the starting point of his tale. German usage calls a sexually indecent and obscene character a "pig" or "swine" (*Schwein*). In Kafka's tale "A Country Doctor," the groom who assaults the doctor's maid walks out of the doctor's pigsty.

Kafka's narratives do not stop with reactivating single metaphors. They connect organically the enactment of one metaphor with the enactments of others; together these establish a narrative development. "A Country Doctor" will serve as an example.

The swinish groom stands in a fateful relation to the protagonist of the story, the country doctor, through whose consciousness alone we witness the events. The doctor had lived next to his maid, Rose, without noticing her as a woman. As soon as she presents herself to him as desirable, the groom steps out of the doctor's *unused*[1] pigsty and seeks to rape her. The unused pigsty belongs to the doctor; it is, in the words of the story, "his own." The groom is, then, literally a dweller of the doctor's forgotten lower depths. He embodies the doctor's unused sex drive in a strikingly literal way. The doctor's consciousness does not acknowledge his responsibility for the event he himself has called forth when he kicked the door of the pigsty open "absent-mindedly" and thus released the groom. The sudden emergence of the "filthy" contents of the doctor's depths—the unacknowledged component of his self—now overpowers his humanity and makes the girl a prey of bestial desire. In Kafka's stories, acts and omissions reveal what consciousness hides from itself. Not consciousness—the explicit comments of the story—but the narrated events show the true meaning of Kafka's tale. "A Country Doctor" begins with a call of the night bell summoning the doctor to a patient. However, his horse had died from overexertion and he cannot follow his call. In his dilemma, he calls "absent-mindedly"[2] (that is, unconsciously) on his forgotten pigsty, releasing the swinish groom and a team of "unearthly horses" and allows the groom to take the girl. Contrary to his verbal protestations, the doctor does in fact leave Rose behind with the groom. She is the price for the groom's aid.

The images and plot of this tale enable us to see Kafka's works as pieces of an autobiography in metaphoric disguise. The "call" of the night bell is a translation into sensory terms of Kafka's "call" to literature, which he understood as an art of healing and self-preservation, a "doctor's" art. Writing for Kafka was night work in two respects: literally, because he had no time for it during the day; figuratively, because he had to delve into the nocturnal regions of his mind, the representation of which he called his fatal talent. The death of the horse shows that no normal and natural way is available for transporting the self to its calling. As the doctor finds his self in absent-mindedness, Kafka notes that he had done his best writing when all rational control was lifted. In one night, with "an outpouring of his soul," he wrote "The Judgment," which remained his favorite work and the model of all others.

"A Country Doctor" presents in the hieroglyphic language of dreams a clear and exact presentation of Kafka's inspirational process and the problems it posed for his life. In a revealing letter to Max Brod, in 1922, he calls his writing a "descent to the dark powers, an unchaining of spirits whose natural state it is to be bound servants." The description fits the groom of "A Country Doctor," who, instead of serving the self, expels it and takes over its vacated house. In that same letter to Brod, Kafka says that in order to devote himself to literature, the writer must sacrifice fulfillment in life. The "unearthly horses" of inspiration, called forth from the unsavory depths, transport the doctor away from life, woman, and home. He is shown literally "carried away," "in the transport" of inspiration, since his unearthly team of horses proceeds without his conscious will and carries him off instantaneously and miraculously to his vocational destination. This destination is an existential encounter, symbolized by his being undressed and put in the same bed with his sick childhood self, the boy patient to whom he has been called.

The two houses pictorialize the two poles of the doctor's existence. In his own house, the house of the self, the doctor abandoned the possibility of erotic fulfillment; in the other house, the house of the patient, he is to dedicate himself to his art, which is the confrontation with the congenital wound of mortality. The hero's ambivalence is such that he cannot be content at either pole. At home he sacrifices the girl to his mission, but at his destination he regrets the price he has paid and wants to return. His split existence, his inability to choose, becomes pure image in the doctor's final condition. He is shown riding aimlessly between the houses; the distance between them has become infinite, and he cannot stay at either place.

"A Country Doctor" became the title story of a volume of Kafka's short pieces published in 1919 and dedicated to his father, which makes the importance Kafka attached to this particular work quite evident. The detailed examination of its plot and images has enabled us to understand the allegorical principle informing Kafka's writings. His images are pictorial translations of overriding personal concerns in which personal meaning acquires universal significance.

Any individual work by Kafka may baffle the reader when considered in isolation. If examined within the context of Kafka's other works and personal documents, the nature and meaning of his images become clear. The individual work will then appear as a variation of a single theme—the inner autobiography of the author—and a step in its development. Each work is aesthetically self-sufficient and, if completed and published by Kafka himself, a complete and satisfying statement of one approach to the master theme.

There is, nevertheless, a difference in the degree of transparency Kafka's images possess in different works. The central images of his long narratives—Gregor Samsa's bug form, the Court in *The Trial,* the Castle in the late novel of that name—are denser and more opaque than the symbols of his shorter pieces. The reason is that the central images of the long works have a variety of functions and meanings. Indeed, they unite mutually contradictory meanings and functions.

Gregor Samsa's metamorphosis, for instance, expresses a number of contradictory tendencies in the single image of the giant bug. Gregor's transformation gives shape to his wish to abandon responsibility as breadwinner and supporter of his family, and thereby returns Gregor's father to his former position as head of the household. At the same time, however, Gregor's metamorphosis embodies his opposite wish to avenge himself of his family's parasitism by turning parasite himself. In the former case the metamorphosis functions as submission, in the latter as aggression and rebellion. The empirical impossibility of Gregor's form of existence serves as objective correlative of his spiritual and psychic contradictoriness.

There are two further factors that make the structure of Kafka's stories analogous to the structure of dreams: unitary perspective and tension between a manifest content and a latent truth.

In fiction, ordinarily, the community of author and reader stands as objective reality outside and above the points of view of the characters and forms a "true" frame of reference. The traditional storyteller or novelist maintains this division by one or both of these devices: he switches the point of view from one character to another, and thus enables us to enjoy a relative omniscience since we can look into all minds of the story, which none of the characters can; or he keeps his own perspective separate, looks into his characters, and comments on their thoughts and actions. These conventions are absent in Kafka's fiction. His stories know only a single point of view, that of the protagonist. Even in his third-person narratives—and his major works are all third-person narratives—objects, scenes, and persons are seen by us only through the protagonist's eyes. An example from *The Trial* may illustrate the means by which Kafka replaces independent authorial comment with his protagonist's interpretation of the action.

The reaction of the Examining Magistrate to a demogogic speech by the defendant Josef K. is described as follows: "The Examining Magistrate kept fidgeting on his chair with embarrassment *or* impatience."[3] The word "or" shows Kafka's radical deviation from the conventional method of narration. Instead of giving us a single authoritative explanation, the author states his ignorance of his fictional world. He blocks and prevents the traditional communication of author to reader "over the head of the character." With this, Kafka achieves the most fundamental realism and removes the last vestiges of the author's presence as an independent, visible personality, thereby fulfilling Flaubert's ideal of an author who is as omnipresent and invisible as God is in his creation. However, he goes further than Flaubert by also taking away the reader's fictional superiority over the protagonist. Together with the protagonist, the reader is thrown into the basic condition of every individual man: he stays imprisoned in the solitary confinement of a limited and subjective consciousness that can only infer, but can never know, the external world. Normally, we accept on trust "the truth" of our fellow man's feelings and motivations. The Kafka hero lacks this *a priori* trust; or if he does start out with it, events take it away from him or, at least, from the reader. This loss of basic trust or faith in the predictability of the world around the protagonist explains the peculiar effect of Kafka's fiction.

For reasons that we shall examine later, Kafka's hero must defend and assert himself, or else be lost. Josef K.'s alternative interpretation, for instance, of the Examining Magistrate's fidgeting results from his need to calculate the effect of his speech. If it was embarrassment that made the Magistrate fidget, Josef K. has scored a victory. If, on the other hand, the Magistrate moved from impatience, K.'s speech has heightened the threat to himself. The fictional reality presented by Kafka is either threat or promise to the protagonist and wholly related to his fears, wishes, and hopes. Therefore, there can be no presentation of facts in Kafka that is not, at the same time, interpretation. The situation of Kafka's protagonist reflects the fundamental insecurity of man's condition as prisoner of his brain.

All aspects of Kafka's narrative form, from individual word and sentence to plot structure and thought, express this fundamental uncertainty of his protagonists, and it is this form that infects the reader and grips him with foreboding. Kafka's vocabulary is one of inference and conjecture. Favorite words are "apparently," "ostensibly," "maybe," "actually." Kafka prefers "it seems" to "it is." His sentences often consist of two clauses: the first states a fact or a guess; the second qualifies, questions, negates it. The conjunction "but" is, therefore, most characteristic of Kafka's thought structure. The frequent use of "even if" clauses expresses the tendency to cancel expectations and refute inferences. Terminal certainty there is in Kafka, but usually of a negative kind, identical with death or final despair. The fragmentary form of most works not ending with the protagonist's death attests to the inability of arriving at certainty.

More than most writers, Kafka favors the subjunctive. The only bridge between the protagonist and his environment is surmise. Kafka's subjunctive acts as the grammatical correlative of the structural device called *anagnorisis*—"discovery"—in Aristotle's *Poetics*. It is the hero's surprise at the unexpected turns of events. However, the anagnorisis in classical tragedy leads to insight on the part of both hero and audience. Its main function in Kafka is to reveal the discrepancy between the protagonist's consciousness and the truth underlying the story.

We have just shown that the protagonist's solipsistic perspective, through which we experience the narrative, does not allow us to speak of authorial truth in Kafka's work. Yet there is an objective and verifiable authorial truth in most of his writings. It is obliquely smuggled in against the consciousness of the protagonist. In the contradiction between the reader's perspective, as given him by the protagonist, and the hidden truth of the work lies the fundamental concern of Kafka's art, the basis of its structure, and the secret of its unsettling effect.

Those who think that the protagonist's perspective is the whole of Kafka are victims of the subtle deception perpetrated by it. In the two K.-novels and several of the longer narratives, the protagonist's motivation is to hide the truth either from himself or from the world, including the reader. However, in most of Kafka's works the truth becomes known. The protagonist's perspective, to be sure, operates for the purpose of blocking access to and comprehension of the truth, but the truth of the story emerges through the defeat of the protagonist's consciousness. In one of his aphorisms, Kafka defined truth as the light reflected upon the retreating grimace (of falsehood) and art as the condition of being dazzled by that light. This aphorism supplies the key to Kafka's poetics, always implicit in his works. The annihilation or refutation suffered by Kafka's protagonist, bearer of the lie, becomes the negative revelation of truth.

This structural principle of Kafka's narratives explains the profound difference between Kafka's method and the stream-of-consciousness technique. The latter assumes the identity of consciousness and truth. It reveals character and, with character, the truth of the narrative. It operates within the framework of psychology. In Kafka's narratives, on the contrary, consciousness hides truth. Therefore, Kafka has to transcend psychology. His concern is not the mechanism of self, but its moral and spiritual justification. In order to express this concern, he must unmask the mechanism, and in doing that he reveals a great deal about it. Kafka is a master in uncovering the subtle workings of rationalization, subterfuge, self-deception. But for Kafka this unmasking is not the end of his art. The end is always the revelation of truth in the defeat of the self.

All of Kafka's works deal with this relationship in one of three ways. Each of them corresponds to one of the three distinct phases of development in his mature writings. In the first phase of his maturity (1912–1914) the protagonist represses his inner truth, but his truth erupts in a catastrophe—accuses, judges, and annihilates him. This is the phase of the punitive fantasies, the powerful tales of punishment and death that are Kafka's most dramatic and popular—"The Judgment" and "The Metamorphosis"; *The Trial,* with important modifications; and partially *In the Penal Colony*. To all of these, *Amerika* forms an "innocent" and "utopian" counterpart. The second phase (1914–1917) begins with *In the Penal Colony* and continues with the short parabolic pieces of the volume *A Country Doctor* that includes "Before the Law" and "A Report to an Academy." In this phase a detached perspective views and contemplates a paradoxical discrepancy between self and truth.

The final phase (1920–1924) is Kafka's greatest and most profound. It comprises the four stories of the *Hunger Artist* volume, the lengthy fragments "Investigations of a Dog" and "The Burrow," and the long fragmentary novel *The Castle*. In the three most important works of that phase—"A Hunger Artist," "Josephine the Singer, or the Mouse Folk," and *The Castle*—Kafka presents the protagonist's deception of the world, perpetrated by his desperate need to create and fulfill his existence.

The punitive fantasies form the foundation for all phases of Kafka's maturity. With "The Judgment," he said, he had achieved his "breakthrough" to his own proper form of expression. We shall, therefore, deal with the punitive fantasies in greater detail than with the two subsequent phases.

The alienation of the protagonist from his true self forms the structural basis of Kafka's punitive fantasies. These fantasies are adumbrated in the early fragment, "Wedding Preparations in the Country." Here the hero—Raban, cryptographic forerunner of Samsa and disguise for Kafka—dreams of literally splitting his self in order to evade visits to his fiancée in the country and other burdensome involvements. His true self, transformed into a giant beetle, would stay in bed, while the unreal image of his body, his façade, would go into the world to represent Raban in the performance of necessary duties. This façade would be a slave, utterly dependent upon the commands of the powerful dehumanized self at home. This buglike true self corresponds to the bachelor self of other early writings and diary entries of Kafka. Raban's façade body, on the other hand, burdened with the task of conducting his engagement, corresponds to the engaged young men who appear in Kafka's juvenilia.

This split prefigures the structure of Kafka's punitive fantasies, with one essential qualification. What the early work presents as a conscious wish becomes in the punitive fantasies a strange destiny, seemingly imposed upon the protagonist from outside and eluding his conscious understanding. What in the early work is a split between façade body and true self reappears in Kafka's mature work as a contradiction between consciousness and truth.

Kafka's punitive fantasies—leaving *In the Penal Colony* out of account for the present—are related to Raban's wish-dream in the following manner. The façade tries to make itself independent of the true self by seeking to repress it. Punishment acts as a recall to the self. Having tried to emancipate itself, the façade is arrested, battered, and dissolved.

With the element of repression, time is introduced as a structural element into the split. What was in Raban's wish-dream an open horizontal coexistence of two halves now becomes a vertical division of two layers; a visible surface layer stands on top of a deeper, submerged layer that the surface tries to "cover up." The protagonist's true self—essentially his childhood self—lies submerged, but erupts one day in a strange guise, arrests him in his course of self-emancipation, involves him ever more deeply and catastrophically in his unacknowledged truth, and destroys him.

Arrest is central fact and symbol in *The Trial,* Kafka's longest and most ambitious tale of punishment. The German word for arrest, *Verhaftung,* carries the additional meaning of entanglement and fatal attachment. In this basic meaning, *Verhaftung* is the theme of all the punitive fantasies. The protagonist's condition of attachment to his childhood self has been repressed and put out of mind, but never truly overcome. The act or happening of his being arrested (literally stopped in his advance) by a catastrophic event is the emergence of the invisible condition of entanglement that had persisted in him all along. Estranged from his conscious intentions, however, his true condition, when it does erupt, manifests itself in an unrecognizable disguise.

The turning point and "breakthrough" to his mature form, which Kafka considered his first punitive fantasy, "The Judgment," to be, lie in two factors: the introduction of the father figure as the authoritative and effective voice of truth, and the consistent shift of perspective to the façade layer of the split. Kafka's juvenilia had been uncertain about perspective and, therefore, hampered by a subjectivism unable to push through to an effective objectification of the themes and problems he sought to express. In Raban's wish-dream the authentic consciousness of the story looks upon the façade, and what the reader obtains is an unformed reverie. The revolution of "The Judgment" consisted in the reversal of the perspective. Kafka made the façade the consciousness of the story, whereby he achieved the powerful alienation effect that we associate with his art. He was able to present consciousness estranged from itself in a way that involved the reader directly, from within the narration, instead of letting him look in from outside.

Since Gregor Samsa's true self manifests itself in the bug form of Raban's wish-dream, "The Metamorphosis" offers an obvious basis for comparison, which can enable us to assess the narrative method and meaning of the punitive fantasies.

In both stories the transformed self is the true self. However, Samsa's transformation, unlike Raban's, emerges from his night dreams and becomes reality. The text clearly refers to the subconscious origin of the metamorphosis by explicitly mentioning that Gregor finds himself changed into vermin upon awakening from "restless dreams." In the early version the transformation expresses what Raban wants to be. In the mature version truth is not what the self wants to be, but what it is. In the early version truth and consciousness are identical; in the mature version they are not. Furthermore, while both versions agree on the retrograde and inhuman nature of the true self, they differ as to the presentation of the façade. Whereas Raban's façade is an unreal body, Samsa's façade is an evasive mind. It is consciousness finding itself imprisoned in a truth it cannot face. In the mature work the split between façade and true self is a discrepancy between a devious human mind and a nonhuman body.

Gregor pretends to himself, and tries to pretend to others, that his metamorphosis is a temporary inconvenience. At the same time he feels a vague uneasiness and sense of guilt for having reneged on his obligations toward his family. His stream of memories reveals that, prior to his metamorphosis, Gregor had indeed thought of giving up his distasteful job. However, for the sake of his family, who depended on his income, he had had to inhibit this wish, and it has received no further attention from him. Seen with this sequence in mind, Gregor's metamorphosis appears and functions as the oblique fulfillment of a wish that had to be repressed. However, Gregor emphatically wards off such suspicions, claiming that he is "still around" and does not intend to abandon his responsibilities. This is the manifest content of the story, which is identical with the protagonist's perspective. The reader tends to accept this content at face value, since he sees all happenings of the story through the protagonist's perspective, and tends also to make that perspective his own.

However, Gregor's avowal to continue as his family's provider offers a glaring contradiction to his condition. The thought does indeed occur to Gregor that his situation must rule out his professed intention. He allows himself the fleeting wish to be left in peace by his family. This wish accords perfectly with his new bodily state and resurrects his previously inhibited thought of abandoning his duties. His physical change can now be seen as a fulfillment of Gregor's wish for seclusion and irresponsibility; it is the abandonment of his family, in fact, which he has indignantly denied in thought. When Gregor wishes to be left in peace, his consciousness and condition meet harmoniously. However, it is so only for a moment. Immediately thereafter, Gregor's false consciousness—that is, thought inconsistent with condition—"covers up" and takes over once more the manifest content of the story.

In the punitive fantasies the repressed part of the self is identical with its childlike component. In a time now long past, the protagonist enjoyed a harmonious relationship with his origins, his parents and family; the loss of this harmonious past plays a very important part in bringing about the vengeance and punishment he suffers. This is most obvious in "The Judgment," least so in *The Trial.* Yet even in *The Trial,* the hero's attachment to his family functions importantly in his punishment. At one point in the novel, Josef K. feels that only the pressures of his family have so desperately involved him in his strange trial. Josef K.'s mother in particular has a vital function in the structure of the novel. On his birthdays Joseph K. had been in the habit of visiting his mother, whom he had left behind in the country. Being preoccupied with his strenuous career at the bank, he had become estranged from her and had given up his visits. On the third birthday after he had stopped seeing her, the mysterious Court visits him to arrest him for an unspecified guilt. His estrangement from his family—indicated also by his annoyance at his uncle, whom he calls "a revenant from the country," and neglect of his cousin—vaguely troubles him. However, like all protagonists of the punitive fantasies, Josef K. easily represses whatever makes him feel uneasy and pays little conscious attention to it.

In all his works Kafka equates truth or objective reality with the family, first in its basic meaning, later in a more and more extended meaning, which became identical with society, stream of the generations, or totality of living things. "The entire community of men and animals," he once termed this total community from which he felt he had defected. It is against this family that he contrasts the self of his protagonists. The representative or spokesman of the family is the father figure.

A close study of the attributes of all representatives of authority in Kafka's entire opus, no matter how universalized and abstract, clearly reveals that these derive from the attributes of the fathers in "The Judgment" and "The Metamorphosis." From "The Judgment" to Kafka's last work, "Josephine," this father figure possesses a power that, however unseen, mysterious, and generalized it becomes, retains a fundamental effectiveness that plays havoc with the assumptions, opinions, and claims of Kafka's protagonist. It is the father figure that proves the hero's consciousness to be illusion.

In Georg Bendemann and Gregor Samsa, heroes of the first two punitive fantasies, Kafka created characters who had tried to rival and succeed their fathers, failed in the attempt, and were horribly punished for it. Indeed, in "The Metamorphosis," Kafka places his protagonist in a condition in which he literally becomes incomparable to his father by ceasing to belong to the same species.

The father is allied with the submerged pole of his son's divided self. He enforces those tendencies in his son that crave regression to a childlike existence, which finds its radical objectification in Gregor's vermin condition. This form of existence combines the son's self-elimination as a possible rival and threat to the father with self-indulgence in a narcissistic freedom.

The composition of the story makes clear this alliance between the protagonist's father and the son's subconscious self. Each of the three parts into which the story is divided shows an attempt on Gregor's part to break out into the world and reassert himself as a responsible adult human being. Each part ends with his being rebuffed and chased back into his prison room. It is Gregor's father, who, as spokesman of the family, administers the first two of these rebuffs. Thereby, he enforces Gregor's own tendency toward withdrawal and seclusion that he expressed by locking himself in his room and emerging from his dreams as a creature unable to communicate. He acts as the executor of Gregor's own innermost force. In "The Judgment," Georg Bendemann's father explicitly calls himself "the representative" of Georg's estranged childhood friend, who exerts upon Georg an effect analogous to the force that erupts in Gregor's metamorphosis.

"The Judgment" shows the son literally "covering up" his apparently senile father after having put him to bed like a child. On the manifest level he acts from filial solicitude. On the latent level, which, as Georg's reactions later show is the true one, he seeks to bury his father and establish his own position as new head of the household. Georg thinks of himself as a good and dutiful son, and seeing him through his perspective we are inclined to agree with him. Actually, however, he has neglected his father, has allowed him to live in the gloomy back room of the apartment while he himself occupied the sunny front (literally the façade), and has not set foot in his father's room for a very long time. He thinks he has taken his father's place in the family business and prides himself on having greatly improved and reformed it. With his impending marriage, Georg consciously plans to move his father to his new apartment and there, reversing the role of child and parent, "take care of him." But Georg is only deceiving himself. He has not succeeded in keeping his father "covered." His father shouts "No!", throws off his covers, leaps up in bed, and reveals himself in his true stature as the giant and supreme judge in the heart of his son.

Truth is revealed to be the opposite of Georg's imaginings. His father is not senile, but "still a giant" whose fingertips reach the ceiling. His fiancée, whom he had thought to be so important in his life, matters so little to Georg that she no longer enters his mind. What counts in his soul is not the girl he wanted to marry, but the friend he thought he had long outgrown and had patronized. This friend now grips and "touches his imagination as never before." This friend (whom Kafka in his own analysis of "The Judgment" called the only common bond of father and son) is Georg's last tie to his childhood and represented an existence "after the father's own heart." Georg loses fiancée, business, status, and power, all in one stroke, but inwardly he had never truly possessed them. For the only loss that matters to him is the loss of his friend in himself. Having lost him, Georg is lost.

The father's accusations prove the entire content of Georg's consciousness to be error and self-deception. They shatter his false consciousness, his wrong self-estimation, and through this shattered façade they reach to and lay bare Georg's hidden childlike self. By rushing to obey his father's death sentence and execute himself, he becomes again the loving, innocent, and obedient child he had once been. The inner division is gone; the façade is removed; harmony has returned. As Georg climbs over the railing to leap from the bridge, his consciousness of loving his parents is his whole truth. It was this truth that his father had demanded of Georg at the beginning of his cross-examination; Georg had been unable to give it except by destroying the untruth that his life had become.

The guilt of the protagonists of "The Judgment" and "The Metamorphosis" is clearly established. In "The Judgment" Georg's guilt is his defection from father and childhood friend, and the "devilish" lechery with which he utilized woman as his instrument for the repression of his friend and childhood self. His father uses the drastic metaphor, accusing Georg of subjugating his friend so that he could "set [his] bottom on him." Georg's guilt above all lies in the unconscious hypocrisy with which he attempted to displace his father while thinking himself a good son. Whether or not we accept the father's harsh judgment as justified is less relevant than the hero's active assent to his death sentence.

Less explicit than "The Judgment" on the verbal level, but equally lucid in poetic terms, "The Metamorphosis" supplies articulated reasons for accusing and condemning its protagonist. Gregor is clearly punished for trying to break out of the "otherness" that he has made his fate. Gregor's sister articulates what amounts to the family's death sentence over him. Her argument is clear and convinces Gregor. If the insect were truly her brother, it would have left them of its own accord. If he had acted according to the inner law that found its visible fulfillment in his ghastly change, he would have continued to withdraw not only from the human form but also from the human community represented by his family. If Gregor had been his true self, he would have gone into ultimate loneliness, and death would have been self-fulfillment. Then his family could have honored his memory. The disgusting monster and parasite is his false self that refuses to die. Instead, it makes forays into the family and seeks to exploit and ruin them. It is this parasitic and hostile self that the sister exposes, judges, and condemns, with uncompromising cruelty.

The sister's judgment in "The Metamorphosis" corresponds to the father's in the earlier story. However, more clearly than there, it is the judgment of the family and life itself that speaks through her. Gregor had withdrawn from the possibility of procreating even before his metamorphosis; he had remained a bachelor who loved to lock himself in when he dreamed. Therefore, the hope for a renewal of the family in the next generation rested entirely with his sister. As the scene after Gregor's death shows, it is through her that the family will continue and the stream of the generations will flow. It is the authority of life itself that judges Gregor through his sister's cruelty.

This clear judgment speaks to him with the voice of his own inner truth. As Georg rushed to execute his father's verdict on himself, Gregor is convinced, more firmly even than his sister, that he must go. Both stories end with statements of inner assent to death. Both protagonists become true sons and truly themselves by dying.

In *In the Penal Colony* Kafka systematized the underlying idea of the two earlier punitive fantasies. The penal machine produces, in a six-hour process of physical torture and laceration, that assent to death which the judgment of their families produced in Kafka's earlier protagonists. In the later work the father's judgment and family consensus have evolved into the law of a penal system. The Old Commander, who invented and operated the penal machine, constitutes the obvious link between the concrete fathers of "The Judgment" and "The Metamorphosis" and the abstract law and collective, anonymous authorities of *The Trial* and all subsequent works. The colony is the first step in Kafka's extension of the empirical family to the societies, nations, and species with which his later work is concerned.

The Old Commander's verdict is inscribed into the flesh of the condemned prisoner who deciphers it with his wounds. As he recognizes the text of the law on his body, he experiences a union with the paternal will more intimate—because physical—than Georg Bendemann's merely symbolic reunion in suicide with his father's will.

The penal machine does not restore, but creates its victim's true self. Before his arrest the prisoner was not much more than an animal. He lived in an unconscious state, ignorant of the law he violated. His dawning recognition of the sentence, as the machine inscribes it into his skin, creates a comprehensible continuity between act and atonement. By connecting his pain with the law he transgressed, he acquires a destiny that is uniquely his and, at the same time, his inward relationship to a superior will.

The continuity of self produced on the penal rack parallels Kierkegaard's idea of the self. (At the time of the punitive fantasies Kafka called Kierkegaard a "friend." He first became acquainted with Kierkegaard through an anthology entitled *Book of the Judge,* a title spelling out a significant affinity between them.) The authentic self in Kierkegaard is not identical with the organism, but with a moral continuity that we create by our choices and actions, and through a special and unique personal relationship to the Absolute. In Kafka's penal system suffering and dying give birth to the same kind of existential self.

Their dying not only restores Kafka's earlier protagonists to the true self of each, but also reconciles them to their families, and through their families, to the world. The sacrifice of Georg's false self reestablishes the harmony of life not in actuality but in principle. Georg's drowning in the river symbolically reunites him with the "stream of life" that proceeds above him in the "unending traffic" over the bridge from which he had leaped to his death.

When, at the beginning of the story, he had looked out upon the bridge, a quiet emptiness, a kind of frozen suspension of life, prevailed. His dying reanimates life. Although, chronologically, only a short time could have passed since the beginning of the action, symbolically a resurrection has taken place. The German word for "traffic"—*Verkehr*—also signifies "intercourse." The word alludes to the sexual and procreative aspect of the "unending" stream released by Georg's death. A remark made by Kafka to Max Brod corroborates the allusion. As he wrote the word *Verkehr* with which he concluded the story, Kafka, according to Brod, had thought of an ejaculation.

The end of "The Metamorphosis" is more directly explicit about the sexual and procreative liberation achieved by the hero's voluntary death. Gregor's demise frees his family from the guilt and shame that had become embodied in him. It allows thoughts of the future, of youth, marriage, and new bloom, to burst forth. Fittingly, the day of his death is the first day of real spring. Gregor Samsa dies as a scapegoat for humanity, represented by his family. In a letter to Max Brod, Kafka designated the writer a scapegoat for mankind. By taking mankind's sins upon himself and suffering for them, the writer allows mankind to sin in freedom.

The idea of the scapegoat led Kafka to find analogous insights in the anthropological research of his time and in the prototototalitarian tendencies becoming noticeable in Central Europe in his day. Both the anthropological and political implications of Kafka's work are most obvious in *In the Penal Colony*. In the officer's report of the penal colony's past, the victim's torture and gradual transfiguration through dying figure as the ritual of a communal cult. Undoubtedly with anthropological discoveries in mind, Kafka presented the human scapegoat sacrificed for the benefit and edification of the community. On the other hand, the "brainwashing" of the subject, who is made to assent joyously to his own destruction, creates obvious parallels to the political and cultural irrationalism of the First World War (*In the Penal Colony* was written two months after its outbreak) and the nascent totalitarianism that was to transform most of Europe into a huge penal colony less than three decades after Kafka had called his story as embarrassing "as our whole age."

At the same time, *In the Penal Colony* illumines the autobiographical character of Kafka's whole work. No matter how interesting and fruitful the anthropological, sociological, and philosophical implications of Kafka's writings are—and they are considerable—the intimate autobiographical meaning must never be lost sight of, since it gives rise to and shapes all the rest. Kafka's greatness lay in his extraordinary ability to picture the universal in the intimate and the intimate in the universal. A multiplicity of referred meanings constitutes the powerful allusiveness and suggestiveness of every image he created. The communal festiveness that surrounds the dying prisoner in the penal colony provides the external correlative to the inner illumination he experiences. It also is an extension of the obviously personal conclusions of Georg Bendemann's and Gregor Samsa's lives. Georg Bendemann dies under a busy thoroughfare, in the center of city life, as it were. After his demise, Gregor Samsa becomes, for a while, the center of his family's hushed attention, a scenic arrangement that anticipates the communal cult of death in *In the Penal Colony* two years later.

As it systematizes in an image the whole first phase of Kafka's mature writing, the penal apparatus is also a metaphoric description of this writing itself. The machine transfigures and kills the prisoner literally by writing, by imprinting a sentence on the prisoner's flesh. The German word for "writing" (*Schrift*) that Kafka uses has the meaning of both "script" and "scripture," enabling Kafka to allude to the literary and religious significance of his penal apparatus at once. Above all, the machine repeats Kafka's own activity as a writer of punitive fantasies who grants his characters illuminating insights as he kills them.

In a diary entry of December 1914, Kafka shows that the penal apparatus is a pictorialized poetics of his writing. He confesses there that he savors in advance his own dying through the vicarious dying of his characters. Here Kafka attributes to himself the same attitude he depicts in the officer of the penal colony. The officer exults in the executions he arranges and supervises. He envies the beatitude his victims seem to attain and craves to take their place. However, when he finally does, the venerated machine merely "murders" him unceremoniously and instantly. No sign of inner illumination can be seen on him. The whole penal system is reduced to the officer's subjective assertion that his own execution contradicts. The objective truth is withheld.

This connects *In the Penal Colony* with *The Trial*, which was begun a little over two months before the story and was left a fragment. Both Josef K., accused and executed without specified charge in the novel, and the officer in *In the Penal Colony,* who executes himself to prove his claim for the penal machine and to savor the happiness he expects it to give, die a meaningless death. Punishment there is, but it no longer shows the truth. Thereby the two punitive fantasies of 1914 are profoundly different from those of two years before. This difference marks a turning point in Kafka's entire development. In *In the Penal Colony* it is literally a change of perspective from the threatening façade to an inquiring objectivity. A detached observer—the explorer—listens to and then rejects the claims made for the punitive machine. Its subsequent collapse comes as the objective correlative of his rejection.

The perspective of *The Trial* is still that of a façade personality. There still is, as in the earlier punitive fantasies, a repressed past embodied in the protagonist's family, from which he has become estranged. However, the family is no longer central. An abstract authority, the Court, takes over the function of the accusing families of the earlier protagonists. It is no longer the intimate drama of father and son that shapes the narrative, but rather a conflict of principles.

Unlike the earlier punitive fantasies, *The Trial* does not specify the guilt for which its protagonist is arrested. The Court that judges Josef K. withholds the clear message given, in the earlier works, by father and family. Indeed, the confrontation of the self with its judge fails to take place. Punishment and annihilation remain, but understanding and atonement are gone.

The physical circumstances of Josef K.'s death reflect its subjective meaninglessness. Whereas Georg Bendemann dies in broad daylight, in the center of life, and Gregor Samsa departs with the first gleam of dawn, Josef K. is knifed in darkness and silence on the deserted periphery of his city. The external darkness surrounding him has its complement in the darkness within him. He does not understand his death. As he fails to see his judges, so he fails to recognize himself. He does not discern within himself a conviction certain and firm enough to be his truth. His inner self remains as unfathomable as the Court.

The Trial is the only truly opaque work among the major writings of Kafka. Its opaqueness results from two factors: the total ambiguity of the Court and the total ambivalence of its hero.

If we understand that the Absolute had two distinct faces for Kafka, we shall do greater justice to his complexity than if we dismiss it as pure paradox. We might define these two aspects of the Absolute by attaching the name of Plato, a philosopher Kafka held in high esteem, to one and the name of Jehovah to the other. With its Platonic face, the Absolute was pure spirit and the physical world illusion; engagement in it was fatally wrong. With its other face—the face of Jehovah, behind whom the features of

Kafka's robust and vital father lurked—it was energy and incessant will, a stream of generations and unending continuity of life. From this ambiguity within the Absolute, it followed that the self would become guilty in two opposite directions. It would become guilty before the Platonic aspect by getting "engaged," not merely sexually but economically and socially as well—by "wanting to snatch at the world with twenty hands," as Josef K. says of himself. On the other hand, the self would become guilty before the creator and progenitor of life by refusing "engagement" in the fullest sense of the word, by keeping itself pure in sterile virginity. In one case, it was the engaged and striving façade, in the other, the celibate true self that sinned and had to be sacrificed. The fate of Georg Bendemann shows the former guilt, while the fate of the misogynist officer of *In the Penal Colony* or of the chaste sister of Barnabas in *The Castle* shows the latter guilt. *The Trial,* however, begun under the immediate shattering impact of Kafka's first break with his fiancée, Felice Bauer, illumines the double and, consequently, total guilt of the self. In Josef K.'s Court the two faces of the Absolute combine to form the enigmatic mask of total ambiguity.

There is a further reason for the novel's ambiguity. It is Josef K.'s inability to decide between the forces battling within him. In Josef K., an unacknowledged *homo religiosus* clashes with the consciousness of economic man. His official impulse of self-preservation and self-assertion resists the upsurge of his unofficial religious impulse, the craving for self-surrender and self-transcendence, objectified by his arrest. It is of highest significance that the Court comes closest to him and appeals to him most directly through a priest. The protagonists of "The Judgment" and "The Metamorphosis" were arrested by the submerged childhood of self within them. In Josef K. the submerged childhood of man, rather than of the individual, arrests the apparently emancipated façade of modern rationality.

By naming his protagonist Josef and adding the name Josef to the initial K. of his own name, Kafka might have hinted at this vertical split in himself and modern man. The "Josefstown" district of Prague, on the edge of which he had been born, had in his childhood still been the site of the ghetto and the center of criminal life. As he once remarked to Gustav Janouch, the new "Josefstown" with its broad streets and bright, airy buildings presented only a "cover-up" surface, beneath which the dark, filthy, and frightful alleys of the ghetto lay merely submerged.

The careful reader becomes aware of this division within Josef K. Verbally, he seems to fight for reason, for man as defined by the rational legal system of the modern state, and denies the possibility of any extralegal guilt. By his acts, however, he seeks out and, in the end, submits to the Court. In his mind he never comes to a clear decision for either one or the other. Consequently, the inner truth can never come to light. His conflicting pulls toward surrender, which would give meaning to his death, and toward resistance, which denies meaning to it, tear the whole concept of a true self apart. To be sure, the pull toward surrender and death does prove stronger. For K. lets himself be executed. He even awaits his executioners and leads them toward his place of execution. His consciousness, however, to the last, withholds definitive assent.

The total ambivalence of the hero becomes the total ambiguity of the story. To appreciate the full extent of this ambiguity, we merely have to compare the last thoughts of Georg Bendemann and Gregor Samsa with the last thought of Josef K. Their last thoughts express not only assent to their death but also affirmation and affection for life as embodied in their families. The last thought of *The Trial,* however, is "shame." Shame, it seems, will survive the protagonist. This final noun of the novel not only emphasizes a desperate negativity in contrast to the tragic affirmation with which the earlier punitive fantasies ended, it also expresses a total ambiguity, which makes it impossible to decipher the final meaning of *The Trial.* For it is entirely uncertain to what the noun "shame" refers. It could refer to Josef K.'s failure to resist his execution, or to the senselessness of his murder, and to the shamefulness of a court that orders such injustices. In either case, "shame" would express Josef K.'s mental defiance coexisting with his physical submission. However, it could also refer to his refusal to kill himself or to understand what the Court expects of him. Then the novel would have the opposite meaning. Josef K. would be justly punished for his stubborn rejection of the possibility of his guilt. Both interpretations are equally justified even though contrary to each other. The unrelieved ambiguity of *The Trial* dissolves, therefore, not only the idea of a true self but also the possibility of discerning a truth altogether.

This ambiguity of the work reflects not only the ambivalence of the character but also the ambivalence of the author. In its last thought the consciousness of the character has become the comment of the narrator. It was Kafka himself who could not come to a decision about the meaning of his novel. He excised passages that would have shown Josef K.'s craving to be united with the Court or his longing to be transfigured in death, and would have made him resemble the officer of *In the Penal Colony.* Kafka crossed out a reverie of Josef K. that would have been the opposite of his actual death in the novel's final scene. In that passage Josef K. succeeds in entering the courthouse whence the warrant of his arrest had been issued, and he experiences a transfiguration, symbolized by a new garment of perfect fit. By eliminating this radiant vision from the novel, that is, from the consciousness of his protagonist, Kafka himself enacted the process of repression that his hero is engaged in. Josef K. exhibits tendencies toward surrender and suicide, which form the powerful subterranean drift that counteracts his ever conscious intention and action and pulls him ever further along toward destruction. These persist subliminally in fleeting thoughts, gestures, and unreasoned acts to which Josef K. seems to be driven. Except for the initial arrest, it is always Josef K. who either actively seeks or welcomes contact with the Court. Josef K.'s longing for contact with the Court emerges perhaps most clearly in the Titorelli chapter. Josef K. rejects the painter's suggestions for compromise solutions and insists on absolute acquittal by the highest Judges. His insistence amounts to a full recognition of their supreme authority over him and, beyond that, implies his wish to be accepted and approved by them. This is the limit to which Kafka allows K.'s wish for the Court to become conscious.

In his preceding works Kafka revealed the strategies of repression that his heroes engaged in and let the truth be said. In writing *The Trial* he imitated his character and threw out anything that might reveal him directly and unambiguously. In the process of creating his protagonist, Kafka himself performed the activity that constituted his character. He excised and refused to show the "whole truth." Consequently, he expunged dreams that would have betrayed Josef K. to himself and to the reader. In *The Castle,* where he deals with a hero much more conscious of his purposes, Kafka leaves K.'s dream in the text and also allows him a revealing childhood memory.

The reasons for Kafka's excisions in *The Trial* are twofold. For one thing they show that he desired to make so complete the division between the conscious surface and the subterranean level in his protagonist's character that Josef K. would be utterly unaware of one level of himself and the reader would be unaware of what compelled Josef K. toward his destruction. Josef K. thus became the precise image of the modern Central European bourgeois who, in our century, would be caught unawares by the eruption of destructive irrationalism around him; yet the tendencies that made this possible were to be found within the bourgeois himself. In this respect Kafka's own art did what he ascribed to the art of Picasso: it portrayed the distortions of reality that had not yet entered consciousness. Secondly Kafka, at the stage of *The Trial,* could no longer bring himself to condone his hero's conscious assent to the judgment that would destroy him.

There is one part of the novel, however, in which the other side of Josef K., which the author elsewhere excludes from the explicit text of the novel, is openly shown. This is the parable "Before the Law," which the prison chaplain tells to Josef K. in the "Cathedral" chapter. Here the radiance that streams from the Court in Josef K.'s repressed dream is allowed to shine forth openly, and the man from the country, who seeks entrance into the Law, is allowed to express freely what Josef K., who thinks of himself as a modern, rational man, can never bring himself to acknowledge: that the desire for union with the mystic Law is the fundamental concern of his existence.

The parable, or "legend" as Kafka himself called it, "Before the Law" presents the split within Josef K. as an explicit coexistence between desire and fear. The man from the country came to join the Law but is prevented by the doorkeeper, who tells him that he cannot let him enter now. He adds that the man might try to go in, but he frightens him with the prospect of more dreadful doorkeepers farther along.

The Law thus presents an ambiguity that the man had not expected. He had thought of it only as highly desirable and enticing. Now it also shows a threatening face. It seems that this ambiguity of the Law offers the key to the parable. This is true, if we restrict ourselves to the perspective of the man. However, as we shall see, here, in the second phase of Kafka's maturity, the perspective of the protagonist is not the perspective of the narrative. For a narrator has been put between reader and protagonist. If we see the man from the perspective of the narrator, we find that the ambiguity of the Law is a tool and catalyst for making the man's ambivalence his destiny. For the ambiguity, introduced by the doorkeeper, merely brings out an ambivalence within the man. His desire for the Law is now complicated by his fear of it. Desire and fear begin to exist side by side in the man.

What connects him with Josef K., and makes his destiny a perfect illustration of the novel, is his inability to opt for either side of his ambivalence. What he decides is to yield to his fear without giving up his desire. He defers his entrance and begins to wait before the door to the Law. He chooses a life of ambivalence. The consequences of his choice are degradation and lifelong frustration. He is literally lowered, by having to spend his life crouching on a footstool at the feet of the forbidding sentry. He is morally degraded by resorting to bribery and cajolery, and he is intellectually reduced to begging the fleas in the doorkeeper's collar to intercede for him. In the end he dies without having attained his goal.

The relationship of this parable to the novel in which it was originally written illustrates very well the different narrative principle of the second phase of Kafka's maturity. The rest of the novel was composed before the parable and indeed before *Penal Colony*. Both parabolic stories helped Kafka to clarify the problem of his novel. What the parable "Before the Law" accomplishes is to illuminate the basic problem of Josef K., his paralyzing ambivalence. In the narrative form of Kafka's punitive fantasies, which used the perspective of the façade, this ambivalence could not be clarified since it could not enter the conscious level of the narrative; Josef K.'s proud rationality, his façade, could not permit his longing for the Court to show itself openly at any time. In the parable, however, there is no façade, and the two conflicting forces within man are clearly presented as existing side by side. In place of the vertical division of layers, which we have found in the punitive fantasies, there is again the horizontal split that we found in Raban's wish-dream, but now it is without the separation of façade and true self.

The man from the country is Josef K.'s repressed truth exposed to view. This emerges clearly from the fact that Josef K., when he hears the parable, spontaneously identifies with the man from the country. Josef K. shares with the subject of the parable an ambivalence of desire and fear. Unlike Josef K., however, the man from the country does not repress his desire; he merely defers it. In contrast to the opaqueness of Josef K.'s fate, the parable, therefore, makes transparent the fatal incompatibility of man's desire for union with the Absolute and his fear for life and safety. By its transparency, the parabolic form, which characterizes Kafka's second phase, goes even further in elucidating the problem it presents. The parable "Before the Law" implies quite clearly that the man from the country could find a "way out" of his impasse by abandoning his fear and entering the gate regardless of the risks awaiting him; if he were to choose to go forward, despite the injunctions of the doorkeeper, he would attain true self-fulfillment. However, the man in the parable could also do the opposite; he could yield to his fear and abandon his desire, leave the gate and turn his back forever on doorkeeper and Law. Such a retreat would amount to an abandonment of self, insofar as his self is identical with its dominant concern. By the same token, it would assure not only his physical survival—which he ensures anyway by choosing not to go into the Law—but also a survival in dignity and independence. He would gain a life emancipated from obsession.

The choice open to the man in the priest's parable defines the problem around which Kafka's subsequent work revolves. In his second and third phase Kafka no longer describes the catastrophic eruption of a hidden truth and the resultant destruction of his protagonist; instead he presents a dilemma attendant upon his protagonist's attempt to realize his true self that would, at the same time, be a union with or recognition by a higher power, authority, or collective. In Kafka's later works the self of his protagonist is undivided and openly dedicated to its craving or quest. The conflict is not between a façade and a true self, but between the true self and an external power that disavows the self's claims or frustrates its expectations. Like the Law in the legend, the external power in Kafka's later works both beckons and forbids entrance to itself. Between the protagonist's imaginings and the behavior of external reality there exists a discrepancy that is the subject of the self's reflections and comments. The protagonist hopes that somehow the contradiction will be resolved. He hopes that reality will conform eventually to his expectations; this hope constitutes his true self and is the mission to which he subordinates and for which he utilizes everything. If he were to give up his hope, he would have to renounce his self and nature, as the ape does in "A Report to an Academy." All other characters of Kafka's later works, clinging to their missions, are yet unable to change reality and influence it according to their desire. They spend their lives waiting in front of closed entrances, locked out from the goal they crave. Indeed, the title of Kafka's last and greatest novel, *The Castle* (*Das Schloss,* 1922), a marvelous elaboration and development of the theme of the legend "Before the Law," carries in German the subsidiary meaning of "lock." For K. the Castle is literally a lock that locks him out. Unable to gain the entrance and likewise unable to resign and turn their backs on it, the protagonists of Kafka's later works stay doggedly loyal and true to their quest. But their loyalty or stubbornness immobilizes them. They waste their lives in visible or invisible cages, prisons of their own devising.

Cage, castle or "lock," underground fortress or burrow are dominant images of Kafka's last works. At the end of his second phase, he presents the image of the cage in "A Report," concluding the volume of parables that "Before the Law" initiated chronologically; and the cage appears again in "A Hunger Artist," title story of his last volume of narratives. The two stories are contrasting approaches to the theme of the cage. We have already drawn attention to the solution of the captured ape who cannot stand life in the cage and finds a "way out" by ceasing to be what he is and becoming something else. The hunger artist takes the opposite course. He voluntarily enters and stays in the cage in order to express his true self.

The hunger artist's wish to be recognized as the incomparable artist he is, is not fulfilled; the public first misunderstands, then neglects and ignores him. Looking at the narrative through the protagonist's perspective, we are inclined to accuse the public of callousness, vulgarity, and cruelty. Similarly, seeing through Josef K.'s perspective in the "Cathedral" chapter of *The Trial,* we are inclined to blame the doorkeeper for keeping the man out of the law. However, Kafka underwent a great change toward analytic clarity and explicitness in the near-decade after he wrote the legend. If we understand the story "A Hunger Artist" as an indictment of the public, Kafka's text convicts us of being wrong. For, at the end of his life, the hunger artist informs the world explicitly that he deserves no admiration. He had been a sport of nature, a freak, unable to find food that satisfied him, and, therefore, incapable of doing anything else but starve. If he had found food to his taste, he would have eaten like everyone else and led a completely undistinguished life.

Like the punitive fantasies, "A Hunger Artist" presents a discrepancy between the official perspective of the story—given by the protagonist—and the truth. The perspective of the punitive fantasies, seeing the protagonists as victims of external injustice and outrageous fortune, tends to prevent us from noting the submerged inner force that drives them to their catastrophes. Similarly, the hunger artist's perspective makes us sympathize with him as the victim of the public and overlook the crucial fact that his exhibition is a fraud. For he makes us accept something as admirable achievement that, as he himself admits in the end, is nothing more than a necessity and, indeed, a debility, for which pity rather than admiration might be the proper response. Knowing his natural defect, the hunger artist should not have expected admiring recognition, but he made us—the readers—believe that this was his due.

In Kafka's final phase we return to the deviousness and deceptiveness of a perspective that distorts and conceals the truth of the story, and is defeated by it. Again the protagonist's claim and grievance against the world are unjustified; they are deceit. His frustration and final refutation or capitulation reveal the truth. As in the punitive fantasies, it is in the dying of the self through which truth conquers and shines forth. Dying, the hunger artist unmasks the fraud his life had been. Like Gregor Samsa, with whom many analogies connect him, he finds in death the contentment that life had consistently denied him.

Yet there is an essential difference between the punitive fantasies and Kafka's final phase. The punitive fantasies unveiled a contrast between the façade and the truth of the self. The late works oppose a unified self to truth. The hunger artist's self is not divided between façade and true self. On the contrary, his mission, symbolized by the cage in which it takes place, is the uncompromising and absolute expression of his true and only self. His starving is the full revelation of his inner truth.

However, this inner truth is, in itself, a deception. Herein lies the paradox of Kafka's last phase. In it the self is a pretense and presumption. The hunger artist's complete "otherness," his inability to eat and, therefore, be like other men, would in itself not be a fraud but a mere eccentricity that would exclude him from humanity. The hunger artist, however, refuses to stay outside humanity. This refusal drives him to proclaim as art the defect with which he was born and exhibit it for public acclaim. Art and fraud are inseparable in him. For he is an artist only by virtue of committing his fraud, or, put differently, his decision to treat his natural want as though it were a skill makes him artist and fraud at the same time. It is this decision that makes him enter the cage. The cage exhibits both untruth and art, yet it also symbolizes absolute subjectivity and otherness. No one but he can fast indefinitely; no one resembles him. His isolated existence in the cage dooms any hope for true appreciation and understanding from the public beyond his bars. For he is on exhibit as a freak. His "art" or, more truly said, his nature is unique—so subjective, so different from the interests and feelings of other men that the hunger artist's monstrous spirituality cannot possibly be more than a short-lived sensation in the life of mankind.

Whereas the hunger artist makes his fraud explicit, the immense deception perpetrated by the Land Surveyor K. in *The Castle* is never stated explicitly, and K. has, therefore, fooled most readers, critics, and exegetes of the novel. K. claims to have been called and appointed land surveyor by the Castle that controls the village into which he has strayed one night. He makes us believe that the Castle authorities, by refusing to honor his claim, treat him unjustly and deprive him of what by right is his. He presses his claim with such urgency and consistency that the reader feels compelled to accept it at face value and to see in K. a victim of soulless bureaucracy or to construct elaborate schemes of interpretation based on the "injustice" done to K. Consequently, *The Castle* appeared in critical literature as a satire on bureaucracy, an adumbration of totalitarianism, an allegory of social injustice or of the religious problem of man's insistence on justice and God's grace. All these interpretations are the result of the critics' being duped by K.'s colossal fraud. A close reading of the text reveals that K. has no legitimate claim on the Castle because he never was appointed land surveyor. This truth of the novel is revealed by inconsistencies in the plot and by a brief passage of K.'s inner monologue. These allow only one conclusion: K. had never been called by the Castle.

K. has no document to prove his call. He promises, however, that his assistants will soon arrive with his apparatus. They never come. Instead K. is given two new "assistants" by the Castle. These assistants know nothing about land surveying and have no apparatus. K. has never seen them before. Thus the "proof" of K.'s appointment, which the promised arrival of his old assistants and apparatus was supposed to be, never materializes. The fact that K. accepts his new assistants without waiting for his old assistants or ever thinking of them shows that, in all likelihood, they do not exist.

A telephone inquiry at the Castle produces the answer that nothing is known of K.'s appointment. Immediately thereafter, a call from the Castle reverses this first answer and confirms K.'s claim. K.'s mental reaction to this information unmasks him as an imposter. Instead of registering with simple satisfaction the news that the "misunderstanding" has been cleared up, K. considers the Castle's recognition of his claim "unpropitious." He takes it to be a "smiling acceptance" of his "challenge," designed to "cow him" by "lofty superiority." The term "challenge," used by K. in this context, shows that he does not expect to step into a promised position but that he comes with the purpose of fighting the Castle and forcing it to yield something to him, either the coveted office or something else. It is clear that he was never appointed land surveyor and called to the Castle. He is a stranger who, for reasons that we shall examine, "challenges" the

Castle to submit to his unfounded claim. The Castle seems to "accept" his "challenge" and plays a game with him that forms the plot of the novel.

This close reading of the text alters the whole basis of interpretation of Kafka's last and greatest novel. It can no longer be maintained that the conflict between justice and injustice, no matter on what level, is its theme. Its theme is rather K.'s attempt to make everyone, including the reader, believe that justice is the problem and that the injustice inflicted upon him is his motive in his struggle with the Castle. Kafka has K. conduct his campaign so skillfully and emphatically that he persuades most readers to believe him, contrary to the textual evidence he himself provides. In his richest and most profound work Kafka depicts the victory of fiction over reality. The deception perpetrated by his character triumphs not over the other characters—for no one in the novel really believes K.—but over the reader.

Kafka achieves this amazing triumph of art by the masterful application of a narrative perspective that misleads the reader into mistaking the protagonist's view for the truth. However, while creating this victory of fiction, Kafka at the same time exposes its falseness through his protagonist's own oblique self-revelations. Furthermore, the fact that the hero's claim never attains true recognition in the novel shows its vanity. In a letter to Max Brod, written in the year 1922, at the time of *The Castle*'s composition, Kafka defined the writer's essence as "vanity." Kafka's late work, especially his artist stories, "A Hunger Artist" and "Josephine," shows vanity both as narcissism and as futility. It shows that the attempt of subjectivity to impose its terms upon external reality must always fail.

The Castle answers K.'s attack with an ironically exact retribution. It meets his unreal claim by an equally unreal appointment. Klamm's letter appoints K. as Land Surveyor, and he will henceforth be addressed as such; but he obtains no land to survey and is never established in an appropriate office. The title given him by the Castle is as gratuitous and empty as his pretended call. The Castle gives him assistants who are irrelevant to his professed profession. They can assist him in his land surveying as little as can the instruments he claims he has but is unable to produce. These assistants also cause him to do to them what he claims the Castle has done to him. As the Castle locks him out and will not admit him, he locks out his assistants and refuses to let them come to him. K. himself displays the cruelty and injustice he ascribes to the Castle. Moreover, even as he took his mistress away from Klamm, his own chief, so he loses her again to one of his assistants. In this late work judgment appears not as destruction, but as ironic retribution.

The Castle counters K.'s maneuver by presenting a universe in which there is no certainty and nothing is what it seems to be. This is the necessary consequence of the fact that the protagonist, too, is not what he seems to be. That is, K.'s self is not a fact but a pretense. It is a desperate experiment, an attempt to impose his fiction upon the reality that confronts and excludes him. He needs this fiction to break into and become part of the reality he faces.

Kafka, in *The Castle,* describes the fundamental situation of modern man, for whom neither the world nor his own self is given and certain. Like every man, K., in order to be, has to be recognized and related as an individual to the whole of society; he must have a specific calling. In order to get his call, he must already be someone, an accredited and required expert. However, K. knows he has no call and is, therefore, nothing. He is a stranger, utterly unconnected, and superfluous—locked out by the *Schloss* functioning in its basic meaning of "lock." Since a human being cannot live permanently outside humanity, K. desperately needs to enter it, that is, to become someone needed and recognized. In order to live, he has to "unlock" the lock with which humanity excludes him. As the dominant necessity of life and the essence of desirability, "*das Schloss*" presents to him its other meaning in the guise of the magically beckoning and unattainable Castle. It is K.'s staggering and superhuman task to create the call he needs. He has to pretend that he already possesses what he has come to get—the necessary prerequisite for beginning an integrated and authentic existence. Therefore, his battle with the Castle is not a whim but a desperate necessity. Precisely because he has no objectively valid claim for recognition, he must force the Castle to honor his subjective pretense—his fiction—as the truth. K. fights to become in truth what he pretends he is—the land surveyor called by the Castle.

K.'s quest is a metaphoric statement of the lifelong struggle that Kafka's entire writing sought to describe. (Significantly, his first work bears the title "Description of a Struggle.") At the time he composed *The Castle* Kafka wrote to his woman friend and lover, Milena, that he was given nothing, that he must create not only his present and his future but his past as well. His task is, therefore, infinitely more difficult than that of other men. For not only must he fight the battle for his future that every man has to wage but, while engaged in that battle, he must also be acquiring a past, a ground on which he can stand and all others can take for granted as their birthright and inheritance.

Kafka related this peculiar predicament to the fate of the Westernized Jew in Europe who, already uprooted and cut off from his ancestral traditions, is not yet permitted to enter fully and truly the life of his hosts. Beyond this personal and national meaning, however, Kafka presents in *The Castle* the task facing modern man in general. Unmoored from his spiritual and social anchorage, expelled from his once secure place in the cosmos, modern man, as the Existentialists point out, has to make his own identity and project his own existence instead of assuming it as given. Kafka's fragmentary novel depicts the tragic irony and ultimate impossibility of this enterprise.

NOTES

1. The original text uses the German word for "unused"—*unbenützt*—which the English translation renders as "uninhabited."
2. The original text uses the German word for "absent-mindedly"—*zerstreut*—which the English translation renders as "confused."
3. Emphasis mine.

SELECTED BIBLIOGRAPHY

NOTE: The first edition of Kafka's collected writings, edited by Max Brod, appeared in Berlin and Prague in 1935–1937. It included the first five volumes listed below. It was revised and reissued by Schocken Books in New York in 1946. This edition still forms the standard edition of Kafka's works in German. Subsequent volumes, edited by Max Brod and, in one case, Willy Haas, were added, as listed below. All were published by Schocken Books in New York.

Principal Works of Franz Kafka

Vol. 1. *Erzählungen und kleine Prosa.* (This volume contains all works published by Kafka himself in his lifetime.)
Vol. 2. *Amerika.*
Vol. 3. *Der Prozess.*
Vol. 4. *Das Schloss.*
Vol. 5. *Beschreibung eines Kampfes. Novellen, Skizzen, Aphorismen aus dem Nachlass.*
Tagebücher, 1910–1923. 1948 and 1949.
Hochzeitsvorbereitungen auf dem Lande und andere Prosa aus dem Nachlass. 1953.
Briefe. 1958.
Briefe an Milena. Edited by Willy Haas. 1952.

Principal Translations of Kafka's Works

Amerika. Trans. Edwin Muir. Preface by Klaus Mann. Afterword by Max Brod. New York: New Directions, 1940. (Paperback edition 1962.)

Amerika: A Novel. Trans. Willa and Edwin Muir. New York: Schocken Books, 1962. Paperback.

Dearest Father: Stories and Other Writings. Trans. Ernst Kaiser and Eithne Wilkins. New York: Schocken Books, 1954.

Description of a Struggle. Trans. Tania and James Stern. New York: Schocken Books, 1958.

Letters to Milena. Ed. Willi Haas. Trans. Tania and James Stern. New York: Schocken Books, 1953. (Paperback edition 1962.)

Parables and Paradoxes. In German and English. New York: Schocken Books, 1962. Paperback. (First edition was titled *Parables* and was published in 1947.)

Selected Short Stories of Franz Kafka. Trans. Willa and Edwin Muir. Introduced by Philip Rahv. New York: The Modern Library, Random House, 1952.

The Castle. Definitive edition. Trans. Willa and Edwin Muir, with additional material translated by Eithne Wilkins and Ernst Kaiser, with a homage by Thomas Mann. New York: Alfred A. Knopf, 1954. (Reissued 1964. First edition 1930.)

The Diaries of Franz Kafka, 1910–1913. Ed. Max Brod. Trans. Joseph Kresh. New York: Schocken Books, 1948. (First edition 1947; paperback edition 1965.)

The Diaries of Franz Kafka, 1914–1923. Ed. Max Brod. Trans. Martin Greenberg, with the cooperation of Hannah Arendt. New York: Schocken Books, 1949. (Paperback edition 1965.)

The Great Wall of China: Stories and Reflections. Trans. Willa and Edwin Muir. New York: Schocken Books, 1946. (Fourth printing 1960.)

The Penal Colony: Stories and Short Pieces. Trans. Willa and Edwin Muir. New York: Schocken Books, 1948. (Paperback edition 1961.) (This volume represents the translation of Volume I of the German edition of Kafka's collected writings.)

The Trial. Definitive edition. Trans. Willa and Edwin Muir. Revised, and with additional materials translated by E. M. Butler. New York: Alfred A. Knopf, 1957. (First edition 1937.)

Biographical and Critical Literature on Kafka

Anders, Günther. *Franz Kafka. Pro und contra. Die Prozess-Unterlagen* Munich: C. H. Beck, 1951.

———. *Franz Kafka.* Trans. A. Steer and A. K. Thorlby. London: Bowes & Bowes, 1960.

Arendt, Hannah. "Franz Kafka. A Revaluation," *Partisan Review* 11 (1944): 412–22.

Beissner, Friedrich. *Der Erzähler Franz Kafka. Ein Vortrag.* Stuttgart: Kohlhammer, 1952.

Brod, Max. *Franz Kafka. Eine Biographie.* Dritte, erweiterte Auflage. New York: Schocken Books, 1954. (First edition 1937.)

———. *Franz Kafka: A Biography.* Trans. G. Humphreys Roberts and Richard Winston. 2d ed., enlarged. New York: Schocken Books, 1960.

Camus, Albert. "Hope and the Absurd in the Work of Franz Kafka," in *The Myth of Sisyphus and Other Essays*. Translated from French by Justin O'Brien. New York: Alfred A. Knopf, 1955, 124–38. (Paperback edition Vintage Books, n.d., 92–102. Original French edition Paris: Gallimard, 1943.)

Dentan, Michel. *Humour et création littéraire dans l'oeuvre de Kafka*. Geneva: Droz, 1961.

Eisner, Pavel. *Franz Kafka and Prague*. Trans. Lowry Nelson and René Wellek. New York: Arts Inc., 1950.

Emrich, Wilhelm. *Franz Kafka*. Bonn: Anthenäum, 1958.

Flores, Angel, ed. *The Kafka Problem*. New York: New Directions, 1946. (Reissued New York: Octagon Books, n.d.)

Flores, Angel, and Homer Swander, eds. *Franz Kafka Today*. Madison: University of Wisconsin Press, 1958.

Gray, Ronald. *Kafka's Castle*. Cambridge: Cambridge University Press, 1956.

———, ed. *Kafka: A Collection of Critical Essays*. Englewood Cliffs, N.J.: Prentice-Hall, 1963.

Janouch, Gustav. *Gespräche mit Kafka. Erinnerungen und Aufzeichnungen*. Frankfurt am Main: Fischer, 1951.

———. *Conversations with Kafka: Notes and Reminiscences*. Introduction by Max Brod. Trans. by Goronwy Rees. New York: F. A. Praeger, 1953.

Järv, Harry. *Die Kafka-Literatur. Eine Bibliographie*. Malmö: Lund, Cavefors, 1961.

Martini, Fritz. "Franz Kafka. Das Schloss," in *Das Wagnis der Sprache. Interpretationen deutscher Prosa von Nietzsche bis Benn*. Stuttgart: Ernst Klett Verlag, 1956, 287–335. (First edition 1954.)

Neider, Charles. *The Frozen Sea: A Study of Franz Kafka*. New York: Russell and Russell, 1962. (First edition New York: Oxford University Press, 1948.)

Politzer, Heinz. *Franz Kafka: Parable and Paradox*. Ithaca, N.Y.: Cornell University Press, 1962.

Robert, Marthe. *Kafka*. Paris: Gallimard, 1960.

Sarraute, Natalie. *L'ère du soupçon. Essais sur le roman*. Paris: Gallimard, 1956.

Slochower, Harry, ed. *A Franz Kafka Miscellany*. Rev. enlarged second edition. New York: The Twice a Year Press, 1946. (First edition 1940.)

Sokel, Walter H. *Franz Kafka: Tragik und Ironie: Zur Struktur seiner Kunst*. Munich and Vienna: Albert Langan-Georg Müller, 1964.

Spann, Meno. "The Minor Kafka Problem." *The Germanic Review* 32 (1957): 163–77.

Spilka, Mark. *Dickens and Kafka: A Mutual Interpretation*. Bloomington: Indiana University Press, 1963.

Tauber, Herbert. *Franz Kafka: An Interpretation of His Works*. Trans. G. Humphreys Roberts and Roger Senhouse. New Haven: Yale University Press, 1948.

Wagenbach, Klaus. *Franz Kafka: Eine Biographie seiner Jugend, 1883–1912*. Bern: Francke, 1958.

3

KAFKA'S POETICS OF THE INNER SELF

WHEN KAFKA began to write, scepticism toward the writer's medium—language—and despair over the limitations inherent in it, were widespread, and not only in German and Austrian letters, although with special acuteness in these. The earliest piece of writing by Kafka, which is preserved, an entry in a young girl's album, dating from the year 1900, is a striking document of this *Sprachkrise* or *Sprachskepsis,* the crisis of faith in language.[1] Kafka, age seventeen, declares his impatience with the inadequacy of words for the task of conveying the intimate and inward aspect of memory, an inwardness that the German word for memory, "Erinnerung," etymologically suggests: "Als ob Worte erinnern könnten! Denn Worte sind schlechte Bergsteiger und schlechte Bergmänner. Sie holen nicht die Schätze von den Bergeshöhn und nicht die von den Bergestiefen" (B, 9).[2]

Kafka's earliest letters to his friend Oskar Pollak are marked by a profound disillusionment with the possibilities of genuine communication through language. The nature of language as a tool of generalizing and conceptual communication endangers the task of expressing essentially personal and intimate truths. Kafka's analogy of words to "bad mountaineers" and "bad miners" of the soul closely resembles another document of the *Sprachkrise,* Maurice Maeterlinck's passage from *Le Trésor des humbles,* which Robert Musil chose as the motto for his novel *Törleß,* composed three years after Kafka's album entry:

> Sobald wir etwas aussprechen, entwerten wir es seltsam. Wir glauben in die Tiefe der Abgründe hinabgetaucht zu sein, und wenn wir wieder an die Oberfläche kommen, gleicht der Wassertropfen an unseren bleichen Finger-

From *Modern Austrian Literature* 11 (1978): 37–58.

> spitzen nicht mehr dem Meere, dem er entstammt. Wir wähnen eine Schatzgrube wunderbarer Schätze entdeckt zu haben, und wenn wir wieder ans Tageslicht kommen, haben wir nur falsche Steine und Glasscherben mitgebracht; und trotzdem schimmert der Schatz im Finstern unverändert.[3]

Here we find the same critical questioning of language, the same denunciation of its inadequacy as in Kafka's earliest extant written statement. Language, in the process of utterance, devaluates and falsifies its content. It cannot do justice to and fails to retain the essence of what we wish to say. In the most famous document of the *Sprachkrise,* Hugo von Hofmannsthal's "A Letter," Lord Chandos says that if we could "think with the heart" expression would present no problem;[4] but such a language of the heart is given to us, if at all, only in rare moments of mystical enchantment. To some extent, this "critique of language," to use the title of Fritz Mauthner's three-volume work of 1903, reveals discontent with the worn-out, cliché-ridden, and pretentious idiom of much of late nineteenth-century writing—a discontent of which Karl Kraus became the outstanding exponent. However, the critique of language also envisages an inherent incapacity of words, insofar as words derive their being from generalizing thought, to express a highly individualized sensibility and inwardness. The social-utilitarian realm that language serves is held to bear no relationship to that inwardness of the individual that Hofmannsthal calls "the heart," and that Maeterlinck and Kafka designate by analogies to the depths of the sea or the interior of the earth. If we were to compare the linguistic concerns of these writers to the problems of communication encountered by Kierkegaard's Abraham in *Fear and Trembling,* the close relationship of the *Sprachkrise* to protoexistential thought would become apparent. The *Sprachkrise* possibly contributed more heavily to the Central European reception of Kierkegaard in the first two decades of this century than might be suspected.

However, even more directly relevant to an understanding of the *Sprachkrise,* and particularly to the role it plays in shaping Kafka's poetics, is an approach that benefits from the intellectual categories of Jacques Derrida. For the *Sprachkrise* provides an excellent example of that "metaphysical nostalgia" that, according to Derrida, finds it difficult to accept "L'impossibilité pour un signe, . . . de se produire dans la plénitude d'un présent et d'une présence absolue," the impossibility of that "parole pleine qui dit être la vérité."[5] What Derrida diagnoses as metaphysical nostalgia is the desire to abolish "la brisure," the gap between the signifier and "the reality" that is posited behind and beyond the verbal sign. The assumptions underlying the phenomenon of the *Sprachkrise,* and particularly the poetics of Kafka, are understandable in terms of that "ineluctable nostalgia for presence that makes of this heterogeneity [of word and being] a unity by declaring that a sign brings forth the presence of the signified."[6] The *Sprachkrise* is a symptom of the loss of faith in the actuality of such a statement. Its preoccupation would best be described by changing the indicative, "a sign brings forth" into the hortatory subjunctive, "a sign should bring forth the presence of the signified."

In the period between the beginnings of his diary and the writing of "The Judgment," Kafka evolved a rudimentary theory of writing that, in its most confident form, seems to embody the intellectual tradition that Derrida associates with metaphysical nostalgia for the "absolute presence" in writing of that reality to which writing refers, a presence that, in Derrida's words, "claims to be truth." Kafka's goal was "truth," i.e., the perfect *adequatio* between word and feeling, between linguistic sign and inner being.[7] This "truth," to be sure, had two aspects pointing in opposite directions. One of those was communal, collective, and universalist, the other deeply personal, individual, and subjective. It is this second aspect of Kafka's "truth" that I want to explore here in some detail. His ideal was "to fill each word entirely with [himself]" (T, 34).[8] He strove for the ability to write a tale that would be linked to his life "from word to word," a tale that he could draw to his breast (T, 39). He graphically described how the length of a word written by him would equal exactly the extent of his "feeling" (T, 60). He spoke of "dwelling" in each of his thoughts (T, 57). He wished to "pour himself" into his writing (T, 230). He exulted in the "miracle" that every thought, "even the weirdest," could find words able to express it (T, 293). The precise agreement between inner experience and linguistic formulation was his criterion for literary value (T, 186 f.), and he insisted that where "the right feeling vanishes, writing loses all value" (T, 391).

This "poetics" presupposes two distinct entities—the inner self or inner world, which is to be expressed, and the medium of expression—language. If perfect correspondence between the two is achieved, writing becomes the true vehicle of being. The fundamental precondition for this harmony does not lie in language, but in the inner world. Being is prior to words. The inner self conquers the word by "filling it out." It stands in a position of dominance to language. It is to take possession of language and, through language, of the social collective world to which language belongs.

In his earliest statement about the nature of his writing, a letter to his friend Oskar Pollak, the twenty-year-old Kafka describes his intention as a writer. It is "to lift, with one single heave, that which I believe I have in me (I do not always believe it)" (B, 17). This kind of writing he called "magic." Ten years later, in a diary entry of 1913, he writes of "the enormous world which I have in my head" (T, 306) and considers it his special mission and destiny "to liberate [himself] and to liberate it," even at the cost of his life: "Die ungeheure Welt, die ich im Kopfe habe. Aber wie mich befreien und sie befreien, ohne zu zerreißen. Und tausendmal lieber zerreißen, als sie in mir zurückhalten oder begraben. Dazu bin ich ja hier, das ist mir ganz klar" (T, 306).

One year after that, he speaks of his special talent of representing his "dreamlike inner life" (T, 420), to which all his other potentialities have had to be sacrificed. His diaries show abundantly that his "dreamlike inner life" consisted not only of the most vivid and powerful night dreams, which Kafka frequently wrote down, but also of hallucinatory visions that obsessed him, especially shortly before falling asleep or immediately after waking up, and that greatly contributed to the insomnia of which he bitterly complained all his life. A tumult of deeply troubling oneiric images obsessed, tormented, and exhilarated him. He called these visionary hosts his "devils," "ghosts," and "demons."[9] One example may stand here for many: "Heute mittag vor dem Einschlafen . . . lag auf mir der Oberarm einer Frau aus Wachs. Ihr Gesicht war über dem meinen zurückgebogen, ihr linker Unterarm drückte meine Brust" (T, 162).

These visions, as noted in his diaries, sometimes formed the point of departure for narratives. In a diary entry of late May 1914, for instance, Kafka begins a fragmentary narrative that tells of a white horse suddenly appearing in an avenue of a city (T, 375). Two pages later, while criticizing the fragment, he makes clear how the inspiration for the story had come to him. The white horse had appeared to him the night before in a vision, as he was about to fall asleep. It seemed to have literally stepped out of his head: "Gestern erschien mir das weiße Pferd zum erstenmal vor dem Einschlafen, ich habe den Eindruck als wäre es zuerst aus meinem der Wand zugedrehten Kopf getreten, wäre über mich hinweg und vom Bett hinuntergesprungen und hätte sich dann verloren" (T, 377).

This close connection between hallucinatory vision and narrative beginning sheds an interesting light on Kafka's creative method or process, in general, even as the specific image of the white horse sheds light on such tales as "A Country Doctor," in which magic horses play a crucial role, or "The New Advocate," in which the protagonist is a horse metamorphosed into a lawyer.

When Dr. Rudolf Steiner, founder of the Anthroposophic branch of the Theosophic movement, visited Prague, Kafka mentioned his visionary states. In his writing, Kafka confessed to Dr. Steiner, he had had experiences "close to the clairvoyant states, as described by you, Herr Doktor" (T, 57). Kafka's statement receives its full meaning, if we recall that Rudolf Steiner had described elaborate methods for attaining extrasensory perceptions and transcendental insights. Perhaps Kafka's visionary states, some of which are described with frightening vividness in his diaries, were similar to hallucinations induced by drugs. In any case, these states seemed to give him feelings of transcending the quotidian self and reaching the frontiers of human potentialities. He found in these states, as he told Dr. Steiner, the "enthusiasm that probably characterizes the clairvoyant," except his peace, and "even that," he adds, was "not entirely" lacking (T, 57).

Thus Kafka equates the call of literature with a hidden, powerful inner world that, as the early letter to Oskar Pollak already clearly shows, stands in complete opposition to ordinary life. Physical health and strength, social intercourse, conversations, particularly with women—these are all seen by him as "the alternative" to "the magic" with which writing beckoned. He compares the conjuring up of the buried treasures of the inner self to "a mole's existence"—anticipating by twenty years the key image of his last fragment, "The Burrow"—and concludes his letter with the question whether an active physical and social life might perhaps not have been the real "magic" of his summer. If so, he implies, he would have been wrong to look for it in "the mole and his kind." The conflicting demands of inner and social self dominated Kafka's entire life and work.[10] Kafka's letters to Felice Bauer definitively show that Kafka tended to view his existence in terms of a struggle between these two selves.[11]

The struggle between the "two selves" can also be seen in terms of two kinds of linguistic intent—expression and communication, or, in Kafka's case, literature and conversation. In his early letter to Oskar Pollak, Kafka viewed his newly found ability *to talk* (to women), in other words, the social art of conversation, an alternative to the inner-directed "magic" of his writing. We thus encounter the paradox that one form of linguistic utterance, writing, stands in radical opposition to the essential function of language as the privileged form of human communication. This paradox has of course been a familiar one since Romanticism, or at least since Mallarmé's distinction between the "parole immédiate" of ordinary, informative discourse, and the "parole essentielle" of purely evocative poetry.[12] In fact, it is already contained in Kant's concept of "aesthetic ideas." An "aesthetic idea" for Kant is one that no language can ever "completely attain and make comprehensible."[13] Insofar as the "aesthetic idea" is transrational, Kafka's visionary utterances, which withhold any aid to the understanding, might be said to conform to "aesthetic ideas" in the Kantian sense. The visionary statement offers no explanatory context. It cannot "make itself comprehensible." Kafka himself considered his art irrational when he insisted that "The Judgment," a visionary work of which he was particularly fond, was utterly inexplicable. This, to be sure, did not prevent him from putting his astute analytic intelligence to work at interpreting the tale.[14]

The problem of communicating the "aesthetic idea" lay of course at the core of the phenomenon of *Sprachkrise.* For Kafka this problem became a particularly acute conflict between the demands of the visionary inner world, insisting on being expressed, and the equally strong moral duty to communicate with the human species. As we have seen, Kafka from the beginning viewed the task of communication as the alternative to the "magic" of writing. The relationship between them, and therewith the strategy of Kafka's writing, will become clearer if we examine the contrast between the poetics of the early diaries and the entirely different poetics outlined in Kafka's famous "Letter to His Father," the only sustained attempt at an autobiography that he left us.

Kafka's "Letter to His Father" begins by calling attention to his difficulty in communicating. The fear that his father had always instilled in him, Kafka claims, had deprived him of the confidence and power necessary for oral communication. By the terror that he struck in his son, his father had condemned him to be a stutterer. In any conversation he found himself at a loss for words. Max Brod contradicts Kafka's self-portrait in this respect. He presents his friend as a very articulate, sociable, and witty companion. However, if we are to believe Kafka's own statements about himself, Brod's image of him must have been Kafka's skillfully maintained social façade. For in his life-documents he, like Jean-Jacques Rousseau, constantly laments his inability to talk coherently and successfully. The archetype of all oral communication remained, for Kafka, communication within his family and, above all, with his father. In this he had miserably failed, in his own view.

Writing, on the other hand, was at the opposite pole. It was the region to which the son could flee and that he cultivated because it was the one area in the world where his father's powerful influence did not extend. Speech was linked to the father's forbidding and threatening presence, but writing dealt with his absence: "Mein Schreiben handelte von Dir, ich klagte dort ja nur, was ich an Deiner Brust nicht klagen konnte" (H, 203).[15]

Thus writing memorialized a twofold absence for Kafka—first the absence of a loving trusted parent, which had caused his grief initially, and then, the absence of the longed-for audience for this grief. In his writing, Kafka, according to his "Letter to His Father," was always bitterly aware of the unbridgeable "difference" between the subject matter and the act of writing. The unreachable father functioned like that "trace," which recalls to us the eternal absence of that which writing is about, and spells out the inevitable heterogeneity that makes writing different from being and gives it its autonomy. What is un-Derridan in the poetics of the "Letter to His Father" is the writer's nostalgia for the presence that is withheld. Writing for Kafka is not the confident assertion and affirmation of the "difference," but the everlasting regret of an imposed autonomy.

What Kafka omits from his autobiography is the substitution that his early diaries triumphantly proclaim. The place of the absent father, as the source of inspiration, was taken by the "inner self." Kafka's poetics, at least up to the composition of "The Judgment," was the attempt to find the way to transcend the need for oral communication that, he felt, his father had made impossible for him. As viewed from Kafka's poetics in the diaries, writing is not the lament over an absence, but the celebration of a presence. This presence, to be sure, is no longer the father, but the inner self and its visionary truth. Kafka's writing, so conceived, represents a victory over the father, and more than that—a victory of the self over the social world of which his father was the earliest representative.

Kafka saw writing, in its ideal form, as a passionate penetration, a taking possession of language, and through language of the social world, originally embodied in the family, that language represents and contains. Kafka's early diaries are filled with recordings of creative experiences in which self-transcendence unites with the sensation of omnipotence. It is this merging of selflessness with self-exaltation that suggests a parallelism between writing and sexuality in Kafka's poetics. Kafka frequently associates inspirational writing with images of flowing, streaming, opening out. He mentions his "pouring himself" into his work and compares his "outpouring" in his writing to an erotic relationship to a girl of his acquaintance (T, 76). Recalling the experience of writing "The Judgment" in the trancelike state of a single night, Kafka writes of an ecstatic self-abandonment, a flowing away of all boundaries of the self, an "absolute opening of body and soul." "Nur so kann geschrieben werden" (T, 294), he proclaims apodictically.[16] While writing "The Judgment," as Max Brod relates, Kafka had experienced an ejaculation.[17] This complete abolishment of the boundaries and limits of the ego, to which the interview with Dr. Steiner also alludes, connects self-transcendence with self-aggrandizement. The loosening of the self seems to bestow magic powers on it: "Das Bewußtsein meiner dichterischen Fähigkeiten ist am Abend und am Morgen unüberblickbar. Ich fühle mich gelockert bis auf den Boden meines Wesens und kann aus mir heben, was ich nur will" (T, 76).

In such moments, Kafka felt, any random sentence written down by him would be perfect (T, 42). It is this merging of selflessness with self-exaltation that suggests the sexual aspect of Kafka's poetics. In the early stages of his courtship of Felice Bauer, Kafka made this parallelism between writing and eros explicit. He saw then in his writing the justification for his hope of winning her. Both writing and eros are, in the framework of

Kafka's life as presented in his "Letter to His Father," triumphs over the parentally induced inhibition of communication.

However, the essential precondition for successful writing, in Kafka's sense, was the genuineness of "the presence" of the truth in the act of writing. The act would have to be the direct outflow, the "unmediated vision," of the inner self. The "draft" or current of inspiration must never be interrupted. If it were, the truth would be gone, and with it, all the value the work might have. The greatest peril for this writing was self-deception—the writer's delusion that he was still in touch with the truth, while it had left him. Kafka's inhibiting perfectionism derives from his insistence upon the presence of the original feeling that inspired the writing. Any word in excess of that feeling, any embellishment or "fill-in," would make the work not only aesthetically worthless, but morally, and one should say ontologically, wrong. This insistence goes beyond the romantic and existential cult of authenticity.[18] The anxiety it engenders can be compared to the worshiper's dread of defilement of the Eucharist.

The consequence of this insistence upon the unadulterated presence of the inner truth in the work is Kafka's conviction that a good work can only be written in a single sitting, unconsciously, without any deliberation and artifice. "The Judgment," he felt, qualified for such standards, and it was the only work of his to which he accorded unmixed and even enthusiastic approval. Having written it in one single night, without interruption, so that his legs were stiff when he rose in the morning, he could exclaim: "Nur *so* kann geschrieben werden, nur in solchem Zusammenhang, mit solcher vollständigen Öffnung des Leibes und der Seele" (T, 294). From this height of a coherent unity—a "Zusammenhang"—achieved between inspiration and result, he could only look down upon the novel—the first version of *Amerika*—with which he had been struggling for a long time, as on "lowlands" where he had wasted his efforts.

Kafka's contemptuous dismissal of the novel and his complete satisfaction with the short tale point to his essential difficulty when faced with narratives that could not possibly be written in one sitting. Inherent in Kafka's approach to writing, it explains the numerous false starts and alternate versions of beginnings of narratives that were never continued beyond a few sentences or paragraphs. Most of his long stories and all of his novels remained fragments; and even *The Trial,* Kafka's only novel with an ending, remained fragmentary in the middle and exhibits a mosaiclike structure of episodic scenes. This poetics, which was of course not an arbitrary and controllable choice, but the way in which Kafka's literary imagination seemed to work, also helps to explain the peculiarly painful conflict Kafka experienced between the demands of literature and human life. All human relationships represented fatal distractions from a work that brooked no interruption. Nothing short of the lifelong self-confinement in the innermost chamber of a deserted cellar, of which he speaks to Felice, would seem to satisfy such rigorous requirements for concentration.

This explains the paradox that an activity conceived of by Kafka as a flowing outward, an inundation of the world by the inner self, seemed at the same time to require an absolute withdrawal, an inhuman solitude. One of Kafka's earliest diary entries states that "loneliness is best" for him. It "metamorphoses" him—Gregor Samsa's fate is here seen as a most positive occurrence—and has "a power over [him] which never fails" (T, 34). For it opens up his "inner self" and allows its deeper layers to come forth. With a dread bordering on panic, he seeks to ward off any disturbance of his creative loneliness. In a letter to Felice, several years later, he describes the ideal way of life for him. It would be to live "with writing utensils and a lamp, in the innermost chamber of a locked spacious cellar." Someone would come to bring him his food, but place it rather far away from his room, "behind the outermost door of the cellar." This arrangement would protect him from contact with the person feeding him. He would return to his desk in the innermost hiding place and, after eating, "immediately commence to write again! And the things I would then be able to write! From what depths I would tear them out! Without effort! For utmost concentration knows no effort!" (BF, 250). To be sure, he adds, at the slightest slackening of inspiration he would probably go mad. He tells her of "invisible chains" binding him "to an invisible literature" and warns her that he would scream "if anyone should come near to touch my chains" (BF, 450). That such auspices would not be favorable for his engagement to Felice was not difficult to see.

In his first attempt at a novel, "Wedding Preparations in the Country," Kafka presented the paradigm for the contradictory structure underlying his poetics. The protagonist, Raban, having to visit his fiancée in the country, wishes he could evade this dreary task by repeating in actual life what he had been accustomed to do in a recurrent fantasy of his childhood years. Faced with disagreeable social obligations, Raban imagined that he would separate his real self from his body. The former would stay in bed, in "the shape of a great beetle" (H, 12), while his body would be sent to carry out Raban's tasks in the world outside. Meanwhile, Raban's true self, reclining in inhuman and solitary serenity, would be the absolute master, not only of his human façade, but of the entire world. The traffic below Raban's window would be utterly dependent on his whims. By withdrawing from humanity and totally identifying with his true desire, by becoming his truth, Raban is able to dominate the world from which he has withdrawn. This wish-dream describes the structure underlying Kafka's inspirational poetics. In Stanley Corngold's formulation, the "omnipotent bug . . . suggests the inwardness of the act of writing."[19] By reducing his empirical person to the zero degree, and uniting with his "dreamlike inner life," the writer by the same token takes possession of society, through its medium—language. His total concentration on his writing immerses him in the essence of his community, as embodied in its language, and enables him to appropriate it so absolutely that he becomes the power that moves it.[20]

That Kafka pursued messianic ambitions in his writing has often been observed. The passage is frequently quoted in which he writes that he would receive permanent satisfaction from his writing only if he could "raise the world into the pure, the true, and the unchangeable" (T, 534). Messianism is the logical consequence of his need "to liberate" "the enormous world in [his] head" into articulated existence. For this inner world would or should be the power that by confronting the empirical world would help it to achieve transfiguration. This messianic task requires the writer to be a Messiah figure. Indeed the state of union between inner self and word that Kafka invokes in his poetics alludes to the incarnation, but reverses its terms. Here it is not the Word become flesh, but the flesh—the living individual of flesh and blood—become Word. "Ich bin nichts als Literatur," Kafka declares. In place of an incarnation we could speak of an "inlogozation." The self achieves divine power through "pouring itself" into the waiting body of language. Kafka, whose writing took place mainly during the night, copies a passage from Roskoff's *History of the Devil* which states that among the Caribs "he who works in the night is believed to be the creator of the world" (T, 314). A fairly crass example of the desire for divine transfiguration by virtue of the creative act appears in a dream that Kafka jotted down in his diary. His "literary projects" come on "an enormous chariot" and naked girls, resembling the houris of Islamic paradise, lift the author upward from his earthly "wretchedness," while his hand commands peace. He feels "the frontiers of human efforts," "at the farthest verge of human endeavor" (D II, 41)[21]

> und mache auf meiner Höhe aus eigenem Antrieb und plötzlich mich überkommenden Geschick das Kunststück . . . indem ich mich langsam zurückbeuge—eben versucht der Himmel aufzubrechen, um einer mir geltenden Erscheinung Raum zu geben, aber er stockt—den Kopf und Oberkörper zwischen meinen Beinen durchziehe und allmählich *wieder* als gerader Mensch *auferstehe*. War es *die letzte Steigerung, die Menschen gegeben ist?* (T, 383 f.; italics mine)

His inspired art, his "Kunststück," literally leads to the artist's "resurrection" and, even though Heaven fails to give the promised special sign to him, and the self-ironic stance is unmistakable, the hybris in this dream clearly alludes to a Faustian striving for the "ultimate" possibilities of man.

In a late diary entry, Kafka sees his literary mission, which is born from "loneliness," as "an assault upon the ultimate frontier of earthly life." "This entire literature," by which, as the context makes clear, Kafka understands his own writing, could have "easily developed into a secret doctrine, a new cabala" (T, 553). Indications for this he sees in his work. However, it is a superhuman task requiring an "unimaginable genius" with the ability to recreate the past and to create the future. We see here how the distant descendant of Kant's "aesthetic idea," which Kafka's visionary poetics represents, likewise entails the corollary to it—Kant's doctrine of transrational genius. In Kant's aesthetics the genius functions like another demiurge giving his own laws to the second nature he creates in his art. Similarly Kafka finds that literature, as he conceives it, demands the strength and power of a demiurge of history. After "The Judgment"—a success that in Kafka's own eyes was never repeated—Kafka increasingly felt that such strength was utterly wanting in himself. Far from imagining that he possessed the quasi-divine powers required for his mission, he considered himself in his diaries and letters the least adequate instrument for his task—sluggish, feeble, sickly, ill-equipped in body, in feeling and in mind. Yet the demand persisted.

However, the gravest threat to this demand came from the nature of writing itself. Kafka's ideal was to give the most faithful expression to the truth within himself, and he thought he had achieved that in writing "The Judgment." Such a faith seemed to justify all sacrifices. This faith required as its formal correlative the restriction of the narrative point of view to a single consciousness and the absence of an omniscient narrator interjecting himself between work and reader. According to Friedrich Beissner, this "unitary perspective" is the chief characteristic of Kafka's art in which its singular truthfulness resides.[22] Despite the profound modifications that Beissner's theory needs to become truly valid for Kafka's actual practice,[23] Kafka's literary judgments, as Hartmut Binder has shown,[24] tend to support Beissner's view. Kafka valued above all else the greatest possible closeness between the feelings of the fictional characters in a scene and those of the author in writing it. The union between writer and text thus established constituted for Kafka the truthfulness of the work in which the reader would naturally share. Thus writing would bring about by a detour that communication which speech had difficulty in achieving, and without which the messianic ambitions of literature would have no basis.

However, after "The Judgment," in the period of *The Trial,* Kafka began to realize that his writing was by no means a vehicle of the truth, but the opposite—an instrument of counterfeit. In looking back on "the best" he "had written" (T, 448), he found that it derived its strength from duplicity. His best passages—according to him, always scenes of dying—were perfectly designed to fool the reader. Kafka enjoyed the dying of his protagonists and luxuriated in death scenes. His writing, however, masked his joy so completely that to the reader these scenes appeared terribly sad and deeply moving. By staying within the point of view of his protagonist, who viewed his death as "an injustice" or at least a harsh fate, the reader, made to identify with the character, shared his grievance, while the author savored "such descriptions secretly as a game":

> ich freue mich ja in dem Sterbenden zu sterben, nütze daher mit Berechnung die auf den Tod gesammelte Aufmerksamkeit des Lesers aus, bin bei viel klarerem Verstande als er, von dem ich annehme, daß er auf dem Sterbebett klagen wird, und meine Klage ist daher möglichst vollkommen, bricht auch nicht etwa plötzlich ab wie wirkliche Klage, sondern verläuft schön und rein. Es ist so, wie ich der Mutter gegenüber immer über Leiden mich beklagte, die bei weitem nicht so groß waren, wie die Klage glauben ließ. Gegenüber der Mutter brauchte ich allerdings nicht so viel Kunstaufwand wie gegenüber dem Leser. (T, 448 f.)

Such artful deceit and clever contriving for aesthetic effect, while attesting to Kafka's subtle mastery of the art of fiction, glaringly contradict his ideal of the writer's absolute faithfulness to and unity with the feeling permeating his work and embodied in his character. The bifurcation of perspectives of author and character, and thus of author and reader, gives the lie to the presence of the writer's "truth" in his text. Thus Kafka failed to find in his own work that indivisible unity between conception and execution that he demanded of literature. The mere restriction of the point of view to the protagonist does not, contrary to Beissner's claim, guarantee the truthfulness of the work. On the contrary, the apparent absence of an omniscient narrator only helps to hoodwink the reader all the more effectively by suggesting an identity between author and protagonist that is not there. The author in his concealment manipulates and dupes the reader, who, one can easily imagine, might be horrified to learn that his "tears" were a calculated side effect of the author's sadomasochistic "play."

There is a striking parallelism between Kafka's literary strategy, as described in this diary entry, and the structure of Raban's dream. Both, first of all, are seen as infantile devices. Raban's split self was originally a child's fantasy, and Kafka compares his literary artifice to the child's device of exaggerating his ailments to get his mother's sympathy. The hidden author, in Kafka's diary entry, corresponds to Raban's inhuman truth. The dying fictional character parallels Raban's pretended human self, and the outside world that is taken in by Raban's human façade has its equivalent in Kafka's deceived reader. Ironically it is the very idea of a "true self" that spells out deception. Raban sends out his "stand-in" to fake his presence in human relationships from which he is "really" absent. Thus precisely by becoming his "truth," Raban cheats. His fantasy, if taken seriously and carried over into life, would entail emotional disaster for his dupes.

Duplicity, Kafka comes to recognize, is built into the very act of writing fiction, since in it the self inevitably splits into the writer and the character, or into the subject and the object of reflection. The "eigene Gestalt" is for Kafka the primary subject of literature, and remains for him the prototype of all fictional characters. But in this self-reflection the unity between the writer and the writing is ruptured. In fact, it can never truly come about, or at any rate, it cannot be sustained for any length of time. For from the moment the writing self reflects on the subject it writes about, the perfect congruence of writer and subject, which is truth, becomes impossible. In its place a playful and coquettish self-regard arises, which for Kafka is the infernal opposite of truth:

> Und das Teuflische (am Schreiben) scheint mir sehr klar. Es ist die Eitelkeit und Genußsucht, die immerfort um die eigene oder auch um eine fremde Gestalt—die Bewegung vervielfältigt sich dann, es wird ein Sonnensystem der Eitelkeit—schwirrt und sie genießt. Was der naive Mensch sich manchmal wünscht; "Ich wollte sterben und sehn, wie man mich beweint," das verwirklicht ein solcher Schriftsteller fortwährend, er stirbt (oder er lebt nicht) und beweint sich fortwährend. (B, 384 f.)

Narcissism for Kafka is only the extreme and logical consequence of reflection, since it is the ultimate result of the separation from being and thus from truth, which occurs in reflection. Multiplication of characters in the literary work does not change the self-reflection at its basis, but merely intensifies it. Since fictional characters are self-projections of the author in varying degrees, "vanity" simply becomes "a solar system" instead of being confined to a single star.

With other authors of the *Sprachkrise,* Kafka held to the superiority of being over thinking, immediacy over reflection. What he dreaded in writing was its mediate character, its referential nature, and separation from being. The inevitably metaphoric nature of writing, its inability to be what it speaks about, describes, or evokes, brought on his despair. Half a year before the letter to Max Brod, from which I just quoted, Kafka noted in his diary: "Die Unselbständigkeit des Schreibens, die Abhängigkeit von dem Dienstmädchen, das einheizt, von der Katze, die sich am Ofen wärmt, selbst vom armen alten Menschen, der sich wärmt. Alles dies sind selbständige, eigengesetzliche Verrichtungen, nur das Schreiben ist hilflos, wohnt nicht in sich selbst, ist Spaß und Verzweiflung" (T, 551).

Kafka's view of writing as "a joke" makes the comparison of his work with a "game"—even a Wittgensteinian "language game"[25]—plausible as long as we realize that it applies to Kafka's "despair," not to his ideal. Writing seen as self-referential "play" of language signals the breakdown of his faith in his own work as the medium of the truth buried in him. Self-reflection capped that fraudulence, which, as the diary entry about his death scenes shows, Kafka found inherent in the strategy of "fiction."

In the ideal of writing, as Kafka conceived it, the author should be nothing but the medium for what wants to be expressed; but self-reflection steps between the inspiration and the act, and dams up and pollutes the flow from within. The self made object shuts out the vision of that "enormous world inside the head" that writing was to bring into view. Literature stifles that which the writer's word is to liberate. A book "must be the axe for the frozen sea within us," Kafka wrote at age twenty-one (B, 28). Any other use of literature, so he felt all his life, was mere "decoration." To demand sacrifices for such a purpose was a sin against life. However, self-reflection, in which for Kafka the nature of fiction resides, separates the self from its inner world and prevents truth from appearing. It perpetuates "the frozen sea" within the self.

We return here to the paradox that underlies Kafka's "Rabanesque" poetics. This poetics attempts to unite two contradictory projects. While it aims for the dissolution of the self to "allow the deeper layers to come to the fore" (T, 34), it also directs the writer toward extreme self-absorption. Its fundamental quest—lifting the inner world into language, and thus into articulated consciousness—also has the dream of the ego's magic and messianic omnipotence built into it. The radiant glimpse of that immense inner world, like the light from inside the law, in the prison chaplain's legend in *The Trial,* can show itself only when the shadow of the self no longer impedes vision. Yet, and this is the paradox that denied to Kafka "permanent satisfaction" with his works, self-regard was inseparable from an art that conceived of itself as "a descent" (B, 384) into the interior of the self. In terms of his own poetics, then, Kafka had to be what Walter Benjamin called him—"ein Gescheiterter."[26]

The poetics, which I have tried to investigate here, alone cannot illuminate the peculiar impact and power of Kafka's writing. Even the impasse to which this poetics led him cannot be fully understood without the communal, collective, and universalist aspect that, in addition to the inward and subjective side on which we have dwelt here, marked Kafka's idea of "truth" and language. Furthermore, a strong desire for clarification and understanding—in the broadest sense, for self-preservation—runs side by side with the visionary element in his art. Only when these other concerns are investigated, can we hope to do justice to Kafka's "poetics."

The present essay must be considered merely a first step toward that objective.

NOTES

1. Cf. Theodore Ziolkowski's "James Joyces Epiphanie und die Überwindung der empirischen Welt in der modernen deutschen Prosa," *Deutsche Vierteljahrsschrift für Literaturwissenschaft und Geistesgeschichte,* 35 (1969): 596.

2. *Briefe, 1902–1924,* ed. Max Brod (Frankfurt am Main: S. Fischer Lizenzausgabe von Schocken Books, New York, 1958). Referred to as B.

3. Quoted from Robert Musil, *Prosa, Dramen Späte Briefe,* ed. Adolf Frisé (Hamburg: Rowohlt, 1957), 15.

4. Hugo von Hofmannsthal, *Gesammelte Werke,* Vol. 2 (Berlin: S. Fischer, 1924), 180.

5. Jacques Derrida, *De la Grammatologie* (Paris: Les Editions de Minuit, 1967), 102.

6. Cf. *Grammatology,* trans. Gayatri Chakravorty Spivak (Baltimore and London: Johns Hopkins University Press, 1976), "Translator's Preface," xvi.

7. Anthony Thorlby, in his stimulating essay "Anti-Mimesis: Kafka and Wittgenstein," crassly contradicts Kafka's own poetics when he writes: "Kafka's stories illustrate the dreadful problem that language *is* something altogether different from what it says. . . ." See *On Kafka: Semi-Centenary Perspectives,* ed. Franz Kuna (London: Paul Elek, 1976), 74. This is precisely what Kafka cannot accept. "Language games" in Wittgenstein's sense are radically inappropriate to the intensely "realistic" and literal-minded seriousness with which Kafka pursues "truth" by means of his writing.

8. Franz Kafka, *Tagebücher, 1910–1923,* ed. Max Brod (New York: Schocken Books, 1948 and 1949). Referred to as T.

9. The close relationship between Kafka's writing and his dream life has frequently been noted. Cf. particularly S. Fraiberg, "Kafka and the Dream," *Partisan Review* 23 (1956): 47–69; Michel Dentan, *Humour et création littéraire dans l'oeuvre de Kafka,* (Geneva/Paris: Librairie Droz/Librairie Minard, 1961), passim; Friedrich Altenhöner, *Der Traum und die Traumstruktur im Werk Franz Kafkas,* Diss., Münster, 1962. Hartmut Binder has also pointed to the flood of visions that "crowded in" on Kafka so that he could consider "die Ausstoßung ins Kunstwerk als grosses Glück." See *Motiv und Gestaltung bei Franz Kafka* (Bonn: Bouvier, 1966), 117. A systematic investigation and analysis of the visionary element in Kafka's work has not yet been undertaken.

10. Cf. Walter H. Sokel, *Franz Kafka: Tragik und Ironie: Zur Struktur seiner Kunst* (Munich/Vienna: Albert Langen/Georg Müller, 1964). Paperback ed. Frankfurt: Fischer Taschenbuch Verlag, 1976.

11. Cf. particularly the long explanatory letter, dated end of October/beginning of November 1914, and the very last letter to Felice, dated October 16, 1917.

12. Cf. my *The Writer in Extremis: Expressionism in Twentieth-Century German Literature* (Stanford: Stanford University Press, 1959), 12.

13. " . . . unter einer äethetischen Idee aber verstehe ich diejenige Vorstellung der Einbildungskraft, die viel zu denken veranlaßt, ohne daß ihr doch ein bestimmter Gedanke, d.i. *Begriff* adäquat sein kann, die folglich keine Sprache völlig erreicht und verständlich machen kann" (*Kritik der Urteilskraft,* Par. 49).

14. Cf. Franz Kafka, *Briefe an Felice und andere Korrespondenz aus der Verlobungszeit,* ed. Erich Heller and Jürgen Born (Frankfurt am Main: S. Fischer Lizenzausgabe von Schocken Books, New York, 1967), 394, 396. (This volume will hereafter be referred to as BF.) Side by side with the oneiric and fantastic tendency of Kafka's art, a strong rational current also runs through his work and forms a powerful complement to the visionary strain in it. His writing can be divided into two distinct types: visions and illustrations. The latter are similes or metaphors, serving basically explanatory purposes, and frequently extended into parabolic narratives. Cf. particularly Karl-Heinz Fingerhut, *Die Funktion der Tierfiguren im Werke Franz Kafkas: Offene Erzählgerüste und Figurenspiele* (Bonn: H. Bouvier & Co., 1969), 37–40, 45–59; and Hartmut Binder, *Kafka in neuer Sicht: Mimik, Gestik und Personengefüge als Darstellung des Autobiographischen* (Stuttgart: J. B. Metzler, 1976,) 7–20. For the distinction between the two types of Kafka's narratives, see Walter H. Sokel, "Das Verhältnis der Erzählperspektive zu Erzählgeschehen und Sinngehalt in 'Vor dem Gesetz,' 'Schakale und Araber,' und 'Der Prozeß'," *Zeitschrift für deutsche Philologie* 86 (1967): 267–300. Stanley Corngold's trenchant essay—"The Structure of Kafka's Metamorphosis: Metamorphosis of the Metaphor"—denies the metaphoric nature of Kafka's art and claims that Kafka "is the writer par excellence who came to detect in metaphorical language a crucial obstacle to his own enterprise." (*The Commentator's Despair: The Interpretation of Kafka's "Metamorphosis."* Port Washington, N.Y.-London: National University Publications Kennikat Press, 1973, 5.) The present essay certainly agrees with Corngold's approach, and particularly with his assertion that "the desire to represent a state of mind directly in language, in a form consubstantial with that consciousness," (7) was Kafka's avowed goal. However, as I shall try to show in a subsequent publication, Corngold does justice to only one aspect of Kafka's poetics and ignores other very powerful and contradictory intentions of his work.

15. Franz Kafka, *Hochzeitsvorbereitungen auf dem Lande und andere Prosa aus dem Nachlaß,* ed. Max Brod (New York: Schocken Books, 1953). This volume will hereafter be referred to as H.

16. Binder points out that Kafka's last great fragment, "The Burrow," was, according to Dora Diamant, also written in one single night. See Binder, *Motiv und Gestaltung,* 118, and J. P. Hodin, "Erinnerungen an Franz Kafka," *Der Monat* 9 (1949): 8–9, 89–96.

17. *Über Franz Kafka* (Frankfurt: Fischer Taschenbuch Verlag, 1974), 114.

18. Cf. Lionel Trilling, *Sincerity and Authenticity* (Cambridge: Harvard University Press, 1971, 1972), passim.

19. Corngold, *The Commentator's Despair,* 21.

20. A crucial image corroborates the link of Raban's wish-dream to Kafka's

poetics. Kafka frequently uses the image of "draft" or "current" ("Zug") to denote inspiration. His work, he states, can succeed only "in ganzem Zug" (T, 267), in a single complete uninterrupted "draft" or "breath." In the passage of his early letter to Oskar Pollak, which I quoted, he speaks of "lifting in one single draft (Zug) that which I think I have in me." (My translation of "Zug" by "heave" obscures the close relationship to Raban's fantasy.) In Raban's dream of omnipotence, a draft of air always blows through his room. This image associates Raban's dream with Kafka's precondition for successful writing.

21. *The Diaries of Franz Kafka, 1914–1923,* ed. Max Brod, trans. Martin Greenberg with the cooperation of Hannah Arendt (New York: Schocken Books, 1974). First Schocken paperback edition, 1965.

22. Cf. Friedrich Beissner, *Der Erzähler Franz Kafka: Ein Vortrag* (Stuttgart: W. Kohlhammer, 1952).

23. Cf. esp. Klaus-Peter Philippi, *Reflexion und Wirklichkeit: Untersuchungen zu Kafkas Roman "Das Schloß"* (Tübingen: Max Niemeyer Verlag, 1966), 14–32.

24. "Kafkas literarische Urteile," *Zeitschrift für deutsche Philologie* 86 (1967/2): 230.

25. Cf. Thorlby, "Anti-Mimesis."

26. "Um Kafkas Figur in ihrer Reinheit und in ihrer eigentümlichen Schönheit gerecht zu werden, darf man das Eine nie aus dem Auge lassen: es ist die von einem Gescheiterten." *Briefe,* ed. Gershom Scholem and Theodor W. Adorno. Vol. 2 (Frankfurt: Suhrkamp, 1966), 764.

4

LANGUAGE AND TRUTH IN THE TWO WORLDS OF FRANZ KAFKA

IN KAFKA'S earliest extant narrative, "Description of a Struggle," a wild exhibitionist attracts the attention of the narrator in a church. Because he is ostensibly praying, while indulging in grotesque antics, the exhibitionist is called the Praying Man, while the obese narrator bears the title Fat Man. The Fat Man accuses the Praying Man of being the bearer of a disease with which he himself admits to being familiar. He calls this disease "a seasickness on dry land."[1] The nature of the affliction is linguistic. Its symptom is the inability to remember "the truthful names of things,"[2] which leads to the compulsive effort to invent ever-new names for them. The victim of this disease cannot recall, for instance, the word "poplar," and in consequence names the tree "the Tower of Babel." Then, having forgotten that name also, he calls it "Noah in his Cups."

We encounter in the victim of such "forgetfulness" the prototype of the poet or literary man. He substitutes metaphor for straight language. The first symptom of his "seasickness" of language is a metaphor. In the word "Tower," there is still contained a recognizable element of comparison. A tall tree, the poplar, can be compared to a tower. However, in this disease, metaphor immediately degenerates into a wildly associative discourse that turns incomprehensible. For the associations that carry it are personal and lead completely away from the original referent. To be sure, the stream of associations can be reconstructed. The comparison of a tall tree to a tower leads to Babel as the place where the highest tower had been attempted. At the same time, "Babel" exemplifies of course the very process

From *German Quarterly* 52 (1979): 364–84.

of forgetting of a shared language and suggests the resulting confusion of human relationships that is the topic of the narrator's complaint. In the Book of Genesis, the building of the Tower of Babel follows closely upon man's first inebriation. The stream of associations thus leads understandably from "the Tower of Babel" to "Noah in his Cups" (literally: "Noah when drunk").[3] However, this sequence of signifiers for "poplar" shrouds the referent, the object signified, in obscurity for all those who are not initiated in this sequence of associations. It destroys the possibility for communication. The languages of personal and social self are sundered. The result is the speaker's imprisonment in total isolation. The Praying Man, as viewed by the narrator, and the narrator himself, are the forerunners of Gregor Samsa, who ceases to make himself understood by everyone else.

Poetic speech, insofar as its essence is metaphor, appears as the first step toward the individual's exclusion from the human species. Mankind is a community of mutually comprehensible communicators. Exclusion from it is the lot of the insane. Appropriately, the Fat Man addresses his alter ego, the Praying Man, as "a perfect lunatic" ("ein gelungener Tollhäusler").[4] The "perfect lunatic" remains bottled up in incommunicable subjectivity. This is not the place to go into the very interesting threads that lead from here to Kierkegaard—Abraham's inability to communicate God's demand.[5] The poetic mode of speech, as viewed in "Description of a Struggle," is born of a defect and ends in disaster. The defect is forgetfulness of the fact that the world receives meaning literally from the consensus of the community that bestows the "truthful" names on things. Metaphor signifies the individual's incapacity to retain his foothold in the community of speakers. By the same token, it signals the disintegration of the self that loss of memory entails. For the extreme individuality of metaphoric speech paradoxically results from the lack of a sense of personal identity. The sense of a coherent and continuous self depends on a functioning memory, which the practitioners of metaphor in "Description of a Struggle" lack. The Praying Man's exhibitionism results from his inability to be convinced of his own existence.

"There has never been a time," he says, "in which I have been able to convince myself of my life."[6] Therefore, he has the need to be "looked at by people, to cast a shadow upon the altar, as it were."[7] He "needs" "to be hammered, by people's regard, into a fixed position, [at least] for the duration of a brief hour."[8] The purpose of his "praying" is to gain a temporary feeling of identity.

The Praying Man is a direct ancestor of the existential hero, plagued as he is by the spiritual seasickness that Sartre will call "nausea." (The etymology of Sartre's term suggests its origins in sea- or ship-sickness.) The lack of a sense of substance in himself corresponds to the dissolution of all appearance of stability in the world. For the Praying Man, things do not hold together when he approaches them. He cannot grasp them. "I grasp the things around me only in such debilitated imaginings, that I always believe that they had once been alive, but are now sinking from view."[9] And in the second version, "things sink around [him] like falling snow, while in front of others even a small glass of schnaps stands on the table firm like a monument."[10] For him nothing is self-evident, nothing induces a feeling of permanence and identity. The untroubled certainty that others seem to enjoy challenges him, as it does Roquentin, the hero of Sartre's *Nausea.*

However, the profound difference between Kafka and the existentialists becomes apparent here as well. In contrast to Sartre, Kafka stacks the cards against the spokesman of his own way of being. (Kafka's identification of the persona of the writer with his Praying Man is shown by his definition of writing as a "form of prayer.")[11] Sartre's Roquentin ascribes the appearance of stability and certainty about the objective world to the conspiracy of the "salauds,"[12] the bourgeois hypocrites who pretend that an orderly cosmos exists in order to protect their self-importance. For Kafka, on the other hand, the spiritual "seasickness" of his protagonists is not necessarily the truth of human reality. Kafka's protagonist is inclined to accept a reliable and harmonious universe that only his own unfortunate peculiarity, his "sickness," prevents him from perceiving. He is eager to concede that it might be *his* perspective that dissolves the calm beauty of a world in which expectations are fulfilled as a matter of course, and no gap exists between individual consciousness and being. Supporting this surmise, he refers to a childhood experience that he describes as follows (in the first version of the tale):

> When as a child, I opened my eyes after a brief afternoon nap I heard, still entangled in sleep, my mother, on the balcony, ask someone downstairs, in a natural tone: "What are you doing, my dear? It's so hot." A woman answered from the garden: "I am having high tea in the green [garden]." They said that without reflecting and without undue distinctness, as if everyone would have to expect it [their statements].[13]

And in the second version of the story, Kafka's protagonist makes this exchange of trivial remarks even more definitely the touchstone and test case for the existence of a profound difference between his own uncertainty and the certainty of all others in regard to the nature of things.

It is a shared language, a dialogue, that seems to guarantee a graspable world, a stable cosmos. This language has to be spoken in such a way "as if everyone would (and could) expect it." It is precisely this condition that the protagonist, because of his forgetfulness, i.e., his lack of a sense of identity, can never attain. His loss of communal memory, stored in the common names of objects, makes his speech radically unexpected, a monologue of capricious, purely subjective signifiers. Whereas for Sartre, meaninglessness and incoherence are the objective characteristics of Being that only the conspiratorial hypocrisy of the pillars of society and "law and order" conceals from us, Kafka leaves the overwhelming possibility open that his protagonists' (and his own) disorientation may only be a pathological deviation, and that the seeming certainties of others may indeed be the truth. If such a truth should exist, its guarantor is a language shared.

The course of the plot of Kafka's earliest tale (and there definitely is a rudimentary recognizable plot in it) shows that the "poetic" and aesthetic way of life in his protagonists[14] leads to the "revenge of things against them" and their "obliteration."[15] Wronged by being wrongly named, creation rebels and drowns those who cannot abide by the order of "truth." Metaphoric signifiers do not contain the communal consensus that lives in the common word "poplar." It is the presence of the "trace" of that community that makes the names of things "truthful" ("wahrhaftig"). From this vantage point, metaphoric speech is untruth. Significantly, lying begins with the Tower of Babel as the primal locus of loss of a universally shared language. Community for Kafka is lodged in the family. As the family disintegrates, community is lost. This is what the sequence of the narrator's associations alludes to. The metaphor following "Tower of Babel," "Noah in his Cups," alludes to the rebellion of son against father, reported in Genesis. When Noah lies in drunken stupor, his son Ham mocks him for his exposed genitals.[16] Man's first inebriation leads to the self-exposure of the second father of mankind—Noah—and his consequent fall from authority. The first rebellion of son against father, Ham's against Noah, is in turn followed by mankind's self-assertion against God in the building of that tower that was to reach into Heaven and ended in the breakup of the human family into isolated, mutually uncomprehending groups of individuals—the atomized, strife-ridden societies of history. What is hinted at in "Description of a Struggle," in thickly veiled form and abstractness, becomes personalized and concretized eight years later in "The Judgment," Kafka's first mature work. Georg Bendemann's sanctimoniously concealed disrespect for his apparently senile father marks that self-assertion of the uprooted ego, which, as in "Description of a Struggle," ends in obliteration by drowning. Between these two works lies Kafka's decisive encounter with the Yiddish Theater and Eastern Jewish culture, the importance of which for Kafka's literary development has been pointed out by Evelyn Beck.[17]

Under the profound influence of the Yiddish Theater and the discovery, through this exposure, of an unbroken link to a communal culture, reaching from the past into the present, Kafka was able to concretize the abstract framework of his youthful tale. For his fanciful protagonists, Fat Man and Praying Man, he now substituted the Westernized German-speaking Jew and made him his prototype for the uprooted and condemned literary individual. When he adopted German as his language, the Central European Jew falsified his relationship to the Jewish way of life, from which he sprang, in which he had his roots, and from which he could not truly extricate himself, but to which he referred in the words of, and therefore with the thoughts of, an alien tongue. In his most intimate relationships, namely those of his family, the referent of his speech remained a Jewish reality with specific emotions attached to it. However, when the signifier of this Jewish referent became German, it designated a world alien to the Jewish reality. The true link between signifier and signified, which is truth, was broken. But the effect of this situation on the individual was a severance from his roots, and the blocking of the path that should lead from words back to the experiences and memories they supposedly referred to. The Jewish speaker of German concealed this rupture from himself. His self was split. He spoke, and therefore thought, differently from the way he felt and remembered. His thoughts became estranged from his emotions, and he became a stranger to himself.

The real self remains bound up with the speaker's childhood and family. It was in diagnosing his lack of warmth toward his mother that Kafka developed the linguistic theory we have sketched. In the same year, 1911, in which the Yiddish Theater exerted its greatest influence on him, Kafka noted in his diary a coldness, a want of love toward his mother that he ascribed to the use of German in a household that was Jewish. The actual human reality of the family had been profoundly un-German, namely Jewish. But the constant use of the German idiom falsified this reality by subverting it and substituting inappropriate associations for the original ones.

> The Jewish mother is no "Mutter"; calling her "Mutter" makes her somewhat comical. . . . [W]e give the name German mother to a Jewish woman, but we forget this contradiction, and having been forgotten, it sinks all the more heavily into our emotional life. "Mutter" is an especially German term for the Jew; below his consciousness, it contains, together with gentile splendor, also gentile coldness. The Jewish woman who is addressed as "Mutter," therefore, does not only turn comical, but alien. Mama would be a better term [name], if only one would not still imagine "Mutter" behind it. I believe that only memories of the ghetto preserve the Jewish family, for even the word father [Vater] by no means targets the Jewish father.[18]

In this early diary passage (October 24, 1911), we find delineated a self-alienation that thereafter finds its expression in the structures of Kafka's family tales, "The Judgment" and "The Metamorphosis," and, in subtler form, but with particular relevance to the mother figure, in *The Trial*.[19] All these works show retrogression and destruction of an adult individual by the eruption of a repressed force, a *revenant*,[20] that finds its strongest ally, and is lodged, within the self. This force stands in a more or less obvious connection to the protagonist's family from which he had, unsuccessfully as it turns out, tried to break away.[21] Analogously, in Kafka's diary entry about his mother, the German linguistic medium is seen as a façade that has usurped the place of the original Jewish childhood self. It alienated the adult son not only from the other members of his family, but above all from himself. This linguistic façade can never become the true expression of his self. Words are arbitrarily imposed on a reality forever different from what they convey. The result is an incurable self-alienation of the German-speaking Jew, which is at the same time an alienation from his family. The inappropriate linguistic medium falsifies his childhood memories and presents to the self a perverted and distorted image of itself. The gentile associations conveyed by the German words for "mother" and "father" can be compared to the decorative "fillers" that creep into writing when the writer's connection with his original inspiration slackens and gives out. But the sociocultural view of truth in language goes further than the poetics of the inner self, which I have tried to delineate elsewhere,[22] in preparing the self-condemnation of Kafka's writing. For even in those rare moments when inspiration seemed sustained, the German medium must falsify it.

For several years Kafka did not follow through this pessimistic logic of the German-Jewish writer's self-alienation from his truth, for, as I have indicated above, he drew somewhat different conclusions from his insight, which proved productive rather than inhibiting for his writing. The disruption of the self-deceiving façade of consciousness by a hidden truth, as exemplified by some of Kafka's most famous and powerful works, from "The Judgment" of 1912 to "A Country Doctor" of 1917, counteracted the inhibitions against his work that his view of the fundamental inner fraudulence of the Western Jew necessarily entailed. But the conviction of the inherent deceitfulness of this German-Jewish literature reasserted itself and became central to Kafka's poetics in the period of his relationship to the non-Jewish Milena.

In 1921, Kafka, in a letter to Max Brod, diagnosed the whole of German-Jewish literature as hopelessly suspended between a Judaic past betrayed by these writers and a German present that they could never make their own in truth.[23] The lack of identity that drove the Praying Man to his fraudulent praying is now presented in terms of a sociology of literature. This literature has no true substance because it does not have a language that it can call its own.

The view of language implied in this wholesale condemnation of all German-Jewish literature partakes of that strange phenomenon of Jewish self-hatred that Stölzl brought to our attention in *Kafkas böses Böhmen* and that Hartmut Binder subsequently elaborated in his *Kafka aus neuer Sicht.*[24] The Central European Jewish intellectuals imbibed a good portion of the anti-Semitic ideology of the culture in which they lived, to which they richly contributed, but from which they also received essential gifts that often proved extremely mixed blessings. As has been pointed out, even the Zionist attack on the Diaspora borrowed from that mystical Central European nationalism that had given rise to anti-Semitism.[25] The anti-Semitic cliché of the Jew was not alien to Zionist propaganda. In this context, the astounding resemblance that Kafka's theory of language bears to the linguistic theory contained in the Bible of modern German nationalism, Fichte's *Addresses to the German Nation* (1807/1808), deserves a brief mention.

Fichte postulates the superiority of the Germans over the West and South Europeans on the premise that the German language, in which the Scandinavian tongues are included, is an original rather than a derived language. The speaker of a Germanic language can immediately see the connections between his words and the objects and concepts to which they refer.[26] The speaker of German, who thinks in a language that makes truth transparent to him, is imbued with the truth of the original thought processes—the Transcendental Ego—from which all reality receives its being. He will therefore be creative and "truthful" in his essence. However, languages such as French, Italian, and English, on the other hand, whose vocabulary largely consists of words transmitted from a dead foreign tongue—Latin—convey the thinking of a dead nation and fail to reflect the living reality of the speakers. Such speakers are alienated from their being.

The assumption common to both Fichte's and Kafka's view of language is the demand that truthful speech be the direct emanation of being. It is this view that Jacques Derrida has exposed as "metaphysical nostalgia" for the impossible presence of the referent—reality or being—in the signifying system that is language.[27] The vast difference between the German Idealist and Kafka lies in the nature of what it is that should be present in truthful speech. For Fichte it is the divine mental activity, the Transcendental Ego, that is the ground of being. For Kafka it is the ideal community.

Language for Kafka should be the proper *adaequatio* for the activities and emotions that bind the members of the community together. Only in such a cohesive community can the speaker of the language be one with himself and with the partners of his discourse. Such wholeness is for Kafka the criterion of truth.

In the social world in which Kafka found himself, this condition was of course utopian. The true community as the basis for a truthful language was a countermodel to Kafka's actual world. It was a projection propelled by the profound lack of and need for the experience of such a community. For Kafka, the nucleus of community, whether actual or imagined, was the family. As we have seen from his diary entry of 1911, it was in his relationship to his mother that the painful lack of a truthful medium of communication emerged. Implicitly he blamed his family for having deprived him of a true language, and thus turned him into a cold son and inauthentic speaker. Social and economic ambition had made his father and his father's class and generation adopt German as their language and thus displace the true language with an alien idiom. The displacement of language was also a tragic displacement of the true self for their sons. The fathers had begun the betrayal to which the sons had fallen victim and that they completed.[28] The Yiddish actors, on the other hand, did show the possibility of a truthful relationship to language. However, for the Westernized Jew, this homecoming to his past must remain practically unattainable.

Already in "Description of a Struggle," the idea of a stable reliable world pertains for Kafka's protagonist to a quasi-mythic, legendary past of his own imagining.

> Always, dear Sir, I am plagued by such a tormenting desire to see things as they might conduct themselves *before* they would show themselves to me. Then they are in all likelihood beautiful and calm. It must be so, for I often hear people talk about them in that way.[29]

This calm and stable world is literally based on hearsay; it is a product of language. The speaker has never experienced it himself. It remains a utopian construct like the definitive acquittals in *The Trial,* the call for a land surveyor in *The Castle,* the free and open entrance into the Law in "Before the Law." Significantly, it is the speaker's mother who, in her dialogue with the woman in the garden, supplies what seems like the guarantee for the existence of a world without anxiety; but that world is withheld from him. Analogously it is, as we have seen, his own mother who induces in Kafka the feeling that he is left without a truthful language and thus without a truthful being.

In a recent "text linguistic" study of Kafka, Rudolf Kreis, applying the psychoanalytic theory of Jacques Lacan and René Spitz, has pointed out the importance of the mother and mother figure for Kafka's language.[30] Spitz stresses the crucial role of the mother in giving the infant, in his prelinguistic stage of development, the feeling of "object constancy," the expectancy of a reliable and stable world, and with that "the formation of a rudimentary self." Where the relationship between mother and infant is disturbed, as it undoubtedly was in Kafka's biography,[31] the sense of predictability concerning the external world and of self-identity fails to develop adequately. The learning of verbal language later on in the child's development constitutes a distancing process in which the mother has to assume the role of naysaying figure to prepare the child for the self-discipline of civilized life. The acquisition of verbal language is thus always associated with denial, withdrawal, and prohibition. The earlier absence of the ego-encouraging function of the mother in Kafka's case prevented the prelinguistic certainties of self and world from being carried over into the language-forming stage. The basis for a trusting and unproblematical acceptance of the necessary distancing and negativity of verbal language was absent in Kafka's life, and its duplicity and "coldness" therefore became intolerable to him.

Our analysis of Kafka's earliest narrative and the diary entry about his mother tend to confirm the link between the mother figure and Kafka's view of language and truth. (The diary entry of October 24, 1911, begins significantly with his mother's constant absence from the home, necessitated by her helping Kafka's father in the business—a circumstance that repeated exactly Kafka's early childhood experience.)[32]

The community that, through a "truthful" language, must underwrite the reliability of the world, remains only a conjecture and presupposition for Kafka's spokesmen. Because he has never known such a community as a fact, the Praying Man, like the later heroes of Kafka, must seek to acquire a sense of identity and existence by pretense, by desperate clamor and antics. Anticipating so many of Kafka's later heroes, he frantically gropes for a "recognition" that would confirm his existence. In the drawing room, which represents society, he desperately seeks to gain the seat at the piano, even though "all seemed to know that [he] was unable to play."[33] Like his descendants in Kafka's later work, he can only *try* to exist; but he can never gain the conviction that he exists. When Kafka calls writing "a form of prayer," he obviously identifies with his early protagonist. The purely religious meaning usually attributed to Kafka's statement must be profoundly modified when we realize that "praying" refers to a desperate need to be "looked at" in order to receive the minimum of stability and identity necessary for existence.

In the whole view of language, as we have traced it so far, language always remains subordinate to being. Primacy belongs to life, to acts and feelings, not to words. Actions and feelings are the touchstone for the right life and its truth. In such a moral universe, literature can only appear as secondary. By spending all his time on describing life, the writer misses his duty to live it. Kafka condemns literature as a mere substitute, a dodging, a "putting of wreaths around the house instead of moving in."[34] In the same vein, in a diary entry of 1921, Kafka condemns writing for its dependence on life, its merely referential character, which lives parasitically on the primary, "autonomous" activities that are reality.

> The dependency of writing. Its dependence on the maid making the fire, on the cat warming itself by the stove, even on the poor old person warming himself. All these are independent, autonomous activities; writing alone is helpless, does not dwell in itself; it is a joke and a despair.[35]

Its referential nature convicts writing of essential insignificance—frivolity; and for the moralist in Kafka frivolity had to spell despair.

So far, we have considered Kafka's view of language and truth from only one of two diametrically opposed perspectives, which accompanied him through his entire life. Kafka saw himself suffering from two mutually exclusive perspectives on life, which he summed up in the following statement:

> [For me] the most important or the most appealing desire has been this: to acquire a view of life (and . . . to be able to convince others of it by writing) in which life would keep its natural heavy falling and rising, but at the same time, with no less distinctness, would be understood as a nothing, a dream, a floating. A beautiful wish perhaps, if I had truly wished it. . . . It is comparable to the desire to hammer together a table, with painfully exact craftsmanship, and simultaneously to be doing nothing, but not in such a way that one might say: "His hammering is nothing to him," but rather that "hammering is real hammering for him, and at the same time, nothing."[36]

One of these contradictory views might be called the naturalist, the other the spiritualist perspective. The difficulty of doing justice to Kafka lies in the equal validity of these two perspectives that seem to vitiate every statement made about Kafka, no matter how justified, by the equal appropriateness of its exact opposite. Yet it is absolutely necessary in speaking about Kafka to insist on the applicability of each pole of this particular dichotomy, and to establish this polarity itself as the essence of his intention.

Essentially the dichotomy goes back to the equal rigor with which Kafka treated the demands of what one might call the social and the inner or spiritual self. As Kafka matured, he tended toward ever greater depersonalization and universality of each "self," extending each into a "Weltanschauung" (in the literal, nonideological sense of the term), which complemented and, at the same time, excluded the other. But even in his earliest extant work, he called this coexistence of the radically contradictory "Proof of the Fact That It Is Impossible To Live."[37]

The demand of the social self becomes universalized as Judaism, the communal ethos, the right action in this life. This side of Kafka corresponds essentially to the image of Kafka given to us by his friend Max Brod. Elsewhere I called this demand "the law of Jehovah,"[38] because its fundamental commandment is the procreation and correct transmission of human life in the continuous chain of the generations that Jehovah vouchsafed to Abraham in His covenant with him. The opposite pole is a profound disgust with earthly life, the yearning for transcendence and total liberation from the flesh. This yearning too becomes universalized into a view resembling Gnosticism, or Indian (and Schopenhauerian) pessimism, a view that posits spirit as sole reality, denies the sensory world as an illusion, and demands a self-destructive asceticism.[39] The following aphorism sums it up succinctly.

> There is only one spiritual world. What we call the sensory world is only the evil in the spiritual one.[40]

This pole corresponds to the mystic whom Walter Benjamin, in sharp opposition to Brod, saw Kafka to be.[41]

Since language only refers to the sensory world, it can never be the instrument of truth.

> For anything outside the sensory world, language can be used only allusively, but never, not even approximately, by way of analogies, since it, in correspondence to the sensory world, only deals with possession and its relationships.[42]

Paradoxically, however, this debasement of language, from this perspective, allows a substantial elevation of the status of literature. For as the above-quoted aphorism clearly shows, there does remain one aspect of language that can be used to allude to the reality that lies beyond our senses and that is, according to the earlier-quoted aphorism of Kafka's, the only true one. This allusive use of language is obviously the kind of writing toward which Kafka aspired, when he tried to present "the enormous world in [his] head,"[43] and put down in his diary his ambition to redeem the sensory world, i.e., "to raise it . . . into the pure, the true, and the unchangeable."[44] The spiritualist perspective frees literature from the servility to which a poetics of referential mimesis reduces it. Here language does not depend on "the autonomous activities" going on in the sensory world. On the contrary, language—i.e., a very special kind of nonreferential, merely allusive language—is a means by which human beings may receive an inkling of the invisible, true world.

The idea of a purely allusive language establishes the otherness of language in regard to truth, not as a defect, but as the necessary condition for the fulfillment of a proper and essential function. To be sure, language can never hope to represent the extrasensory reality, but it can hope to point toward it and thus to sharpen human awareness for it. Here, writing does not aim at the *adaequatio* of linguistic formulation and reality. Such a "true" referentiality is completely beyond its reach. Language can only hope to capture the trace of something that has to be essentially and eternally absent from the sensory world.

The way for literature is therefore not to try to express the truth, but to hint at it by showing the undoing of untruth.

> Our art is a being blinded by the truth. The light on the retreating grimace is true, nothing else.[45]

It is not difficult to see that this aphorism applies to a basic feature of all of Kafka's work, in which some falsehood, some self-deception or deception, is contradicted and exposed. The protagonist, who embodies this falsehood, is forced to retreat, one way or another. The official viewpoint of the work, represented by the protagonist, is found to be untrue. Since the reader does not gain access to any other consciousness in the work, and since the narrator withholds all revealing commentary, the reader first tends to be persuaded by the protagonist and to side with him. Closer reading calls this support into question. Too many indications emerge that make the protagonist's claim untenable. His defeat at the hands of his antagonist or antagonists—his "counterworld," in Martin Walser's term[46]—is revealed as the refutation of a false claim. Beyond that the reader is not able to go. He may witness the negation of an untruth. The truth itself remains shrouded from him. The defeat of the protagonist by no means entitles him to assume that the "counterworld" represents the truth. The structural feature reflecting this withholding of the truth is the absence of a reliable and authoritative narrator.

In the poetics implied in the aphorism about art and truth, Kafka's two perspectives converge. It accommodates his community-oriented naturalism as well as his gnostic spiritualism. If truth is seen to reside in the collective, the stream of life and procreation, the totality of existence, then the defeat of the individual subjectivity, embodied in the protagonist, vindicates the collective and establishes it as the truth. If, on the other hand, truth is seen as transcending this world and residing in an extrasensory beyond, or spiritual realm, the withholding of the truth alludes to its ineffability. The only "trace" of the truth is its absence made manifest by the refutation of what the reader had thought to be true. From his naturalist perspective, it would seem that Kafka tends to equate vitality, energy, and power—characteristic of his father—with truth, and to endorse the collective in which these qualities are lodged as the repository of truth.[47] Weak in his isolation, and impotent in his subjectivity, the individual qua individual must be wrong. The reader, having first sided with the protagonist, on second thought is tempted to rectify his mistake, and is inclined to see the counterworld (what I would prefer to call "the power figure") as being right. However, on a third "reading"—each "reading" standing for a level of meaning further removed from the surface—he would realize that not even that equation holds, and that there is no way of establishing the "truth." All that can be uncovered are successive layers of untruth. With this insight, the spiritualist perspective is approximated. For such a procedure demonstrates the inadequacy of all language to express the truth. All language can show is the "retreat" of untruth. The process of making untruth evident is the only "light" that language can shed on truth.

In his late phase, following the Zürau period, Kafka tended to equate the spiritual world with literature. Literature, however, was not the finished work; it was the process, the act of writing, not its result. Because it was not the product but the act that counted, Kafka could ask that his writings be burnt and yet continue to write to the last, and correct printer's proofs on his deathbed. The finished work catered to the ego and its narcissism that afflicted Kafka, but that he loathed and hated as the writer's fundamental curse. Consideration for work done was self-caressing and a sin against the law of Jehovah with its commandment to live fruitfully, to engage, to care, to procreate, to love. Vanity was the original sin against the self's duty to be part of the communal world. But living the work, not basking in it, constituted fulfillment of the law of the spirit. In the act of writing, Kafka felt closest to existing in a purely spiritual world, as a member of another universe, differently organized from the physical and social world of bodies and possessions, free of the imperfections and the cruelties built into Jehovah's realm. Living in and as literature, Kafka felt as close as anyone could be to that unity which he called truth. Writing, Kafka formulates in a late diary entry, gives supreme happiness. It enables one to step out of "murderer's row," which is this life, and gain an observation post on it. However, writing gradually evolves from a point of observation into a pure autonomous realm, a universe of its own, operating in complete heterogeneity from life, according to its own laws and needs.[48]

The impression that one of the two "laws" ever superseded the other would be wrong. To the end of Kafka's life, the demand of "Jehovah's law" persisted as inexorably as the demand of absolute spirituality. Kafka's "double bind," to use Bateson's term, could never be truly resolved. But near the end of his life, in the parable "Von den Gleichnissen" (usually translated as "On Parables"), Kafka seems to have attempted to reconcile to some extent the two mutually exclusive laws. This parable seems to me to be the final statement of his poetics.

The key word, "Gleichnis," is translated into English as "parable."[49] But its meaning in German is "simile" as well as "parable."[50] Grimm's *Wörterbuch* allows a rather broad range of meanings for the term. "Gleichnis" is "a poetic or rhetorical figure," "a means of artistic expression," "a symbol," and "a sign with a definite meaning." It is "closely related" to metaphor from which it is distinguished by its consisting of two parts—"image and referent" ("Bild und Sache")—ranged "independently alongside each other."[51] (As we shall see, Kafka uses the term in a way that does also include the meaning of metaphor.) The subject of Kafka's parable is not only the traditional parable form, known to us from the Bible, but a whole range of meanings that embrace the essence, the very mode of poetic writing or literature insofar as it resides in the circumlocutory indirectness of language represented by simile and metaphor. We have to keep this broad range of meanings of "Gleichnis" in mind as we read Kafka's parable. In Kafka's play with the various meanings of the term lies, as we shall see, the meaning of this piece and its important relationship to the whole problematics of his work, as it is first encountered in "Description of a Struggle." It is the relationship between the parable at the end of his life and the problems of his earliest protagonists that shall interest us here particularly.

> Many complain that the words of the sages are only *Gleichnisse,* again and again, and inapplicable to everyday life, and that is all we have. When the sage says: "Cross over," he does not mean that one should cross over to the other side, which one could still manage, after all, if the result were worth the effort; but *he* means some legendary Beyond, something which we do not know, which he cannot in any way define more concretely, and which therefore cannot be of any help to us here. All that these *Gleichnisse* intend to say is this, that the incomprehensible is incomprehensible, and that we have known all along. Thereupon someone said: "Why do you resist? If you were to follow the *Gleichnisse,* you would have become *Gleichnisse* yourselves, and thereby already you would be free of daily care."
>
> Another said: "I bet that is another *Gleichnis.*"
>
> The first one said: "You have won."
>
> The second one said: "But alas only in the *Gleichnis.*"
>
> The first one said: "No, in reality; in the *Gleichnis* you have lost."[52]

The starting point of the parable is the complaint of the many that poetic speech—literature—is ineffectual in real life. For poetic speech is unclear and therefore cannot be acted upon. Since in the real world only action "helps," poetic speech is pointless. Literature can never save the world. Kafka states here, through the mouths of the many, the irreconcilability of writing and being. Any attempt to transfer hope for salvation from literature to life is doomed.

In this context, the shift that the meaning of *Gleichnis* undergoes in the telling of the parable is of crucial importance. The many want the *Gleichnisse* of the sages to be understood as precepts for action and conduct, as examples that would instruct and "help" one to master the problems of life and death. *Gleichnisse* here appear in a practical-religious, a moral-salvational context. The meaning is clearly that of "parable," in the Biblical sense of the genre. The sayings of the sages are, as in most higher religions, to prescribe the right behavior that would "help" and save human existence. *Gleichnis* here relates to desirable and imitable conduct. Literature appears as a servant of life, a tool of action.

When the first speaker says that if the many were to follow the *Gleichnisse,* they would become *Gleichnisse* themselves, and thus be liberated from daily care, the meaning of the word undergoes a radical shift, which has escaped previous commentators, as far as I know. The statement can be divided into two parts: Part one is the conditional phrase, "If you were to follow the *Gleichnisse.*" Part two is the hypothetical condition fulfilled: "You would have become *Gleichnisse* yourselves and thus be free of daily care." The shift of meaning takes place between part one and part two. In part one, *Gleichnis* still means "parable." It conveys this sense: If the many were to imitate and carry out the precepts of the sages perfectly, "follow" them as disciples "follow" their masters, they too would become paragons of desirable behavior, emulated by all. Being supported by action, literature would and can make a great difference in life. However, this is not the meaning, at least not the literal meaning, of *Gleichnis* in part two; in fact, it clashes with it. For part two literally advises an empirical impossibility: the transformation of human beings into linguistic structures. If taken literally—and in Kafka the text has to be taken literally—*Gleichnis* here denotes a rhetorical figure.

This interpretation receives decisive corroboration from the one actual example of a *Gleichnis* given by the many as characteristic of the speech of the sages. It is a single sentence, expressed in the imperative: "Geh hinüber" ("Cross over"). Obviously this *Gleichnis* is not a parable. For a parable always "narrates . . .'a particular case.'"[53] A single imperative sentence can therefore never qualify as a parable. It is an imperative, commanding a movement with a destination. But the destination "hinüber" ("over") is, as understood by the many and made the object of their grievance, a metaphor of which the tenor, namely the place, remains undefined, "legendary" ("sagenhaft"). We thus confront here the problem of metaphoric speech, which brings Kafka's late piece on *Gleichnisse* into close connection to his earliest work, "Description of a Struggle."

The second speaker's remark, "I bet that is another *Gleichnis,*" confirms the nonparabolic meaning of the term still further. Henceforth the word has clearly the sole meaning of rhetorical figure. Any implication of narrative, which "parable" must contain, is gone. Now *Gleichnis* refers only to a device of literary speech. "Von den Gleichnissen" emerges as a parable not about parables, but about literature, i.e., about literary or poetic discourse and its applicability to life. By turning into *Gleichnisse,* the addressees would become nothing but literary, and thus linguistic figures. They would become denizens of a world in which significance has replaced life.

The prescription of becoming a *Gleichnis* is itself only a *Gleichnis* and cannot be lived. Therefore, the second speaker is told that he has won the bet in reality. From the point of view of real life, becoming a *Gleichnis* can only be understood metaphorically. While one stays alive, the first speaker's advice remains "only" a metaphor. One cannot live it. However, in the realm of *Gleichnis* the second speaker has lost the wager.

The contrary to *Gleichnis* at the end of the parable is not nonfigurative language, as one might expect, but empirical reality or actuality—"Wirklichkeit." The identical spatial preposition "in"—"*in Wirklichkeit* you have won," "*im Gleichnis* you have lost"—establishes a parallelism between two localities or realms. One is the realm of action and life, what Kafka in the above-quoted diary entry called "autonomous activities" ("eigengesetzliche Verrichtungen"); the other is the realm in which significance takes the place of action, the "legendary" realm of the *Gleichnis.* In the realm of empirical reality, the second speaker has won the bet. In this realm, the first speaker's advice can only be taken as a *Gleichnis;* it cannot be translated into action. Yet, if someone were to attempt the empirically impossible, take the first speaker's advice literally, and actually "follow" the *Gleichnisse* spatially, into their realm, he would leave empirical reality behind and become a *Gleichnis.* Thus if actually carried out, the first speaker's advice would paradoxically cease to be "merely" a *Gleichnis.* It would become counsel for action actually performed. Following his advice, however, means to cease to be part of life and to become a denizen of literary discourse. To become literary language, the self has to die in this life, as Josef K. has to die in his dream, if the artist's immortalizing script is to be completed on his grave.[54] The radical incompatibility between the modes of being represented by life, on the one hand, and by literature on the other, is unflinchingly proclaimed in the first speaker's advice. It recalls the youthful Mallarmé's program for an existence devoted to absolute poetry: "c'est t'apprendre que je suis maintenant impersonnel et non plus Stéphane que tu as connu, mais une aptitude qu'a l'Univers Spirituel à se voir et à se developper à travers ce que fut moi."[55]

Yet to put matters this way is to stress only one of the two paradoxes implied in the advice of the spokesman of Kafka's parable. The self that becomes a *Gleichnis* and thus a linguistic figure becomes part not only of the order of literary language; it also becomes a part of the even larger order, language itself, of which literature in turn forms only a part. By entering language, however, the self enters the community that language expresses. Thus the radical self-banishment from human life, which becoming a *Gleichnis* implies, also leads back to humanity, in a roundabout way. If taken literally, and followed, the first speaker's counsel would, as we have noted above, cease to be a *Gleichnis* and become reality. His advice advocates an approach to reality, from the direction of linguistic, i.e., mental or spiritual structures, rather than from the direction of life.

Understood in that way, the advice of Kafka's spokesman aims at the abolishment of the difference between writing and being. Since *Gleichnisse* are first and foremost linguistic structures, the spokesman of the parable advocates entering language with one's whole being. The self that is to become a *Gleichnis* will be absorbed in language and disappear in it. He who enters language with his whole being, and becomes one with it, would achieve that freedom from "daily care" that human beings will vainly look for as long as they exist as empirical beings in this world.

Kafka's aversion to metaphors is well-known. The reason for his impatience with metaphoric language was the gap between writing and being, which we pointed out in connection with the diary entry that lamented literature's lack of the ontological dignity and independence of the "autonomous activities" that make up actual life.[56] By its referential nature, writing spells separation from autonomous being. Metaphor, a writing to the second power, widens this gap still further. However, becoming a metaphor is not only different from writing one; it is actually the opposite. For it abolishes that distinction between writing and being, which all writing that is less than a total way of life enhances and perpetuates. As Stanley Corngold has reminded us, Kafka wanted his saying "I am nothing but literature" to be taken as literally as possible.[57] In becoming a *Gleichnis,* rather than in showering metaphors on things, the self establishes its participation in the community that is language. The first speaker's advice thus seems to answer the problem of the protagonists of "Description of a Struggle." For the speaker, who is afflicted with the "fever" of metaphoric speech, becoming a *Gleichnis* is the only hope of rejoining the human family. He reenters it, not, to be sure, as its living son and brother, but in the way Kafka actually did, as an addition to, and enrichment of, its language.[58]

NOTES

1. Franz Kafka, *Beschreibung eines Kampfes: Die zwei Fassungen,* Parallelausgabe nach den Handschriften, hrsg. und mit einem Nachwort versehen von Max Brod, Textedition Ludwig Dietz (Frankfurt am Main: S. Fischer, 1969), 88. Hereafter listed as B. All translations from Kafka's writings are my own.

2. B, 88.
3. Ibid.
4. B, 80.
5. Cf. Søren Kierkegaard, *Fear and Trembling* and *The Sickness Unto Death,* trans. Walter Lowrie (Garden City, N.Y.: Doubleday Anchor Books, n.d.; copyright Princeton University Press, 1941, 1954), 87.
6. B, 90.
7. Ibid., 87.
8. Ibid., 87–89.
9. Ibid., 90.
10. Ibid., 91.
11. Franz Kafka, *Hochzeitsvorbereitungen auf dem Lande und andere Prosa aus dem Nachlass,* ed. Max Brod (New York: Schocken Books, 1953), 348. Hereafter listed as H.
12. Jean-Paul Sartre, *La Nausée* (Paris: Editions Gallimard, 1938), 124.
13. B, 90.
14. The Fat Man and The Praying Man are variations of the I-narrator who in turn commands the magic power of the poetic imagination that transforms the world in accordance with his wishes. Cf. Walter H. Sokel, *Franz Kafka: Tragik und Ironie: Zur Struktur seiner Kunst* (Munich, Vienna: Langen-Müller, 1964), chap. 1.
15. B, 68.
16. Genesis 9:21–25.
17. Evelyn Torton Beck, *Kafka and the Yiddish Theater: Its Impact on His Work* (Madison: University of Wisconsin Press, 1971).
18. Franz Kafka, *Tagebücher, 1910–1923,* ed. Max Brod (New York: Schocken Books, 1948 and 1949), 115 f. Hereafter listed as T.
19. Cf. the fragmentary chapter "Fahrt zur Mutter" in Franz Kafka, *Der Prozess,* ed. Max Brod, 5th ed. (New York: Schocken Books, 1946).
20. Josef K. calls his uncle "das Gespenst vom Lande." Kafka, *Der Prozess,* 112.
21. Cf. Sokel, *Franz Kafka: Tragik und Ironie,* passim, and Sokel, *Franz Kafka,* Columbia Essays on Modern Writers, no. 19 (New York and London: Columbia University Press, 1966), passim.
22. "Kafka's Poetics of the Inner Self," *Modern Austrian Literature* 11 (1978) (3/4): 37–58.
23. Cf. Kafka's letter to Max Brod of June 1921, *Briefe, 1902–1924,* ed. Max Brod (Frankfurt am Main: S. Fischer Lizenzausgabe von Schocken Books, New York, 1958), 336 f. Hereafter referred to as Br.
24. Christoph Stölzl, *Kafkas böses Böhmen: Zur Sozialgeschichte eines Prager Juden* (Munich: edition text + kritik, 1975), passim. Hartmut Binder, *Kafka in neuer Sicht: Mimik, Gestik und Personengefüge als Darstellungformen des Autobiographischen* (Stuttgart: J. B. Metzler, 1976), xiv f., 265 ff., 374–95.
25. Cf. Stölzl, *Kafkas böses Böhmen,* chap. 4, and Binder, *Kafka in neuer Sicht,* 376–81.

26. Johann Gottlieb Fichte, *Sämmtliche Werke*, ed. J. H. Fichte (Berlin: Veit & Comp., 1846), vii, 316–27.

27. Jacques Derrida, *De la Grammatologie* (Paris: Les Editions de Minuit, 1967), 17, 21–41.

28. Cf. also "Die Forschungen eines Hundes," in Franz Kafka, *Sämtliche Erzählungen*, ed. Paul Raabe (Frankfurt am Main-Hamburg: Fischer Bücherei, 1970), 341.

29. B, 90.

30. Rudolf Kreis, *Die doppelte Rede des Franz Kafka: Eine textlinguistische Analyse* (Paderborn: Ferdinand Schöningh, 1976), 16–19, 22–39.

31. Ibid., 16 f.

32. T, 115.

33. B, 102.

34. Br, 385.

35. T, 551.

36. Franz Kafka, *Beschreibung eines Kampfes: Novellen, Skizzen, Aphorismen aus dem Nachlass*, ed. Max Brod (New York: Schocken Books, 1946), 293 f.

37. B, 44.

38. Sokel, *Franz Kafka*, Columbia Essays, 28. I used here the term "the face of Jehovah" to define one of the two faces that "the Absolute" tended to assume for Kafka.

39. This aspect of Kafka has been most consistently presented by Peter Foulkes, *The Reluctant Pessimist: A Study of Franz Kafka*, Stanford Studies in Germanics and Slavics, vol. 5 (The Hague-Paris: Mouton, 1967). For the relationship of Kafka to Schopenhauer see T. J. Reed, "Kafka und Schopenhauer," *Euphorion* 59 (1965): 160–72.

40. H, 44.

41. Walter Benjamin sees in Kafka's work an "ellipse" of which one focus is "mystische Erfahrung," and the other "die Erfahrung des modernen Grosstadtmenschen." *Briefe*, ed. and annotated by Gershom Scholem and Theodor W. Adorno (Frankfurt am Main: Suhrkamp Verlag, 1966), II: 760. See also Benjamin's polemic against Brod's interpretation of Kafka; II: 756 ff.

42. H, 45.

43. T, 306.

44. Ibid., 534.

45. H, 46.

46. Martin Walser, *Beschreibung einer Form*, Schriftenreihe Literatur und Kunst (Munich: Carl Hanser Verlag, 1961), 64–69.

47. I maintained this view in my earlier work on Kafka.

48. T, 563 f.

49. Franz Kafka, *The Complete Stories*, ed. Nahum Glatzer (New York: Schocken Books, 1971 [1946]), 457.

50. Cf. *Harrap's Standard German-English Dictionary*, Part One, German-English, ed. Trevor Jones (London and Toronto: George G. Harrap & Co., 1963); *Langenscheidt's Enzyklopädisches Wörterbuch*, ed. Otto Springer, 1st rev. ed.

(Berlin, Munich, Vienna, Zürich: Lagenscheidt, 1974); *The New Cassell's German Dictionary,* ed. Harold T. Betteridge, rev. ed. (New York: Funk & Wagnall's, 1962).

51. Jacob and Wilhelm Grimm, *Deutsches Wörterbuch,* hrsg. Deutsche Akademie der Wissenschaften zu Berlin, bearbeitet von Hermann Wunderlich u.a. (Leipzig: S. Hirzel Verlag, 1949), Bd. 4, 1. Abt., 4. Teil.

52. "Von den Gleichnissen," in *Sämtliche Erzählungen,* 359.

53. Klaus-Peter Philippi, "Parabolisches Erzählen: Anmerkungen zu Form und möglicher Geschichte," *Deutsche Vierteljahrsschrift für Literaturwissenschaft und Geistesgeschichte* 63 (1969): 297–332. For the difference between parable and *Gleichnis,* see p. 314.

54. Cf. "Ein Traum," *Sämtliche Erzählungen,* 145 ff.

55. Quoted by Claudio Guillén, *Literature as a System* (Princeton, N.J.: Princeton University Press, 1971), 240.

56. See esp. T, 550.

57. "The Structure of Kafka's *Metamorphosis:* Metamorphosis of the Metaphor," in *The Commentator's Despair: The Interpretation of Kafka's Metamorphosis* (Port Washington, N.Y.-London: Kennikat Press, 1973), 24.

58. I wish to acknowledge my gratitude to Dorrit Cohn for her valuable comments on the original version of this paper.

5

SYMBOL, ALLEGORY, EXISTENTIAL SIGN

Three Approaches to Kafka

IN THE long-standing debate about the applicability of the terms "symbol" and "allegory" to the writings of Kafka, there exists in addition a third point of view. Existentialism is a semiotic feature of Kafka's work that is of central importance to his writing. Since the debate between "symbol" and "allegory" provides the appropriate setting for introducing this feature, let us first briefly review the debate and its poetological significance.

The debate between "symbol" and "allegory" has taken place in a frame of reference set by Goethe's distinction between them.[1] For Goethe allegory attempts to illustrate a concept and therefore tends to be unambiguous. It translates from the abstract into the concrete or figurative and, like an equation, it permits only one interpretation. The symbol, on the other hand, is polysemous. The Idea is still evident in the representation, but not, as in allegory, in a conceptually understandable way, as a translation of thought into specific image, event, or character, but rather in a way that allows one to think of many different things.

A second difference lies in the autonomy of symbols as opposed to the contingency of allegories. Symbols are understood intuitively, without the need of a conceptual explanation, without a key. A conceptual key is needed to grasp the meaning of allegory. This distinction between symbol and allegory implies the coinciding of symbols with mimetic representation. While allegories depend on conceptual thought from which they originate, symbols represent life and its truth directly. Ideas are evident in them, emotionally affecting and intuitively understandable, without having to be

---

Translated by Harold Brubaker. The essay is published here for the first time.

grasped conceptually. They enlighten us through the artistic representation they are. They can be so effective only because they are a form of mimesis. Mimesis, as representation of reality, causes the spectator or recipient of art to experience directly, sensuously, and emotionally what is represented. If symbols were not mimetic, one would not be able to appreciate them as mere representation, without conceptual understanding of the idea embodied in them. Like mimesis, symbols are based on an unspoken harmony, a concordance between representation and reality or truth, between the work of art and the world.

With regard to Goethe's differentiation of symbols and allegories, three main currents are discernable in the reception of Kafka's works: positive allegorical, symbolic, and negative allegorical interpretation.

Max Brod's readings of his friend pointed in the first direction, which dominated the reception of Kafka up until the late 1950s.[2] The classical Goethean concept of allegory underlay Brod's influential interpretation of Kafka. For Brod, Tauber,[3] and others, Kafka's texts were religious allegories, whereby authorities such as Josef K.'s Court and K.'s Castle were seen as allegorical representations of God. According to Herbert Tauber, for example, the father in "The Judgment" signified God in an everyday bourgeois disguise.[4] This allegorical approach to Kafka was furthered in secular form, for example, in Norbert Fürst's Kafka interpretation, which has the characteristic title *Die offenen Geheimtüren Franz Kafkas* (*Franz Kafka's Open Secret Doors*). Fürst thinks he discovers a quite specific allegory in each of Kafka's works discussed by him.[5] Even Kafka's tuberculosis must serve as a concept to which Kafka's text is an allegorical translation.[6] In this positive allegorical interpretation of Kafka, one inquires about the extratextual meaning of the puzzling figures or groups of figures, such as Court and Castle, that dominate the text. The answer is found in a specific concept, which can be God but can also be Kafka's tuberculosis. The presumption is that figures and events in the text are signs for things that are outside the text. If one has the key to the translation of the signs, then Kafka's texts appear to be very clear.

Erich Heller spoke out against this approach to Kafka as early as the 1950s, focusing his attack above all on Brod's interpretation of *The Castle*.[7] For Heller, Brod's theological reading of the novel as an allegory of the problem of divine grace reduced Kafka's literary stature. Heller approaches Kafka by way of Goethe and applies Goethe's idea of the symbol to Kafka. Kafka was a true artist, and, according to Heller, abstract conceptuality and, even more, the explicitness of the allegorical contradicts the polysemous wealth of "true" *Dichtung*, which in the German classical tradition of poetics has the meaning of great inspired writing of literary genius in sharp distinction from the ordinary hackworklike writing of the "mere writer" or *Schriftsteller*. Heller raises Kafka to the status of a *Dichter*, a poet in that special German sense of a literary artist of sublime rank. Only if he is seen as a true poet can the profound effect of Kafka's works be explained. A true poet, however, can never be an allegorist. A poet proceeds to representation not from conceptual thinking, but rather from the mysteriously creative processes of the imagination. A poet creates symbols. *Dichtung* presupposes symbols because it creates worlds, and worlds are symbols whose multivalence is inexhaustible. Unlike allegories, Kafka's works are not comprehensible as offering single conceptual meanings. They are multivalent. Although Heller, then, in his interpretation of the Castle as the seat of gnostic demons denies the novel the symbol's multivalence, one must recognize that his turning of Kafka criticism away from the allegory back to the Goethean symbol had a liberating effect on Kafka's readers. From our contemporary viewpoint the multivalence of the symbol appears to serve Kafka significantly better than the preciseness of the classical allegory, and we would therefore be inclined to agree with Heller in the Heller-Brod controversy.

As far as the second aspect of Goethe's concept of the symbol is concerned, namely mimetic independence, we can in no way associate Kafka with Goethe. During the first reading of Kafka's texts it becomes clear to the reader that the imaginativeness of his texts is inconsistent with mimesis, that his texts fly in the face of mimesis as representation of empirical reality. Kafka's texts lack mimetic obviousness. They demand explanation. They provoke interpretation and are, because of that, more closely related to allegory than they are to Goethe's symbol. Going beyond Heller's criticism of Brod, we would have to say that Kafka's texts are a blend of symbol and allegory. In their ambiguity they conform to symbols; in their antimimetic need for interpretation, however, they are allegories. Essential here is the momentous change made to the concept of allegory by Walter Benjamin in *The Origin of German Tragedy* (*Ursprung des deutschen Trauserspiels*).[8] Kafka criticism owes a great deal to this change.

Benjamin stands in a polemical relationship to Goethe. His opposition to and protest against Goethe is sparked by Goethe's devaluation of allegories and his view of symbols. For Benjamin, this is typical of Goethe's glossing over the world's true condition and covering up its terrible reality with the propagation of a harmony in which individual and universal happily coincide. Not unlike mimesis, the Goethean symbol rests on a harmonizing view of the world. The Idea or the Absolute can show through the representation of the particular only if the particular, the individual, can be seen as somehow attuned to and reflecting the universal and absolute, if harmonious agreement reigns between the fundamental constitution of the world and individual existences in it. However, in a fallen world, which, according to Benjamin, our world is, an unbridgeable gap yawns between individual existence and the Idea. Goethe's symbol denies this chasm. It fakes a harmony that is nonexistent.

Benjamin rejects the Goethean symbol not only for ontological, but also for ethical reasons. For him, the Goethean symbol is based on the autonomy and priority of the aesthetic dimension. The cosmic harmony underlying Goethe's notion of the symbol holds true only if the view of the world restricts itself to purely aesthetic rather than moral and ontological terms. In light of the quite transparent misery and frailty of existence in the world, aesthetic harmony and beauty must seem mendacious. Far from letting the truth shine through, the self-sufficient and "beautiful" work of art is a metaphysical lie, profoundly immoral, close to kitsch. With rose-colored glasses, symbols conceal the truth of the world in its fallen condition.

Allegories, by contrast, faithfully reflect that condition. They are more truthful than symbols because they openly admit their own deficiency, as signs rather than symbols, in supplying meaning by themselves, thus revealing the deficiency of the world's condition. With their lack of transparency, their advertising of a need for a meaning that by themselves they cannot supply, the signs of allegory disclose the fundamental rift symbols repress. They reveal the chasm between representation and meaning, between image and significance. Thus they correspond to the truth of the world. They mutely proclaim its fallenness that does not allow a recognition of meaning. It is not in the self-contained symbol, but in the fragmentary and enigmatic allegory, crying out for interpretation, in which we encounter an art truthful to the needy state of being.

Benjamin's concept of allegory, however, radically differs from the classical one presupposed by Goethe. In the traditional concept of allegory, two distinct aspects or phases can be distinguished. The first emphasizes the contingency of the sign, its lack of transparent meaning, the element calling for interpretation. The second phase provides the meaning. Goethe's view of allegory reverses that order. For him the conceptual meaning comes first, and only then one supplies a sign that can make the concept manifest. Benjamin, in contrast to Goethe, returns to the original sequence. For him, the sign comes first. The sign seeks meaning. Differing from the classical view of allegory, however, Benjamin holds that meaning never becomes transparent. Rather, allegory is a sign of meaning withheld. Calling out for meaning, but not supplying it, allegory turns into a signal of the absence of illumination in a darkened world. Allegory signifies existence that is denied redemption in understanding.

Allegory for Benjamin is neither unambiguous like the classical notion of allegory nor polysemous like the Goethean symbol. It resists the goal of interpretation, the arrival at meaning. True, it appears to insist on a search for meaning, but it frustrates all attempts to deliver it. Craving for meaning and eternal denial of it is the statement allegory makes about the world. For precisely that reason it reveals its truth. It calls attention to the deficiency of being, its hopeless alienation from a meaning that would justify it. However, it does not rest content with accepting a senseless existence. Desperately it clamors for meaning but refuses to pretend it when it cannot be discerned.

The remarkable relevance of Benjamin's notion of allegory must readily suggest itself to a reader of Kafka. It has been Stanley Corngold's merit to have, clearly and persuasively, pointed it out.[9] The applicability of Benjamin's theory of allegory to Kafka's texts resides in the concurrence of the need for meaning and the withholding of it. Neither side of this concurrence by itself applies to Kafka. It is precisely in the coincidence of provoking interpretation and thwarting it that the sirenlike fascination, the hermeneutically seductive temptation of Kafka's texts, lies. They attempt to lure us toward metaphysics and theology, but frustrate and appear to mock anyone who allows her or himself to be swept beyond their appearance of a call for meaning to the attempt to find one.

By way of Benjamin, Kafka interpretation becomes linked to poststructuralism and its tireless striving to demonstrate the ultimate irreconcilability of sign and referential meaning, language and "truth." Corngold's reading of Kafka indeed proceeds from the fusion of Benjamin with poststructuralism. A perspective critical of such an approach to Kafka would enable one to discern the limits of relevance to Kafka of a reading solely based on the incompatibility of sign and meaning.

In basic respects, Corngold's semiotic-allegorical reading of Kafka's works as the denial of referential meaning continues into poststructuralism Heinz Politzer's theory of Kafka as the writer of parables of paradoxical meaninglessness.[10] For Politzer, Kafka is interpretable neither in terms of the nonambiguity of classical allegory nor in terms of the multivalent symbol. Kafka's works are for him parables of pure contradiction, of total incomprehensibility, of absolute denial of meaning. Politzer is close to Benjamin's theory of allegory without making this closeness explicit. Replacing Politzer's term "parable of paradox" with Benjamin's term "allegory" would make that quite clear. Then one would be able to recognize Kafka's presumed parables of paradox as allegories in Benjamin's sense.

Politzer's great opponent in the history of Kafka's reception, Wilhelm Emrich, is also, in his interpretation of Kafka, much closer to Benjamin's theory of allegory than it first might appear.[11] Emrich's reading of Kafka is connected to, and at the same time differentiated from, Benjamin's concept of allegory through its Heideggerian historicizing of the negative theology that lurks in Benjamin. In Emrich, Benjamin's deeply theological idea of a fallen world appears varied into a sociocultural critique of modernity, at once metaphysical and anticapitalistic. Projecting its golden age backward into the era of Goethe and German Idealism, it envisions it as an epoch in which individual and universal, human existence and the absolute Idea, had still been in glorious harmony. Aesthetically this harmony was represented by the poetic symbol.[12] Through the development of capitalism and the scientific-technological demystification of the world promoted by it, modern life has become utterly bereft of this harmony. The Idea, the meaning of human life and the spiritual cement holding society together, has become invisible and incomprehensible. The aesthetic consequence of this process of modernity has been the disappearance, and indeed the impossibility, of the symbol.[13] In modern art, mimesis ceases to let the Idea shine through and instead becomes, in Realism and Naturalism, an end in itself, imitation of banal everyday reality with no inkling of transcendence. Or else, art climbs into the realm of abstraction and turns nonrepresentational and utterly obscure, into a signlessness in which the artwork literally ceases to signify.

For Emrich, this is where Kafka's towering and unique significance for the modern world is to be found. Just as Karl Barth's Negative Theology retains the Godhead, even if in the form of the negation of all assertive statements, so does Kafka's work retain the Universal "negatively," by calling attention to its absence. As a genuine contemporary of modernity, Kafka, to be sure, is no longer capable of representing the Idea, the Universal and Absolute, in self-evident symbols. In his work, which belongs to the modern age, the Idea no longer shows itself. Unlike Naturalists and Abstractionists, however, Kafka alludes to the Universal, repressed by modernity into total concealment, by refuting all expectations held by rationality, and by representing a search for meaning, even though that search follows an absolutely futile course.[14] Kafka alludes to the Universal by evoking the shatteringly powerful effect of its nonappearance. In the absurdity of Kafka's world, the Absolute reveals itself negatively through the bafflement of reason that had believed itself capable of managing without it. The Idea is still felt in Kafka paradoxically through its absence, through the negation of its negation by utilitarian rationality, even as God, in Negative Theology, is present in the refutation of all statements defining Him. In Emrich's interpretation of Kafka, the symbol has become the sign of a *deus absconditus.*

By comparison with Benjamin and Politzer, Emrich takes a step back toward the symbol. Even though, in Kafka's texts, the Universal or Absolute is hidden, to be sure, the texts constantly allude to it. In Kafka, allusion inherits the place emptied by the symbol. Emrich explains the frustration of Kafka's readers with the fact that, in the modern age, meaning can be approached only through negation, because every affirmative declaration of meaning can in this age only be a lie, and pretending it must tend toward kitsch. However, precisely in the negative, the frustration and defeat of all search for meaning, exiled meaning expresses itself in Kafka's work. Kafka stands for Emrich midway between the nihilisms of modernity—pure naturalism, on the one hand, and empty abstraction, on the other, neither of which has any ken of the symbol—and premodern Classicism, which could still represent the Idea by symbols. It is through the reader's alienation and bewilderment that Emrich's Kafka alludes to lost meaning. For Emrich, Kafka is the master of allusion.

Allusion differs from symbol as well as from allegory—from symbol in that it does not allow the Idea, the meaning, to shine through anywhere in the work, from allegory because it does not function as the sign in an equation. In Kafka's allusive works, no static relationship prevails between sign and signified, but rather a dynamic process that goes on between them. It is this process of which Kafka's narratives consist. The debate over symbol and allegory, preoccupied with the meaning of Kafka's texts, neglected the connections between the events they describe, their narrative element. It is in this element that for Emrich the process of alluding manifests itself in Kafka's works.

In the emphasis on Kafka as a narrator, Adorno goes beyond Emrich. Adorno stresses the function of narrative details,[15] which seem to him much more essential to understanding Kafka than the question of what his themes "mean." When considering Kafka's narrative elements, one should not ask about a meaning that transcends them, but rather about their function in the context of both the individual text and the totality of Kafka's texts. The concept of function supplements the concept of allusion. Instead of concentrating, as does allegory, on a meaning that is either outside the text or missing, allusion and function play up the textual structure. The functionalism of textual details, which points toward the total structure of the text, approaches the Aristotelian concept of mimesis, but in a way that is very different from Goethe's symbol. Aristotelian mimesis—art as *representation* (not mere copy) of reality—has two different aspects. One is the similarity between what is represented and reality, the static reference to it. But the other one is the event or process, the action, the mythos, the sequence of statements and depicted incidents, and their coherence, what we would now call the structure of content. This is also mimesis, because mimesis signifies representation, an active, creative process that represents a process in life. We do not inquire about the relationship of the textual elements to anything outside the text—that is, reality—but about the relationship of the textual elements to one another, about their "work-immanent" interrelatedness. Here the detail or sign is not a translation or an expression of something outside the work, but a function internal to the work, a performance of the internal mechanism of the text.

In the wake of Emrich and Adorno, I considered in my own work on Kafka the course of events, the narratives enacted in his writings, to be of central importance.[16] Examining them, I believed I discovered in his work a single overarching myth, or mythos, in the Aristotelian sense of a narrative representation of a process. Kafka's mythos appeared to be the "description of a struggle," which also happens to be the title of Kafka's earliest text. This struggle proceeds within a self divided between life in society, in the human family, with the emotional and moral obligations that entails, and a special inner mission in which the uniqueness of the self expresses itself. A supplemental aspect of this struggle I perceived to be the subject's self-assertion against and simultaneous quest for recognition by patriarchal power stretching in a huge arc from the father in "The Judgment" over the bureaucracies of the K.-novels to society and community, collective existence as a whole. Certain images, descriptive or scenic elements in Kafka's texts, mark very specific positions, tendencies, attributes, and functions in the mythos that represents this twofold existential struggle. Examples of such textual elements are coldness and winter landscapes, the flow of water, food and starvation, dirt and cleanliness, children and childlike behavior, music, certain animals, and enclosed spaces. These descriptive and scenic elements possess more or less constant semiotic functions within the whole of Kafka's mythos. They act as signs that receive their full significance only in the context of the totality of Kafka's writing, including his life-documents, such as diaries and letters.

I propose to name those narrative elements that retain a more or less constant semiotic function in the description of the struggle about existence that Kafka's work is, existential signs. They are not directly, but indirectly mimetic. That is, they do not indicate and depict scenes and events conforming to empirical experience, but they are the content of metaphors built into and constituting everyday language. Günther Anders had pointed out as early as the 1930s that Kafka made the metaphors buried in ordinary language into the fictional reality of his texts.[17] Let us choose as an example the metaphor with which language designates a person as "cold." Here language turns a signifier referring to an attribute of physical nature into a metaphor that signifies the behavior of a person lacking in affection and emotional warmth. In Kafka's texts, coldness, wintry landscapes, regions of the far north represent withdrawal and seclusion of the self from human bonds—familial, social, and erotic—a hermitlike ascetic lifestyle, which Kafka himself considered an indispensable condition for his writing. In his fiction, cold, winter, and the far north are the scenery that sends out to the fictional self a call to abandon its ties to domesticity and to venture forth into estrangement, uncertainty, and existential homelessness, into a solitary existence, deprived of all security, and exposed to grave risks and dangers. In Kafka's late work, this call becomes a calling, a vocational or professional mission, which, analogous to the fasting skill of the hunger artist, becomes the metaphor for an art that, like Kafka's own writing, is incompatible with the demands of life in the human community. Kafka's fictional scenes of cold and winter function as existential signs signifying a way of existence that necessitates isolation.

This particular signification of cold, winter, and the north can be traced from the walk out into the cold night in "Description of a Struggle" through the friend's self-exile to Russia in "The Judgment," to the doctor's summoning through a snowstorm in "A Country Doctor," and the "call" of the self-proclaimed "land surveyor" K. to the wintry scene of *The Castle*. In all those texts from the most varied periods of Kafka's writing, we see that coldness, north, and winter have a relatively fixed signification. They always signify a form of existence that leads away from family, household, social gatherings, and homeland into aloneness, insecurity, adventure, and, finally, in the late work, to the claimed exercise of a vocation, a special skill, in the broadest sense an art, whether it be medicine in "A Country Doctor" or land surveying in *The Castle*. In all instances, it is the sign of a compulsion toward an ascetic, solitary, fanatically committed and enigmatically driven existence.

Kafka's texts are thick webs of such existential signs. Their close investigation would be a fascinating undertaking, far exceeding the limits of this essay. Here, I shall be able to restrict myself only to a brief examination of the relationship of the existential sign—illustrated by a single example, coldness and winter in *The Castle*—to the concepts of mimesis, symbol, and allegory.

The existential sign is in no way self-evident. That alone makes it different from the symbol, as understood by Goethe. Using the winter landscape of *The Castle* as our illustrative example, we note that in the Castle region it is almost always winter. Summer, it is said, lasts only two days, and even then it snows sometimes.[18] Such a climate is mimetically impossible. It could never support the big village and the huge Castle bureaucracy. Because of its fantastic and absurd character, this detail provokes interpretation. It therefore cannot be seen as a symbol in Goethe's sense. The urgent need for interpretation that is built into the Kafkan existential sign seems to bring it closer to allegory.

However, it also differs from allegory because of the mimetic translucency of its signification, an aspect linked to its derivation from metaphor embedded in speech. Coldness is intuitively understood and indeed transparent as the sign of an environment of inhospitableness and hostility to life. Avoidance of and flight from it would appear to be the expected, "natural" reaction of life to such an environment. K.'s stubborn insistence on being summoned to this inhospitable region alludes to something in him that contradicts "normality," the common sense of self-preservation. It signals an ambition out of step with what is presumed to be natural. Like the art of the hunger artist, it appears to aim for a transcendence of nature. In this intuitively felt signification of the existential sign we thus come upon an aspect that seems to contradict the antimimetic alienation effect we have noted before. While the eternal winter in the Castle region shows that the novel does not portray an empirically recognizable world, making it difficult for the reader to grasp at first the function exercised by the existential sign, the sign becomes readily understandable when its derivation from metaphoric speech is perceived. It becomes still clearer when looked at in conjunction with the signifiers of cold, winter, and far north, and their closely analogous function in other texts by Kafka.

The functional similarity of the existential sign of cold, winter, and far north in Kafka's total oeuvre makes the significance of eternal winter in *The Castle* much clearer. It becomes recognizable as a descriptive setting of the will to follow a call, to practice an art that, like the healing art of the country doctor, the starving art of the hunger artist, and, in Kafka's own case, the art of writing, is a mission conditional upon self-banishment from family, homeland, normal and "natural" human life. It would lead us too far from our topic here, which is the existential sign in general, to discuss the fact that K. in *The Castle* seems to strive for a synthesis of his ascetic-fanatical commitment to his strange calling and establishing a "natural" and "normal" emotional bond to a woman, Frieda—a synthesis that finds an analogy in the last year of Kafka's own life in which he was able to unite, for a short period, his lonely devotion to writing with cohabitation with a beloved young woman, Dora Dymant.

We have thus seen that the existential sign in Kafka's work has a mimetic as well as a nonmimetic aspect. Moreover, like the Freudian dream symbol, it has not only a more or less definite, but also a universal meaning. The signifier denoting coldness functions in many languages as a metaphor for a certain quality of human behavior because it expresses an analogy between the physical feeling caused by low temperatures and the emotional effect that emanates from persons who distance themselves from and avoid intimacy with their fellow human beings. The metaphor that Kafka's text turns into scenery reflects an analogy with experiences in human life. It raises Kafka's work far above the private, the particular, and the autobiographical and lends the mythos of the struggle of existence, which Kafka's work represents, a much wider significance. Since the existential sign unites nonmimetic and mimetic aspects of Kafka's writing, it helps to explain the peculiar combination of the alienating, disconcerting, dreamlike mysteriousness of Kafka's texts and their strong and vivid emotional appeal to many readers.

The existential sign likewise combines the equationlike semiotic specificity of traditional allegory with the universal, intuitively understandable power of symbols. In this respect, the existential sign has less to do with Goethe's than with Freud's concept of symbol. Dream symbols are for Freud images of objects and beings that, like Kafka's existential signs, signify something quite specific. What they signify remains essentially constant.[19] Freudian dream symbols are symbols in a pre-Goethean sense, in which, as in common parlance, the word "symbol" is used interchangeably with "sign." The climbing of stairs, for example, signifies in Freud's dream interpretations always the sexual act, while all "lengthy objects, sticks, tree trunks, umbrellas . . . knives, daggers, pikes," occurring in dreams, "represent the male organ."[20] Not in terms of content, but in terms of function, the Kafkan existential sign corresponds closely to the Freudian symbol.

The two are also in accordance in so far as both are signs whose roles are significant only in the context in which they appear, for Freud in the dream as an expression of the psyche of the dreamer, for Kafka in the individual text as an expression of the total work. Extending this analogy, we might say that Kafka's individual texts correspond to dreams, while Kafka's total oeuvre could be compared to a whole psyche. That is, the individual text of Kafka, like the individual dream for Freud, allows a particular view of a general situation. In the case of Freud, the general situation is an individual's psyche. In the case of Kafka, it is the struggle that his entire work describes in variations of fascinating diversity.

The analogy to the Freudian dream symbol also illuminates the marked difference between Kafka's existential signs and allegory in both its classical and its Benjaminian sense. Allegory addresses itself to the question of meaning of a whole work and finds that meaning in a concept, or does not find it. The existential sign, however, is only a detail in a text. It does not supply a meaning but fulfills an expressive function that connects a particular text to other texts by Kafka. Through their existential signs Kafka's texts tend to illuminate each other, but the former do not provide overarching answers to the questions raised by the texts. They merely shed, admittedly important, light on the terrain in which the myth that the totality of Kafka's texts relates takes place. Since this myth is not an equation, but a narrative, its "meaning" is left in charge of the readers to whom it speaks.

NOTES

1. Johann Wolfgang Goethe, *Maximen und Reflektionen.* Neu geordnet und erläutert von Günther Müller (Stuttgart: Alfred Kroner Verlag, 1943), 104 f.

2. Max Brod, "Nachwort," Franz Kafka, *Das Schloss.* Roman (Munich: Kurt Wolff, 1926), 492–503, esp. 495 f.

3. Herbert Tauber, *Franz Kafka: Eine Deutung seiner Werke* (Zurich-New York: Verlag Oprecht, 1941).

4. Tauber, *Franz Kafka,* 24 f.

5. Norbert Fürst, *Die offenen Geheimtüren Franz Kafkas: Fünf Allegorien* (Heidelberg: W. Roethe, 1956).

6. Fürst, *Die offenen Geheimtüren Franz Kafkas,* 36–52.

7. Erich Heller, "The World of Franz Kafka," in *The Disinherited Mind: Essays in Modern Literature and Thought* (Cambridge, U.K.: Bowes & Bowes, 1952), 155–81, esp. 160–69.

8. Walter Benjamin, *Ursprung des deutschen Trauerspiels* (Frankfurt am Main: Suhrkamp Verlag, 1963), 174–268. First edition 1928. English translation, *The Origin of German Tragic Drama.* Trans. John Osborne (London: NLB, 1977), 160–235.

9. Stanley Corngold, "Symbolic and Allegorical Interpretation," in *The Commentator's Despair: The Interpretation of Kafka's Metamorphosis* (Port Washington, N.Y.—London: National University Publications, Kennikat Press, 1973), 31–38.

10. Heinz Politzer, *Franz Kafka: Parable and Paradox* (Ithaca, N.Y.: Cornell University Press, 1962), esp. 1–22.

11. Wilhelm Emrich, *Franz Kafka* (Bonn: Athenäum Verlag, 1958).

12. Ibid., 11, 23 f.

13. Ibid., 25 f.

14. Ibid., 30–73.

15. Theodor W. Adorno, "Aufzeichnungen zu Kafka," in *Prismen. Kulturkritik und Gesellschaft* (Berlin-Frankfurt am Main: Suhrkamp Verlag, 1955), 302–42. English translation "Notes on Kafka," in *Prisms,* trans. Samuel and Sherry Weber (London: Neville Spearman, 1967), 244–71.

16. Walter H. Sokel, *Franz Kafka: Tragik und Ironie: Zur Struktur seiner Kunst* (Munich-Vienna: Albert Langen, Georg Müller, 1964), passim.

17. Günther Anders, *Franz Kafka. Pro und Contra. Die Prozess-Unterlagen* (Munich: C. H. Beck), 1951, 40–44. English translation *Franz Kafka,* trans. A. Steer and A. K. Thorlby (London: Bowes & Bowes, 1960).

18. Franz Kafka, *Das Schloss,* ed. Malcolm Pasley (Frankfurt am Main: S. Fischer Lizenzausgabe von Schocken Books, New York, 1982), 488. First edition, ed. Max Brod (New York: Schocken Books, 1926). English translation, Franz Kafka, *The Castle,* a new translation based on the restored text, trans. and with a Preface by Mark Harman (New York: Schocken Books, 1998), 312. It is true that it is the chambermaid Pepi who says "in one's memory spring and summer seem so short, as if they didn't last more than two days, and sometimes even on those days,

throughout the most beautiful day, snow falls." But because it is winter during the entire novel, Pepi's comment has objective plausibility for the reader.

19. Sigmund Freud, *The Standard Edition of Complete Psychological Works of Sigmund Freud,* translated from the German under the general editorship of James Strachey in collaboration with Anna Freud, assisted by Alix Strachey and Alan Tyson (London: Hogarth Press and Institute of Psychoanalysis, 1953). Vol. 5 (1900–1901), *The Interpretation of Dreams* (Part 2), 350–404.

20. Ibid., 354.

6

THE RELATIONSHIP OF NARRATIVE PERSPECTIVE TO NARRATIVE ACTION AND MEANING IN "BEFORE THE LAW," "JACKALS AND ARABS," AND *THE TRIAL*

IN HIS book on Kafka's "poetic theory and poetic form" ("Dichtungstheorie und Dichtungsgestalt"), Heinz Hillmann distinguishes five basic types of narration in Kafka's work, which he calls "meditation" ("Betrachtung"), "parable" ("Parabel"), "story" ("Geschichte"), "novel" ("Roman"), and "report" ("Bericht"), whereby "novel" is to be seen as a subcategory of "story."[1] Leaving aside the category "meditation," as a special case, we deal in Kafka's mature work with three narrative genres: parable, story (to which the novel belongs), and report. Hillmann considers the Kafkan parable form to be determined above all by "dispensing with details through simplification, abstraction and generality," which "results in conciseness and brevity."[2] On the other hand, he sees "the succession of situations" as the defining characteristic of the category "story."[3]

This distinction based on structure is certainly very useful, but it needs an important amendment. A still more precise differentiation is possible when one examines a particular structural feature, namely the relationship of narrative perspective to narrative action. Then the essential differentiation between "parable" and "story" is not only expanded and made more precise, but the categorization is also simplified, in that from this

---

Originally published as "Das Verhältnis der Erzählperspektive zu Erzählgeschehen und Sinngehalt in 'Vor dem Gesetz,' 'Schakale und Araber' und 'Der Prozeß': Ein Beitrag zur Unterscheidung von 'Parabel' und 'Geschichte' bei Kafka," *Zeitschrift für Deutsche Philologie* 86 (1967): 267–300. Translated by Harold Brubaker. Translations from Kafka are my own.

viewpoint the "report" appears to be a subcategory of "parable." Thus remain two basic narrative groups in Kafka's mature work: "parable-report" and "story-novel."

Before the appearance of Hillmann's book and also without knowing about him, I made a similar distinction between two basic narrative forms in my essay "Kafka als Expressionist" and in my book *Franz Kafka: Tragik und Ironie.*[4] I found the distinguishing characteristic between Kafka's two forms in the narrative perspective. The one narrative form I called "expressionistic." But this terminology mixed characteristics of form and content. In addition, the terms "expressionistic," "tragic," and "ironic" proved to be too inexact to allow the distinction to be made sharply enough. Above all, what was essential, the relationship of narrative perspective to narrative action, was not sufficiently established. The object of this study is the clarification of this difference on the basis of two parables and a novel.

The writing of *The Trial,* which went very quickly at first, began to cause Kafka difficulties in the late summer and early fall of 1914.[5] One of those crises arose that Kafka always seemed to experience during the writing of longer works and that caused his novels to remain fragments.[6] During this particular crisis, Kafka wrote *In the Penal Colony* while on vacation (October 1914)[7] and soon thereafter the legend of the doorkeeper, later titled "Before the Law" (December 1914).[8] In these two relatively short stories he developed for the first time what was for him a new form, which we shall call parable. It served first of all to clarify the problems that had developed during the writing of the novel. After *In the Penal Colony* he was able for an extended period to continue his work on *The Trial* with renewed energy, and the two parables, especially the legend, made the meaning of the novel significantly clearer.

When one applies Hillmann's standards, *In the Penal Colony* must be counted among the stories. From the viewpoint of narrative perspective, however, it is part of the transition to the parable form. What contrasts the new from the old form is not merely the brevity and the unitary perspective of the new parable form, because "The Judgment" is also short and "The Metamorphosis" is also unimental, yet both of them are stories and not parables.[9] It is in the first instance in the new narrative perspective where the contrast is to be found.

The narratives from Kafka's breakthrough period from September 1912 up through *The Trial*—"The Judgment," "The Metamorphosis," *Amerika,* and *The Trial*—show the radicalness of the "personal narrative situation" ("personale Erzählsituation") that was discovered in Kafka's work by Friedrich Beissner and Martin Walser.[10] Kafka takes to its logically consequential extreme the elimination, programmatically practiced by Flaubert and Henry James, of the omniscient, sovereign, auctorial narrator.[11] In these narratives from his "breakthrough period"—so called because Kafka dated from "The Judgment" his "breakthrough" to a narrative style appropriate to him—the reader sees with the eyes of the protagonist. The narrator is so closely connected to the perspective of the protagonist that he becomes invisible to the reader, even if, as Keith Leopold has shown in the case of *The Trial,* the perspective of the narrator does not completely meld with that of the protagonist.[12] The reader never learns thoughts and feelings of other characters, only their words, gestures, and actions. The reader, like the protagonist, is dependent on conjectures and inferences, based on the words and the behavior of the other characters, which, however, can never be certainties. The true inner life of these figures remains unknown. Also in the physical world, the reader sees only what the protagonist sees and in the same chronological sequence in which objects and scenes come into his field of vision. The reader sees the protagonist "directly" just as little as the protagonist sees himself (if we exclude the closing scene of "The Metamorphosis").

This single-perspective narrative style corresponds to what one could call "existential realism," for it represents exactly what every human being experiences during his/her entire life. Condemned to lifelong solitary confinement in his/her own brain, no human being can achieve incontrovertible certitude about the inner life and consciousness of his/her fellow human beings, but is always dependent on indirect information and conjecture. He/She can never climb into another person's body and soul, never perceive from the viewpoint of another person's brain. Kafka's extremely personal narrative perspective therefore corresponds formally to the unavoidable fact of individuation. Seeing and acting, perceiving and suffering are united in one and the same person as a result of the limitation and isolation of the individual, who can never step out of his skin.

That is not the case in the legend, which the priest tells to Josef K. in the "Cathedral" chapter of *The Trial* and which Kafka included in the volume *A Country Doctor* with the title "Before the Law." Here seeing and experiencing are separated. A narrator, the figure of the priest, and the listener Josef K. get between the main character of the legend and the reader. The reader's perspective is thereby twice removed from the object of the narrative. With this doubling of the perspective, the narrative ceases to be a "story" and becomes a "parable."

The first time a nonauctorial perspective gets between the reader and the main character in Kafka's work is *In the Penal Colony.* In the larger opening section of *In the Penal Colony,* the main character, the one who acts and suffers, is the officer. He is the hero of the narrative. In contrast to "The Judgment," "The Metamorphosis," *Amerika,* and *The Trial,* we do not see the events caused by the hero and suffered by him with his eyes. The

Explorer, who as observer and listener steps between the Officer and the reader, sees them. We no longer see with the eyes, we no longer sit in the brain of the figure experiencing the action; rather we experience indirectly through the senses and the brain of the observer. That is a step away from the personal narrative situation, in which the reader identifies as closely as possible with the narrative, toward the distance between the narrative and the reader that an auctorial narrator creates. This distancing results from the doubling of the narrative perspective. On the one hand, as we view the Officer through the eyes of the Explorer, we are distanced from him; but, on the other hand, because of the length, liveliness, and passion of the Officer's evocation of the execution machine and its procedure, the reader comes to identify with the Officer's vision to such a degree that some readers have been led to believe that the penal procedure actually takes place in scenic representation even though it is merely the report of a fictional character. Although for a time we seem to see from the Officer's perspective, we return definitively to the Explorer's perspective at the conclusion of the report. Kafka thereby consciously breaks the law of unity of perspective that he followed in the larger narratives from "The Judgment" to *The Trial.*[13]

In *In the Penal Colony* this distancing and doubling of perspective is not consistently maintained. After the death of the Officer, the observer becomes the active and experiencing main character. This creates a break in the narrative form that disrupts the uniform mood of the narrative. Kafka himself felt that this disruption was awkward. In a letter from September 4, 1917, he asks his publisher not to publish the piece. "Two or three of the final pages are bungled, and their presence points to some deeper flaw; there is a worm somewhere which hollows out even the successful parts of the story" ("Zwei oder drei Seiten kurz vor ihrem Ende sind Machwerk, ihr Vorhandensein deutet auf einen tieferen Mangel, es ist da irgendwo ein Wurm, der selbst das volle der Geschichte hohl macht.").[14] We see that Kafka was dissatisfied with the part of the narrative that follows the death of the Officer and in which the observer becomes the active character, where the detachment of perspective from action stops. Around the same time he tried to alter the concluding section, as shown by drafts in his journal.[15] The main section, however, which shows the new doubled perspective, he called "the successful part of the story" ("das Volle der Geschichte"). This expresses his satisfaction and high opinion, which is the attitude he generally displayed toward *In the Penal Colony.*[16] He welcomed the new principle and developed it further in the following work, the legend "Before the Law."

In the legend, though, the new principle of perspectival distancing from narrative action is only apparent when we read it in the context in which it was originally written, in the "Cathedral" chapter of *The Trial.* There it is clear that the legend is told by a character in the novel and is therefore an example of detached perspective. The priest narrates and therefore looks at what is narrated from the outside. As listener, Josef K. is twice removed from the character of the legend, and the reader of the novel is therefore actually three times removed from the legend's narrated action. In its original place in the novel, the legend literally fulfills the function of a parable. It is an allegory, an illustration, a figurative commentary on the plot of the novel.

This new way of seeing necessitates a new style of representation, already noticeable in the first sentences of the legend.

> Before the Law stands a doorkeeper. A man from the country comes to this doorkeeper and asks for admittance into the Law.
>
> Vor dem Gesetz steht ein Türhüter. Zu diesem Türhüter komt ein Mann vom Lande und bittet um Eintritt in das Gesetz. (P, 255)[17]

The perspective at the beginning originates outside of the narrative, outside of the two figures, the doorkeeper and the man from the country. The two participants in the narrative are literally presented to us, placed before us. One needs only to put the introduction of the legend next to the beginning of the novel in order to recognize the difference in perspective and style:

> Someone must have slandered Josef K., for without his having done anything bad, he was arrested one morning. The cook of Frau Grubach, his landlady, who brought him his breakfast every morning around eight, did not come this time. That had never happened before. K. continued to wait a while, watching from his pillow the old lady who lived across from him and who was observing him with a curiosity quite unusual for her, but then, both unsettled and hungry, he rang.
>
> Jemand mußte Josef K. verleumdet haben, denn ohne daß er etwas Böses getan hätte, wurde er eines Morgens verhaftet. Die Köchin der Frau Grubach, seiner Zimmermieterin, die ihm jeden Tag gegen acht Uhr früh das Frühstück brachte, kam diesmal nicht. Das war noch niemals geschehen. K. wartete noch ein Weilchen, sah von seinem Kopfkissen aus die alte Frau, die ihm gegenüber wohnte und die ihn mit einer an ihr ganz ungewöhnlichen Neugierde beobachtete, dann aber, gleichzeitig befremdet und hungrig, läutete er. (P, 9)

In contrast to the legend, the novel does not provide a three-dimensional, all-encompassing external view of the scene. The first thing that is expressed is not an occurrence, but rather a conjecture, a thought. It remains uncertain who thinks this thought, Josef K. or a narrator. It could be one or the other or even both thinking the thought. The subjunctive form of the auxiliary verb "hätte" does appear to point, as asserted by Kudszus, to an auctorial narrator.[18] This ambiguity regarding the one who thinks here, the narrator or Josef K., is effectively described by Kudszus: "On the one hand we sense a narrator distanced from Josef K.; because with the reporting of the arrest something is anticipated that K. does not experience until a few sentences later. On the other hand, Josef K.'s perspective makes itself noticeable because the 'hätte' indicates suspiciousness on the part of the hero and is probably consciously chosen over the reporting 'hatte,' which would point to a distanced narrator."[19] Narrative object (hero) and narrative perspective (narrator) are so close to one another that their viewpoints are not clearly distinguishable. This is a typical example of the personal narrative situation, which Franz Stanzel calls the highest degree of emotional presentation possible in narratives.[20] The following sentences of the novel, which report the interruption of Josef K.'s breakfast routine, are spoken from his viewpoint. Here it would be completely possible to replace the third-person with the first-person pronoun, to say "me" instead of "him," without changing the meaning. Why Kafka did not write his novels in the first-person—*The Castle,* as is well-known, was begun in the first person, but revised consistently to be in the third person—has reasons we can't go into here.[21] In the fourth sentence of the novel we encounter for the first time a description of the situation. It is indicative that what is described there is not Josef K., but rather what he sees. Our perspective takes Josef K. as its point of departure.

Let us now return to the legend. In the further course of the text we notice a shift in perspective, reminiscent of the novel, to that of the man from the country. But this is true only up to the point when the doorkeeper gives him a stool and allows him to sit to the side of the door. Here the objectification of the perspective begins anew. "There he sits for days and years" ("Dort sitzt er Tage und Jahre.") (P 256). We see the main character from outside, as we saw him come to the doorkeeper in the second sentence. He is shown to us, whereby we remember that the parable, called a "legend" by Kafka, is a demonstration, an example. In *The Trial,* it functions as an example of Josef K.'s self-deception.

The following sentence marks the complete objectification of the narrative perspective in the legend.

> He makes many attempts to be allowed in and *wearies the doorkeeper* with his pleas.

> Er macht viele Versuche, eingelassen zu werden, und *ermüdet den Türhüter* durch seine Bitten. (P, 256; emphasis mine)

This is proof of a traditional-auctorial narrative perspective in Kafka's work, which went completely unnoticed by Beissner and Walser. The narrator allows us an (when we leave out of consideration the end of "The Metamorphosis," which also went unnoticed by Beissner and Walser) unprecedented direct look into the inner life of a character who is not the protagonist. A second example is found at the end of the legend:

> The doorkeeper *realizes* that the man is already at the end and *in order still to reach his fading hearing* he roars at him.
>
> Der Türhüter *erkennt,* daß der Mann schon an seinem Ende ist und, *um sein vergehendes Gehör noch zu erreichen,* brüllt er ihn an. (P, 257; emphasis mine)

Here we become certain of the thoughts and intentions of the antagonist, thanks to the authority of the omniscient narrator.

The two breaks established here in Kafka's otherwise uniform personal narrative perspective go far beyond the deviations from the third-person perspective, which Leopold and Kudszus noticed and commented on.[22] Leopold and Kudszus show that the K.-perspective is supplemented by the perspective of a narrator who knows more than the K.-figures and reports things that the protagonist himself cannot be aware of. In the legend, however, something much more fundamental takes place: for in the passages I have emphasized the narrator's position is outside of and above the two figures of the narrative and he sees into them in a traditional manner. Above all Kafka allows us, even if it is only fleetingly, a look into the consciousness of the antagonist, which he had up until then refused. Nowhere else in *The Trial* is the conscious content of a figure other than Josef K. imparted to us with certainty. Like Josef K. himself, the reader is dependent on conjecture and has no advantage over K. When the content of the consciousness of other characters is related, the information is robbed of its absolute validity by the adverb "surely" ("gewiß"): "The director, who *surely* recognized the distress in K.'s eyes" ("Der Direktor, der *gewiß* an K.s Augen die Not erkannte") (P, 241). "In the darkness prevailing down here the priest could *surely* not recognize K. exactly" ("*Gewiß* konnte der Geistliche in dem Dunkel, das unten herrschte, K. nicht genau erkennen") (P, 254; emphasis mine). Whatever transpires in other characters is not communicated as objective information secured by the auctorial narrator, but rather as a conjecture by Josef K. In another example, where we learn of the anger of the priest, the text says: "It was an angry cry" ("Es war im Zorn geschrieen.") (P, 254). We do not know if the priest was really angry. We only get the impression of his scream on Josef K., the acoustic phenomenon in Josef K.'s interpretation. But we are not told that the priest actually *felt* anger. The priest's actual feeling remains unknown to Josef K. and the reader. In the legend, on the other hand, we do get, even if most sparingly, direct insight into the consciousness of someone other than the main character. Consequently, an objectification takes place here that distinguishes the legend stylistically and formally from the novel and moves it closer to the traditional autonomy of an omniscient narrator.

This narrative form, which we encounter already in the earliest text in the volume *A Country Doctor,* is dominant in the following period—1916–1917, during which the remaining stories in the collection were written.[23] It consists to a large degree of separation of the narrative perspective from the action and suffering of the characters prominently involved in the events, while in the preceding period (1912–1914) seeing and action largely coincided. Typical for this shift in perspective and climaxing is the change from third-person narrative dominant in the breakthrough period to the first-person form in the volume *A Country Doctor*. In this regard the doorkeeper legend is a mark of the transition. It is one of the few pieces in *A Country Doctor* that retains the third-person narrative. Only three others are told in the third person, "A Dream," "Up in the Gallery," and "A Fratricide." All others—a total of nine of fourteen stories in the volume—are told by a first-person singular or plural narrator. A middle position between the larger group of first-person and the smaller group of third-person narratives is occupied by "An Imperial Message," because it is basically reported in the second person as a communication or an address to a subject, who appears to be identical with the listener or the reader. If we disregard the title story, "A Country Doctor," which deserves its own study in terms of narrative perspective, all the first-person narratives have in common with the legend of the doorkeeper a considerable distancing of perspective from action or happening. The first-person narrative form accommodates this separation because in the first-person narrator, an observing consciousness stands opposite an observed happening and registers it. The first-person narrative is a transition to the report. Not without reason does the last piece in the volume, "A Report to an Academy," carry the word "report" in its title. This shows that it was not just coincidentally put at the end, but rather represents the crowning and logical culmination of the formal tendencies of the whole volume. As Stanzel shows, the I-form borders with one pole on the auctorial and with the other on the personal narrative situation.[24] Kafka was poetologically consistent in resorting to the first person when his narrative called for auctorial distance from the narrated action, even as he likewise preferred the first person as the natural form for his "meditation" ("Betrachtung").

Providing a complete proof of the function of this new formal principle in all the narratives of *A Country Doctor* would go beyond the frame of this essay. I must limit myself to a striking example on the basis of which to define the Kafkan parable and to delimit it from the story form. "Jackals and Arabs" is chosen for the following reasons. First, the content of this parable shows astonishing parallels to that of the "Whipper" chapter, the fifth chapter of *The Trial,* so that the thematic analogies allow the formal differences to stand out with particular clarity. Second, in Kafka's arrangement of the volume *A Country Doctor*, this parable, written at the beginning of 1917,[25] is placed immediately after the legend "Before the Law." Kafka's story collections were always or were always supposed to have been arranged according to a conscious principle,[26] which means that this sort of juxtaposition often indicates a thematic and structural relationship. The present investigation will yield such relationships between "Jackals and Arabs" and the legend of the doorkeeper. It should be said in advance that the last section of "Jackals and Arabs" functions exactly like "Before the Law" as an example and illustration of a certain way of being. In the parabolic spectacle, the essence of the jackals is put on display for the benefit of the first-person narrator in the same way the behavior of the man from the country is related to Josef K. as an example of his own essence, of his self-deception. The contrasting effects of this viewing on the first-person narrator in the parable and on Josef K., the character in the novel, provide another key to the essential difference between "parable" and "story" in Kafka's work. Let us now compare "Jackals and Arabs" with the whipper scene in *The Trial.*

In "Jackals and Arabs" and in the fifth chapter of *The Trial,* there are three parallel figures or groups of figures—the viewer, the tormentor, and the sufferers. In the parable the viewer is the first-person narrator; in the novel it is Josef K. In the parable the tormentor is the whip-swinging Arab; in *The Trial* the whipper is summoned by the Court. In the parable the suffering victims are the jackals; in the *Trial* chapter the two guards Franz and Willem, about whom Josef K. had complained, are beaten in the storage room of his bank because of his complaint. In both narratives, the victims implore the viewers to save them from their tormentors. In both cases the request is fulfilled either only partially or not at all. Even the two tormentors resemble one another. Both look down mockingly upon their victims and try to prove their worthlessness. The parallelism in narrative perspective becomes very apparent if we realize that in the "Whipper" chapter of *The Trial,* a first-person narrator could easily replace the third person. This remarkable common ground makes it possible to clearly show the tremendous differences in the narrative situation by very carefully tracing the course of action of the two narratives with regard to the relationship of perspective to action, of looking to doing and suffering. Kafka's narrative principles will be clearly established and differentiated, and the intricate relationship between narrative form and content will likewise become apparent.

One evening Josef K. sees in the storage room of the bank where he works the two guards who had arrested him, Franz and Willem, with a whipper who had been summoned by the Court. The whipper is about to flog the guards because Josef K. had complained to the examining magistrate about the theft of his laundry. Although a spectator, K. is therefore immediately drawn into what he sees. He has a causal connection to the event, one that tends to make him guilty. Accordingly, he feels driven to justify himself and to give a reason for his behavior. He excuses his reporting of the guards by saying that he had not requested their punishment and had had no idea at all that his complaint would lead to punishment. He asks the whipper if it would not be possible to spare the guards the beating. The whipper says that it is not possible. Thus K. cannot remain a spectator as the rod falls down on Willem. He tries to bribe the whipper, but can only do so with averted eyes, thereby admitting the shamefulness of his conduct. This attempt to do away with the results of his earlier action, namely the reporting of the theft, to shift the blame from himself, only makes him guiltier because through bribery he would also make the whipper punishable. The whipper reproaches K. for that and brusquely rejects his offer. K. declares that he really is serious about freeing the two. Would he stay there otherwise? If he were not serious about it, he would shut the door, close his eyes and ears, and go home. He accuses the Court of being the guilty one and presses the whipper's switch down. But the whipper does not let himself be swayed. Franz, in a manner evoking the greatest sympathy, now implores K. to save him, clings to K. and dries his tears on K.'s coat. The whipper lashes into Franz relentlessly. The victim's screams of pain sound through the whole building. K. panics. He pushes Franz to the floor, where the whipper's blows continue to hammer down on him. Servants appear in the distance. K. quickly slams the door shut in order to conceal the compromising scene, thus doing exactly what he had not wanted to do. He does exactly what according to his own statement he would have done if he were not serious about freeing the guards—he steps to the window facing the courtyard. When a servant asks him if something untoward has happened, he lies, saying that a dog had been whining in the courtyard, and sends the servant back to work. What follows now is narrated in K.'s narrated monologue. He is left with a feeling of agony and failure because he did not succeed in preventing the beating. He tells himself, however, that it had not been his fault. Had Franz not screamed, K. would "probably" have found the means to persuade the whipper. It was Franz's screaming that made all intervention impossible. K. certainly could not allow the servants to find him negotiating with that group in the storage room. He could have just as well offered himself to the whipper as a replacement for the guards. Based on the reasoning that the whipper would not have accepted this replacement, K. rejects the idea as absurd. He justifies his behavior to himself with the idea that there was nothing he could do but close the door.

This passage is typical for Kafka's breakthrough period. Witnessing provides the occasion to illustrate the behavior of the spectator, his self-contradiction. The spectacle in the junk room tells us nothing certain about the victims and the tormentor, but very much about K. What determines the behavior of the protagonist is the attempt at self-justification, the shifting of guilt from oneself to others, the refusal to recognize the irrepressible bubbling up of a guilty conscience. Ingeborg Henel applies to this typical behavior of Josef K. Kafka's concept of "Motivation."[27] Kafka understands motivation as follows:

> No one can be content with knowledge alone, but rather must strive to act according to it. However, for that, he is not endowed with the necessary strength; he must, therefore, destroy himself, even at the risk of not attaining even by such means the necessary strength; however, nothing else remains for him but that one ultimate attempt. (That is also the meaning of the threat of death accompanying the prohibition of eating from the tree of knowledge; perhaps that is also the original meaning of natural death.) He happens to be afraid of that attempt; he would rather revoke his knowledge of good and evil (the term "Fall of Man" goes back to that fear); but what has occurred cannot be made undone, it can only be obscured. For that purpose the motivations arise. The entire world is filled with them; indeed, all of the visible world is perhaps nothing but a motivation of man wishing to rest for a moment.

> Niemand kann sich mit der Erkenntnis allein begnügen, sondern muß sich bestreben, ihr gemäß zu handeln. Dazu aber ist ihm die Kraft nicht mitgegeben, er muß daher sich zerstören, selbst auf die Gefahr hin, sogar dadurch die notwendige Kraft nicht zu erhalten, aber es bleibt ihm nichts anderes übrig, als dieser letzte Versuch. (Das ist auch der Sinn der Todesdrohung beim Verbot des Essens vom Baume der Erkenntnis; vielleicht ist das auch der ursprüngliche Sinn des natürlichen Todes.) Vor diesem Versuch nun fürchtet er sich; lieber will er die Erkenntnis des Guten und Bösen rückgängig machen (die Bezeichnung "Sündenfall" geht auf diese Angst zurück); aber das Geschehene kann nicht rückgängig gemacht, sondern nur getrübt werden. Zu diesem Zweck entstehen die Motivationen. Die ganze Welt ist ihrer voll, ja die ganze sichtbare Welt ist vielleicht nichts anderes als eine Motivation des einen Augenblick lang ruhenwollenden Menschen. (H, 49)

The concept of "motivation" has striking relevance to the "Whipper" chapter. K. tries to undo the consequences of his original action, at which of course he does not succeed and only entangles himself in worse guilt. He only manages to obscure the meaning of what has happened by shifting the blame and attempting to ease his guilty conscience by repressing the insight that would make him sacrifice himself for the victims of the beating and take their place. He conjures this thought away with hollow attempts of self-justification that cannot convince. The carrier of the narrative perspective is, at the same time, the source of a continual cover-up, of maneuvers of deception that are essential to the narrative content and emotional effect of Kafka's "stories." The bearer of its point of view is both the subject and the object of the narrative action, which in turn illustrates his "Motivations." He constantly feels it incumbent upon himself to intervene in the event he witnesses. He appears to demand from himself a decisive deed, but fails to perform it, substituting for it a kind of para-action, efforts marked by halfheartedness, insincerity, and futility. Those conform exactly to Kafka's meaning of "Motivations."

In order to carry out our planned comparison between the story and parable forms in Kafka's work we must now turn to a strictly formal element concerning narrative technique. We need to distinguish between the depiction of objective and subjective behavior on the part of the character whose perspective the reader shares. As objective behavior I understand the distancing of the character from the action he witnesses, linking the action to its observer at one remove. I term as "subjective behavior" those narrative passages in which the seeing and experiencing character is also the direct object of the narrative action—be it through conduct, suffering, and speaking or reflecting on his own conduct in narrated monologue. In the section of the "Whipper" chapter examined above, we find the following numerical relationship between Josef K.'s objective and subjective behavior. Of one hundred sentences or parts of sentences considered, fifty-eight describe objective and forty-two subjective behavior on Josef K.'s part. Thus, although K. arrives at the scene as a spectator, he becomes the center and chief vehicle of the action as often as he stays an onlooker. K. feels obliged to keep meddling in the action and finally he takes it over completely. The observer becomes the carrier of the action. His behavior becomes the exclusive object of the narrative. An objectifying separation, a knowledge-enriching distance does not arise between the viewer and the viewed.

Josef K.'s subjective behaviors have the following relationship to one another. What K. says is contradicted by what he does. He declares that he is serious about freeing the guards because if he were not he would just shut the door and not see or hear anything. He does exactly that shortly thereafter. The last part of the section consists in Josef K.'s attempt to justify to himself the inconsistency between his speech and conduct. The actual object of the narrative is therefore not what Josef K. sees and hears. That is just the trigger that allows the actual object, Josef K.'s inconsistencies and his motivations, to become apparent. This is the way in which not only this scene but the entire novel is constructed. The arrest is the trigger that sets off the *Prozeß* of the contradictions and motivations in Josef K.[28] In this sense one can say that the Court is "drawn in" by Josef K.'s guilt (P, 15). The trial against Josef K. is nothing more than a series of examples that shows how K. always tries to shift his guilty conscience onto the Court, turns the Court into his "Motivation."[29] It is the process of his repeated attempts and repeated failures to shift guilt from himself. The comment of the priest in the "Cathedral" chapter applies to this motivational maneuvering: "the guilty tend to talk" like Josef K. (P, 253).

The parable "Jackals and Arabs" contains the following numerical relationship between objective and subjective behavior on the part of the observing character, the first-person narrator. Of 128 sentences and sentence parts, ninety-six depict an objective, only thirty-two a subjective behavior by the first-person narrator. But of those thirty-two sentences and sentence parts, three are questions, and one other sentence expresses the narrator's desire to keep his distance from the events. That leaves merely twenty-eight sentences or sentence parts that contain active subjective behavior. In the "Whipper" chapter subjective behavior takes up almost half, here barely a fifth of the statements in which perspective and action are directly connected. In more than three-quarters of the narration they are separated. This numerical variation points to an essentially different narrative style.

Even more instructive, however, is the direction in which the relationship between narrative perspective and events changes in the course of the narrative. In the "Whipper" chapter we saw that the events returned to the onlooker himself. But in the parable we observe the opposite development. Seeing and acting move further and further apart. If we investigate this distancing process in greater detail, we can come to a better understanding of structure, function and meaning of the parable form for Kafka.

At first the observing "I" of the parable, the first-person narrator, appears almost as intimately involved in the action as Josef K. in *The Trial*. At the beginning of the narrative, the first-person narrator had separated himself from his companions and sought sleep in an isolated, therefore dangerous, location. The mournful howling of the jackals prevents him from falling asleep. The jackals disturb the peace and quiet of the perspective figure. Their relationship to him is the same as that of the Court to Josef K. The Court jolts Josef K. out of his routine existence, "hounds" him (P, 244), never again allows him to find peace. The first-person narrator of "Jackals and Arabs" gets involved in the affair of the jackals, as does Josef K. in the trial that is imposed on him. He forgets to ignite a fire to frighten away the jackals and, because of his excessive friendliness, allows them to involve him more and more deeply in their cause.

However, an essential difference between the narrator and Josef K. lies in the fact that the first-person narrator is linked to the vehicle of the action by his desire for knowledge, instead, like K., by a need for self-justification. The narrating "I" counters the surge of the Jackals toward him with a question: "What do you want, then, jackals?" ("Was wollt ihr denn, Schackale?") (E, 147). While Josef K. feels obliged to justify himself and takes the offensive against the Court, the first-person narrator of "Jackals and Arabs" limits himself to asking questions and seeking to learn. He wants to know the facts. What he represents is reason. In fact, to the jackals he embodies the principle of rationality:

> "We know," the eldest one began, "that you come from the North; on that fact our hope is built. There rationality is at home that cannot be found here among the Arabs."

> "Wir wissen," begann der Älteste, "daß du vom Norden kommst; darauf eben baut sich unsere Hoffnung. Dort ist der Verstand, der hier under den Arabern nicht zu finden ist." (E, 147)

To the jackals the "I" represents the extreme opposite of the much-hated Arabs. "'Out of this cold arrogance (of the Arabs), you know, it is impossible to get the least spark of rationality. They kill animals in order to eat them and they look down on carrion'" ("'Aus diesem kalten Hochmut (der Araber), weißt du, ist kein Funken Verstand zu schlagen. Sie töten Tiere, um sie zu fressen und Aas mißachten sie.'") (E, 147) But here the jackals' fundamental error becomes apparent. They identify reason with repugnance at flesh killed by violence. Anyone who kills animals and eats their flesh lacks reason and anyone who gets his nourishment from carrion has it. But ascetic revulsion at freshly slaughtered meat has nothing to do with reason. Seen from the standpoint of reason, represented by the "I", this revulsion is the expression of an instinctive conflict based in the blood. This is how the first-person narrator phrases it in an answer to the jackals:

> "Maybe, maybe," I said. "I do not presume to have any judgment in matters that are so remote from myself; it seems to be a very ancient dispute; it probably lies in the blood, and thus will perhaps end only with the blood."

> "Mag sein, mag sein," sagte ich, "ich maße mir kein Urteil an in Dingen, die mir so fern liegen; es scheint ein sehr alter Streit; liegt also wohl im Blut; wird also vielleicht erst mit dem Blute enden." (E, 147)

He thereby already draws a sharp line of separation between himself, the onlooker, to whom "these things" ("diese Dinge") (the action) are distant, who would not presume to pass judgment, and the ones making demands, the ones who suffer from them. The "I" does not allow himself to be causally linked to the victims, rather he distances himself as a true observer. As such the "I" can observe the contradiction in the jackals, whose concern is not a matter of reason, but rather of the blood, of fate. The observing "I" evades the action. By rejecting all judgment, it establishes its objectivity. It wants to keep its distance from the conflict and to witness it without involvement.

For the sake of contrast, we can now refer to Josef K.'s reaction to the priest's parable. Josef K. makes an immediate judgment. Without troubling to take into account all the facts ("die volle Wahrheit") (E, 59) contained in the parable of the doorkeeper, he rushes to the judgment that the doorkeeper deceived the man. In complete contrast to that, the ape in "A Report to an Academy" says: "By the way, I seek no man's judgment, I only want to spread knowledge, I am only reporting" ("Im übrigen will ich keines Menschen Urteil, ich will nur Kenntnisse verbreiten, ich berichte nur" (E, 177). In that statement of the reporting ape, the new attitude of Kafka's protagonists that begins with the traveler of *In the Penal Colony* culminates.

The jackals misunderstand the comment of the first-person narrator. With "it probably lies in the blood" ("liegt also wohl im Blut") he meant innateness, the fatefulness of the conflict between the jackals and the Arabs. The feud must endure as long as life. It cannot end until death. This has overtones of original sin, of unregenerate creation. There is no way to mitigate such a feud. The "I" anticipates the viewpoint of the Arab, who calls the jackals' "hope" for liberation absurd. But the jackals understand the word "blood" in a completely different way. They hope that the ancient feud will end in a bloodbath among the Arabs. This misunderstanding angers the "I" who sees no possibility for the fulfillment of this murderous hope for liberation. In the case of a rebellion, the Arabs would shoot the jackals down in swarms. But the jackals instruct the first-person narrator that not they themselves will kill the Arabs, but rather the first-person narrator would. For that purpose they offer him an ancient rusty pair of scissors. The jackals see in the European their liberator, their Messiah.

In their hope for a Messiah there lies an admission of helplessness. Belief in a Messiah arises from the inability to liberate oneself. The act of liberation is to be performed with scissors that are to cut the Arabs' throats. However, the jackals lack hands with which to work their scissors. They have "only their teeth" ("nur das Gebiß") (E, 149). Hands are the tools and symbols of reason, a sign of the exceptionality and power of *homo faber* in the universe. Reason must assist the jackals, in order to accomplish the work of their instinctive, blood-borne hate.

> Therefore, oh my lord, therefore, oh my dear lord, with the help of your all-capable hands, cut their throats with these scissors!

> Darum, o Herr, darum, o teurer Herr, mit Hilfe deiner alles vermögenden Hände, mit Hilfe deiner alles vermögenden Hände schneide ihnen mit dieser Schere die Hälse durch! (E, 149)

Because they lack the skill that hands bestow, the power of *homo faber,* they must resort to the Other, a stranger, to do their work of liberation for them.

However, a self-contradiction inheres in their request that thwarts its fulfillment. The jackals have to turn to reason as their savior, begging reason for a deed founded on irrationality. Their revulsion at freshly killed meat and their longing for purity free of violence and murder cannot be established rationally. They are a deep-seated, psychic, indeed instinctual, blood-borne necessity—an existential need. Because the first-person narrator represents reason, he cannot identify with the irrational, blood-borne demand of the jackals and must refuse it.

The question arises, why must the jackals resort to the hands, which is to say to the reason, of *homo faber* in order to accomplish the work of their blood-borne hate? Why could they not express their hate by physical means, by their teeth, and bite through the necks of the Arabs instead of cutting through them with scissors? Cowardice alone is not the answer. The answer appears in the text. It says that the Arabs are so unbearable to the jackals that they must flee "at the mere sight of their living body into the cleaner air, into the desert, which for that very reason is their home" ("schon vor dem bloßen Anblick ihres lebendigen Leibes weg, in reinere Luft, in die Wüste, die deshalb, Heimat ist") (E, 148). They would therefore never be able to attack the Arabs. Because if you cannot stand to smell someone, you cannot very well jump on him and rip his throat out.

Here a new and even more hopeless self-contradiction in the jackals' cause surfaces. Their revulsion at the Arabs thwarts their longing for liberation from them. The negative aspect of the jackals' cause—hatred of the Arabs—cancels its positive aspect—the wish to be free of them. That is why the jackals need an artificial aid, a pair of scissors, and must wait for a Messiah instead of liberating themselves. It is their insurmountable disgust at the carnality and the filth of the Arabs that hinders any effort to realize, by their own means, a clean and pure world.

In *The Trial* the contradictoriness is found in Josef K., that is, in the narrative figure, from whose perspective we experience the action. He does not want to recognize a Court from which he nonetheless seeks acquittal. He fights and derides the Court, yet seeks it out and makes every effort to penetrate its secrets. In the "Whipper" chapter he promises to help those suffering, yet instead pushes one of the victims down to the floor, and then conceals their torture even as the opportunity beckons to save them by making their victimization public. He contradicts his words with his deeds.

In the parable "Jackals and Arabs," on the other hand, the contradictoriness is not found in the character through whose mind we witness the events, but rather in the object of his vision, the jackals. Thus while in the novel the self-contradictoriness is in the subject of the narrative perspective, in the parable it is the object of contemplation. In the novel, the motivations, the obfuscating and repressive maneuvers take place in the carrier of the perspective. The reverse is the case in the parable. In it, the bearer of the perspective, the traveling first-person narrator, serves as the agent of clarification. Through him, the self-contradiction implicit in the objects of parabolic observation emerges to the reader's conscious awareness. The observer figure facilitates a transparency of the core problem that the self-justifying maneuvers of the protagonists' consciousness obfuscates in Kafka's "stories."

Even in the parable, the action temporarily overpowers the observer figure. The first-person narrator is "arrested" by the narrative object. Two young jackals hold onto him with their teeth and rob him of his freedom of movement, which corresponds to Josef K.'s arrest by the two warders in *The Trial.* This shows the great power that, in Kafka's world, the observed exercises over the observer. A strong and uncanny bond exists between reason and the ascetic yearning for transcendence of the carnal sphere. In Josef K., an analogous situation leads to the death of the empirical self. In contrast to Josef K., the first-person narrator of "Jackals and Arabs" faces no such danger. For here the bearer of the perspective, the "I," is not burdened by inner contradictions. He is only expected to observe from the outside, as a spectacle, the inner contradictions in which creatures become involved because of their striving to transcend the flesh and earthly filth. He himself is beyond the disastrous temptation that arises from the jackals' ascetic purism.

Actually, the first-person narrator is not freed from the throng of jackals until the Arab arrives. However, despite his predicament, the narrator refuses to move any closer to the jackals' position. On the contrary, upon his energetic protest and insistence he is released, but the jackals' speaker still asks him to hear their case. The arrest of the "I," as the speaker explains, should be taken as an honor. Although indignant and annoyed, the narrator grants the speaker's request.

Thus we see that the dangerous identification of the onlooker with the action, the structural principle of "The Judgment," "The Metamorphosis," *Amerika,* and *The Trial,* turns out to be nothing more than an episodic misunderstanding in the text of the volume *A Country Doctor* and has no further consequences. Immediately upon the observer's "arrest," which turns out to be a misunderstanding, the action moves away from him. The narrator's energetic protest against being held down forces the jackals to justify themselves to him. They excuse themselves by referring to their helplessness. Here it is not, as in "The Metamorphosis" or in *The Trial,* the observer who has to justify himself to the observed, but rather the observed who have to justify themselves to the observer. The onlooker does not take on the role of the defendant, but rather of the judge, who can make reproaches but not receive them.

The jackals implore the "I" to save the world from the "filthy" Arabs. The narrator is supposed to cut their throats with the rusty old scissors. Then there would be no more violent death on the peaceful earth, and the jackals could drain the blood of dead animals in peace and quiet.

Then the Arab suddenly steps between them and swings his whip. The jackals disperse hastily, but remain in the distance, huddled close together, waiting. Now the narrator becomes a true spectator. The cheerfully laughing Arab puts on "a show" for him, in which the jackals are the actors. The show proves the foolishness of the jackals' hope. "These animals entertain a senseless hope; they are fools, true fools. We love them for it; they are our dogs; more beautiful than yours" ("Eine unsinnige Hoffnung haben diese Tiere; Narren, wahre Narren sind sie. Wir lieben sie deshalb; es sind unsere Hunde; schöner als die eurigen.") (E, 149).

The rotting carcass of a camel is brought to the scene. As if magnetically attracted, the jackals cannot resist coming closer, craving to drain the blood. The blood in the carcass seems to them to have the power to quench their inner fire. The carrion is their deliverance. They are the possessed perpetrators of the action and it is literally passion that they embody. The reader has forgotten the narrator. The scene viewed by the narrator displaces him in the reader's consciousness. In the following sentences, the perspective shifts from him to the jackals:

> They had forgotten the Arabs, forgotten their hate, the all-extinguishing presence of the strongly odorous carcass bewitched them. . . .
>
> At that moment the leader powerfully cracked his stinging whip all across them. They raised their heads, half-intoxicated and swooning, *saw the Arabs standing before them, got to feel the whip with their snouts;* they withdrew in a leap and ran back some distance.

> Sie hatten die Araber vergessen, den Haß vergessen, die alles auslöschende Gegenwart des stark ausdunstenden Leichnams bezauberte sie. . . .
>
> Da strich der Führer kräftig mit der scharfen Peitsche kreuz und quer über sie. Sie hoben die Köpfe; halb in Rausch und Ohnmacht; *sahen die Araber*

> *vor sich stehen; bekamen die Peitsche mit den Schnauzen zu fühlen;* zogen sich im Sprung zurück und liefen eine Strecke rückwarts. (E, 150; emphasis mine)

The places emphasized by me show clearly that we are seeing with the eyes of the jackals, are experiencing the action through them. The perspective has moved to them and we empathize with their fate. This change in perspective serves to enliven the action. Along with the observing narrator, the reader is shown the context of the relationship between jackals and Arabs, which clarifies its significance. Obsession with the blood of dead animals makes the jackals a defenseless object of their oppressors. The desire for cleanliness, for purity, is exposed as bloodthirsty parasitism and passionate addiction, which degrades the jackals into victims of a self-inflicted disaster.

The narrative perspective, transferred to the jackals for clarifying the situation, now returns to the narrator. Now that he has thoroughly observed it, he puts an end to the gruesome "spectacle." He asks the Arab to stop. The Arab agrees. The last word of the story is his. He sums up the meaning of the situation.

The show that the Arab puts on for the narrator completes with gruesome clarity the image of the absurd "motivations" of the "madness" of the jackals. Not only can they never hope to attack the Arabs because they find them revolting, beyond that they are condemned to always exist in the hated proximity of the Arabs, for the very reason that makes the Arabs so odious and repulsive to them. From the Arabs they receive the carrion, which they love and cannot live without. Precisely because they are so exclusively and greedily addicted to their striving for pure bloodsucking, they are at the mercy of the "filthy" Arabs. Their lust for blood enslaves them to their enemies. The longing to transcend a world based on murder turns out to be parasitism.

The jackals are literally parasites, that is, creatures that feed on what others have accomplished. They feed on the bodies of animals killed by the Arabs. Kafka's images come out of the literalness of language, which for its part is a metaphorical interpretation of the world as experienced by human beings.[30] In nature jackals are parasitic animals and consequently become a metaphor for parasitism in linguistic usage. In his parable, however, Kafka links the parasitic with the religious. Kafka's jackals are parasites also because they need a Messiah figure. The hope for a savior who "can do everything" that the creatures themselves cannot accomplish obviously points toward the heart of the religious, the feeling of absolute dependency. Like the jackals, the homo religiosus believes in an omnipotent savior expected from afar, from the hereafter. The analogies that can be drawn between

Kafka's parable and basic tenets of the Jewish and Christian religions are too obvious to be overlooked. Among them are the longing to overcome the flesh and its compulsion to kill; the hope for a future, pure, and peaceful world free of earthly filth, in which blissful pleasure alone will dominate; the flight into the desert away from the dreadfulness of worldly life; the tradition embodied in the old scissors of belief outlasting generations "because we have been waiting an endlessly long time for you; my mother waited and her mother and further back all mothers right back to the mother of all jackals" ("denn wir warten unendlich lange auf dich; meine Mutter hat gewartet und ihre Mutter und weiter alle ihre Mütter bis hinauf zur Mutter aller Schakale") (E, 146). By choice of vocabulary and word sequence, above all, Kafka strikingly alludes to the imagery, the world of emotion and ideas of the Judaeo-Christian tradition. "Believe it!" ("Glaube es!") shouts the jackals' speaker at the traveler in an unconditional imperative. "How can you stand it in this world, you noble heart?" ("Wie erträgst nur du es in dieser Welt, du edles Herz?") they ask themselves. And of the Arabs they say: "when they lift their arms, hell stirs forth from their armpits" ("und heben sie den Arm, tut sich in der Achselhöhle die Hölle auf") (E, 149).

The jackals and Arabs illustrate the contrast between "ascetic ideals" and noble life as diagnosed by Nietzsche in *The Genealogy of Morals.*[31] Two types of being are compared: the ascetic, ritualist, fanatic, and priest on the one hand, who flees from the filth of the earthly into the "purer air" ("reinere Luft") of "the desert" ("der Wüste") (E, 148) and dreams of a world without violence, but all the while is filled with resentment and hate and wants to destroy the world as it exists; and on the other hand the worldlings, the vigorous conquerors and killers who freely enjoy their power and feel comfortable in the "filth" of this world, do not even consider it filth because they are at home in nature. The sovereignly cheerful mockery and the ultimately good-natured tolerance exercised by the contemptuously benevolent figure of the Arab stands in remarkable contrast to the irrational and murderous hatred of the ascetic spiritualist. Evil, the monstrous product of impotent hate, exists only for the ascetics, the jackals. "The hell" they see in the Arabs is their point of view, their fabrication. For the dominant Arabs, who, thanks to their strength, feel secure and free from jealousy, there is no evil.[32] Their archenemies are nothing more than cause for amused astonishment. The Arabs' opinion of the jackals has nothing to do with morality; it is rather a matter of aesthetics. The existence of these wondrous animals does not anger them, but provides an entertaining game for them. Fully aware of his superiority, the powerful can afford the luxury of magnanimity. "We love them for it [their madness]; they are our dogs, more beautiful than yours" ("Wir lieben sie deshalb; es sind unsere Hunde; schöner als die eurigen.") (E, 149). By contrast, the bloodthirsty fanaticism, the resentment felt by the "ascetic spiritualist," originates from pitiful impotence. The waste and refuse left over and tossed away by the merry hunters and killers, the Arabs, enables the scavenging jackals to engage in their bloodsucking rituals in the first place. And while the powerless are consumed by hate, the powerful can allow themselves to be interested in and tolerant of those who hate them. Thus Kafka's parable depicts certain basic ideas of Nietzsche's *Genealogy of Morals.*

At the end of the parable the jackals' purity-seeking species no longer appears to be as innocent a victim of the Arabs as it attempted to present itself at the beginning. It is exposed as a victim of its own obsession, a perverse beneficiary of its own agony. In the figure of the jackal the narrator witnesses a demonstration of the pathetic paradox that underlies the ascetic existence. In Kafka's parable the deeds and sufferings of the observed figures reveal to the viewer the essence of what is seen. The Arab in "Jackals and Arabs," who corresponds to the whipper in *The Trial,* is not only his victims' tormentor and whipper, but also their exposer. The torment serves to illuminate the meaning of the victims' behavior. The parallel to the penal apparatus in Kafka's earliest parabolic story is obvious. The penal machine likewise has the function of revealing his offense to the body of the prisoner. But in the later parable the one who benefits from the illumination is not the one who suffers and who is punished, but rather the spectator, who corresponds to the explorer in *In the Penal Colony.* The show put on by the Arab demonstrates to the narrator the nature of the wondrous animals and their plaint. This show is an example, a parabolic lesson. It grants allegorical insight into the situation and makes clear to the narrator what it was that had beset him in his sleeplessness.

In the "ancient" conflict between ascetic-otherworldly spirituality and "filthy"-vigorous, earthly, carnal lust, the rational "I" is supposed to take sides with the spiritual and kill the worldly. Then the world would be transformed into a pure and peaceful paradise. But the rational "I" does not want to take sides. He does not presume to make a judgment, and he insists on remaining a neutral spectator. Yet he is overpowered and "arrested" by the longing for release from the prison of the flesh that appears out of the desert night, the nocturnal and forsaken realm of being, even as the bank official Josef K., who likewise embodies the rational ego-principle of modern Western man, is arrested by a Court that emerges from unknown attics and hiding places. The Court also, in the words of Frau Grubach, represents "something learned" ("etwas Gelehrtes") (P, 30), thus intellectual or spiritual, and which significantly touches Josef K. most deeply and intimately in a house of God and through a priest. Of course, the Court unites aspects of the jackals and the Arabs that battle each other in the parable. If the Court, on the one hand, anticipates the jackals' call for the overcoming and extirpation of the carnal, some of its representatives, on the other hand, appear to Josef K. just as carnal and bestial as the Arabs do to the jackals.

In the parable the "I," the rational perspective of the modern European emerges victorious over the call for deliverance from the flesh that had burst forth from the unexplored and marginal regions of the world. To understand this victory, it is necessary to investigate why the jackals need to beg for help from the European's intelligence. They themselves have "only their teeth" ("nur das Gebiß") (E, 149). They are able to oppose to the instinctual fleshly being of their enemies only instinctual physical means of their own, their teeth. The nocturnal rebellion against the flesh, which puts reason under "arrest," functions every bit as instinctually and compulsively as the being of the Arabs. It, in its turn, is nothing but a manifestation of an instinctual need. Thus the representative of reason acts quite consistently when he refuses his assent to the instinctually driven hatred of the jackals, even though he experiences the tremendous pressure of its nocturnal eruption into his life of rationality.

What saves reason is the vigorous carnality, the brutal zest for life embodied in the Arab. By means of the simple power of the whip, a threatening situation is transformed into an instructive spectacle that demonstrates the true nature of the instinctually driven enmity. It is not truly spiritual; it is itself an irrational instinctual drive. At the same time it is forgetful of the true sign of intelligence—freedom. Nothing is less free, more dominated by physical urges, than the jackals' insistence on purity, which reveals itself as an addiction to blood. Like a metaphorical commentary, it anticipates this passage from Kafka's letter to Milena: "I am filthy, Milena, forever filthy; that is the reason why I make such a fuss about purity" ("Schmutzig bin ich, Milena, endlos schmutzig, darum mache ich ein solches Geschrei mit der Reinheit.") (BM, 208).

The vivid instruction it receives liberates the "I" who now relates to the conflict in such a superior way that he can actively intervene without himself being detrimentally affected. The "I" can provide, if not lasting help, which is denied to the jackals by their nature, at least some temporary relief and a break from their dreadful "trial." He is able to persuade the Arab to halt the whipping.

By contrast, we have seen Josef K., whose unconfessed guilty conscience, whose shame, prevents him from keeping a rational distance toward his arrest, remain incapable of intervening in the mechanism of the Court. Instead he is victimized again and again. In the "Whipper" chapter the victims of the switch initially beg K. for help even as the victims of the whip in the parable beg the rational "I" for succor. But, unlike the "I" of the parable, Josef K. cannot achieve distanced and reflective insight, which would make considered and effective action possible. For he falls out of the role of spectator into that of an acting participant and thus a suffering victim. K. maneuvers himself out of the part of the observing "I" into the jackals' role. In that shift an instance of the overall structural principle of the novel can be seen. The observer becomes a rash and compulsive agent, thereby giving up true freedom to act and becoming a helpless victim. Again and again he stops being the subject of the seeing and turns himself into its object. The execution, in which he is finally and ultimately reduced to an object, in which with his last glance he sees himself defined as the object of his butchers' observation and dies "like a dog" ("wie ein Hund") (P, 272), is only the last example of Josef K.'s reification, a whole series of which makes up the novel's action. The "Whipper" chapter shows us one of those reifications with special clarity.

While the "I" of the parable reacts to what he sees only with questions, not with judgments, K. feels compelled to bribe the whipper, which leads to even deeper involvement. He ends up going completely against his wish to help the victims and participates actively in their oppression. He does, thus, the exact opposite of what he wanted to do and not only deprives himself of his goal but also acts in such a way that it makes him in human and ethical terms guilty.[33] Instead of learning from what he sees, he himself becomes the object viewed by the reader because he exposes his own contradictoriness. Not the events perceived by him, but Josef K.'s own behavior becomes the action of the story. The vehicle of the perspective becomes an example of human self-contradiction, the incapacity of uniting will and action. K.'s self-contradiction is grounded in shame, which his never-admitted guilty feeling triggers in him. Shame is his trial itself, starting, in the third sentence of the novel, with the old lady's looking over at him until the last sentence, which reads "as if shame should outlive him" ("als sollte die Scham ihn überleben") (P, 272). This shame is his inner entanglement, his inability to achieve distance from himself. If he could liberate himself from shame, he could act consistently according to his spontaneously human feelings. He could put an end to the beating by beckoning the servants, in whom humanity appears to be rushing to help. But the contradiction between human sympathy and shame prevents goal-oriented action. Thus his unadmitted inner self-contradiction puts Josef K. helplessly at the mercy of events.

That the same scene (the guards in the storage room with the Court-appointed whipper) repeats itself on the following day gives further proof of that. Indeed, this time K. breaks into a fit of rage and commands the servants to clean out the storage room. This is not goal-conscious action, but compulsive reaction. It brings no clarification, only greater guilt, as K., instead of helping them, has the victims removed from his sight and consciousness. Such behavior is symptomatic of Josef K. The tendency to repress problems instead of courageously pursuing solutions to them marks Josef K.'s general behavior in the novel and makes up its plot structure. It is, indeed, the "trial" in which or the "process" by which Josef K. defines and reveals himself.[34]

It is essential for *The Trial* that seeing and acting coincide again and again, that the onlooker K. gets emotionally involved and consequently becomes the instrument of the narrated action. Whenever such a linking between perspective and action takes place in Kafka's work, we can speak of "story" in contrast to "parable." Stories are Kafka's larger narratives and novels, in which looking, acting and suffering are united in one character—"The Judgment," "The Metamorphosis," *The Trial, Amerika,* "Blumfeld," "A Hunger Artist," *The Castle,* and others are typical examples. To be sure there are differences of degree among the stories. *Amerika* and *The Castle,* to some extent, approach the parable form insofar as Karl Rossmann and the land surveyor K. show a stronger tendency to look and to listen to and learn from what they see and hear than do Georg Bendemann, Gregor Samsa, or Josef K. Nevertheless, even in these cases, the bearer of the perspective remains the vehicle of the action. The heroes in the stories never succeed in gaining the calm and distance necessary for observing properly, no matter how hard they might try. Gregor Samsa reminds himself "that much better than reckless decisions would be calm and calmest deliberation" ("daß viel besser als verzweifelte Entschlüsse ruhige und ruhigste Überlegung sei") (E, 74). And Georg Bendemann "had decided long ago to observe everything with utmost care, so that he could not be surprised somehow unexpectedly, from behind or from above" ("hatte sich vor einer langen Weile fest entschlossen, alles vollkommen genau zu beobachten, damit er nicht irgendwie auf Umwegen, von hinten her, von oben herab überrascht werden könne") (E, 63). But it is impossible for them to carry out these intentions. The heroes of Kafka's "stories" always react hastily to what they see, feel deeply affected by the events, interfere in them, and block with hasty reactions the path to understanding. A formal feature, the union of perspective with action, is the precise functional expression of content, of the protagonist's nature.

The parable form, on the other hand, shows a factual or implied separation of two levels—the level of events and the level of meaning. Events become meaningful through the process of seeing. The one who sees does not necessarily have to figure in the narrative itself. In his place, as in the legend of the doorkeeper, there can also be a narrator and a listener. But it remains essential that seeing and action are separate, that the onlooker maintains distance from the events. The "I" of the parable "Jackals and Arabs" is indeed deeply affected by what he sees and, as we have seen, is literally "arrested." But he never allows himself to be emotionally caught up in those events. Even in the face of external arrest he preserves an inner distance and leaves all action up to the jackals and the Arabs. The "I" is nothing more than an observing intelligence. He thereby affirms, even if in a completely different way than hoped for by them, the compliment paid him by the jackals. Through this behavior he shows that he actually does represent reason, objectively pondering rationality, the contemplative *theoria* of the narrative (in the Aristotelian sense of the term). Theory is originally unadulterated contemplation and the narrative "I" remains true to it. In Kafka's "stories," however, this kind of unadulterated observing is nowhere to be found. Josef K.'s behavior in the cathedral illuminates even more clearly the contrast between him and the "I" of the parable because the similarities are even more remarkable than in the "Whipper" chapter. Both—Josef K. in the cathedral and the first-person narrator in "Jackals and Arabs"—are put into the role of listener or onlooker. Both are shown a performance, respectively told a legend, as an illustration. Before we investigate Josef K.'s reaction more closely, we need to establish the common ground of both parables—"Jackals and Arabs" and "Before the Law."

As we have seen, the show put on by the jackals makes clear that the longing to overcome addiction to the flesh, the striving for release from the prison of "this world" and for attainment of another world of complete purity, is revealed to be nothing more than lusting after blood. Only if the jackals could free themselves from lusting after blood would they be truly free. It is not the Arabs who enslave them, but rather it is their own passion, their addiction to carrion and blood. This bloodlust is the doorkeeper who does not allow them access to the goal of their yearning, to the Law of Purity, to whom they must remain hopelessly subjugated. Of course they shift the guilt to the Arabs and accuse them of oppressing them. However, the Arabs are only the means of bringing the jackals' dependency and addiction to light. The jackals relate to the Arabs the way Josef K. does to the Court. The Arabs and the Court alike are the jackals' and Josef K.'s "motivations," in Kafka's sense of the term, attempts at self-justification by accusing the Other.

The jackals fail to achieve salvation and turn their existence into a living hell for two opposite reasons: On the one hand because they strive for spiritual or rather noncorporeal existence and can see nothing but filth in the natural vitality of the Arabs, as Kafka himself experienced the sexual only as filth.[35] On the other hand because they cannot truly achieve the spiritual, but rather distort it into parasitic bloodlust. They try to get beyond the animalistic-murderous existence of nature and despise it, but precisely because of this passionate striving they fall completely under its spell. They are enslaved to their physical need to an even greater degree than the carefree, unashamedly sensual Arabs.

The same problem appears in the legend of the doorkeeper. The figure of the doorkeeper corresponds to the Arabs, the man from the country to the jackals. Just as the Arabs only *appear* to be responsible for the misfortune of the jackals, but are not, so does the doorkeeper appear to be responsible for the fact that the man from the country is held back from the Law. But just as it is the dual guilt of the jackals that leaves them at the mercy of the Arabs—namely desiring purity beyond the flesh and nevertheless being addicted to blood—so the man from the country is at the mercy of the doorkeeper because he strives for the Law on the one hand and on the other hand allows himself to be intimidated and kept from entering the Law at the offered moment. It is not external force that holds him back from the entrance. It is his fear of the menace in the description of the inside that he hears from the doorkeeper.

> As the doorkeeper notices that, he laughs and says: "If it tempts you so much, try to enter despite my prohibition. However, take note: I am powerful. And I am only the lowest doorkeeper. In one hall after the other doorkeepers are placed, each more powerful than the one before him. Even I cannot bear the sight of the third one." The man from the country had not expected such difficulties; the Law is supposed to be accessible to everyone and at all times, he thinks; but in looking now more closely at the doorkeeper in his fur coat, at his large pointed nose, his long thin black Tartar beard, he decides after all to wait until he will get permission to enter.

> Als der Türhüter das merkt, lacht er und sagt: "Wenn es dich so lockt, versuche es doch, trotz meinem Verbot hineinzugehen. Merke aber: Ich bin mächtig. Und ich bin der unterste Türhüter. Von Saal zu Saal stehen aber Türhüter, einer mächtiger als der andere. Schon den Anblick des dritten kann nicht einmal ich vertragen." Solche Schwierigkeiten hat der Mann vom Lande nicht erwartet, das Gesetz soll doch jedem und immer zugänglich sein, denkt er, aber als er jetzt den Türhüter in seinem Pelzmantel genauer ansieht, seine große Spitznase, den langen, dünnen, schwarzen, tatarischen Bart, entschließt er sich doch, lieber zu warten, bis er die Erlaubnis zum Eintritt bekommt. (P, 256)

The man was given the opportunity to make a decision, and he did make one—namely to wait. He wants access to the Law, but not absolutely; that is, he does not want to put his life at risk. But that is the only way he could gain access to the Law he desires. Instead he allows himself to be "arrested" by the doorkeeper and subjugates himself to him.

Two contradictory factors subject him to the mercy of the doorkeeper: the desire to gain access to the Law and the fear that holds him back.

Thus his life turns into a self-inflicted servitude caused by suspension between fear and longing. The simultaneity of fear and longing regarding one and the same object is ambivalence. Ambivalence prevents all action and freedom. The fate of the man from the country shows the situation of the homo religiosus who does not want to admit that entrance to the Absolute includes an element of the awful, the *tremendum,* and is only possible as absolute risk. Whoever cautiously holds back and wants to protect his/her physical life should not ask anything at all of the Law. For the sake of his dear life he should do without the bliss of union with that for which he longs the most. As the ape explains in "A Report to an Academy," with which quite significantly *A Country Doctor* ends, the price of physical survival and relative well-being amounts to the renunciation of the Absolute of one's desire. The alternative is to possess the heroism of Kierkegaard's Abraham and with fear and trembling, but without any thought of physical security, push onward toward the Absolute he craves. Either/Or—either infinite resignation—in the sense of Kafka's ape, not in the sense of Kierkegaard—or the infinite determination of faith. Choosing neither the one nor the other leads to that terrible paralysis of life that the fate of the man from the country demonstrates. The priest's legend shows it to Josef K. as a warning mirror image.

The legend shows, however, not only the inner contradiction in the behavior of the man from the country. It also shows the self-deception that underlies his opinion of the Law. It was his naive opinion that the relationship of man to the Law would be simple. But that is by no means the case. After all, the Law itself had appointed the terrifying doorkeeper. Thus the Law contains in addition to temptation and splendor also the menace of unbearable horror. Only those who are ready to act "despite" the threat of the unbearable, to take on the risk of annihilation, can approach the radiant mystery of the Law. The man deceives himself when he believes that the entrance meant only for him guarantees an innocuous and unproblematic path to salvation. It is not the doorkeeper who deceives the man, but rather the man himself who is mired from the beginning in a self-deception to which he clings tenaciously, impervious to learning.

The self-deception of the man from the country mirrors that of Josef K. The priest, after all, relates the legend as an example of a self-deception.

> You are deceiving yourself about the Court, said the priest, in the introductory writings to the Law it says about that deception: Before the Law stands a doorkeeper.

> In dem Gericht täuschst du dich, sagte der Geistliche, in den einleitenden Schriften zum Gesetz heißt es von dieser Täuschung: Vor dem Gesetz steht ein Türhüter. (P, 225)

With these words the legend begins. It relates to Josef K.'s perpetual self-deception regarding the Court, of which the priest warns him. The analogy to the man from the country becomes clear as soon as we recall that the priest's actual warning relates to the fact that Josef K. seeks "too much help from others" ("zuviel fremde Hilfe") and does not notice "that it is not the right kind of help" ("daß es nicht die wahre Hilfe ist") (P, 253). The man from the country also depends on "outside help" ("fremde Hilfe"), on the doorkeeper, instead of risking the entrance that he desires. Similarly Josef K. deceives himself in hoping that with other people's help and by taking detours and finding out special paths he can bring about his acquittal.

Like Josef K., the man from the country is also arrested and both are detained even while they remain free. Josef K. can continue to practice his occupation, and the man from the country can at any time choose to go away from the door to the Law. That the arrest leaves them with their freedom is emphasized in both cases. "You are arrested, certainly" ("Sie sind verhaftet, gewiß"), says the warden to Josef K., "but that shall not prevent you from fulfilling your professional duties. You shall not be disturbed in your accustomed lifestyle" ("aber das soll Sie nicht hindern, Ihren Beruf zu erfüllen. Sie sollen auch in Ihrer gewöhnlichen Lebensweise nicht gehindert sein.") (P, 24–25). "The man is in fact free" ("Nun ist der Mann tatsächlich frei"), says the priest about the man from the country; "he can go anywhere he wants, only the entrance to the Law is forbidden to him, and moreover, only by one person, the doorkeeper. If he sits down on a stool to the side of the door and stays there for his entire life, he does it voluntarily; the story mentions no compulsion" ("er kann hingehen, wohin er will, nur der Eingang in das Gesetz ist ihm verboten, und überdies nur von einem einzelnen, vom Türhüter. Wenn er sich auf den Schemel seitwärts vom Tor niedersetzt und dort sein Leben lang bleibt, so geschieht dies freiwillig, die Geschichte erzählt von keinem Zwang.") (P, 262).

In addition to the parallel of being arrested while retaining freedom, there is the parallel of the voluntary decision to wait. In the scene of his arrest, Josef K. wonders about whether he could not simply open "the door of the next room or even the hall door" ("die Tür des folgenden Zimmers oder gar die Tür des Vorzimmers") (P, 16) and thereby be rid of his trial.

> Perhaps the two would not dare to impede him at all if he were to open the door to the adjoining room or even the door to the hall, perhaps it would be the simplest solution to this whole matter if he were to push ahead to its extreme consequence. But perhaps they would then grab him after all, and, once he was thrown down, all his superiority to them which, to some degree, he was at present still preserving would be lost. Thus he preferred the definiteness that the natural course of events had to bring, and returned to

his room, without a single further word about the matter being uttered either by him or by the warders.

> Vielleicht würden ihn die beiden, wenn er die Tür des folgenden Zimmers oder gar die Tür des Vorzimmers öffnete, gar nicht zu hindern wagen, vielleicht wäre es die einfachste Lösung des ganzen, daß er es auf die Spitze trieb. Aber vielleicht würden sie ihn doch packen und, war er einmal niedergeworfen, so war auch alle Überlegenheit verloren, die er jetzt ihnen gegenüber in gewisser Hinsicht doch wahrte. Deshalb zog er die Sicherheit der Lösung vor, wie sie der natürliche Verlauf bringen mußte, und ging in sein Zimmer zurück, ohne daß von seiner Seite oder von der Seite der Wächter ein weiteres Wort gefallen wäre. (P, 16)

Here we find in Josef K.'s behavior, dictated by caution and apprehension in the early stages of his trial, the exact parallel to the timid decision of the man from the country to wait in front of the entryway rather than risk entering the Law. Josef K. and the man from the country are the same in that they both prefer the safety of waiting to the free, all-risking deed, and thereby seal their fate. However, it would be incorrect to deduce from that, as Gesine Frey does, that the problem is the same in both cases.[36] To be sure, the characters are the same in that they do not walk through the door and decide to wait rather than risk a decisive step, but the direction in which each door leads is completely different. The door to the hall would lead Josef K. into freedom from the Law of his trial, into an existence without problems of guilt, without existential involvement and decisions. For the man from the country, the door would lead into an exactly opposite direction, into the Law and into fulfillment or even annihilation of existence.[37] The obscurity of the legend's relationship to the novel comes from the fact that the arrests are on the one hand similar, but on the other hand the opposite of each other. In the legend the arrest means being held back from the Law; in the novel it means being impeded in the routine existence of a bourgeois professional. In the legend it keeps one away from the Law; in the novel it draws one's attention to the existence of the Law, making him for the first time aware of it. The parable is therefore not simply a parallel, but rather a kind of mirror writing, not a direct, but a reverse commentary. Upon first sight, the man appears as a seeker of the Absolute, Josef K. as a clueless worldling. But precisely this contrast provides an illuminating correspondence, which lies in the similarity of what, in each case, follows upon the arrest. Josef K. and the man from the country reveal themselves as parallel cases by their reactions to the arrests. The arrest by the doorkeeper makes it clear to the reader that the man from the country does not absolutely seek access to the Absolute. He allows himself to be intimidated by threats and permits his fear to hold him back from his goal. Since he is not willing to put his physical well-being and his life at risk, he shows that the Law is not the most prized, the ultimate value for him. He is given over to his physical existence even more than he is to the Law. However, neither does he want to leave the Law. Thus he becomes for the gatekeeper what the jackals are to the Arabs—his "fool" ("Narr"), his "dog" ("Hund").

Josef K.'s arrest makes an analogous situation apparent, but one in which the direction of the movement that it suggests is reversed. K.'s reaction to his arrest, his unwittingly sliding into involvement with the representatives of the Court, shows that his professional career, his bourgeois life and worldly freedom are not his supreme value. Josef K. is not ready to take the most extreme risk for the self-sufficient independence of a modern rational-empiricist city-dweller.

With his arrest a change of direction begins in K.'s existence. He, who previously had had no inkling of the Court, gets involved with it, becomes curious, goes on the attack, and ultimately seeks access to the highest judges. In the course of his trial and as a result of it he gets closer and closer to the initial position of the man from the country. He becomes a seeker after the Law. However, his original tendency, K.'s intention "to escape from the trial" ("aus dem Prozeß auszubrechen"), "to circumvent it . . . to have a life outside the trial" ("ihn zu umgehen . . . außerhalb des Prozesses zu leben") also persists (P, 254). It is precisely for that purpose that he hopes for advice from the priest, shortly before the latter tells him the legend of the doorkeeper.

As in the man from the country, there exist in Josef K. two incompatible tendencies. The man wants to enter the Law but is afraid to do so. Josef K. strives for acquittal by the Court—as is shown by his behavior at Titorelli's—but he wants, at the same time, to avoid the trial, to live outside the trial and not to recognize the Court. He believes that he can achieve both of these objectives only with other people's help—women's, lawyers', other defendants', Court servants', Titorelli's, the priest's—just as the man from the country believes that he can only enter into the Law with the help of the doorkeeper. The legend of the doorkeeper is therefore a metaphor of Josef K.'s self-contradictoriness. The priest emphasizes this analogy when he expressly warns K. about looking for "too much help from others" ("zuviel fremde Hilfe") (P, 253) and then again in the exegesis of the legend when he advises K. "not to blindly accept the opinions of others" ("fremde Meinung nicht ungeprüft zu übernehmen") (P, 257). He insists that K. should observe the "literal wording of the text" ("Wortlaut der Schrift") (ibid.). Now the wording of the parable reports that the man allows himself to be swayed by another's opinion to put off entry into the Law, since the threatening description of the interior of the Law expresses, after all, only the opinion of the doorkeeper. But the wording also refers to the error of the man, to the misconceptions, with which he came to the Law and which led him not to expect any difficulties. This does not prove that the doorkeeper deceived the man, but rather that the man was ignorant of the Law. In this he resembles Josef K., who admits at his arrest that he was ignorant of the Law of the Court, but nevertheless asserts his innocence. What that proves is only K.'s ignorance of the Law, not his innocence. "Look, Willem, he admits that he does not know the Law and yet he claims he is innocent" ("Sieh, Willem, er gibt zu, er kenne das Gesetz nicht, und behauptet, gleichzeitig unschuldig zu sein.") (P, 15). Even according to the rules of customary jurisprudence, ignorance does not protect one from the Law. Likewise, the ignorance of the man from the country does not mean that he is a victim of deception, but of his own delusion. He had imagined the entrance to the Law to be different from what it actually is. He had been mistaken about the Law. The priest recounts the parable as an example not of deception, but of self-deception. " 'You are deceiving yourself about the Court,' said the priest, 'in the introductory writings to the Law it says about this deception: . . .' " ("In dem Gericht täuschst du dich, in den einleitenden Schriften zum Gesetz heißt es von dieser Täuschung: . . ."). "Nothing is said in it about deception" ("Von Täuschung steht darin nichts"), the priest says reasonably at the end, whereby he uses "deception" ("Täuschung") in the sense of "being deceived by someone else," not in the sense of "self-deception" (P, 257).

Josef K. misinterprets the text by reading "deception" into it. "So the doorkeeper deceived the man" ("Der Türhüter hat also den Mann getäuscht"), he rashly concludes (P, 257). Instead of recognizing the man's self-contradiction and his ignorance of the Law, he identifies with the error the figure in the parable makes, uncritically assuming the latter's perspective as his own. This shows, in a decisive way, that he is incapable of seeing from the perspective of one who truly sees, of one who can overview a total situation. In telling him the legend, the priest offered him the opportunity to attain such comprehending vision. But Josef K. continues to identify with the position of the man from the country instead of seeing through it. He cannot achieve a distance from the events because he is "drawn in strongly by the story" ("von der Geschichte sehr stark angezogen") (P, 257). He feels himself and his own problem reflected in the figure of the man from the country but does not reach an insight into it. He is not capable of achieving that detachment, which is the basis of understanding. Like the man from the country, he persists in his error, remains a captive of his self-deception and his futile hope to be saved by others. The "Cathedral" chapter proves more clearly than the "Whipper" chapter that in Kafka's novel, the large form of the "story," the main character, who is also the vehicle of the perspective, never arrives at true observation, at understanding himself. Rather, he remains a mere object of the reader's observation, revealing his self-contradiction without seeing it.

Kafka's story figure prevents himself from becoming a true spectator. Therefore, he cannot be a true actor either, since he lacks knowledge and his actions represent only impulsive drives. The actual spectator, the one who is able to gain insight, can only be the reader. However, the narrative perspective makes this difficult for him/her because it so closely follows that of the main character that he tends to identify with him and to see from his false, limited, and distorting perspective. The undistanced, uncritical reader of the novel makes the same mistake as Josef K., the listener to the legend. He adopts the main character's way of seeing, believes his self-justification and "motivation," and remains convinced that the protagonist is the innocent victim of an unjust course of events. As Josef K. dogmatically asserts that the doorkeeper deceived the man from the country, so does the reader tend to see in Josef K. an innocent victim of the Court and thereby misunderstands the nature of his trial. The priest's warning is also an indirect guidance for the reading of the novel.

> "Do not be hasty," said the priest, "do not take over the opinions of others unexamined. I have told you the story literally the way it is written."

> "Sei nicht übereilt," sagte der Geistliche, "übernimm nicht die fremde Meinung ungeprüft. Ich habe dir die Geschichte im Wortlaut der Schrift erzählt." (P, 257–58)

This advice is just as valid for the reader as it is for Josef K. The parable within the novel invites the protagonist, and the novel itself invites the reader, to distance seeing from acting, which the observing "I" achieves in "Jackals and Arabs." Kafka's step from the story form, in which perspective and action are merged, to the parable, which distances the perspective from the action, can be seen as a step from a radically empathizing, in the Brechtian sense, "Aristotelian," to an, again in the Brechtian sense, alienating and (even if quite subtle) didactic poetics. Consistent with that, Kafka more and more frequently had speaking animals appear in his parables, bringing him closer to the poetic genre that always served didactic distancing—the fable.

In the collection *A Country Doctor,* which was written between December 1914 ("Before the Law") and June 1917 ("The Cares of a Family Man" and "A Report to an Academy"),[38] Kafka's new narrative form dominates. This form, in stark contrast to the single-perspective stories from "The Judgement" to *The Trial,* is based on the use of a perspective figure distanced from and observing the narrated action. Apparent exceptions, the investigation of which must be reserved for a later study, are merely the title story "A Country Doctor" and in part "Up in the Gallery," "A Fratricide," and "A Dream." If one goes through the volume in the chronological order of the individual stories' dates of composition, one perceives a more and more pronounced development toward didactic objectification and explicitness of commentary. In the earliest piece "Before the Law" there is not yet an observing spectator figure in the text itself. (The narrator, the priest, is positioned outside the narrative and is only visible in the text of the novel, not in the legend.) In the novel, the legend remains an uncomprehended allegory. In the volume's later narratives, however, an observing figure appears, more or less removed from the action, from whose point of view the reader is enabled to contemplate the narrated happenings. This figure embodies in the form of a first-person narrator the new perspective for Kafka, characterized by its objectifying and distanced point of view. This figure views, respectively describes, the narrated course of events, offering a first-person (singular or plural) report of them. Thus a carefully observing, meditative, and reportorial "I" or "We" focuses on Bucephalus, the former war-horse of Alexander the Great, in "The New Advocate"; the nomads and the emperor in "An Old Manuscript"; the jackals and Arabs; the most senior engineers, in "A Visit to a Mine"; Odradek in "The Cares of a Family Man"; the "Eleven Sons"; and the past of the reporting ape in "A Report to an Academy." Even where, as in "Up in the Gallery," "A Fratricide," "An Imperial Message," and "A Dream," the narrating voice reports in the third person, this distinction is not essential since in these texts as well the narrative principle resides in viewing and contemplating the object and process of narration from a detached and distanced point of view. The same principle also forms texts composed around the same time span but not included in the volume *A Country Doctor,* such as "A Crossbreed."

In the chronologically last narrative, which concludes *A Country Doctor,* "A Report to an Academy" (May/June 1917), Kafka lets the tendency of the entire volume culminate. While the preceding parables stage the contemplated events and characters without, or with only rudimentary, commentary, the ape analyzes the self that he had been and explains how his new self had been constructed. With this turn toward genetically proceeding interpretation and analytical reflecting on the causal chain and history of a problem, "A Report" represents a radical, but logically consistent continuation of the distanced viewing that distinguishes the whole volume. In the earlier pieces, the situations to be contemplated are shown as parabolic illustrations, mutely illuminating what they show; later they serve as material for a bemused spectator. In the case of "A Report," however, they are presented as the process by which a thinking, self-comprehending, and analytically reporting subject comes into being. In "A Report" we encounter an application, in terms of a biography, of what Kafka has Sancho Pansa, in "The Truth about Sancho Pansa," describe as the external projection of a subject's inner problem into a viewable character, which saves the subject's sanity and his life. It is the process of objectively "representing" ("Herausstellen") and thus objectifying psychic disturbances in and through the sublimating work of art:

> Sancho Pansa, who by the way never boasted of this, succeeded, in the course of the years, by procuring a lot of romances of chivalry and brigandry for the evening and night hours, in diverting his devil, whom he subsequently named Don Quixote, from himself, in such a manner that the latter kept performing the craziest deeds that, however, for want of a predetermined object that should have been Sancho Pansa, harmed no one. A free man, Sancho Pansa followed with equanimity, perhaps also from a feeling of responsibility, Don Quixote on his wanderings and derived from that a great and useful entertainment till the end of his life.

> Sancho Pansa, der sich übrigens dessen nie gerühmt hat, gelang es im Laufe der Jahre, durch Beistellung einer Menge Ritter- und Räuberromane in den Abend- und Nachtstunden seinen Teufel, dem er später den Namen Don Quixote gab, derart von sich abzulenken, daß dieser dann haltlos die verrücktesten Taten aufführte, die aber mangels eines vorbestimmten Gegenstandes, der eben Sancho Pansa hätte sein sollen, niemandem schadeten. Sancho Pansa, ein freier Mann, folgte gleichmütig, vielleicht aus einem gewissen Verantwortlichkeitsgefühl, dem Don Quixote auf seinen Zügen und hatte davon eine große und nützlich Unterhaltung bis an sein Ende. (BK, 96)

NOTES

1. Heinz Hillmann, *Franz Kafka. Dichtungstheorie und Dichtungsgestalt* (Bonn: Bouvier, 1964) 161–94.
2. Ibid., 165.
3. Ibid., 171.
4. Walter H. Sokel, "Kafka als Expressionist," *Forum* 10 (1963): 288 ff. and 363 ff., and *Franz Kafka: Tragik und Ironie* (Munich and Vienna: Albert Langen, Georg Müller, 1964), 19–23.
5. Cf. journal entries from August 21, 29, and 30, September 13, and October 7, 1914. Franz Kafka, *Tagebücher, 1910–1923* (New York: Schocken Books, 1948 and 1949), 435–38.
6. Regarding Kafka's tendency to leave longer works incomplete, cf. Hillmann's remarks in Hillmann, *Franz Kafka*, 153–60.
7. Kafka, *Tagebücher*, 437–38, 453.
8. Ibid., 448.

9. Hillmann, *Franz Kafka,* 168–70, sees "The Metamorphosis" as a combination of parable and story, but because of its epic-narrative breadth, individualizing characterization, keenness for detail, and depictive thoroughness it clearly belongs to the story form that is characterized by a "sequence of situations, movement and plot" ("Abfolge von Situationen, Bewegung und Handlungsablauf") and not to the parable form that tends toward "blankness" ("Aussparung"), "simplification" ("vom Detail absehenden Vereinfachung"), "abstraction" ("Abstraktion"), and "generality" ("Allgemeinheit") (165).

10. Friedrich Beißner, *Der Erzähler Franz Kafka* (Stuttgart: Kohlhammer, 1952), and Martin Walser, *Beschreibung einer Form. Versuch über Franz Kafka* (Munich: Carl Hanser, 1961). On the concept "personal narrative situation" see Franz K. Stanzel, *Typische Formen des Romans* (Göttingen: Vandenhoeck & Rupert, 1964).

11. Cf. Percey Lubbock, *The Craft of Fiction* (London: Jonathan Cape, 1926), 60–76, 156–71, and Stanzel, *Typische Formen des Romans,* 40–42.

12. Keith Leopold, "Breaks in Perspective in Franz Kafka's *The Trial,*" *The German Quarterly* 36 (1963): 31–38.

13. Indeed in "The Stoker," as a result of the stoker's complaints about his treatment on the ship, the perspective appears to move from Karl Rossmann to another figure, namely the stoker, but for a far shorter stretch than in Kafka's *In the Penal Colony.*

14. Franz Kafka, *Briefe, 1902–1924,* ed. Max Brod (Frankfurt am Main: S. Fischer Lizenzausgabe von Schocken Books, New York, 1958), 159. English translation *Letters to Friends, Family, and Editors* (New York: Schocken Books, 1977), 136.

15. Kafka, *Tagebücher,* 524–28.

16. Kafka's note in his journal on December 2, 1914 (ibid., 444), that he was not completely dissatisfied with *In the Penal Colony* can be seen as high praise in consideration of his tendency toward extreme self-criticism.

17. From now on all references to Kafka's works will be made within the text. The abbreviations preceding the page numbers refer to the following volumes:

- B *Briefe, 1902–1924.* Ed. Max Brod. Frankfurt am Main: S. Fischer Lizenzausgabe von Schocken Books, New York, 1958.
- BK *Beschreibung eines Kampfes.* New York: Schocken Books, 1946.
- BM *Briefe an Milena.* Ed. Willy Haas. New York: Schocken Books, 1952.
- E *Erzählungen und kleine Prosa.* New York: Schocken Books, 1946. 2d ed.
- H *Hochzeitsvorbereitungen auf dem Lande und andere Prosa aus dem Nachlaß.* New York: Schocken Books, 1953.
- P *Der Prozess.* New York: Schocken Books, 1946. 5th ed.

18. Winfried Kudszus, "Narrative Attitude and Timeshifting in Kafka's *The Trial* and *Das Schloss,*" *Deutsche Vierteljahrsschrift für Literaturwissenschaft und Geistesgeschichte* 38 (1964): 192.

19. Kudszus, "Narrative Attitude," 192.

20. See note 8 above.

21. Cf. the penetrating comments by Lothar Fietz, "Möglichkeiten und Gren-

zen einer Deutung von Kafka's 'Schloss-Roman,'" *Deutsche Vierteljahrsschrift für Literaturwissenschaft und Geistesgeschichte* 37 (1963): 73.

22. See note 10 above and Kudszus, "Narrative Attitude," 192 and 195.

23. On the dating of Kafka's works, see Malcolm Pasley's and Klaus Wagenbach's "Versuch einer Datierung sämtlicher Texte Franz Kafkas," *Deutsche Vierteljahrsschrift für Literaturwissenschaft und Geistesgeschichte* 38 (1964): 149–67, and their "Datierung sämtlicher Texte Franz Kafkas" in *Franz Kafka—Ein Symposion* (Berlin, 1965), 55–83.

24. Stanzel, *Typische Formen des Romans,* 25–39.

25. See Pasley and Wagenbach, *Franz Kafka—Ein Symposion,* 76, 78–80, 82.

26. Cf. Kafka's plan to bring together the stories "The Judgment," "The Metamorphosis," and "The Stoker" in one volume that was supposed to have the title "Sons" and his justification for this desire in a letter from April 11, 1913, to his publisher Kurt Wolff: "'The Stoker,' 'The Metamorphosis' (which is one and a half times as long as 'The Stoker'), and 'The Judgment' belong together, both inwardly and outwardly. There is an obvious connection among the three and, even more important, a secret one, for which reason I would be reluctant to forgo the chance of having them published together in a book, which might be called *The Sons.*" Letters, 96 ("'Der Heizer,' 'Die Verwandlung,' und 'Das Urteil' gehören äußerlich und innerlich zusammen, es besteht zwischen ihnen eine offenbare und noch mehr eine geheime Verbindung, auf deren Darstellung durch Zusammenfassung in einem etwa 'Die Söhne' betitelten Buch ich nicht verzichten möchte") (B, 116). He tried as well to express the inner unity of "The Judgment," "The Metamorphosis," and *In the Penal Colony* in a volume with the title *Punishments* (see the letter to Kurt Wolff Verlag from October 15, 1915 [B, 134]). Heinz Hillmann has convincingly shown the inner unity and the compositional principle of the *Hunger Artist* volume (Hillmann, *Franz Kafka,* 107–12).

27. Ingeborg Henel, "Die Türhüterlegende und ihre Bedeutung für Kafkas 'Prozeß'," *Deutsche Vierteljahrsschrift für Literaturwissenschaft und Geistesgeschichte* 37 (1963): 57–58.

28. Gerhard Kaiser sees the meaning of the trial similarly ("Franz Kafka's 'Prozeß.' Versuch einer Interpretation," *Euphorion* 52 [1958]). "K.'s 'guilt' lies in his relationship to the trial itself (33)." Ingeborg Henel as well sees the arrest not as an "action of the Court," but as the "situation, in which K. already finds himself at the beginning of the novel" ("Die Türhüterlegende," 57).

29. Cf. Ingeborg Henel, "Die Türhüterlegende," 59.

30. See Günther Anders, *Franz Kafka. Pro und Contra. Die-Prozess Unterlagen* (Munich: C. H. Beck, 1951). Anders pointed out Kafka's literalness and literal revival of metaphors hidden in language usage.

31. Especially "Erste Abhandlung": "Gut und Böse," "Gut und Schlecht."

32. Friedrich Nietzsche, *Werke in drei Bänden.* Ed. Karl Schlechta. 2. Band (München: C. Hanser, 1955), 778–80, 782–88.

33. See note 28 above.

34. Ingeborg Henel's analysis leads to the same result. K.'s own actions and justifications create the conditions, which, seemingly originating in external forces,

act against him in the trial. But he himself creates his visible world out of his justifications. "He, and not the Court, transfers the proceedings to the suburban apartment house, which is as dirty and rundown as his own inner self; and he himself turns the employees of the Court into what they are—weak, ignorant, corrupt officials" ("Er, und nicht das Gericht, verlegt die Untersuchung in das Mietshaus der Vorstadt, das schmutzig und verkommen ist wie sein eigenes innere; und er selbst macht die Angestellten des Gerichts erst zu dem, was sie sind—schwache, unwissende, korrupte Beamte.") (Henel, "Die Türhüterlegende," 59). According to Henel, the trial is the signature of Josef K. himself. Cf. also Sokel, *Franz Kafka: Tragik und Ironie,* 151.

35. In a letter to Milena, Kafka explains that for him "abomination and filth" ("Abscheuliche und Schmutzige") are "inwardly very necessarily" ("innerlich sehr notwendig") associated with the sexual act (BM, 181–82). In another letter, he expresses the belief that sexual intercourse with a beloved person must mean the loss of that love (BM, 149).

36. Gesine Frey, *Der Raum und die Figuren in Franz Kafkas Roman "Der Prozeß"* (Marburg: Elwert, 1965), 146–51.

37. Cf. also my criticism of Frey's position in my review of her book in *Welt der Literatur,* September 15, 1966, p. 12.

38. Pasley and Wagenbach, *Franz Kafka—Ein Symposion,* 76–82.

7

FREUD AND THE MAGIC OF KAFKA'S WRITING

To CALL Franz Kafka "the Dante of the Freudian age" would not be without justification. The statement implies this analogy: as Dante had given poetic expression to the world view developed conceptually in scholastic philosophy, Kafka presented in fictional terms the image of man as conceived by Freud. Like all such sweeping statements that seek to pinpoint an extremely complex relationship, the analogy would call for far-reaching and profound qualifications. As I shall briefly point out, at least one half of it would have to be negated from the start. Yet let us look further into the possibility of its validation.

Historically, Kafka's writing career coincided with the appearance of the fundamental texts that established psychoanalysis. In 1895 Freud and Breuer had published the pioneering *Studies in Hysteria,* which was followed in 1900 by Freud's *Interpretation of Dreams,* and, the year after, *The Psychopathology of Everyday Life.* In 1905 followed the case history, *Dora, Three Essays on the Theory of Sexuality,* and *Jokes and Their Relation to the Unconscious.* It was the publication of these works that laid the foundations of Freud's fame and that quickly spread his notoriety. In Kafka's most formative decade as a writer, the influence of Freud radiated through the intellectual avant-garde of Central Europe and, in his native Prague, Kafka could not escape it. Freud was discussed and lectured on in the literary salon of Frau Berta Fanta, which Kafka frequented. He became personally acquainted with and was greatly attracted to the psychoanalytic thinker and reformer Otto Gross, whom the avant-garde of

Kafka's day hailed as a martyr to the Oedipal family institution. Kafka frequently referred to psychoanalysis in general, and in his correspondence showed himself familiar with psychoanalytic concepts and literature. He was very interested in a book in which the psychoanalyst Wilhelm Stekel had referred to his "The Metamorphosis," and Kafka's immersion in the thought, if not the actual writings, of Freud could not be more tellingly confirmed than by the tone of stating the obvious with which Kafka lists Freud among the associations that came to him in reading over "The Judgment," the evening after it was written. "Thoughts of Freud, naturally," Kafka observed.

Kafka shared with psychoanalysis the genetic approach to human existence. He agreed with Freud in attributing overwhelming importance to early childhood experience and upbringing and, like Freud, accused the Central European variant of the late Victorian middle-class family of twisting and crippling human life. This statement of Freud's, from one of his essays of 1908, seems to have been echoed by Kafka whenever he viewed his own life in relation to his father:

> Those who succumb to nervous illness are precisely the offspring of fathers, who, having been born of rough but vigorous families, living in simple healthy country conditions, had successfully established themselves in the metropolis, and in a short space of time had brought their children to a high level of culture. (IX, 182)[1]

Kafka's long autobiographical "Letter to His Father" of November 1919 reads like an elaboration of Freud's sentence. This letter is a remarkable document, not least because of its cultural-historical significance as one of the most consistent applications of Freud's theory of the Oedipus complex to one particular life. In his letter, which represents Kafka's basic autobiography, he employs the perspective of the Oedipus complex with so pure and radical a consistency that the French "anti-Oedipal" psychiatrists Deleuze and Guattari have been persuaded to see it as a deliberate caricature of Freud's fundamental doctrine, "a magnifying of Oedipus to the point of the absurd."

Analogies that center on the Oedipus complex, or on the masochistic component underlying the themes of Kafka's life and oeuvre, seem all too obvious for comfort. They tend to obscure the equally, or even more important, fundamental differences between the founder of psychoanalysis and the creator of the "Kafkaesque" mode of perceiving and presenting human life. Despite the many striking thematic parallels, Kafka was by no means a Freudian or a follower of any psychoanalytic persuasion. The most important difference lies in Kafka's categorical rejection of psychoanalysis as a means of therapy. In sharp contrast to Freud, Kafka saw emotional illness not as something remediable and extrinsic to human existence. What Freudian psychoanalysis diagnosed as "neurosis" was for Kafka a spiritual or existential anguish, inseparable from the whole being of the one who suffered it. "There is only one illness," Kafka said in one of his letters, "and medicine hunts it blindly like a beast through unending forests."[2] The illness of which he speaks is neither psychological nor physical; it is individual existence itself. Kafka rejected the irreligious humanism that lies at the basis of Freud's psychoanalysis. He completely and resolutely despaired of Freud's rationalistic faith in the curative power of scientific knowledge. Since Kafka could not accept its therapeutic hopes, he had to dismiss the very raison d'être of psychoanalysis. For him, sensuous life as such was the disease for which there was only a single cure—death. Kafka's violent condemnation of sexuality makes him a radical opponent of the naturalism firmly believed in by Freud. Physical life, propagated by what Freud called "eros" and aided by intelligence, always remained Freud's supreme value, even when, in his later stages, he saw a well-nigh tragic dilemma for man in the ineradicable conflict between the life-affirming instinct of eros and the equally powerful death instinct, which manifests itself in self-destruction and aggression. Kafka's antinaturalistic abhorrence of the flesh and all its works—"the sensuous world is only the evil in the spiritual one,"[3] he noted—could be viewed by Freud as nothing but a symptom of a severe neurosis. For Kafka, on the other hand, what psychoanalysis would consider neurosis, such as the *Angst* that forever haunted him, was a "fact of faith," an "anchoring of man in distress," "preformed in his being and subsequently continuing to shape it. . . . And here one tries to cure?"[4]

In an informative essay, "Kafka and Psychoanalysis," Hartmut Binder has argued that the basic opposition of Kafka to Freud, as it emerges from passages such as the one just quoted, resides in the Freudian restriction of neurosis to the individual case and family situation. According to Binder, Kafka, in contrast to Freud, sees "forces at work [in neurosis] which far transcend the individual's experience." For Kafka, the therapeutic process of psychoanalysis fails to grasp the roots of illness "in the suprapersonal anthropological dimension."[5] Binder overlooks the presence of the anthropological dimension in Freud's theory. The Oedipal family situation is seen by Freud, even in his early work, and progressively more sharply as his theory develops, in anthropological terms. It is viewed by him and his followers as the foundation of human society and civilization, and it is held to have worked its traumatic effects on all mankind. Kafka himself acknowledges the anthropological side of Freud, when he remarks that psychoanalysis views neurosis as the foundation of all religion. The main point of difference thus does not lie in the absence of a collectivist angle in Freud, but rather in the existential direction that Kafka's view of neurosis takes in contrast to the sociocultural view of Freud. For Kafka, *Angst,* like religion, is man's desperate attempt to find a resting-place in his "distress," his frantic search for the "anchor" in his "thrownness" (to use Martin Heidegger's peculiarly apt term here), for a refuge "in any maternal soil" that promises stability. Freud sees man capable of overcoming his original *Angst* by the strengthening of his ego in the face of super-ego and Id—a process of maturing that is both socializing and individuating. For Kafka, as for the existentialists, *Angst* constitutes the very "essence" of the person, the forming element that "continues to shape him" as long as he lives. For Freud, man would prosper and be properly himself if freed from his neurosis; while, for Kafka, without his illness he would not exist. Since individuated life itself is the illness from which man suffers, Kafka is able to call "the therapeutic part of psychoanalysis" "a helpless error."

Having said all this, we should recall that the case against too close a Kafka-Freud connection must not be overstated. It does justice only to one side of Kafka, and not necessarily the dominant one. Among the strongest "Freudian" components of Kafka is his ambivalence, and one of the main critical tasks is to follow the various ramifications of this ambivalence. Kafka's avowed pessimism about the sensory world is counterbalanced by professions of fervent belief in the blessings and joys of physical fitness, practical energy, and vitality, which link him to turn-of-the-century vitalism, to Thomas Mann's nostalgia for the *Bürger,* and also to Freud's struggle in the cause of mental and emotional health. It is by no means clear whether Kafka's "reluctant pessimism" was usually meant to be extended to the human condition, or whether it was not mainly restricted to himself and those he considered similarly afflicted. His preoccupation with the kind of education that would protect a future generation from falling victim to his own plight speaks against his exclusive immersion in mystic spirituality. There are similarities between Kafka's views on education, as they emerge in his letters to his sister Elli, and Freud's essay "Civilized Sexual Morality and Modern Nervous Illness." Here, for all their differences, Kafka seems to share with Freud the general outlook of enlightened humanism.

Because of a deep split between Kafka's nature and his contrasting allegiances to pure spirit on the one hand, and Freud's concept of eros, on the other, Kafka's opinions can never provide a consistent world view. If we restrict ourselves to his opinions, all we can say is that he was close to Freud at the naturalistic or vitalistic pole of his being, and radically opposed to him at the spiritualist or mystical pole. However, if we proceed to examine the striking analogies between the working of the human mind, as expounded by Freud, and certain structural peculiarities of Kafka's fictional world, we shall arrive at an aspect of Kafka that is not only compatible with Freud's thought, but almost incomprehensible without it. Let us recall that

Kafka, after writing the work of his "breakthrough," mentioned "thoughts of Freud" as "*naturally*" occurring to him in connection with it. That is, he found a "natural" link to Freud in the form and theme (he does not distinguish between them) of what he considered to be his best and most authentic writing. Kafka's own awareness of this connection emerges as a factor of crucial significance for the case, which this essay will attempt to argue, for a close kinship between the structure of the human mind, as conceived by Freud, and the principles of Kafka's creative method.

I shall concentrate on the structural role of the magic or fantastic element in Kafka's work and its relationship to two key concepts of Freudian psychoanalysis—repression and projection. Such a focusing might help to illuminate not only the relationship of Kafka's writing to the psychoanalytic view of man, but also to clarify the function of one of the most striking features of Kafka's work. By "fantastic" I understand those narrated events in which the reader finds startling and puzzling deviations from his normal expectations, unexplained violations of what he would consider possible in the empirical world. Among very many examples are the unexplained metamorphosis of a human being into an animal, the apparently self-propelled movements of inanimate objects, the miraculous condensation or expansion of spatial distance. The fantastic is the other side of the magic. In magic, to use Freud's words, we encounter "omnipotence of thought" or will, and its victory over the laws of nature. In the fantastic, the same seems to hold true, but the thought or will to which we could ascribe this victory over empirical experience is not perceived. At the very beginning of his writing career, the twenty-year-old Kafka, in a letter to his friend Oskar Pollak, called his own writing "magic." In his first extant work, "Description of a Struggle," the first-person narrator performs acts of magic, altering features and dimensions of the landscape at will. The "magic omnipotence of thought" here exhibited is transformed in Kafka's mature work into the fantastic, in which events defying the laws of nature happen, or seem to happen, without, and even contrary to, any discernible will. This important shift from the magic to the fantastic in Kafka's work corresponds to the difference between conscious and unconscious wishes in Freudian thought. Magic, with which Kafka equated his writing, remained its hallmark in a figurative sense, too. What we have come to call "Kafkaesque" designates the peculiarly unsettling effects that radiate from the unexplained mysteries in his fiction and make for its special place in literature.

The most systematic attempt to explain the fantastic in Kafka, or at least in one of his most famous works, "The Metamorphosis" of November/December 1912, was undertaken by Tzvetan Todorov within the framework of a general treatise on the fantastic in literature. Todorov (not unlike Jentsch, in his definition of the central concept of "the uncanny" in Freud's essay on "The Uncanny," 1919) sees the fantastic as the effect produced on the reader by uncertainty as to the appropriateness of a natural or a supernatural understanding of the events depicted. What distinguishes Kafka from traditional authors of the fantastic genre is the reversal of direction, in his work, of the movement between natural and supernatural. In the traditional fantastic, text and reader move from a natural to a supernatural ambience. In Kafka's tale (Todorov argues) the opposite occurs. The story moves from the supernatural—the mysterious insect—to the acceptance, by himself and his family, of this mystery as "natural." Its final "naturalization" appears as "the banality of evil," the brutal callousness of the petty-bourgeois family in which the miracle dies, while the trivial round of everyday life triumphs.

Todorov's reading, certainly persuasive on one level, ignores a countermovement, from the natural to the supernatural, that clearly emerged when we take Gregor's reflections on his past life into account. Gregor recalls how badly he had wished to quit his job and tell his hated boss his true opinion of him, which would make the exploiter tumble from his high seat. However, consideration for his family, whose debt to the firm had to be paid off first, had forced Gregor to silence his own rebellious wish. Instead he had, in his sleep, managed to get transformed into an insect. His metamorphosis, at a gruesome price, fulfilled at least part of the wish he had not dared to carry out himself. It freed him from his job and obligations as the breadwinner of his family. The sequence of events in the story thus initially describes the opposite of the movement discerned by Todorov. It shows a natural desire preceding and leading to the supernatural event. In this respect it is not Todorov, but Freud, who will help to illuminate the function of the fantastic in Kafka's work.

The connecting link between Freud's theories and Kafka's tale is Freud's concept of repression, which he declared to be "the cornerstone . . . of the psychoanalytic theory of the neuroses" (XIX, 196). Repression results from the rejection by the ego of a wish the ego finds incompatible with its need for parental and societal approval. The rejected wish, if strong enough, does not simply go away. It is pushed back into the unconscious. Freud carefully distinguishes between unconscious and preconscious systems of the mind. The preconscious is the locus of thoughts eventually admissible to consciousness, while the unconscious is the lower depth of the self, where all forbidden wishes gather and fester and from where they constantly seek to reemerge into consciousness. The mind is then split between a consciousness that refuses to know and an unconsciousness in which the repressed seeks to gain expression and fulfillment. The ego, through its preconscious censor, constantly beats back the efforts of the unconscious to reenter the light of consciousness. If a forbidden wish happens to be particularly powerful, the ego is forced to yield, up to a point. What then results is a compromise. The wish is allowed to slip into consciousness, but only in unrecognizable disguise. Our dreams are such compromises. Sleep weakens the ego sufficiently to permit the forbidden wish to slip past the censor, but the ego is still strong enough to force a disguise on it. What is allowed to appear to consciousness, the "manifest content" of the dream, is a product of concessions made by both sides. Analogous compromises appear in waking life as parapraxes—malfunctioning of the self, such as slips of the tongue; forgetfulness in regard to appointments, duties, or words; and "accidental" injuries—and as neuroses. Like the dream, neurosis arises in instances in which both the repressed wish and the repressing ego are particularly strong. Their conflict results in a pathological condition. That part of the neurotic compromise that is allowed to emerge into consciousness is the neurotic symptom. It is analogous to the manifest content of a dream.

These characteristics of the psychic compromise are found again as structural and functional features of the apparently supernatural event narrated in Kafka's "The Metamorphosis." Gregor's metamorphosis is preceded by his inhibition of a wish. For the time being, Gregor has repressed his desire to walk out of his job. At the time when his transformation takes place, in his sleep, he is not conscious of this desire. No connection between his former wish and the strange event is made explicit. However, by choosing to narrate Gregor's wish in the casual context of his musing and reminiscing, the author creates an implicit link. It places the reader in the role of the Freudian analyst, whose hermeneutic task it is to be aware "that even the apparently most obscure and arbitrary mental phenomena invariably have a meaning and a causation" (XIX, 197). As the Lacanian sequel to Freudian psychoanalysis has made explicit, the patient's life and associations, communicated to the analyst and "read" by him, form as much of a "text" to be interpreted as do literary texts. The parallelism of hermeneutic tasks between analyst and textual critic must not be overlooked simply because of a difference in "texts"—lives as against words—and ultimate purpose. Both have to discern patterns in a multiplicity of signals, and both ultimately depend on communications with which they are confronted. The distinction between lives and texts is not as absolute as the New Critics wanted to make us believe.

If we consider the function of the metamorphosis in the total context of all phenomena narrated in the text, we find that it fulfills the function that a neurotic symptom, particularly hysterical illness, fulfills in the total context of a life communicated to the psychoanalyst. Its function is to fulfill a rejected wish in a disguise that makes it unrecognizable as such a fulfillment.

It appears as a calamitous malfunctioning, a gigantic "parapraxis" of Gregor's body, as an inexplicable blow of "outrageous fortune," which relieves its victim of all responsibility for the fulfillment of his wish, and punishes him for it in the bargain. In contrast to his previous, openly acknowledged desire, its present "unintended" fulfillment is divorced from Gregor's ego. On the contrary, his ego seeks to demonstrate by most strenuous efforts that he is eager to continue to support his family, and is prevented only by his "unfortunate" situation from doing so. Gregor's metamorphosis is a divorce of bodily behavior from conscious intention. It seems to exemplify the concept of the "compromise," which is crucial to the psychoanalytic theory of the neurotic symptom. Freud writes,

> A symptom is not merely the expression of a realized unconscious wish; a wish from the preconscious which is fulfilled by the same symptom must also be present. So that the symptom will have *at least* two determinants, one arising from each of the systems involved in the conflict. (V, 569)

The metamorphosis, in Kafka's mature version of the theme, functions exactly like a symptom as here described by Freud. It is the synthesis of two opposed tendencies. While it fulfills the rebellious wish of the repressed unconscious and liberates Gregor from his hated job and obligations to his family, it also satisfies the preconscious ego's craving to appear innocent, to exhibit good will, and ultimately to atone for what it has allowed to occur. Gregor has realized his wish for freedom unconsciously, literally in his sleep. But the shape in which his unconscious wish-fulfillment appears literally embodies the disapproval with which his consciousness views his own act. From the perspective of his conscious, or preconscious, ego, which is the perspective the reader shares, Gregor's unconscious revolt appears not only unfortunate, but in a most reprehensible guise. Upon waking up, Gregor appears to himself unrecognizable. The product of his unconscious emerges as an object of supreme disgust, alien to himself, a "colossal" specimen of what is most parasitic and contemptible—"vermin."

The fantastic in Kafka's tale thus behaves like the uncanny as seen by Freud. It is a "return of the repressed." The unconscious reemerges in unrecognizable disguise to haunt the conscious ego. It is the ego's humiliation and punishment. In the split self, of which the metamorphosis provides such a clear and drastic example, the wish fulfillment of one part of the self acts as the humiliation and punishment of the other. Kafka's work narrates as an individual's fate what Freud describes as a general problem of wish fulfillment in a divided self:

> No doubt a wish fulfillment must bring pleasure, but the question then arises "To whom?" To the person who has the wish, of course. But, as we know, a dreamer's relation to his wishes is a quite peculiar one. He

> repudiates them and censors them—he has no liking for them, in short. So that their fulfillment will give him no pleasure, but just the opposite. . . . Thus a dreamer in his relation to his dream-wishes can only be compared to an amalgamation of two separate people who are linked by some important common element. . . . [I]f two people are not at one with each other, the fulfillment of a wish of one of them may bring nothing but unpleasure to the other. (V, 580, footnote 1)

We find an analogous structure in "Blumfeld, an Elderly Bachelor," another example of a miraculous occurrence narrated in Kafka's oeuvre—the strange story of the two small celluloid balls that follow the "hero" wherever he goes until, ashamed of these unwanted companions, he succeeds in interesting two children in them who, he hopes, will take them away. As in "The Metamorphosis," Kafka suggests that the fantastic is the return of a repressed wish in unrecognizable disguise. Aware of the monotony and unrelieved isolation of his bachelor's life "in secret," which no one observes, Blumfeld thinks of acquiring a young dog as a "companion." But the ego, appearing in Blumfeld in its most narcissistic form, brushes this desire aside. Such "companionship" would involve cares and responsibilities that would impose too great a strain on Blumfeld's self-centered addiction to absolutely unmolested privacy and comfort. Therefore, Blumfeld dismisses his wish. But immediately, as if in direct answer to it, he perceives a "noise which paws produce when pattering one after the other over a floor."[6] These "paws" turn out to be the two celluloid balls that, virtually inseparable from him, will provide him with the companionship for which one part of his self longed, while the other denied it.

This is the place to introduce into the discussion a second structural principle, closely related to repression and equally vital to both Freud and Kafka. This is the concept of projection, which holds that what appears as external fate, accident, illness, or the behavior of the outside world towards us, may sometimes be a projection of our own unconscious will and thus be of our own doing. Such a dominance of the inner over the external world occurs in our dreams, in which all phenomena express only the dreamer's mind and will. Schopenhauer pointed this out long before Freud, in a remarkable passage about dreams of frustration: "That which creates the obstacles and frustrates our lively desire . . . is after all only our own will; operating, however, from a region that lies far beyond the image-producing consciousness . . . and, therefore, appears as inexorable fate."[7] Schopenhauer goes on to suggest that human life itself may behave analogously to dreams. What appears to befall us from outside may be the fulfillment of our unconscious wish. What Schopenhauer arrived at by philosophical speculation, Freud extended and systematized by what was, at least to his view, scientific observation and reasoning. He established the sway of the psychic and inward over the physical and external world basically in three areas.

1. In his early studies of hysteria, he discovered that there were illnesses in which the body obeyed the unconscious mind. The relationship between body and mind thus was not always a one-way street, with the body swaying the mind (as in the view of nineteenth-century materialist science), but that in certain, not infrequent, cases the reverse held true.

2. In the many instances of parapraxis of "the psychopathology of everyday life" he showed that accidents and failures ascribed to chance may often be the result of the individual's inner conflicts.

3. He added to the stature of dreams by demonstrating for them a significance that they had not appeared to possess in the view of science prior to him. What is more, he sought to prove dreams to be the product of deep-seated inner forces, and essentially independent of stimuli from the sleeper's physical environment or from somatic sources in which science had hitherto seen the main cause of and explanation for dreams.

In the light of Freud's theories, much of what used to be ascribed to the material world external to the individual was now seen as a projection of his inner life. Reversing the centuries-old direction of natural science, Freud reclaimed much lost ground for the human "soul." Ultimately, of course, Freud also saw the psyche as subject to the physicochemical universe. However, before the ultimate explanation was reached, there was an area where the opposite chain of command prevailed, where the physical world merely appeared to be the cause of what turned out to be the work of the (unconscious) mind of man. This area harbored psychosomatic illnesses, parapraxes, dreams, and neuroses and psychoses in all their forms.

It is this dominance of the inner over the external world that makes the insights of Freudian psychoanalysis touch so intimately on the nature of Kafka's narratives. The fantastic in Kafka is a projection or prolongation of psychic tendencies in the protagonist, a fact that is clearly hinted at by the texts. In Blumfeld's case, we have already seen how the mysterious appearance of the balls in his flat is the oblique fulfillment of his rejected wish for "companionship." It is the function of Kafka's "miracles" to make the external world of his fiction conform to the unacknowledged wishes of his characters. This, of course, is precisely the method of dreams, as seen by Freud. Kafka indicates in subtle ways that Blumfeld's bouncing "companions" are the embodiment of an inner need. As we have seen, his very first perception of them reminds him of a "pattering of paws." The narrator thus provides a very obvious link to Blumfeld's wish for a dog. Furthermore, the time sequence, in which the noise is heard immediately after Blumfeld has dismissed his desire for a "droll" and playful young creature, strongly suggests that the miraculous toys are the extension of, and the answer to, his repressed longing for escape from his solitary and routinized adulthood into companionship, playfulness, and youth. The balls are heard before they are seen; they are sounds before they appear as objects. The perception of the miracle thus proceeds from what Herder called the "inner sense," in contrast to the distancing and objectifying sense of sight. Hearing makes the distinction between subjective and objective reality more difficult to discern. Even when Blumfeld finally sees the balls, they seem to try to stay behind him, thereby reducing his chances to scrutinize and examine them. Furthermore, they behave in exact conformity with Blumfeld's movements, as though they were a part of him, and, what is most crucial, the text gives no evidence that the balls are ever perceived by anyone except Blumfeld. The possibility of a hallucination thus remains open.

But even where such a possibility is excluded, as in "The Metamorphosis," where the miraculous is an objective fact of the fictional world, Kafka hints at a connection with those nocturnal hallucinations that we call dreams. Although it is explicitly stated that the metamorphosis is no dream, the text also tells us that Gregor was transformed in a night of "unquiet dreams." His vermin shape thus emerges from among his dreams, as though one of them had been projected into external reality and become part of it.

In "Blumfeld," the relationship of the miraculous to the protagonist's psychic conflict is even more explicit. During the night, after Blumfeld has managed to keep the balls temporarily quiet under his bed, he frequently awakens from his "dreamless" but "unquiet" sleep, with the "delusion" that someone is knocking on his door:

> He knows quite well that no one is knocking; who would knock at night and at his lonely bachelor's door? Yet although he knows this for certain, he is startled again and again and each time glances in suspense at the door, his mouth open, eyes wide, a strand of hair trembling over his damp forehead.[8]

It is his own perception, and not an objectively external sound, that Blumfeld "hears," as he himself lets us know in no uncertain terms. Thus it is clear that what he hears is a message from himself to himself—the message of his desire for a companion, which his egotism had repressed. He perceived his own desire for the other as the other's attempt to come to him—a constellation of psychological factors expressed much more subtly in Kafka's last fragment, "The Burrow." The "suspense" with which Blumfeld stares at the door, and the symptoms of extreme excitement that the narrator describes, clearly reveal the ambivalence between longing and fear with which the Kafka protagonist always experiences his relationship to "the other."

One of the most common disguises used by the preconscious censor, according to Freud in *The Interpretation of Dreams,* is the "reversal, or turning a thing into its opposite" (V, 362). The dreamer's own thought or wish is projected into and perceived as someone else's behavior towards him. For instance, a death wish directed at one's father may be disguised as the father's assault upon the son, a fact that sheds interesting light upon Kafka's "The Judgment" and its forerunner, "The Urban World."[9] The "knocking" on Blumfeld's door is a striking example of such a reversal. Blumfeld perceives his own wish for the open door, for breaking out of his solitude, which was evident in his initial wish for a dog, as someone else's attempt to come to him. Here the narrator makes this "reversal" obvious, and it is even clear to the protagonist. In other works, such as *The Trial* and "The Burrow," the disguise is much more difficult to detect.

As in a Freudian slip of the tongue, it is the words of Blumfeld's thought that betray what his consciousness conceals. When Blumfeld, in his narrated monologue, names the activity of the balls, he comes up with the verb "locken"—"to entice" or "to tempt." By this choice of word, the narrator makes Blumfeld inadvertently admit that the balls embody a "lure," a temptation for him. Like the knock on his door, they are a message to him from a part of himself that the "elderly bachelor" has tried to deny. The fact that they are two, perfectly attuned to each other, demonstrates a lesson in that "companionship" and "loyalty" that Blumfeld, feeling these qualities painfully lacking in his life, had hoped to get from a puppy. By clinging to him and to each other, the celluloid balls seem to make light of his principle of self-sufficiency and wear away his narcissism. They behave as the projection of his own longing for "the other," and they encounter the same resistance from the official part of his divided self that had made him suppress his original wish for a dog.

Kafka presents the perplexing element in his work as the projection of unacknowledged forces in his protagonists. To take a famous example, the mysterious Court of Josef K.'s trial is rung in by Josef K.'s own hand. In response to his ringing for his breakfast, the "stranger" appears, who turns out to be Franz, one of the warders arresting Josef K. (Franz and Josef K. are, of course, transparent allusions to Franz Kafka's divided self.) Josef K.'s intention had been to call the maid; the result of his act is his arrest. Josef K.'s ringing constitutes a parapraxis, a *Fehlleistung.* It reveals the same kind of self-alienation that we find at the beginning of "The Metamorphosis." Gregor Samsa fails to "recognize" the part of himself that has emerged from his unconscious, and Josef K.'s wish for punishment appears to his consciousness as a "stranger." This stranger tells him that he and his fellow-warder are "closer to [him] than any other people in the world." As an analysis of *The Trial* would bear out, Josef K. does not recognize, either literally or figuratively, what is "closest" to him—namely, his twin needs for exculpation and punishment. He is ashamed of these needs, and tries to keep their expression, his trial, hidden from the world. Appropriately, "shame" is the last noun of the novel: "It was as if the shame of it must outlive him." Yet shame is evident in Josef K. even before the plot begins. At the very opening of the novel, before "the stranger" appears, Josef K. notes that he is being watched from a window across the street. He feels annoyed and bothered by it, as though something secretly shameful were connected with him. That resistance to scrutiny, that need to hide, which is shame, precedes the reason for it. The emotion comes before its motivation. In a sense, it generates it.

This is the method of dreams. It characterizes the beginnings of Kafka's writing, and he remained faithful to it to the end. In his first work, "Description of a Struggle," the sad fate of a character, the Fat Man, profoundly upsets the first-person narrator. However, long before the Fat Man appears on the scene, an unexplained moaning has disturbed the narrator's sleep all night. The Fat Man and his tragic misfortune function as the materialization of that sadness which the narrator has heard in himself. The miraculous contraction and expansion of distance in Kafka's work likewise confirm and extend what the protagonist expresses by words, thoughts, or behavior. Like the dreamer in his dream, Kafka's protagonist is the secret source of the mysteries that assail him.

THE CONVERGENCES of Kafka's and Freud's views of the working of the mind—explicitly and systematically analyzed by Freud, implicitly shown by Kafka—are numerous, profound, and amazing. Here I have not been able to do justice to more than a small number of them. The significance of these convergences for Kafka's art can become fully clear only from an exploration of the most fundamental difference between Kafka and Freud: their contrasting attitudes toward the ego. Such an exploration, however, would go beyond the limits of this essay.

NOTES

NOTE: All translations from German in this essay, except for those from Freud, are my own.

1. All quotations from Freud are from *The Standard Edition of the Complete Psychological Works of Sigmund Freud.* Translated from the German under the general editorship of James Strachey in collaboration with Anna Freud, assisted by Alix Strachey and Alan Tyson (London: Hogarth Press and the Institute of Psychoanalysis, 1953–1974). The volume number is indicated by roman numerals in the text.

2. Franz Kafka, *Briefe, 1902–24*, ed. Max Brod (Frankfurt am Main: S. Fischer Lizenzausgabe von Schocken Books, New York, 1958), 320.

3. Franz Kafka, *Hochzeitsvorbereitungen auf dem Lande und andere Prosa aus dem Nachlass*, ed. Max Brod (New York: Schocken Books, 1953), 44.

4. Franz Kafka, *Briefe an Milena*, ed. with a postscript Willy Haas (New York: Schocken Books, 1952), 246.

5. Hartmut Binder, *Motiv und Gestaltung bei Franz Kafka* (Bonn: Bouvier, 1966), 103.

6. Franz Kafka, *Sämtliche Erzählungen*, ed. Paul Raabe (Frankfurt am Main-Hamburg: Fischer Bücherei, 1970), 307.

7. Arthur Schopenhauer, *Sämtliche Werke*, ed. Arthur Hübscher (Leipzig: F. A. Brockhaus, 1937), Vol. 1, 230.

8. Kafka, *Sämtliche Erzählungen*, 312.

9. The unfinished story of another father-son relationship; see Kafka's diary entry after 21 February 1911.

KAFKA'S BEGINNINGS

Narcissism, Magic, and the Function of Narration in "Description of a Struggle"

FROM THE beginning, Kafka connected his writing with magic.[1] In one of his earliest letters, Kafka refers to his writing as "Wunderdinge" (miracle things),[2] and twenty years later, near the end of his life, he still, in speaking of his writing, points to the sphere of sorcery, Satanism, and magic.[3] In *Totem and Taboo,* Freud calls art the last refuge of magic, because art is the last territory on earth where the omnipotence of the psyche is still possible.[4] In Kafka's earliest preserved work, "Description of a Struggle," the central sections entitled "Ride" and "Promenade" serve as a strikingly literal[5] and "prophetic"[6] illustration of this insight, which Freud incidentally formulated eight years after Kafka's tale was written. In these sections, the first-person narrator performs feats of magic omnipotence, and the world obeys his wishes.

> The rocks vanished according to my will. . . . Since I love pine forests, I walked through pine forests, and, since I am fond of looking quietly into the starry sky, the stars rose slowly and calmly in the vast spread-out heavens. . . . This sight gladdened me so that, like a little bird swaying on a branch, I forgot to let the moon rise. (BK, 48)[7]

This blissful domination of nature by the self is art. The German word for art, *Kunst,* derived from *können* ("to be able to") makes clearer this basic meaning of art as superior ability and singular skill, as "magic" that heals, compensates, and elevates its practitioner to divine heights of power.

From *Kafka and the Contemporary Critical Performance,* ed. Alan Udoff (Bloomington: Indiana University Press, 1987), 98–110.

In the art of magic, Kafka's literalizing language presents us with the magical in art, the immediate *können* of *Kunst,* art's self-fulfillment in the act, which is the mark of what has traditionally been associated with inspiration and genius. It is the utopia of art in which effort is instantaneous accomplishment. Its "medium"—if one can call it that—is the immediately effective will, and the enjoyment of this power is its sole object. This art needs no public. It is sublime self-amusement. Kafka's text calls it "Belustigung."

As I have tried to show elsewhere,[8] Kafka sought to reach the infinite power and happiness of such magic in his writing. In fact, what he presents in "Description of a Struggle" as a deliberate performance remains the underlying principle of his work. What in this work looks like external fate can, upon closer reading, be seen as accommodating and obliquely fulfilling inner needs and tendencies of the protagonist.[9] Kafka's fictional world seems to obey the rule of the psyche.

Yet, Kafka also viewed magic, and thus his writing, with the suspicion and hostility with which the Western religious tradition—Judaic and Christian alike—has always met the *magus.* In an important letter to Max Brod, Kafka calls his writing "the reward for Satan's service," "descent to the dark powers," "an unleashing of spirits bound by nature," the fruit of "questionable embraces," of which the writer "writing stories up in the sunlight is no longer aware."[10] The eros offered the writer by the infernal powers is not "natural" love. These "questionable embraces" are onanistic, as the continuation of Kafka's self-condemnation makes very clear, for he finds "the properly diabolical" element of writing in its "vanity and lusting for pleasure which perpetually whirls around and enjoys one's own figure [*Gestalt*], or else another—in that case, the motion merely multiplies; it becomes a solar system of vanity."[11] Kafka condemns his writing because it is narcissism.

To understand the connection between narcissism, magic, and art, which is crucial for Kafka, it will be useful for us to turn to Freud's concept of narcissism, not because there can be any question of "influence,"[12] but because Freud provides a structural pattern and a vocabulary extremely suitable to illuminating Kafka's literary beginnings.

For Freud, too, magic was closely related to narcissism. His awakening anthropological interest in magic closely preceded his introductory treatise "On Narcissism."[13] What connects magic with narcissism for Freud is the belief in the "omnipotence of thoughts."[14] Freud discovered this belief first in cases of compulsion neurosis,[15] then "in primitive peoples" as "overestimation of the power of wishes and psychic acts . . . vis-à-vis the external world,"[16] and soon thereafter in the small child. Thus shortly after *Totem and Taboo,* Freud arrived at the idea of a "primary narcissism" in which the libido is still directed entirely toward the child's own body or self. The infant enjoys a feeling of omnipotence that rests on his ability to feel the world as an extension of the self. However, with the development of the child, as with that of humanity as a whole, a new object-directed libido conflicts with self-directed pleasure. Beginning with the child's mother, object libido extends to his fellow creatures and leads to the adult ability to love. Where, however, severe disturbance of emotional maturation occurs, libido may be withdrawn from others and redirected exclusively toward the self. Then the "pathological" phenomenon of "secondary narcissism" arises.

Freud's concept of narcissism enables us to articulate the profound appeal that magic had for Kafka. It represented for him the "omnipotence of thought," the primacy of the mental-spiritual over the physical, the psychic over the empirical. But the narcissism in it made it reprehensible to him. For Kafka, the ego was the *moi haïssable.* His extraordinarily strong moral, religious, social, and mystical sense recoiled from an activity of supreme self-indulgence.

How could Kafka's radical condemnation of his writing be compatible with his intense dedication to it? Even though he asked Max Brod to burn his manuscripts, he corrected proofs even on his deathbed. One answer to this question lies in the existence of conflicting poetological intentions underlying and informing his work. Narcissistic magic combines with opposing tendencies to produce the uniqueness of this work.

I shall restrict myself here to only one of these. "Writing," says Kafka, "is a form of prayer."[17] Kafka thus defines writing as an appeal to something beyond the writer's self. This definition obviously contradicts the infernal self-enjoyment with which he identified writing in his letter to Max Brod. The conflict between these two functions of art was enormously fruitful for Kafka's work. The most important form that writing as appeal took for Kafka was narration. Narration, by showing the punishment of the narcissistic *magus,* made it possible for him to use writing as the antidote to itself.

I propose to show this conflict between magic and narration in the first version of Kafka's first extant work, "Description of a Struggle," of 1904/1905. This work of the twenty-one-year old makes the fundamental concerns of his total oeuvre and the genesis of his method of composition transparent to a degree unmatched in his later works. This transparency might have been Kafka's reason for excising and condensing crucial passages of the text. Like Georg Trakl and other classics of modernism, Kafka sought to obscure his tracks. I shall, however, not respect his motivation here, because the original wording represents Kafka's true beginnings and blatantly reveals intentions fundamental to his entire work, and with these I am concerned here.

The struggle mentioned in the title refers to a conflict between two reactions to a temptation. The temptation is life as erotic and social existence. In the midst of an evening party, the narrator sits alone "at a little table, sipping from his third jigger of Benedictine" (BK, 10), when a "new acquaintance" steps up to him and tells him of his happy love affair. The acquaintance embodies the challenge not only of eros and life, but also that of narrative action, which he initiates with his intrusion. As a "*new* acquaintance," he brings into the solitary bachelor's existence the element of novelty and change. He does not allow the narrator to rest. By repeatedly prodding him on, he keeps the action going. Only by eliminating him can the narrator attain peace. But this peace will prove to be temporary and illusory because narration itself, as we shall see, will take over the disturbing function of the acquaintance.

From the beginning, narration has eros as its content. The acquaintance starts the plot with a narration of his love affair. In Kafka's beginnings, narration is the formal correlative of eros and life, even as magic is the formal correlative of narcissism. Narration has in common with eros that it always aims to go beyond itself. It does so in two ways: in trying to communicate with a public, and in straining from any given moment it has reached toward the next. It is directed outward from the narrator to the recipient and forward from the present to the future. Thus it mimes life itself as movement, growth, and development. Contrary to the circularity of narcissism, which is libido wishing to flow back into the self, narration strives toward a telos, an ending that is essentially different from beginning and middle. Thus narration mimes not only life, but death as well.[18] The thematic and structural relationships in Kafka's first story adumbrate with uncanny accuracy the conflict between eros and narcissism in the Freudian myth.

The whole first part of the "struggle" describes the narrator's counter-challenge to the other's challenge. He seeks to draw the other's eros to himself. His relation to the acquaintance becomes an appeal, a supplication for being admitted into a genuinely human life. The narrator is the first of Kafka's many supplicant figures, and the acquaintance becomes for him what the doorkeeper in the legend of *The Trial* will be for the man before thc law.

> [M]y acquaintance became very valuable to me as one who gives me worth before people without my having to earn it myself. I looked at my acquaintance with eyes of love. (BK, 20)

The medium of the narrator's supplication is art "as a form of prayer." In the second half of the story, a variant of the narrator is called "der Beter," "the praying man."[19] His "prayer" is a frantic exhibitionism, wild contortions and convulsions of his body, and its purpose is "to be looked at by people" (BK, 86). He seeks to draw the literal "regard" of people—pointing to the figurative meaning of respect—in the church away from the proper object of their worship, God, to himself—a variation of the narrator's attempt to gain, through the acquaintance, a standing in humanity, and to participate in the other's erotic life: "and I partook of the kisses he had received tonight from two girls / Oh tonight was amusing" (BK, 22). "Amusing" and "amusement"—key words in "Description of a Struggle"—signify the libidinal element that the German origin, "lustig," "Belustigung," through the root connection with "Lust"—lust, joy, desire—makes much more transparent; but at the same time, they also point to the objective of the activity that both the narrator and the Praying Man pursue. Both seek to amuse or at least to arouse attention, and the medium of their performances is the body. The Praying Man's convulsions are preceded in a less macabre way by the narrator's acrobatics. He leaps, "throws [his] hat in the air and catch[es] it boastfully" (BK, 14). This is art at its most primitive. In contrast to magic, it is art as a form of appeal. It courts a public; it aims to impress. It does not offer gratification to the artist but performs for the diversion of spectator or audience. Of course, through and beyond the other, the desperate objective of this art is the self's salvation. We have seen the narrator's need for the acquaintance whose "life became dearer to [him] than [his] own" (BK, 22). As to the Praying Man, the second version of the story spells out the implications of his need for "the regard" of others. His exhibitionist behavior, the Praying Man explains, "is no jest; it is a need for me, a need of being hammered fast by those looks, even if only for a brief hour" (BK, 87–89). Others are to help him acquire—no matter how fleetingly—a sense of being. His exhibitionism is a plea for existence. It is therefore literally as well as ironically appropriate that Kafka shows it as "a form of prayer," taking place in a church, and thus identifies it semantically with his own "form of prayer"—writing.

Despite the self-seeking in it, supplication entails a measure of concern for the addressee. The narrator represents this altruistic or eros-related element in the art of appeal. We remember his saying: "His life became dearer to me than my own." In "Description of a Struggle," narration is the form of appeal in which concern for the other replaces self-seeking as the primary aim. In the plot, narration succeeds the body as the medium of the narrator's courtship of the other. It also makes self-display give way to consideration.

It occurs to the narrating self "that [his] tall stature might perhaps be annoying to [the acquaintance]" (BK, 26). He tactfully hunches over to minimize the difference in height. Immediately thereafter, he thinks of entertaining his acquaintance by "inventing love stories . . . containing remarkable situations and not lacking even a little coarseness and robust rape" (BK, 26). Thus narration functions as the direct successor of the delicate considerateness that the narrator just displayed by his physical behavior. As his hunching over was to accommodate the other's physical and emotional comfort, the love stories are to satisfy the acquaintance's interest, which from the beginning had seemed to be erotic. In trying to meet the other's needs, the narrator becomes explicitly concerned with the art, the method or skill, of narrating. He reflects on the most effective means of relating his stories. "One might narrate it in this way," he thinks before beginning his attempt (BK, 24). It is the form of communication that troubles him. Accordingly, "invention" is called a "strenuous" effort. "Love" as the subject of the intended "stories" establishes the obvious link between eros and the narrative genre. In "Description of a Struggle," narration functions literally as the art of love.[20]

The thematization of narration represents the climax of the self's wooing of the other. It ends in failure. The other does not respond. Thus the narrator withdraws. Accepting the failure of art as appeal and communication, he turns to art as self-gratifying magic.

The genesis of the self's art of magic is described as a process of withdrawal of libido from the other and a retreat into fantasy. It provides an alternative to the mere wish to escape that had characterized the self's initial reaction to the acquaintance. Unlike mere retirement, withdrawal into the imagination leads not to the contraction but to the expansion of the self. Corresponding to narcissism rather than the death wish, it withdraws libido not from life itself but only from the other, in order to lavish it generously on the self.

This process can be followed fairly precisely in five distinct stages: metaphor, in which magic is not yet completely divorced from eros; projection, the attribution of one's own thoughts to another; sublimation; repression; solipsistic world dominion by the power of the wish.

METAPHOR

The first instance of magic occurs when the self responds to its neglect by imagining itself as the possessor of ineffable powers of attraction. The relevant passage of the narrator's inner monologue runs as follows:

> Tomorrow my acquaintance will be talking to Fräulein Anna; at first about ordinary things as is only natural; but then suddenly he will say: "Last night I was with someone the like of whom, dear Annerl, you surely have never seen. . . . I almost forgot you. I felt as if with the breathing of his hollow chest, the solid dome of the starry heavens lifted. The horizon burst open

> and, amidst flaming clouds, landscapes appeared, endless ones, that make us happy." (BK, 22)

The supernatural power with which the narrator sees himself endowed is quite literally the power of poetic speech. Magic power is contained in a simile: "I felt as if. . . ." It resides in the metaphoric capacity of language, and it is invoked as an aid in communication. For the imagined—not the real—acquaintance wishes to convey a contrast to that "ordinariness" and "naturalness" that characterize eros—the relationship of the acquaintance to his girl as the narrator imagines it. Magic power is a metaphor that alludes to a pole of existence opposite the earth-bound life of love. Magic is associated with the heavens, with distant horizons, with sudden illuminations. It is a sign of something utterly incommunicable in "straight" language. Even metaphor can only "allude to" the unnameable.[21] A happiness is being hinted at that, not entirely unlike that which Martin Heidegger understands by "being,"[22] is definable only by its contrast to the happiness of love. Over the powerful impression made by the magic self, the imagined acquaintance "almost forgets" his sweetheart.

The self's fascination for the other occurs only inside the self. It is not the "real," objectively existing acquaintance who sees the narrator as a heaven-moving magus; it is the acquaintance inside the narrator whom the narrator fascinates. His imagined self-elevation follows his inability to keep the "real" other's attention. Thus the text shows imaginary omnipotence resulting from real impotence. The narrator replaces the real other, who ignores him, by a desirable other who bestows magic power upon him. This process is a step toward "secondary narcissism." The imagined other is the means by which the self fascinates itself, and self-fascination appears as magic power.

Yet, in this first instance of magic power, narcissism is still incomplete. Its precondition, withdrawal of libido from the other, has not yet occurred. Magic is here still bound up with appeal and contained in communication. The ego's magic power is evoked in an imagined act of communication. It is a metaphor in the service of eros as imagined by the lonely self. The speaker, the acquaintance in the narrator's head, finds himself between two competing sources of attraction—the narrator and Anna. He seeks to explain one source of attraction to the other. Thus he mediates between two objects of eros. The form this mediation assumes is, typical of Kafka, narration. Narrating the events of the evening, the imagined acquaintance describes the I-narrator as endowed with extraordinary powers. Thus eros provides both theme and recipient of communication. In the ineffable fascination exerted by the narrator, eros occasions and originates narration; but in Anna, it provides recipient and conclusion. "My God," the imagined acquaintance ends, "how I love you, Annerl . . . your kiss is dearer to me than any landscape. Let's not talk of *him* any more and let's love each other" (BK, 22; italics mine). Love of the girl overcomes the fascination of the self. This victory of eros leads immediately to the narrator's above-discussed effort to entertain the real acquaintance with love stories in which eros and narrative art are so obviously welded.

After the failure of the self's attempt to woo the other with love stories, projection becomes central in the self's attempt to withdraw. The narrator suddenly attributes to the acquaintance the wish to kill him. The text offers no objectively discernible cause for this panic. On the contrary, it makes quite clear that the narrator projects into the acquaintance his own anger at being ignored and his envy of the other's presumed happiness and then reacts in paranoid dread to his own projection.

> But I told myself: "How heartless is this person! How typical and how flagrant is his indifference to my humble words! Well, he is happy and that is the [cruel] way of the happy ones. . . . [I]ndeed, *if the mood were* to come over him—a happy man *is dangerous,* that's *unquestionable—he would kill me* like a highwayman. *That is certain.* . . . For God's sake." *I looked around in fear.* (BK, 28–30; italics mine)

I italicized certain words to illuminate the process. The sudden jump from the conditional subjunctive, "if the mood were to come over him," to the indicative of certainty—"that's unquestionable"—makes the process of projection completely transparent. As a threatening assassin, the acquaintance becomes of course the earliest example of the Oedipal father and hostile power figure that was to dominate Kafka's oeuvre.[23] The text presents an obvious psychic act that transforms the other into a deadly menace for the narrator, but not for the reader. For it allows the reader to be aware of the subjectivity of the narrator's attribution. Thus the reader is able to witness a pathological development, a distortion of the actual state of affairs. This tends to devaluate in advance the narrator's subsequent magic feats. The close connection of his magic to paranoid behavior tends to place this "art" in a highly ironic light. The moral implications in the self's turn to total subjectivity become clearer in his subsequent treatment of the other, which is presented as the final step to magic omnipotence.

SUBLIMATION

Kafka's text shows a difficult learning process preceding such magic mastery. This process can be seen as a humorously pictorial presentation of the idea of sublimation. Wounded in the knee and able to walk only with pain, the first-person narrator teaches himself to swim in the air. Deprived on earth, he raises himself into a literally higher element. Three years prior to Freud's fundamental essay "The Poet and Daydreaming," Kafka enacts its poetics of sublimation. He shows the wound giving birth to the bow.[24] The narrator's self-liberation from the laws of gravity is art in its most fundamental sense.

In sublimation, magic is still aided by internalized eros. As the narrator tries to swim in the air, the thought of a girl in love with him inspires him. However, eros—even a purely imagined one, as seems to be the case here[25]—does not help much in the exercise of magic skill. As long as the thought of love inspires him, the narrator's efforts in overcoming the restraints of nature remain modest and uncertain. Only the deliberate withdrawal of libido from all fellow humans—real or imagined—enables him to rise to the mastery of magic.

The fellow creature in whom all others are embodied is of course the acquaintance. He has to become an object of utter indifference to the self, and finally be eliminated, for magic art to succeed.

> So then [the narrator tells himself] this man is of no account to you—repeat it—of no account. Besides he is harmless, as has been shown, he presents no danger. . . . So then . . . let him talk and you amuse yourself in your fashion; thereby—say it softly—you also protect yourself best. (BK, 40)

To use Hegelian terminology—quite appropriate here—the other has to cease to be a being-in-himself and become a being-for-the-self (of the narrator). The narrator reduces the other to a mere instrument of his self-gratification. He makes the acquaintance a beast of burden and rides on him. Immediately the landscape, too, begins to comply with his wishes.

> Already I jumped with unaccustomed skill upon my acquaintance's shoulders and pummeling his back with my fists, I got him into a gentle trot. . . . I succeeded, and at a goodly speed, we came into the interior of a large but as *yet unfinished region* where it was evening. (BK, 441; italics mine)

Belustigung—self-amusement—culminates when the other is eliminated and the "ride" on him becomes a "promenade" without him. The narrator abandons the acquaintance, leaving him wounded on the rocks, and, whistling down a few vultures to guard him,[26] walks into an unpeopled landscape in which he exercises divine power. The acquaintance was the last bond to the external and human world. With his removal, the narrator is enabled to triumph in a world in which there is nothing but his ego. The laws of nature, ultimate restraints on the ego, are repealed, and solipsism, the epistemological fulfillment of narcissism, makes for omnipotence. Through repression and excision of the other, the self becomes God.

RETURN OF THE REPRESSED

However, nothing characterizes Kafka's universe more aptly than the remark that "Kafka manifests a counternarcissistic tendency."[27] He presents the triumph of narcissistic self-fulfillment only to show it as illusory. Anticipating Kafka's last work, "The Burrow," a mysterious sound begins to disturb the narrator in his self-enjoyment and deprives him of rest. This enigmatic disturbance is a voice that is—to use another Freudian term uncannily appropriate to Kafka's work—quite literally "the return of the repressed." For this voice assumes the function of the eliminated acquaintance. When the self decided to rid itself of him, he had mainly been a voice for it. "Let him talk and you amuse yourself in your fashion." Now a voice functions as a reminder that elimination of the other cannot grant peace to the self. In his effort to keep the voice away, the narrator repeats his former intent to ignore the other. He tries "violently" "to roll off [the voice]" (BK, 56) and "to forget it stubbornly" (BK, 58). But this time repression does not succeed. The mysterious sounds do not cease to torment the narrator. They cause him "furious anxiety" (BK, 56), drive him down from his heights, and force him to flee the landscape of his making "in order to escape all ghostly people at last" (BK, 58). The "Promenade" that had begun with the self's omnipotence ends in its desperate impotence.

What returns here in "ghostly" guise is not only the other. It is quite literally a part of the narrator's self. For the words that the narrator hears uttered by the mysterious voice are his own, which he had used when trying to entertain the acquaintance by narrating to him a scene from his life. Now the disembodied voice literally echoes the narrator, quoting bits of his attempted narration: "Bench by the river," "cloudlike mountains," "trains with luminous smoke" (BK, 52). These words, with which the narrator had once expressed his need to communicate, now come back to haunt him and show him the limits of the magic power of solitude.[28] The incessant babble of the voice turns into "a weeping" and "a sobbing," sounds of mourning for something omitted or lost. It proves repression ineffectual. In a ghastly and ironic reversal, the self's former appeal to the other comes back as an appeal to the self, which the self does not acknowledge as its own. The principle of self-alienation of which Kafka's later works, such as "The Metamorphosis" and *The Trial*, have become classic examples is born here. In the disembodied voice of the "Promenade," we meet the first ancestor of Josef K.'s mysterious Court. As Josef K. does not acknowledge the Court, which he had rung for literally with his own hand, as having any connection with him, so the narrator of "Description of a Struggle" does not acknowledge that the voice gives his own words back to him.

As the return of the repressed forms the basis of the uncanny for Freud, it supplies the foundations for the fantastic in Kafka. The narrator perceives his own words as issuing from "ghostly people," a ghostly presence that frightens him and that he seeks to flee. The popular belief in ghosts—*revenants,* literally "returners," in French—perfectly illustrates the psychic constellation of the Freudian uncanny. Something that had once been familiar and shameful in the ego's past that had to be buried and forgotten comes back in a strange and frightening disguise to haunt the present.

The fantastic in Kafka is countermagic. It is the structural principle with which he purges his writing's magic of its narcissism. Through the fantastic, magic ceases to be the tool of consciousness, which, for Kafka as for Freud, is the seat and pride of the ego. It turns against consciousness and confounds it. Those startling deviations from empirical probability, which have come to be considered the "Kafkaesque" in Kafka's work, no longer proceed, as they do in "Ride" and "Promenade," from Kafka's narrator or protagonist, whose consciousness is the organizing center of perception in his work and who furnishes its perspective to the reader. With the enigmatic voice, a power emerges that seems to lie beyond the ken and control of consciousness. With it, the narrated events emancipate themselves from the narrator. Behind the explicit narrator, the presence of an infinitely greater, implicit narrator makes itself felt. He seems to know much more than the explicit one but is never heard speaking in his own voice. He remains "ghostly." He is identical with narration itself, which now appears as an autonomous process. It renders impotent the consciousness through which the reader perceives the fictional world.

We recall that from the beginning in "Description of a Struggle," narrative action had been associated with the representative of eros. The acquaintance had started the action by forcing the passive self to react, to "struggle," against the intrusion. Throughout the text, the attempt to communicate ignited the faltering action. After the other had been removed, speech as such resumed the attack. Through the voice that compels the self once more to act, the narrative renews itself. Thus narration works as a waking and a shaking up, a menace to and an overthrow of the self that seeks to evade it. It imitates the flow or "Fluss," the river, in which, while narrating his story, the Fat Man—enormous version of the ego—will be carried away and drown. The flow of narration turns against the narrating ego and sweeps it away.

The emancipation of narration from the consciousness dominating it enables Kafka to unite two fundamental but mutually inimical intentions in his writing—writing as magic power and writing as refutation of the self. By letting narration magically turn against the narrator, Kafka was able to use magic to vanquish the ego instead of serving it. He divorced the subject of his writing from the power that carried it forward. Dumbfounding and defeating the subject, the protagonist's or narrator's consciousness, Kafka could guiltlessly indulge in the power of writing. He was able to keep the principle of magic, the power of spirit and psyche over the empirical world—in Freud's words, "the omnipotence of thoughts"—while removing this power from the grip of the ego.

The turn from a magic employed by the narrator-protagonist to one without identifiable agent also unsettles the reader. The reader's superiority over text and characters vanishes when the text no longer permits him to explain a particular textual event, such as the unidentifiable voice. Does the narrator imagine these sounds? Are they his projection? Or do they issue from the acquaintance who is taking his revenge? Or are they "supernatural phenomena"? The reader has no means to decide. This inability shakes his superiority over the fictional characters and events, which Northrop Frye calls the mode of irony, dominant in modern literature.[29] The reader can no longer, as in irony, see through and look down upon the fictional world. The ironic mode gives way to what T. Todorov calls the fantastic.[30] A close reading of texts such as "The Judgment," "The Metamorphosis," *The Trial,* and *The Castle* shows that the mysterious fates from which Kafka's protagonists suffer obliquely meet certain needs and tendencies that are discernible in them. Yet the texts never truly sanction a reading that would see these happenings as mere projections by the characters. The withholding of the sanction for any definite answer topples the reader from ironic superiority and throws him nearer the opposite end of Frye's spectrum—myth.

Frye speaks of myth where the narrated events radically transcend the human sphere. In the case of Kafka's texts, however, the mythic does not reside, as it does for Frye, in the superhuman stature of the characters. In Kafka's texts, the mythic shows itself as the transcendence of the reader's human understanding. It is the reader's inability, built into the texts, to decide on a definitive answer to fundamental questions raised by his reading that humbles his accustomed confidence in the powers of his rational mind. Thus the ego is routed not only in Kafka's characters but also in his reader.

But Kafka's reader does not stay in the mythic mode. He is tossed back and forth between myth and extreme irony. For his inability to find explanations that are not immediately made questionable forces him to adopt an ironic stance not only toward the character whose predicament he shares but toward himself as well. Kafka's method extends the humbling of consciousness in narrator or protagonist to the reader. In this lies the greatest triumph of narration over ego. This triumph was a principal aspect of the "breakthrough" that Kafka felt he had achieved in writing "The Judgment," where he baffled himself as the reader of his own work.[31]

Actually, as I have tried to show here, it already occurred in his earliest work.

Yet Kafka subsequently decided to cross out the passage in which this "breakthrough" had taken place. By excising it, he removed the possibility of his reader's return to the superiority of the ironic mode. The original version, which we have analyzed, enabled the reader to see through the narrating character. He could recognize the narrator's evasion of the obvious fact that the mysterious voice echoed himself. The reader could thus conclude that the narrator committed bad faith in refusing to acknowledge what he could have recognized. Such transparency flatters the reader and returns him to the ironic superiority from which the undecidability of the voice had dislodged him. Cutting out the revealing passage was in keeping with Kafka's tendency to humble the ego, even in his reader.

NOTES

1. Cf. his letter to Oskar Pollak of September 6, 1903. *Briefe, 1902–1924*, Gesammelte Werke, ed. Max Brod (Frankfurt am Main: S. Fischer Lizenzausgabe von Schocken Books, New York, 1958), 17.

2. Cf. note 1. This letter represents Kafka's earliest comprehensive reference to his view of his writing.

3. *Briefe*, 384.

4. Sigmund Freud, *Studienausgabe, Conditio humana*, ed. Alexander Mitscherlich, Angela Richards, and James Strachey, Vol. 9 (Frankfurt am Main: S. Fischer Verlag, 1974), 378. All references to Freud will be from this edition, and quotations will be in my own translation.

5. See Günther Anders, *Franz Kafka. Pro und Contra. Die-Prozess Unterlagen* (Munich: C. H. Beck, 1951), passim. English translation by A. Steer and A. K. Thorlby as *Franz Kafka* (London: Bowes & Bowes, 1960). Cf. also Walter H. Sokel, *Franz Kafka*, Columbia Essays on Modern Writers, no. 19 (New York—London: Columbia University Press, 1966), 4–8.

6. Cf. Sokel, "Von Marx zun Mythos: Das Problem der Selbstentfremdung in Kafkas *Verwandlung*," *Monatshefte* Vol. 73, No. 1 (Spring 1981): 6–7, and Sokel, "From Marx to Myth: The Structure and Function of Self-Alienation in Kafka's *Metamorphosis*," in *The Literary Review, Kafka: Centenary Essays* 26(4) (Summer 1983): 485.

7. All references and quotations are from the first version of "Beschreibung eines Kampfes." Franz Kafka, *Beschreibung eines Kampfes: Die zwei Fassungen*, ed. Ludwig Dietz (Frankfurt am Main: S. Fischer Verlag, 1969). All quotations are my own translations from this edition. References with page number will be marked parenthetically in the text as BK. For a comparison of the two versions of "Beschreibung eines Kampfes," see Judith Ryan, "Die zwei Fassungen der 'Beschreibung

eines Kampfes.' Zur Entwicklung von Kafkas Erzähltechnik," in *Jahrbuch der deutschen Schillergesellschaft* 14 (1970): 546–72.

8. "Kafka's Poetics of the Inner Self," *Modern Austrian Literature,* Special Franz Kafka Issue, 11(3/4) (1978): 37–58.

9. Cf. Walter H. Sokel, *Franz Kafka: Tragik und Ironie: Zur Struktur seiner Kunst* (Munich-Vienna: Albert Langen-Georg Müller, 1964; paperback edition Frankfurt am Main: Fischer Taschenbuch Verlag, 1976). See also Sokel, *Franz Kafka,* Columbia Essays, passim.

10. Letter of July 5, 1922, *Briefe,* 384.

11. *Briefe,* 385.

12. The first version of "Beschreibung eines Kampfes" dates from 1904/1905. (See Malcolm Pasley and Klaus Wagenbach, "Datierung sämtlicher Texte Franz Kafkas," in *Kafka Symposion: Datierung Funde Materialien,* ed. Jürgen Born et al. [Berlin: Verlag Klaus Wagenbach, 1965], 58.) There can, therefore, be no question of influence by Freud's treatise on narcissism, which was published in 1914. I should like to emphasize that I am not concerned here with the problematic concept of "influence" but rather with structural analogies that are extremely suitable to help illuminate Kafka's literary beginnings. What Freud understood by the term "narcissism" had already been an important preoccupation in the literature of the Dual Monarchy at the turn of the century, as seen in works such as Leopold von Andrian's *Garden of Knowledge* (*Garten der Erkenntnis*), Beer-Hofmann's *The Death of Georg* (*Der Tod Georgs*), and above all Hugo von Hofmannsthal's lyric poetry, poetic plays, and *The Fairy Tale of the 672nd Night* (*Märchen der 672. Nacht*). A thorough exploration of Kafka's Hofmannsthal reception has, to my knowledge, not yet been attempted but would surely yield significant insights. Interesting parallels exist, for instance, between Hofmannsthal's "The Emperor of China Speaks" ("Der Kaiser von China spricht") and Kafka's figure of the Fat Man in "Description of a Struggle." A first step toward an investigation of the Hofmannsthal-Kafka link can be found in Klaus Wagenbach's biography of Kafka (*Franz Kafka: Eine Biographie seiner Jugend. 1883–1912* [Bern: Francke Verlag, 1958], 121).

13. Cf. the discussion of narcissism in *Totem and Taboo.*

14. Sigmund Freud, *Studienausgabe,* Vol. 3, 43.

15. Ibid.

16. *Studienausgabe,* Vol. 9, 375.

17. *Hochzeitsvorbereitungen auf dem Lande und andere Prosa aus dem Nachlaß,* Gesammelte Werke, ed. Max Brod (New York: Schocken Books, 1953), 348. Henceforth this volume will be cited as H.

18. However, death in narration is not the restoration of a past, as in the death wish of Freud's *Beyond the Pleasure Principle,* but a radically new condition, even though it derives from and continues what has come before.

19. On the parallelism between the I-narrator and the figures of the Fat Man and Supplicant or "Praying Man," cf. Judith Ryan's exemplary analysis, "Die zwei Fassungen," 561–62. Also Sokel, *Tragik,* ch. 1, and Henry Sussman, *Franz Kafka: Geometrician of Metaphor* (Madison, Wis.: Coda Press, 1979), 62.

20. In the original version, formal-generic considerations are even more obvious. The narrator emphasizes narrative objectivity by shifting from the first to the third person and substituting "a young man" for himself as the hero of his tale. Narration serves detachment from and subordination of self.

21. Cf. Kafka's aphorism: "For anything outside the sensory world language can be used only allusively. . . ." (H 45).

22. Cf. *Being and Time,* Introduction, ch. 2, par. 7.

23. Concerning the father- and power-figure of Kafka's oeuvre, cf. Fred Peters, *The Transformation of the Father Image in the Works of Franz Kafka,* M.A. thesis, Columbia University, 1963 (Typescript); and Sokel, *Tragik,* passim.

24. Cf. Edmund Wilson, *The Wound and the Bow: Seven Studies in Literature* (Boston: Houghton Mifflin, 1941).

25. This sublimation of suffering is initially linked to the interiorization of eros. The narrator's sudden thought of being loved by a girl in a white dress helps him attain his first success in overcoming gravity. The text has not mentioned this girl before. On the contrary, the reader is made to think that the narrator is an unloved, totally solitary bachelor. Consequently, the girl in white might very well be understood as purely imaginary, as a mere function of the narrator's need.

26. The vultures, variants of the Promethean eagle, foreshadow Kafka's brief tale "The Vulture" as well as his version of the Prometheus myth. They seem to represent a threat to the acquaintance lying helplessly on the rocks. In a fit of "generosity," however, the narrator merely commands them to guard the vanquished Other.

27. Gerhard Kurz, *Traum-Schrecken: Kafkas Literarische Existenzanalyse* (Stuttgart: J. B. Metzler, 1980), 14. Quoted in my translation.

28. In the later version of his text, Kafka drastically reduced the conflict between the voice and the self. The original version describes in great detail the narrator's frantic efforts to ward off and suppress the intruding voice.

29. *Anatomy of Criticism: Four Essays* (1957, 1971; repr. Princeton: Princeton University Press, 1973), 42, 46.

30. Tzvetan Todorov, *The Fantastic: A Structural Approach to a Literary Genre* (Ithaca, N.Y.: Cornell University Press, 1975; Cleveland: Case Western Reserve University Press, 1973). Translated from the French by Richard Howard, with a foreword by Robert Scholes. (Original French version *Introduction à la littérature fantastique* [Paris: Editions du Seuil, 1970]).

31. Cf. Franz Kafka, *Briefe an Felice und andere Korrespondenz aus der Verlobungszeit,* ed. Erich Heller and Jürgen Born. (Frankfurt am Main: S. Fischer Lizenzausgabe von Schocken Books, New York, 1967), 394.

9

PERSPECTIVES AND TRUTH IN "THE JUDGMENT"

"THE JUDGMENT," the work of Kafka's "breakthrough" of September 1912, is thematically, i.e., in terms of mythos or plot content, a continuation of his earliest extant work, "Description of a Struggle" (1904–05). In the frame story of that work, an engaged young man comes to grief under the influence of a bachelor. In the inner story, the Fat Man is separated from the girl he dates by the appearance of a weird, solitary figure, the Praying Man. He comes under the latter's spell and is subsequently drowned—a striking anticipation of Georg Bendemann's fate. Six years after "Description of a Struggle," in a diary entry of July 1910, Kafka describes an encounter between a party-going, socially "engaged" young man, who is the narrator, and a hideously pathetic bachelor in whom the narrator anticipates the perilous eventuality for his own development. The threat of drowning appears here as an analogy to the bachelor's dangerous clutch on the narrator. "The Judgment" carries this theme farther. Here the engaged protagonist, Georg Bendemann, actually drowns himself as a consequence of his bachelor friend's "alliance" with the protagonist's father. Proclaiming himself the "representative" (Kafka 1970, 30)[1] of his son's bachelor friend, the father accuses Georg and ultimately condemns him to death by drowning.

The introduction of the father into the conflict between bachelor and

From *The Problem of "The Judgment": Eleven Approaches to Kafka's Story*, ed. Angel Flores (New York: Gordian Press, 1977), 193–237. Some of the ideas expressed in this paper were first presented in my book *Franz Kafka: Tragik und Ironie* (1964) and monograph *Franz Kafka* (1966), but have been thoroughly revised, reformulated, expanded, and combined with new ideas.

engaged man ties "The Judgment" to an even earlier period of Kafka's writing. In a diary entry of January 1911, Kafka outlines the plan of a novel, conceived in his childhood or earliest youth, that was to relate the fate of two brothers, one of whom had emigrated to America, while the other stayed at home, imprisoned (Kafka 1948, 39 f.). The two childhood friends of "The Judgment" easily appear as a later variant of the two brothers of the early project. Like brothers, Georg Bendemann and his friend descend from the same womb—shared native city and common past. Corresponding to one of the two brothers, Georg stayed at home, while his friend, counterpart of the other brother, emigrated into exile. In "The Judgment," the empire in the East, Russia, replaces the Western continent of the planned novel, which reappears at the same time as "The Judgment," in Kafka's new novel, *Der Verschollene,* which Brod called *Amerika.* But what in particular connects the two friends of "The Judgment" with the brothers of the early plan is the presence of the father.[2] While no father is mentioned for the planned novel, in "The Judgment" Georg and his friend function like Old Bendemann's two sons. Old Bendemann says of the friend that he would be a son after his own heart, while he terms his actual son a "devilish human being," who has to be condemned to die. We learn nothing about the friend's family. For all we know his only ties are to Georg's family. Nor are we supplied any reasons for his original discontent that made him "flee" to Russia. He functions only as an alternative to Georg's way of coming to grips with a frustrating home situation that he had experienced prior to his mother's death. In a letter to his fiancée-to-be, Felice Bauer, Kafka himself pointed out that the friend should not be seen as an autonomous character, but as the common element between father and son.

> The story is perhaps an inspection tour around father and son, and the changing figure of the friend is perhaps the perspectivistic change in the relations between father and son. (Heller and Born 1967, 397)

Both in the early planned novel and in "The Judgment," one member of each pair is "good" and the other "bad," but the criteria of evaluation are reversed. In the early novel plan the brother who stayed at home in prison was to be the good one, while the one who had left would be bad. Now, if we take Old Bendemann's perspective as our standard of evaluation, the opposite prevails. The friend who emigrated into exile is the ideal son; his exile and misery serve as equivalents for the good brother's imprisonment at home. But the stay-at-home, Georg, now corresponds to the "bad brother." According to the father's judgment, he is a bad friend and a diabolical son. This shift in moral evaluation is easy to explain. The two friends, read "brothers," represent two alternative attitudes toward home and origin, translated into two contrasting life styles.

Georg and his friend started out with an identical discontent with their situation at home. The word "discontent" is explicitly mentioned only in reference to the friend. However, as we are cursorily told, his father's overpowering, self-willed nature that forced his own opinion on everyone around him had overshadowed Georg's youth: profound "discontent" is thus implied in his life, too. The two young men's reactions to this discontent, however, are markedly different. The friend "practically fled" his native land. The word "fled," Georg's word, only slightly weakened by the qualifier "practically" (*förmlich*), implies extreme frustration, even fear. Usually one "flees" a scene posing danger. Georg too could have removed himself from his father's domain by following his friend's example and explicit invitation to join him in exile. The friend had urged Georg to come, for the last time when Georg's mother died. But upon his wife's death, the father's powers began to wane. The giant's apparent decline permitted Georg to rise rapidly in the family business and he began to take it over. Given the father's self-willedness, an Oedipal combat seemed likely to result from the son's option to stay in the father's domain. The friend showed a possible way out that Georg chose not to follow.

Georg and his friend, it must be said here parenthetically, correspond to the two sides of the fundamental choice that Kafka had seen confronting him all his life. Kafka presented himself as split between the bachelor's ascetic hermitlike withdrawal from the world and the wish to engage himself fully in it, with particular stress on the obligation to marry and raise a family. In "The Judgment" he depicted this split most clearly in the two representative antagonists—Georg's friend, the bachelor in Russia, and Georg himself, engaged to "a girl of a well-to-do family" (Kafka 1970, 25).[3] Essentially Kafka himself veered toward the friend's way.[4] In his "Letter to His Father," written more than seven years after "The Judgment," he depicts himself as one who had to withdraw from his father's realm and presence. Given a progenitor as tyrannically self-righteous and as brimming over with robust vitality as Herrmann Kafka, the weakling sensitive son's only possibility for survival was flight. In his diaries, Kafka also compares himself to one exiled by his father from Canaan, the land of fertility and life, to the desert, a region not dissimilar to the desolate solitude of the friend's Russian existence. Only eight months prior to his writing of "The Judgment," Kafka links the terms "Russian" and "friend." "Russian" describes the most extreme loneliness that results from having removed oneself from one's family into an isolation more thorough "than the most distant journeys can achieve." Then, he adds, "you have lived through an experience of solitude so extreme by European standards that it can only be termed Russian" (Kafka 1948, 233). The link to the friend is expressed in the paradoxical afterthought that this loneliness is heightened by dropping in late at night on "a friend" to see how he is doing. In this strange link of "Russian" and "friend" we can see the seed of this enigmatic figure of "The Judgment."[5]

But Kafka's own engagements distinguish him from the friend and link him to Georg. The writing of "The Judgment" followed soon upon Kafka's first meeting, in August 1912, with Felice Bauer, about whom he noted in his diary that he had formed "an unshakeable judgment" (Kafka 1948, 185). As Politzer points out, it could not have been a judgment about her, but only "a judgment of himself" in relation to her.[6] The story is dedicated to Felice Bauer and carries her initials in the name of Georg's fiancée, Frieda Brandenfeld. This name is also an allusion to Felice's residence in Berlin, as Berlin is the capital of the province of Brandenburg. Kafka's professional career as an official in an insurance agency, which kept him in daily touch with the world of industry; his helping out in his family's factory and his, albeit most reluctant, partnership in it; his staying in his native city and continuing to live, as an adult of marriageable age, in his father's household—all these facts point to close analogies with Georg Bendemann. Kafka made his identification with his protagonist clear when he pointed out that "Georg" had the same number of letters as "Franz," the "Bende" had as many letters as "Kafka," and that the vowel "e" is repeated in "Bende" exactly at the same place as is "a" in Kafka.

In this connection, a striking structural analogy between "The Judgment" and one of Kafka's autobiographical observations should be mentioned. Georg's fall from a considerable height of achievement, repeated later by Josef K., and to a lesser extent Gregor Samsa, has its analogue in Kafka's recounting of his forebodings of doom in the face of any success of his, no matter how modest. Shortly before writing "The Judgment," he records in his diary that as a child and adolescent he had been convinced of having only temporarily postponed disaster whenever he had managed to pass an examination or was promoted to the next grade in school. Any success had to be short-lived because it was based on a "swindle" (Kafka 1948, 225) and entailed catastrophic exposure to come. For him "the great manly future" appeared as an impossibility, and any provisional sign of it must be a façade hiding a terrifying failure soon to be revealed. Kafka thought he would be "found out" sooner rather than later, but in any case eventually, and would marvel that he could have come as far as he had. In the "Letter to His Father," he attributes this utter lack of self-confidence to his father's threatening presence in his life, a circumstance that establishes an even closer analogy to "The Judgment." The difference between the author's forebodings, as described by him, and his protagonist's fate is of course even more significant. Kafka expected the "unmasking" that Georg experiences as an unforeseen blow. Unlike his creator, Georg does not perceive the provisional façade, which all worldly success axiomatically represented for Kafka; he lives it.

Although its roots can be traced to Kafka's own life, the juxtaposition of Georg and the friend must be viewed in more universal terms. The friend functions not only psychically, as a rejected possibility for Georg, but also socially, morally, and existentially as the choice of a noneconomic way of life, an existence defined by the rejection of the struggle for power as its guiding principle. It is Elias Canetti's merit to have pointed out the drive for power, and its radical condemnation, as Kafka's central concern.[7] It is the conflict between the son's drive for self-assertion and the father's insistence on the absolute dominance of his will that ended the golden age of harmony that had at one time existed in the Bendemann family. The origin of discord in "The Judgment" offers a significant parallel to Kafka's "Letter to His Father." The letter is an indictment of the father's stifling and crippling influence on the son's natural need for independence and ego-development. By the sheer weight of his personality and largely unconscious "pedagogy," the father had thwarted and deflected the son's growth as a person. In "The Judgment" this deflection of the will to assert himself is split off from the protagonist and embodied in the friend. Georg, on the other hand, asserts the will to attain his "great manly future" and takes up the struggle for succession to the father's role with a directness that his author never dared or desired to assume. He represents an unrealized tendency lurking in the writer of the "Letter to His Father."

By the same token, the two hostile "friends" or "brothers" of "The Judgment" represent two universal possibilities for human existence. These possibilities can be expressed in terms borrowed from Freud's *Totem and Taboo,* a work written almost simultaneously with "The Judgment";[8] but they can also be couched into socioeconomic, existential, and religious terms. In the terms of *Totem and Taboo,* the friend's way parallels the wifeless sons whom the father of the Primal Horde to whom all the women belong deprives of sexual fulfillment and casts out into the wilderness, while Georg corresponds to one of the unsuccessful challengers of the primal father who, too weak to overcome him, is defeated and killed before the father in turn is killed one day by the band of rebellious brothers. Transcending the framework of the Oedipal combat, the friend represents the way of the ascetic and holy man, the way of the monk loyal to the three vows: poverty (his business failures), chastity (his bachelorhood), and obedience (his self-removal from any chance of rivalry with the fathers). He comes in touch with the sphere of spirit and religion. It is in connection with the friend that Kafka introduces into "The Judgment" the single reference to a priest. Moreover, this priest embodies a religion of self-mortification. He cuts a "broad cross of blood into the palm of his hand" (Kafka 1970,

29). The image adumbrates Georg's self-punishment in obedience to his father. The attribute "broad" unites the cross and Georg's father whom Georg sees as "broad"—"How broad he is, sitting there" (Kafka 1970, 27)—until it forges the semiotic link between the symbol of martyrdom and holiness on the one hand, and Georg's father whom Georg's ultimate act of obedience reveals as being "the cross" his son bears. At the same time the image also points to a larger tradition in which the religious life entails celibacy, asceticism, and mortification of the flesh. It likewise alludes to the existential exposure into which the friend ventured when he took the step of exiling himself and "fleeing" the bourgeois circumstances in which Georg has opted to remain. For the friend's Russia, which, as Georg insists on reminding us, is not identical with the actual country of that name, is a realm of disquiet, turbulence, savage mobs, and spiritual fanaticism. It is a place far too unstable for the friend to leave in order to journey back home into the snug comforts of Central or Western European respectability.

In all these respects, Georg at first seems to be the opposite of the friend. By choosing to stay at home, trying to succeed his father, he has followed the ways of the modern bourgeois. His engagement is a token of his socioeconomic success, as the emphasis on the financial standing of his fiancée's family clearly underlines. To put it more precisely, both the socioeconomic and the sexual realm represent areas of the—in the broadest sense—"political" sphere, the arena in which the struggle for power takes place. The appearance, in contrast to the substance, of a woman's love is essential for the exercise of power in Kafka's world, as is evident in "Description of a Struggle," where the mere mention of being engaged, or the mere thought of being loved by a girl, suffices to boost the combatant's position decisively. Marriage then is the sign of physical power and worldly success; it is the most visible evidence of male strength and a primary means of its exercise. Georg has to wait for his mother's death to make his ego felt in the father's business, because immediately upon the loss of his wife, his father weakens and begins to decline. Yet, the socioeconomic aspect of power has priority over the erotic in "The Judgment." Georg's apparent supplanting of his father in the firm antedates his engagement. The economic sphere determines the nature of the Oedipal conflict. It is as economic man that Georg stands in opposition to his father and to his friend. It is in the business that he first perceives his father as one who blocks him; and by his economic success he automatically assumes an antagonistic position vis-à-vis his father whom he threatens to overshadow. It is from the vantage point of his bourgeois success that Georg looks down upon his childhood friend and senses his increasing alienation from him.

Georg has assumed a patronizing stance toward the friend. In his reflections on their relationship, which initiate the story, Georg dwells on the friend's poverty, economic ineptitude, and social isolation, from which his other peculiarities and above all his "adaptation to permanent bachelordom" derive. In Georg's eyes resignation to remaining a bachelor only crowns an existence of total failure. His friend had ended in a cul-de-sac, as we might translate Georg's term "*verrannt.*" It is from the perspective of the successful bourgeois that Georg judges his friend's life to be a failure. As he looks down physically upon the world at his feet—street, river, bridge, and nature at the opposite bank—he looks down socially upon the friend's exile. Separating him inwardly from the childhood friend, his bourgeois outlook alienates Georg from his own childhood and past that, in a certain sense, stay embodied in the distant friend. Precisely because of his total failure in bourgeois terms, the friend has remained in touch with the characteristics of childhood. His lack of means would make him a dependent if he were to return home, his celibacy keeps him in the condition of sexual immaturity, and his social ineptness illustrates his unfamiliarity with the conventions that rule adult society. The ultimate sign of this permanent immaturity is of course his inability to found a household of his own. The German word for bachelor, "Junggeselle," includes the word "young" and thus graphically conveys the friend's near-childlikeness. In the friend is preserved Georg's link to his own childhood, otherwise apparent only in his tie to his father. Everything points to the friend's emblematic connection with childhood. Although he wears a "fremdartige Vollbart" (foreign-looking beard), this token of masculinity can only poorly conceal "the face well-familiar since childhood days" (Kafka 1970, 23). For Georg the friend has remained "an old child." Like a child, he would simply have to obey his successful friends who had remained at home (Kafka 1970, 23).[9] This condescension toward the friend betokens the loosening of Georg's bonds to his own past. This self-alienation surfaces in the frequent occurrence of the word or syllable "fremd" ("alien" and "strange") in the two paragraphs describing Georg's thoughts about his friend.

Georg's bourgeois perspective on the friend, and therewith on his own childhood, with which the story opens, also establishes Georg's life as a façade existence hiding unacknowledged realities. To show this fully, it will be necessary to return for a moment to the earlier versions of the bachelor-engaged man conflict. In the frame story of "Description of a Struggle," the narrative perspective is still that of the bachelor, who also functions as the narrator. In the inner story, which the Fat Man relates to the narrator, the perspective briefly shifts to the "engaged," i.e., dating, partner of the struggle. This shift is fully worked out in the diary entry of July 1910. There the socially engaged, party-going narrator views the lonely bachelor with distaste and anxiety, and yet with fascination. With the same apprehensive concern, Georg Bendemann looks down on his bachelor friend in Russia. In both diary scene and "The Judgment," a sense of mortal danger emanates from the bachelor. However, in the diary scene, the engaged protagonist explicitly acknowledges the danger; it forms the topic of his conversation and reflections. The decisive switch in "The Judgment," two years later, lies in the protagonist's failure to admit the peril that the bachelor's existence constitutes. The shift from first- to third-person narrative facilitates the presentation of a rift between admitted and unacknowledged elements in the protagonist's attitude toward the bachelor. This rift between conscious acknowledgment and actual behavior constitutes the real "breakthrough" toward the narrative structure that we have come to call "Kafkaesque" and that, among other things, is a masterful and unique exposition of the bad faith lodged in consciousness.

Georg Bendemann's fear of a menace from the exiled bachelor can only be inferred, but never proved. It can be inferred from Georg's attempts to keep the friend away from himself. However, Georg never admits this as his motive. Instead he claims that it is his solicitude for the friend's feelings that makes him wish he would not come back. He reasons that his friend's self-esteem would be shattered if he were to return and witness the successes achieved by his friends at home. But the friend's presumed feelings of offended self-respect are only attributed to him by Georg. They are feelings imagined by Georg but not necessarily felt by the friend. Georg, however, fails to make this thought process clear to himself. Neither does the narrator ever intervene to inform the reader of Georg's mental maneuverings. Georg's arguments resemble a sleight-of-hand. He projects onto his friend what he wants to prove, and then reasons as though his projections were fact. By imputing to his friend his own bourgeois criteria for self-esteem, he persuades himself and us that it would be in the friend's interest to stay away. He builds up in his mind a bogus "friend" for whose sake he displays great delicacy of feeling that, by the nature of the case, has to be spurious. For Georg persuades himself that he tries to spare feelings that, as far as the text shows us, exist only in his imagination.[10] The friend's real feelings remain unknown to us. Georg, however, utilizes these imagined feelings to argue against the real friend's reappearance.

Georg's deliberate self-deception, which is the essence of bad faith in the Sartrian sense of the term, arises from his ambivalence toward the friend. Despite his wish to keep him in distant Russia, he continues to write to him regularly. Something in Georg attaches him to the friend and prevents him from making a clean break with this exiled remnant of his past. But something else in him disallowed this channel to the past to remain honestly open. This unadmitted and unresolved conflict between two tendencies in Georg, one for keeping the bond to the friend and the other against it, makes for a structure of his behavior that closely resembles the structure of the human psyche as Freud described it in *The Interpretation of Dreams, The Psychopathology of Everyday Life,* and *Wit and Its Relation to the Unconscious.* There is no evidence that Kafka had read any particular work or works by Freud; but there is no doubt that he had absorbed Freudian thought by the time he wrote "The Judgment," particularly as he noted "thoughts of Freud" as "naturally" accompanying his composition of "The Judgment" (Kafka 1948, 294).[11] Georg's behavior toward the friend resembles the quasi-ludicrous character of Freudian "slips" or accidents. Georg cannot bring himself to tell the friend of his engagement. He conceals the fact from the friend, thus acting like the repressive Freudian "censor." Yet he cannot help writing to him three times in a row about the "engagement of an unimportant girl" until the friend, made curious by this "slip," begins to show interest in it.

Georg also conceals his economic success from his friend. As in the case of his engagement, he thereby inadvertently reveals his own unadmitted negative thoughts toward both tokens of success. While pretending that he would find these negative thoughts in his friend's mind (for instance wretchedness and "discontent" if informed of Georg's forthcoming wedding), he suppressed the fact that these thoughts are only in his own mind, since we get no evidence of the friend's actual thoughts on these matters.

This highly critical view of both business career and impending marriage is a part of himself that Georg will not acknowledge. At least to his friend, Georg still seeks to appear as the unsuccessful bachelor he had once been. His letters perpetuate the image of a son innocent of the recent successes that have made him his father's threatening rival. Having chosen to challenge his father by following the route of economic man and sexual maturity, he yet wants to retain a realm in which his earlier, pure, childlike self can be preserved. Georg's bad faith lies in his unwillingness either to allow this bachelor self to persist as a true reality or to give it up entirely. Instead he abstracts this self to an idea in the mind of his friend. As the course of the plot shows, his tie to his friend will prove, in the end, much stronger than his desire for marriage and his ambition to succeed economically. But as the story opens, Georg seeks to indulge adult and bachelor self simultaneously by the device of keeping his actual life separate from the idea of his "pure" self. Reflecting the constancy of "existential symbols" in Kafka's work, the abode for this image of the bachelor self is the vast Northern empire of Russia, associated with those regions of cold, winter, and snow in which, from "Description of a Struggle" to *The Castle,* Kafka's bachelor figure finds his being.

By insisting on this split Georg exhibits bad faith in both directions. He indulges the adult's sexual appetite, but only furtively, shamefacedly, keeping it hidden from his "pure" friend, while at the same time degrading his friend by attempting to keep him as the mere receptacle for his own self-image. In this light his father is right when he accuses Georg of having known "only of yourself" (Kafka 1970, 32), of having approached his fiancée only "because she lifted her skirts" (Kafka 1970, 30), i.e., for sheer lewd self-gratification, and of having tried to "get his friend down" so that he could "sit on him with his behind" and immobilize him.[12] This is precisely what Georg does. He "sits" on the actual person, whom he shuts out from visibility, and substitutes for him a carrier of his own ideas, feelings, and desires.

Georg's "repression" of the friend manifests itself most obviously in the form of the deception that his letters perpetrate. Georg omits from them the essential truth of his present life—his financial successes and his intention to marry. His correspondence is a false façade, a "cover-up." His relation to his friend, and through him to his own past and "pure self," has become profoundly inauthentic. Georg is able to write only about "unimportant matters," making his "literature" an inessential enterprise. For Kafka only the most conscientious comprehensiveness could ever hope to approximate "truth" in literature, as in life, and truth alone was the ultimate, although practically unattainable, vindication for both. By having his protagonist practice in his letters the kind of deceit, based on self-serving selectivity, that Kafka attacked in other writers and above all in himself, he conveyed his condemnation of this character. The father's "judgment" of his son merely puts in explicit terms the author's "judgment."

In "Wedding Preparations in the Country," the giant beetle into which Raban transforms himself in his dream sends his human façade out to do his work in the world. In "Description of a Struggle," the bachelor-narrator reduces the engaged man to the status of a horse, which transports him into a landscape that reflects the wishes of his imagination. In both cases the imagination debases physical reality by making it serve as the instrument of its self-gratification. In "The Judgment," Georg Bendemann repeats the process, but reverses the roles. He, the engaged man, exploits his bachelor friend, to be no more than the repository of the dream of chastity and purity that his actual life has betrayed. The narrator ironically highlights Georg's unacknowledged subjectivity in regard to the friend's feelings, when he lets us have that rare glimpse into the actual friend's behavior, which we have already mentioned. By making the friend evince an unexpected interest in the "engagement" of "an unimportant girl," which Georg had mentioned to him three times in a row, the narrator suggests that the real friend might be less hostile to the idea of engagement and marriage than Georg makes him out to be. There is here also the innuendo of a possible revenge threatened by the friend, which would account for Georg's "disquiet" at the friend's interest.

Typical of Georg's hidden repressive design on the friend is his unwitting self-revelation in musing about the friend's possible return. No one, he thinks, would "intentionally suppress" him—or "repress" or "oppress" or "depress," since the German word "niedergedrückt" has all four meanings—if he were to come back. The insertion, "not intentionally," gives Georg away. It shows that he has to defend himself in advance against the accusation that "someone" might "oppress" his friend "on purpose." It is easy to see that this "someone" is of course Georg himself. He literally anticipates his father's subsequent charge of his having tried "to get his friend down." We might add that Georg never denies the charge. His final answer to it is suicide.

The other side of the coin is his concealment of his engagement, which makes the latter appear as something shameful for which he feels guilty, at least toward that aspect of his existence that the friend represents. Indeed, in his conversation with Frieda Brandenfeld, as remembered by him, he admits that their engagement was their "guilt" (Kafka 1970, 25). "If you have such friends, Georg, you should not have become engaged at all," Frieda tells him, whereupon he answers: "Yes, that is the guilt of both of us" (Kafka 1970, 25). (The English translation fails to bring out the word "guilt" present in the original German.) J. P. Stern raises the question: "Is [Georg] guilty because he intends to get married?" and then claims that we cannot answer because we know too little about Georg's relationship with his fiancée.[13] However, he overlooks the crucial fact that it is Georg himself who "answers" the question, first by hiding his engagement from his friend and then by literally declaring it to be "guilt." It is of course Georg's view alone that counts as the criterion for judgment in Kafka's tale.

Georg immediately covers up this admission of "guilt" by kissing his fiancée with an ardor that threatens to "choke" her. This scene is also structured in a manner reminiscent of a "Freudian slip." Georg has just concealed his guilt feeling about the engagement. He now seeks to erase the impression by adding an afterthought in which he emphatically affirms his engagement. "But now I would not have it otherwise," he adds. The ambivalence of his protagonist, which Kafka himself eminently shared, as his *Letters to Felice* show, requires the cancellation of any "truth" by the assertion of a "countertruth." However, the now suppressed "truth" continues to have its effects. It manifests itself in the very act of being denied. Georg's kisses, which are to bury his guilt feeling about his engagement, turn out to be so excessively impetuous that they threaten to "suffocate" his fiancée and thus to do away with the object and cause of his "guilt." That is, the real intent of Georg's feelings expressed in the word "guilt," but repressed by his "change of mind"—"now I would not have it otherwise"—reemerges in the guise of an overzealous display of affection. The very manifestation of his love acts as both a cover-up and an unacknowledged expression of his true hostility toward the fellow conspirator in his "guilt."

Even prior to this, the text, as we have seen, revealed a "Freudian slip" of Georg's feelings about his engagement. We have already remarked that Georg, instead of informing his friend about his own engagement, reported the engagement of an "unimportant fellow" to an "unimportant girl" (Kafka 1970, 25). By the narrator's choice of the word "unimportant" ("gleichgültig") in describing Georg's thinking, the unimportance of his engagement is inadvertently revealed. For what the use of the word "unimportant" lets show here obliquely will later emerge as Georg's truth. In the decisive confrontation with his father, Georg can no longer think of Frieda but only of his friend. The father ironically challenges his son to summon Frieda to his aid, but Georg cannot even live up to the challenge. Frieda fails to move him in the crucial encounter in contrast to the friend who "gripped him as never before" (Kafka 1970, 30), but whom he has lost. The father boasts that he will simply "sweep" the girl "off [Georg's] side." But Georg himself has already accomplished what the father predicts. He fails to have Frieda in his heart and therefore does not have her by his side to call on her for aid. Not his bond to Frieda but his tie to his friend is shown to be Georg's true or essential self. His engagement turns out to be no more important to him than the engagement of the "unimportant" couple he had reported to his friend.

By entering his father's room instead of sending off to his friend the letter that was finally to announce his engagement, Georg obtains the verdict of "guilty" on this engagement, which he himself had uttered spontaneously, but then had failed to face and acknowledge. We note a phenomenon of crucial importance for the structure of "The Judgment"—the two-layered duality of perspectives linguistically expressed by the coincidence of literal and figurative, or basic and derived, meanings of certain crucial words. Georg seeks to give to his word "Schuld" ("guilt") a superficial and casual meaning according to which it would convey something like "that was our fault." The father, however, applies the full force of the literal meaning of "Schuld" as a debt that has to be paid and an offense that has to be atoned for. This layered semantic duality of perspectives corresponds to the multiplicity of layers comprising Georg's attitude toward his father that the encounter with him lays bare.

First of all, we discern a striking parallelism in Georg's relationship to the two figures who dominate each half of the story—friend and father. The earliest points discernible in each relationship represent an era of closeness and harmony. In Georg's early youth, he had been the true friend of his friend. At the same time, his father had loved him; he had been the pride of his parents, and had loved them in return, as we learn at the end of the story. That was a happy, harmonious time; the natural order of things, an original state of paradise, seemed to prevail. The beginning of Georg's alienation from both his friend and his father marked the fall. Georg's contempt for his friend's failures has its complement in his growing indifference toward his father that marks the period between his mother's death and his entrance into his father's room. He had separated his life from his father and seems to have become autonomous. For a young man preoccupied with the rapid progress of his business and his own career, there is no reason to set foot in an aged father's room. His father has simply receded from Georg's consciousness, and significantly he is mentioned only once in the story prior to Georg's abrupt and apparently unmotivated entrance into his room. Before that, the son had paid scant attention to his father's physical decline, was unaware of the sorry state of his cleanliness and bodily care, and had not realized the gloom enveloping the room in the back of the apartment. Occupying the bright and wholesome front room, Georg had not bothered to look after his father's condition. It never occurred to him to question the propriety of the occupancy of the two rooms: this spatial structure eloquently expresses the change in status between father and son. The father is literally relegated to the back, pushed into the background, and the son has literally become the front, the representative of the family toward the world. It is he, and not his father, who is greeted with respect from the street below, a sign of deference to family and firm that is no longer given to the father, but to the son.

Yet this reversal of roles is not a conscious rebellion. That is, Georg does not permit himself to view it as such. His indifference to and neglect of his father are allowed to appear as explicit revolt and hatred after the father literally "uncovers" them as such. A thoughtlessly accepted development, the "natural" pushing aside of the aged parent by the ambitious child becomes a rebellion with a parricidal wish only after the father's perspective is focused on it. It takes the father's accusatory "resurrection" in his bed to make the son's potentially murderous hatred explicit. Implicitly the Oedipal displacement of father by son had been present as soon as the father withdrew his full energies from the business and the son jumped, "decisively," to use his own word, into the power vacuum thus created. From the perspective of the son this was a natural assertion of the normal adult ego. From the perspective of the father, it entailed a criminal displacement of the rightful chief of family and firm. The father accuses Georg of having perpetrated, or at least having caused or allowed, "certain things" to occur in the business "that were not nice" (Kafka 1970, 27). The father alludes to information having been withheld from him and his rightful control over the firm having been undermined. The reader cannot determine the factual "truth" of this. Nor is that the point of Kafka's story. The point lies in the father's automatically assuming an accusatory view of the natural succession of the generations. Important is not the factual and legal question. Whether or not "things that aren't nice" have actually occurred is not important. What matters is Georg's "decisive" stepping into his father's shoes. That by itself is "the thing that isn't nice," the change that should never have occurred, and that cries out for retribution, "some day—sooner than you think" (Kafka 1970, 27). In Kafka's world, natural man, who is identical with economic man, stands condemned by the paternal perspective. The father in "The Judgment" assumes the perspective of Shakespeare in *King Lear.* For all his foolish caprice and self-willed stubbornness, the old king is justified as soon as the rebellion against him breaks out, precisely because this rebellion, as Edmund sees it, is an assertion of mere nature—"Thou, nature, art my goddess; to thy law my services are bound" (*King Lear,* I.2, lines 1–2)—against the sanctified law that protects the privilege of feeble old age as it espouses lawful wedlock against natural lust. As in *King Lear,* nature in "The Judgment" stands condemned from the perspective of a higher law. In nature the brute strength of youth prevails over the wielders of authority who are weakened by age. But in the eyes of another law, external to nature and opposed to it, the natural process itself becomes guilty. Georg's neglect of his father is "natural" and to be expected from a young businessman intent on the pursuit of the battle for survival and success, in that extension of Darwinian nature that is modern capitalist society. But it literally becomes a crime when looked at by Georg's father. Decisive is Georg's taking over and incorporating into himself his father's accusatory view of natural self-assertion. A declining father's displacement by an energetic son, sanctioned and justified by the natural order of the Darwinian age, will then be revealed as Luciferian revolt and parricide.

It is this duality of perspectives that has to be kept in mind if we are to understand what makes the father's "uncovering" a revelation of the truth, and what kind of truth it is that is revealed. The coinciding of two perspectives—one "natural" and the other parental—is inseparably linked to the division within Georg between his "natural" wish to assert his ego at his father's expense and his original self that lived in love and approval from his parents.[14] It is surely significant that Georg remembers once having been the object of his parents' pride. Side by side then with his growing independence and the neglect of his father, a solicitude persists that makes him accuse himself for his neglect. We encounter here the same dichotomy that we have seen displayed in his relationship to his friend. But since he does not acknowledge his negative feelings toward either father or friend, and fails to face his ambivalence honestly, its unacknowledged existence tends to make the positive feelings a façade in his mind that covers up the unacknowledged presence of negative sentiments. For instance, no sooner has Georg allowed himself to believe that his mother's death facilitated his rise by weakening his father, than he takes back the thought and covers it up by "blaming" accidental factors for his rapid ascent. Or as soon as he comes up against the damning thought that he had not set foot in his father's room for months, he at once adds the exculpating afterthought that there had indeed been no need to do so, since he meets his father regularly at meal times and also spends some evenings with him in the shared living room. Ironically, however, we learn that these evenings spent with his father can only nominally be viewed as time together, since each is absorbed with his own newspaper. The close parallel to Georg's letters immediately suggests itself. In both cases Georg maintains the semblance of a relationship, but its essence, its soul—genuine communication—has departed. His life with his father, outwardly a sign of filial loyalty, has become a façade hiding their essential isolation from each other. Georg's neglect of his father has become the actual and effective state of affairs, while his continuing solicitude literally appears as an afterthought. When he discovers the unclean condition of his father's underwear, he reproaches himself for having neglected the old man. His former affection still appears but it is now something negative—self-accusation. As with the letters to his friend, the unacknowledged simultaneous presence of two opposed wishes constitutes bad faith. Georg's continuing cohabitation with his father, like the continuing letters to the friend, has become a cover-up for his wish to be free. And his living a life of façade is expressed in terms of spatial logic by his occupying the *front* room of the common dwelling.

As in the relation to the friend, Georg's marriage would act as the final decision for a severance of the umbilical cord—his final separation from his father's household. Georg and his fiancée had tacitly assumed that they would leave his old apartment to his father. However, upon entering his father's room, and seeing his apparent decrepitude, Georg has to change his mind. His "duty" makes him decide to take his father along into the new household. There the son will be head and master, and his father a childlike dependent to be looked after. Georg's solicitude paradoxically causes his father's subjugation. With this, the meaning of his forthcoming marriage also changes. From a mere affirmation of the son's independence, it becomes the father's reduction to dependence, his unmanning, as it were. Georg's plan in itself constitutes a disenfranchisement of the old man. For the young man makes the decision without consulting his father's own wish and preference. Georg disposes of his future fate as though his father had no will and mind of his own, and his solicitude ironically turns into the instrument of its own negation. Loving care in intent, it is overthrow in effect. The nature of Georg's intended marriage is thus revealed as Oedipal revolt aiming at a reversal of roles between father and son, a symbolic slaying of the old by the young. Filial devotion turns out to be the cover-up under which displacement of the father may proceed.

This reversal of roles and the subsequent cover-up are literally enacted by Georg as he undresses his father, carries him to bed in his arms, and covers him "well." This covering of the father calls to mind the premature burials of still living fathers by impatient heirs, as exemplified in Schiller's drama *The Robbers*. Georg literally lays his father to rest and when his father lies finally "covered" it "seems" "well" done to Georg. The real meaning of this "covering" emerges soon thereafter when Georg explicitly wishes for his father's death. "If he were to fall and get smashed! This word hissed through his head" (Kafka 1970, 31). The subjunctive used in the German text expresses Georg's thought as a wish now unrestrained by the appearance of filial duty. The façade has burst open and bares the inner truth of his presumably solicitous actions. By uncovering himself and rising in his bed, the father explicitly refutes the son's cover-up as working well. At the same time, he uncovers the true content of Georg's devotion as murderous revolt.

The reader, sharing Georg's perspective, would object by insisting that the text shows that Georg has no intention of subjugating his father, that he is motivated merely by understandable alarm at his father's apparent deterioration, and that his subsequent thought of his father's death is only the reaction to the old man's "irrational" accusations, which in turn can be attributed to his senility.[15] We must therefore take a look at the father's appearance of senility as the crucial clue to the interpretation of "The Judgment."

The father's senility is seen by the reader from Georg's perspective. What is it then that makes us feel that Georg is justified in treating his father as though he were in need of special care and had, because of senility, lost the right to be consulted about his own fate? That he is toothless is a physical fact and does not necessarily entail mental decline. His "peculiarities" appear as the symptoms of an enfeebled organism when seen through Georg's eyes. They do not necessarily require such explanation, as we shall see. To be sure, Old Bendemann himself admits his loss of vigor, his weakening memory and decreased ability to pay full attention to the whole range and complexity of the business. However, the very insight allowing him to make such an admission also shows that he may yet be far from senile. The main impression of senility derives from one particular circumstance more than from any other. It is the father's question: "Do you really have this friend in Petersburg?" (Kafka 1970, 28). It is, however, Georg's reaction to the question rather than the question itself that suggests the father's senility.

The question is ambiguous. It could mean: "Is there a person in Petersburg whom you call your friend?" In that case, the question would address itself to a fact, and the father's asking would indicate loss of memory. For we know that Georg has been writing to such a person, and we also know that this person has visited the Bendemann home in the past. However, the question can also have another meaning. "Is this person whom you call friend truly your friend?" Then it would not relate to fact, but to meaning and to truth, if truth is, as Kafka often assumed it was, in regard to his writing, an adequate relationship between word and feeling, name and thing, language and existence. If taken in that deeper meaning, the question would imply not a loss of memory, but a search for truth. The text shows that truth rather than fact is the purport of the father's question. For before asking, he urges Georg to tell him "the full truth." Understood with this demand in mind, his question would have this sense: "Is there a person in Petersburg, to whom the term 'friend' applies in truth?" Then the answer must be negative. We have seen that Georg has stopped treating his friend as a true friend; he looks down upon him with patronizing contempt, has tried to forestall his possible return, and has deceived him. But Georg, and with him the reader, fails to perceive the other meaning of the father's question; i.e., he chooses to relate it only to the factual location in Petersburg of a person whom he *calls* "friend."

We see in these two interpretations of the father's question a bifurcation of perspectives that broadens and generalizes the semantic duality we have already touched upon in relation to the term "Schuld." The difference between Georg's and the father's understanding of the meaning of "friend in Petersburg" amounts to the distinction between an empiricism or positivism for which truth is fact and a spiritualism or idealism that searches for agreement between language and essence. Georg understands "friend" to be nothing but a person *called* "friend." His view of language is nominalistic. The conventionally accepted label suffices to designate the truth. The father, on the other hand, is concerned about the essence of "friend." Does the name correspond to "friendness," a view that implies the presence in language of a moral ideal or command to which we should conform and aspire?

The discrepancy between the two understandings of the word "friend" is closely relevant to Kafka's view of language and literature. Kafka aimed for an ideal of complete "correctness," i.e., the complete agreement between the emotion and the word used to convey it (Kafka 1948, 11). The agreement should be so thorough that no gap whatsoever would open between speaker and speech, or writer and sentence. Any distracting, extraneous element inserting itself between the speaker and his sentence or word, such as the aim for rhetorical effect, vitiates meaning and makes the statement untrue. Ideal speech and writing would reveal a truth in the sense of an intimate connectedness, an indissoluble link of every word with the speaker's or writer's life (Kafka 1948, 39). One should be able, Kafka says, to take one's writing to his breast, or be carried from his place by it (ibid.). He felt the word to be part of his flesh, part of himself (Kafka 1948, 77). It is in this sense that the father's searching question for Georg's meaning of the word "friend" has to be understood. Does a total agreement prevail between Georg's existence and his use of the word "friend"? Is there a friend in Petersburg to whom the word applies not as a mere rhetorical designation, or a cliché employed by habit, or a pretense of feeling no longer felt, but as a living reality equal to Georg's total being? The father asks for "the full truth" of Georg's friend *qua* friend, not for a label to which an incomplete or contradictory reality corresponds. Such a discrepancy would make the word "untrue." A speaker uttering a word for which he cannot supply in himself all the emotions corresponding to its meanings would, according to this perspective, be a liar.

The thought might suggest itself that we are dealing here with something akin to Platonism in which the word should be adequate to the concept or archetypal idea. Such a connection would be misleading. Kafka demands the total coincidence of the linguistic unit—word, sentence, paragraph, speech, story—not with a universal idea, preexisting and external to the speaker, but with the speaker's individual existence. At most one might call this an individuated, existential Platonism, if such were not a contradiction in terms. Yet precisely such a paradoxical formulation would be necessary to do justice to Kafka's view of language that is bound up with his idea of truth. A good example that closely relates to the dialogue between father and son in "The Judgment" is Kafka's stricture against the German-speaking Jews' false relationship to language, which implies a false relationship to themselves and their total existence. Not long before writing "The Judgment," Kafka reflected in his diary on his loveless attitude toward his mother. He tried to understand his lack of true love for her at least partly in a linguistic context. Between his actual Jewish mother and his feelings for her, the German language had interposed an alien emotional complex contained in the German word "Mutter." *Mutter* is associated with a very different world, a different "feel" and contrasting actuality of human relationships. Its use distorted the relationship between Franz and his Jewish mother that it was supposed to express. The word "Mutter" carried for Kafka a coldness, hauteur, and reserve alien to the warm affectionate atmosphere of the Jewish family. On the other hand, it brought with it also a kind of sentimentality incongruous with the particularly Jewish emotionalism that the speaker would intend to convey. "Christian" feelings were conjured up whenever the word "Mutter" was used. These imported a falsifying tone into the talks between Jewish mother and son. Eventually they marked and covered the original emotional reality of the Jewish son's life with his Jewish mother. "We give to a Jewish woman the German name 'mother,' but forget the contradiction [between them] which then sinks all the more heavily into our feeling" (Kafka 1948, 116). Since Kafka ties mind intimately to language, inauthentic language, i.e., language that inadequately conveys the speaker's external and inner life, makes for an inauthentic, inwardly divided existence. Expressing, as it does, the uprooting of the Westernized Jew, the use of German creates a façade that first covers and later alienates him from his original Jewish self. The significance of the friend's Russian, i.e., Eastern, domicile for the Judaic implications of "The Judgment" cannot be gone into here. But we can emphasize the analogy between the language-related duplicity that the Westernized Jew assumed for Kafka and the bad faith underlying the concept of his protagonist Georg Bendemann.[16] Georg's linguistic nominalism, evident in his superficial understanding of the word "friend," reveals his restricting himself to his façade existence, to a way of looking only at surface meanings and to his avoidance of the deeper issues and responsibilities involved in the use of language as communication, not only between human beings, but also within each person, since language is the medium of one's dialogue with oneself.

The contrast between Georg's empiricist nominalism and the father's "existential Platonism," for which "absolute morality"[17] or spirituality might be a more appropriate term, forms the essence of the entire confrontation scene. Entering his father's back room, Georg confronts a world, new and strange to his bourgeois ego, but familiar, as we shall see, to a forgotten and repressed layer of his self. Unconsciously, without explicit and deliberate challenge or claim, he embarks on the quest in which Kafka's later protagonist, K., will engage when he penetrates the village of the mysterious Castle. He enters a counterworld, different from and opposed to empirical nature and bourgeois society. Immediately upon his entrance, he notes the darkness of his father's room, which is caused by the interiority of its location.[18] A high wall cuts off the view of the external world. Shut off from the light of nature, the room affords no opportunities for observing external phenomena. It tends to draw the occupant inward to himself and to the inner reaches of his mind. Georg, on the other hand, has occupied the front room. He has been accustomed to looking out into and over the world, surveying it from his window (anticipating in this respect, too, the land surveyor), enjoying the external light of nature. He finds the darkness of his father's habitation unsettling and slightly menacing. He praises the bright airiness of the front room and asserts that his father's health will improve by a move to the front. He is intent on promoting the benefit of light, wishing to spread it to the dark regions and to save his literally "benighted" old father from himself. This "crusade" for light and open windows, nourishing food (he implicitly criticizes the abstinence of his father who has hardly touched his breakfast), and cleanliness and hygiene (we know that his father's unclean underwear greatly disturbs him) mark Georg as a representative of a perspective that could be termed one of "enlightenment." The family firm has benefited from his management, he has achieved great economic progress measurable in statistical terms, and the employees side with him against his father, as we learn from the elder Bendemann's complaint of a disloyal staff. Georg does not merely wish to take his father's place. He wishes to outdo the old man and move the world ahead to a richer, healthier stage than his predecessor bequeathed him. He even wishes to reform his father's life. These "reforms" are all directed toward the body, toward physical health and comfort. But like any enlightened despot or any revolutionary vanguard in the forward march of history, Georg will not consult the desires of the presumed beneficiary of his reforms. The father is to be moved, a doctor is to be consulted, fresh air is to be let in, all without ascertaining—and sometimes even going against—the father's specifically expressed preference.

In Georg and his father two perennial antagonists of Kafka and of the world confront each other. Georg initiates the procession of rational, empiricist, rebellious, and ultimately self-defeating protagonists, son figures, representatives of the modern liberal-progressive and bourgeois outlook. The father heralds the "counterworld" of obscure and archaic organizations and power structures, hidden away and irrational, apparently obsolete and decrepit, yet in a sinister and mysterious way all-powerful. We meet a later development of the son/father confrontation in the New Commander and the old penal system of *In the Penal Colony,* in Josef K.'s fight against a Court lurking in filthy attics and dark cathedrals, and in the land surveyor's reputation of bringing reform and a breath of fresh air into the timeless, snow-covered, and frozen corner of the world in which the Castle holds sway. In "The Judgment," the opposition between hero and "counterworld" is least explicit, because it is contained in a family setting and thus obscured by the appearance of a "realistic" frame. But even here the allegorical implications of this opposition are clearly discernible. When the father complains that the employees have become "disloyal" to him, siding with the usurping son and "persecuting" the legitimate chief, Georg's ascent to the top of the business assumes the nature of a displacement of ancient legitimacy by a progressive and efficiently capitalistic force. The father's counterworld, his conspiratorial "alliance" with Georg's friend, with the spirit of Georg's dead mother, and with the loyal customers, is cast in the corresponding role of a reactionary party seeking to regain the rights of dethroned power. Between the father's alliance and the Habsburgs' desperate rearguard action in the empire whose subject Kafka was, a subtle connection cannot be ruled out. But it is the spiritual-philosophical and ultimately religious context in which the father-son conflict must be seen. What makes such a context discernible is the combination of spatial and temporal terms in the structure of "The Judgment."

As Georg enters his father's room he moves back not only in space from front to rear, from wide-sweeping vision to blocked vision, from light to darkness; he also steps back in the time dimension from his forward-looking, future-bound career to a backward-looking realm in which mementos of the dead mother and archaic newspapers seem to mock and stubbornly resist all change. In this dark back room, time seems to have stopped. The newspaper that his father has been pretending to read is so ancient that Georg cannot remember it. As the father, deprived of the love and physical presence of his wife, has nothing but the past to sustain him, the son has everything to expect from the future.[19] Further success is imminent and marriage beckons to him on the near horizon as the crowning of his ascent. As if to emphasize the "modernity" of his fiancée and the opposition to the past she signifies, Georg pointedly mentions to his friend that she did not settle in their town until long after the friend's departure. Like the oppressive new Pharaoh in *Exodus* who knew nothing of Joseph, she comes from a new generation that knows nothing of the friend. Insofar as a reader of "The Judgment" herself comes from an intellectual climate that shares the "progressive" outlook, Georg's orientation toward the future would appear to her to be correct and worthy of approval, while the father's attachment to the past would seem to be a pathetic sign of a wrongheaded, demented condition. All the more disconcerted and astonished must this "progressive" reader be when she later sees Georg carrying out his "mad" father's verdict.

What this reader would fail to see is another aspect of the temporal structure of the confrontation scene. By living in the past, the father also lives outside the sensory world in a realm of inwardness in which feelings refuse to bow to the onward march of time. Memory creates, as in the universe of Proust, a purely spiritual realm in which the aged widower has his being. The father's loyalty is extended over spatial separation as well when he cultivates the bond with Georg's distant friend, while for Georg physical distance has meant dilution and corruption of friendship. The temporal opposition between past and future thus takes on the additional meaning of a confrontation between the power of the invisible, the power of spirit, and reliance on physical and empirical strength. If this is recognized, then the father's clinging to a dead past will no longer appear merely as a pathetic oldster's sentimentality or a reactionary's nostalgia, but also as a confident assertion of the primacy of inner bonds over physical change, including death. This confidence in the invisible enables the father to draw, as he says, on his dead wife's support from beyond the grave. His power is rooted in a constancy of spirit and emotion that, in Rilke's term, comes from "the world's inner space."

Against the possibility of such strength, Georg's initial strategy in the struggle is the attempt to view the spiritual itself as a sign of senility. Initially, seen through Georg's eyes, old age appears as toothless enfeeblement, loss of rational control, as utter decline—in short as the breakdown of human dignity and personality. Later, by virtue of the father's "revelation," it emerges as a fearful and mysterious power confounding and overthrowing the rational and empiricist perception of the world. It has to be stressed, however, that in the beginning Georg chooses to impose a negative interpretation on his father's behavior. This behavior would appear in a very different light if perceived from an "unnatural," spiritual, and transcendent perspective. But Georg uses his one-sided perspective to "declare" his father senile, i.e., to act toward him as though he were senile.

The first example of this use of perspective is seen in Georg's reaction to the "closed" window in his father's room. He finds this strange and objectionable since the weather is warm. The state of the external world determines his values. The father's answer that he prefers the window closed might indicate a primacy of personal will and choice, and his independence of external circumstances. The preference for shutting oneself off from the external world regardless of the weather might point to a deliberate withdrawal into an interiorized life. It might express a determination to place the memory of his dead wife, and loyalty to her, above all considerations of physical health and hygiene. However, from a naturalistic perspective for which physical health and an outward-looking stance are ipso facto superior to withdrawal to an inner world, the father's choice represents the caprice of a mind slipping into dotage. It deserves the same apprehensive disapproval as the friend's asocial existence in Russia. Georg's perspective and its values subtly prejudice the reader who sees the father through Georg's eyes, and he is therefore likely to share Georg's feeling that there is something "queer" about the old man's insistence on keeping his window closed. Henceforth we are prepared to expect further signs of decrepitude and craziness from the oldster. Georg's perspective deliberately shuts out any possible spiritual and existential interpretation of his father's words and actions, and justifies in our eyes his treatment of the father as senile. Georg, we feel, is right in disregarding his father's wishes and in depriving him, presumably in the interest of the old man's health, of his right to self-determination. The son's naturalistic value system, implied in his perspective, then gives him the pretext to pursue a naturalistic, i.e., Darwinian, policy that places the aged, as physically unfit, under the tutelage of the young and strong. Power being a matter of the body, and the body being subject to time and to change, this subjection of the old is accepted and even espoused as beneficial. Moreover, the reader by her own conditioning in a naturalist-empiricist civilization is in any case inclined to affirm Georg's course as the only "natural" and only sensible one to follow, and is prepared to disregard whatever might contradict Georg's view of his father. The younger man's deliberate ignoring of the deeper meaning of his father's question about the friend in Petersburg is likely to escape the reader.

The narrator, however, unmasks Georg's perspective as a cover-up. He does so above all by the subsequent plot and Georg's own behavior in it. In a more subtle way, however, he lets the textual structure of the passage immediately following the father's question reveal the cover-up. He describes Georg as "embarrassed" and shows him evading the answer to his father's question. Instead of addressing himself to the question regarding the friend, Georg answers: "A thousand friends do not replace my father" (Kafka 1970, 28). He distracts attention from the question to his father's presumed need for rest and care. By Georg's evasive maneuver and shifting of the ground, the narrator has him betray his uneasy conscience and dishonesty. At the same time, a hint is given that Georg is already thinking of his father's demise. Otherwise he would not allude to its possibility in his uncalled-for answer to the father's question. To be sure, the thought of his father's death is clothed in the guise of solicitous apprehension for his well-being. But soon it will, as we have already mentioned, erupt undisguised.

Typical of Georg's "cover-up" is the continued maintenance for the reader of the two perspectives throughout this scene, culminating in the actual "covering" of his father with a blanket. Georg's suggestion that his father retire from the business is sugarcoated by his addition that he would rather close the business than allow his father's health to be endangered. The brutal aspect of retiring the father without questioning his wishes in the matter is "covered up" by this display of seemingly unselfish, indeed self-sacrificing, regard for the father's well-being. Georg would rather sacrifice his own promising career than allow his father to continue to overwork himself to the point where, as Georg by his tactics insists, his mental health is giving way under the strain. Thus the son presents himself as the soul of consideration. But from another perspective this very consideration appears as a forcible elimination of his father from the business he had founded, in which he works, and from which, as he indicates, he has no desire to be removed. On the contrary, the father makes it plain that he resents being shut out from its control by Georg's deviousness. From this perspective, solicitude is a guise for taking away the old man's self-determination.

Undressing his father and putting him to bed can be seen as marvelous kindness and subordination of Georg's self to his father's needs. On the other hand, it is the father's crass reduction to the status of a small child. While carrying his father, as though he were a child, Georg is terrified when he notices him playing with Georg's watch chain. Thereafter Georg has difficulty in putting him to bed because the old man "held on so firmly to this chain" (Kafka 1970, 29). Here the two perspectives follow each other in time. First we see the scene from the point of view of the anxiously solicitous child. What terrifies Georg is this new evidence of his father's apparent senility. The word "playing" seems a strong indication that the old man has finally lapsed into his second childhood. However, immediately after that, when Georg finds it extremely difficult to put his father to bed, a very different perspective takes over. Now he has to face his father's powerful strength and ominous hold on Georg's life. The sequence clearly shows that the two perspectives do not have the same validity. By being able to displace the first perspective, the second shows its greater strength, which is moreover borne out by the plot. Already when he entered his father's room, the troublesome thought had fleetingly occurred to Georg that his father "was still a giant," and the subsequent plot shows that Georg has every reason to fear not his father's senility but his powerful hold on him. In pre—World War I Europe, the watch chain represented a symbol of male maturity and bourgeois respectability. Thus we see the father weighing down with his full force on Georg's adulthood, and his "playing" with Georg's watch chain now appears in the light of a deliberate and terrible irony.

Georg's fear of his father is now hardly disguised. Otherwise he would not be comforted by the observation that his father is looking up to him in a "not unfriendly way" (Kafka 1970, 29). The use of the negation implies that he expected "unfriendliness" from his father. His consciousness is now literally the cover that he spreads over his fear. His perspective merges with an anxious desire to render his father harmless. The physical blanket with which he covers him acts as the "objective correlative" of the tendency to bury "the giant." Consciousness itself functions as the cover of the Oedipal rebellion. If taken literally, Georg in covering his father is only acting out the duty of a good son. But if "cover" is taken figuratively, his consciousness itself is the cover of the Oedipal wish for his father's final disarming. The two perspectivist levels of meaning correspond to what the father will later identify as "the innocent child" and "the devilish person" in Georg. "Actually you have been an innocent child . . . , but even more actually you have been a devilish human being!" (Kafka 1970, 32). The "actually" expresses the literal, the "more actually" the figurative level of meaning on which Georg's act of covering his father is seen. The literal level is the son's and the reader's perspective; the figurative level is the father's and the narrator's.

The father's second decisive question in the dialogue is his: "Am I well covered?" It has again the two levels of meaning contained in his question, "Do you have this friend in Petersburg?" If understood as referring to physical fact, Georg is right in answering that his father is "well covered." But if referring to the figurative, metaphoric meaning of covered as being buried, retired, done away with and finished, Georg is proved wrong. With his resounding "no," his throwing off the wraps and rising in bed like one "resurrected," the father establishes the figurative perspective as the only one on which the mythos will be conducted. The perspective of Georg's consciousness is now swept away and annulled.

Georg's immediately avowed open hostility toward his father shows that he too has accepted the figurative perspective, and that his former solicitude and unselfish devotion prove to have been a façade destroyed by the eruption of truth.

However, the Oedipal rebellion that the father uncovers is not Georg's ultimate truth. As soon as his antagonism toward his father is liberated from the cover-up of "duty" and solicitous concern, a still deeper force counteracts and defeats the Oedipal revolt. The father's "revelation" does not immediately bare a unified, authentic self in Georg, but a profound cleavage. The simultaneous presence of two perspectives in Georg's thoughts, speeches, and behavior, now stands revealed as an inner conflict. The terms of this conflict too have radically shifted. Prior to the father's "uncovering," dutiful devotion had been in conflict with a concealed Oedipal hostility. Now that the revolt is openly visible, it is challenged in turn by a still unacknowledged drive for self-defeat and adoption of the father's will as Georg's own. In the dramatic denouement of "The Judgment," the father's will and the son's actions combine to smash Georg's ego, the conscious self-willed part of his self.

Georg's Oedipal revolt shows itself undisguised as his explicit wish to defend himself against a father threatening from everywhere. He remembers a decision he had made long before to protect himself by constant wariness and close observation from a surprise attack. The text leaves it open when he had made this decision. "A long while ago" (Kafka 1970, 30) might at first sight refer to the beginning of his father's present tirade. But since these accusations had just begun, it is much more likely that the "long while ago" is to be taken literally as a distant past. In that case, we see here the first open acknowledgment that Georg had been living in a state of war in his father's apartment, and that his now open hatred cannot be merely a reaction to what is happening at this moment.[20] The purposeful ambiguity of the text still hints at the two perspectives, one of which would view

Georg's hostility as a reaction to his father's sudden attack of "madness," while the other would see it as a permanent state of hostile preparedness that had hitherto been concealed. But in either case Georg's resolve can only be seen as an act of self-defense of the ego and its integrity against the ever-lurking danger from the powerful Oedipal father. Elsewhere I have called this ego, armed with the powers of accurate observation and acute awareness, the ideal of the concentrated self, which occurring here for the first time in Kafka's entire opus plays an important role throughout his work, from *Der Verschollene* to "The Burrow."[21] Connections between this ideal and one important aspect of Kafka's writing can be established. But what concerns us here is the immediate cancellation of Georg's posture of self-defense by a distractedness or absent-mindedness that makes him forget the resolve of preparedness each time he remembers it. A force within him, hostile to his ego, disarms him before any defense against his father can get under way. His Oedipal struggle is nipped in the bud by something stronger within himself. Georg does not permit himself to gather strength against his father. Since it is this deeper force that prevails over his conscious will to resist, I propose to call this self-defeating force his true or effective self.

Georg's next assault upon his father is verbal. He shouts "Comedian!" at him. But immediately he regrets the epithet and as his first act of actual self-punishment, he bites his tongue so fiercely that "the pain made his knees give" (Kafka 1970, 30). Thus he anticipates his final fate soon to come.

After Georg's wish for his father's death openly declares itself, the narrator informs us that the father now expected his son to approach him, but that he failed to come nearer. A physical assault upon the father would be the logical consequence of the son's murderous wish. His failure to realize his wish assures the father's victory. Rightly the father now exults and proclaims his triumph over Georg who, he declares, is deluded into believing that he still has the strength to carry out his own will. It is the father's strength that dominates now.

Finally, Georg's intention of mocking and undercutting his father changes, literally in Georg's mouth, into achieving the opposite effect of confirming and even outdoing his progenitor's berating statements. When the father jubilantly announces that Georg's friend knows everything "a hundred times better" and then "a thousand times better" than Georg, Georg multiplies this by another ten and says "ten thousand times." He raises his father's bombastic assertion to the second power "in order to deride" him—having even before wished to "make him impossible in the whole world"—"but even in his mouth the word assumed a deadly serious ring" (Kafka 1970, 31). Georg's own mouth, Georg's body, now turns against his conscious will. A force inside him supports his father against himself. This force wins out and demolishes the self, even as Gregor's body transforms the salesman Samsa into vermin, and thus liberates his father from the son's rule in the household. Georg's true, i.e., effective, self has risen against him to do his father's work on himself. The alliance between father and friend extends to Georg's own innermost and ultimately prevailing self. Even as the façade of duty toward the father had given way to the Oedipal revolt, the latter in turn has yielded to the wish for defeat and surrender. Georg's last assertion of rebellious independence is to accuse his father of having lain in wait for him treacherously. Like Josef K., he views his downfall as resulting from a sneaky attack by an external foe. But actually he blames his father for something that has arisen against him from within himself. Because of this mistaken perspective his father calls his remark outdated, long overtaken by events. It would have fitted earlier when Georg's Oedipal ego still had seemed to have a chance of battling the father. "Now it is no longer apropos."

When Georg carries out his father's judgment, his father's command has taken the place of his autonomous will. Without applying any physical force, by the sheer spiritual power over and psychic hold on the son, the father drives him out of the room, down the stairs, and into the river. His perspective has taken over Georg and becomes one with the core of his being, which in Freudian terms we would call the Unconscious or Id. The grammatical structure that describes Georg's self-execution bears this out. Kafka changes the subject of Georg's act from the personal "he" to the impersonal "it"—"it drove him across the roadway, toward the water" (Kafka 1970, 32). By his syntax Kafka shows that Georg's Id now executes and dissolves his person. Long before Freud's *The Ego and the Id,* but in close analogy to it, Kafka shows the alliance of Superego and Id doing away with the Ego.

Yet it is not the unconscious Id that remains as the last truth of Georg, but the articulate consciousness of his original self reaffirmed. His last words are a declaration of love for his parents, a conscious avowal of moral stance, a deliberate assertion of his return to what he had originally been. Climbing over the railing of the bridge, he becomes the reincarnation of the child who had once been the object of his parents' pride. With his statement, "Dear parents, all the same I have always loved you," he denies, cancels, revokes his Oedipal ego and rebellion, his years of dissatisfied ambition and attempted displacement of his father, and his alienation from both parents. That the dry tone Georg had noted in his friend's words of condolence reflected Georg's own lack of proper sadness over his mother's death appears obvious from the context in which he dated his success from the moment of her demise. By proclaiming with the last sentence of his life that he had loved his parents always, he takes back and wipes out the entire intervening period between his original and his ultimate self. That is, he erases himself as an independent ego at loggerheads with its origin, since his ego had been the element contradicting the love for his parents.

To be sure, the moment of Georg's murderous wish for his father's fall seems to belie his claim of having loved his parents always. How is that earlier wish to be reconciled with his final statement? It can be reconciled if we see his ineffectual revolt itself as the instrument of his self-punishment and thus as the necessary station on his road to the reattainment of his original self. Georg's rebellion is its self-judgment. Only by bursting open and manifesting itself explicitly can his true self be freed from the oppressive façade—"the closed face of the man of honor," as his father calls it—of his hypocritical dutifulness with which he masked self-indulgence and ambition. Georg's dutiful devotion toward his father necessarily entailed bad faith as long as it was coupled with his existence as economic man. For the basic principle of economic man, hedonistic egotism, runs counter to the filial reverence and self-subordination that Georg felt bound to express as well. As long as the rebellion of the ego remained unconscious and covered up by the pretense of duty and devotion, it festered unchecked and corroded the self. As with an abscess, purification came only when it broke open.

This came about with Georg's final letter to his friend in which, at his fiancée's bidding, he openly acknowledged his engagement and invited him to the wedding. The letter was to establish Georg at last as the successful engaged adult he had apparently become. But instead of sending off the letter he entered his father's room. This entrance has initially two opposite aspects. On the one hand, it appears as the final step toward emancipation from the father as well as from the friend. By letting his father frankly know that his engagement is irreversible and marriage imminent, Georg flaunts before the father his liberation from his childhood bond. The bald and brutal spareness of tone with which he informs the father of the fait accompli, the use of the belittling word "only" ("Actually I only wanted to tell you") (Kafka 1970, 27), the arrogance of the word "tell" with its decisive preclusion of asking for his father's opinion—all these point toward a defiant, humiliating triumph over both "bachelors"—father and friend. Georg seems to wish to "rub in" the fact that he has won the victory at last over his dependency. In fact, he appears intent on arousing his bachelored father's painful envy of the good fortune of the son. For we know, and Georg knows, how profoundly deprived the father has felt by the loss of his spouse. On the other hand, going to his father's room functions as a substitute for actually sending off the letter. It takes the place of the act that his fiancée had wished Georg to perform by writing the letter in the first place—namely to openly proclaim himself engaged and thus achieve the integrity of his divided self. By sealing the letter but not sending it, Georg first of all postpones and finally undoes what the letter was to bring about. And moreover, from the perspective of the end, we must say that Georg tacitly concedes his father's right to advise him and ultimately to judge his intention and prevent him from carrying it out. His stepping into the rear of the dwelling is also a stepping back in time to his childhood, when all his plans and acts were subject to his father's judgment, and his father's will was Georg's law. Walking into his father's room, in place of sending out the letter, he becomes implicitly what his self-punishment makes him explicitly—his father's obedient child. The Oedipal rebellion, the flaunting of his engagement, thus serves as the detour to and the very occasion for his punishment.

Georg's self-punishment, however, contradicts his father's judgment. His father had discerned the "innocent child" in Georg, but then expressly stated that the "devilish human being" in him was the more basic layer of his self, was in fact his "more actual" self; and he makes this analysis the reason for his death verdict:

> Actually you have been an innocent child, sure enough, but still more actually you have been a devilish human being! And therefore you should know: I now sentence you to death by drowning! (Kafka 1970, 32)

But if the "innocent child" is to be equated with obedience and love, and "the devilish human being" with rebellion, then the order of layers in Georg does not conform to the father's diagnosis, but is its reverse. Loyalty to his father and self-punishment are, as we have seen, in every instance of the confrontation, more effective, still "more actual" than the devilish revolt. The very structure of the scene, and above all Georg's final act of carrying out his father's sentence, refute his father's analysis. Georg contradicts his father—this is the story's final paradox—by obeying him. His self-execution appears as a last act of protest and as a disproof of the justice of the judgment.

The paradox changes into a clear, albeit complex meaning if we realize that Kafka incorporated two perspectives into the story, both of which are ultimately found in Georg. The father's perspective uncovers and condemns the son's Oedipal rebellion and self-deceiving bad faith, and establishes these as sufficient reasons for justifying a death verdict. Georg accepts this perspective and identifies himself with it by acting in accordance with it. But his own perspective takes over and goes far beyond his father's. For he also sees his punishment as his vindication. Thereby he questions the basis of his father's sentence. He is, Georg seems to say and proves it by his obedient suicide, in his fundamental essence a loving innocent child, and no longer the devilish person the father condemns. His declaration of love for his parents denies his father's view of him as ultimately devilish. On the contrary, this declaration proves he is the very opposite of his father's view of him. While his father sees nothing beyond the villain in him, Georg looks upon himself tragically. To be sure, he implicitly admits by his suicide that his adult life had gone wrong, and therefore he consents to his death sentence. But he does not see in his punishment a mere erasure of his person. He considers it an atonement and therewith a symbolic reinstatement of the original harmony that, in agreement with the structure of tragedy, can only be achieved at the price of death.[22] His self-punishment is a self-sacrifice that calls to mind Nietzsche's view of tragedy in *The Birth of Tragedy*. The tragic action liberates and reaffirms the species as it slays the individual in the person of the hero. At the beginning of the story, the bridge, like the whole scene of the world surveyed by Georg from his window, had seemed empty and lifeless, except for an isolated sign of deference offered the mighty individual Georg, enthroned in his contemplative Apollonian repose above the scene. This mute and still Apollonian world is brought to life at the moment of his leap. Now it suddenly teems with "a well-nigh infinite traffic" (Kafka 1970, 32). The individual's destruction calls the collective life into being.

The traffic collectivizes the family. It represents a symbolic broadening, a token of the universalization, of the family context. The German word "Verkehr," which Kafka uses in this last sentence of "The Judgment," means not only traffic but "intercourse," which is its more basic meaning. It thus refers to the sphere of sex and procreation as well as to communication and commerce. "Verkehr" thus relates to Georg's parents and their intercourse to which he owes his life. It is to them he returns in his dying profession of everlasting love. "Dear parents, all the same I have always loved you." Max Brod underlines this link between the intercourse on the bridge and that of the parents. In a conversation recorded by Brod, Kafka explained that the last sentence of "The Judgment" had evoked in him the thought "of a strong ejaculation."[23] The self-elimination of his hero from the life proceeding unendingly on the bridge above him, his letting himself fall under the "intercourse" of living, henceforth undisturbed by his presence, provided the author with the thought of intense pleasure. A later diary entry of Kafka's corroborates this meaning that self-punishment and death possessed for him. He writes that

> the best I have written is founded in this ability to die contentedly. . . . For me . . . such dying scenes are a secret game, in fact, I am happy to be in my dying protagonist. (Kafka 1948, 448)

Behind the back of the overt text, as it were, or underneath it, embedded in the key word "Verkehr," a secret connection exists between the traffic on the bridge and the sexual intercourse to which Georg owes his being. The parallelism between commercial and sexual intercourse is established in the text by the coinciding of Georg's utterance of eternal love for his parents with the unending traffic that drowns out his fall. The attribute "unendlich," meaning both "unending" and "infinite," describes the stream of life that Georg restores by surrendering to the river beneath him. By drowning, he, too, reenters that universal current, one form of which coursed through his parents' love, while another streams "unendingly" on the bridge, and a third flows in the river beneath. The stream of existence, which development into an autonomous, and thus separate, individual had interrupted, re-forms when the son returns to his father the love that his father had earlier extended to him. Just before Georg wanted him to topple and smash, the father had professed his love for him. "Do you think I had not loved you—I from whom you issued?" (Kafka 1970, 31). His father's love was founded explicitly on his procreative powers, on the affection of the begetter for his offspring as for a part of himself. Then Georg had answered this love with his Oedipal wish for his father's fall and death. But that answer was provisional. The true answer is given at the end with Georg's own self-propelled fall. Literally echoing his father's "I love you" by his own, "Dear parents, I have always loved you," the son links himself directly to his father's love. In his own interpretation of the story, Kafka mentions "the circle of blood . . . around father and son into which the fiancée cannot enter" (Kafka 1948, 296). This "circle of blood" is now allowed to flow once more, reuniting father and son in the "dialogue" formed around the verb "love."

However, this reunion is achieved only on a linguistic and symbolic level. It can no longer come about in the actuality of the story. River and bridge traffic are only signs, tokens standing for, but not identical with, the living blood stream, "the circle of blood . . . around father and son" that Kafka mentions. By restricting reconciliation to a symbolic act, to atonement in place of restitution, the narrator establishes the tragic dimension of the tale. For the broken law of an original harmonious state cannot be restored in actual life. It is achieved only in representation on a token plane, by the protagonist's sacrificial death. It is not the family that is restored but only its token, the intercourse on the bridge. It is not the actual stream of the generations that flows again, but only the current of the river symbolically accepting the son. And it is the bridge, mere sign of conjunction, rather than the actual reembrace of parent and child, that is left in the end.

On this symbolic and representational level, Georg attains what all tragic heroes attain. By becoming a victim, he is vindicated as a martyr and symbolic savior. His sacrifice of self assures the infinite life of the bridge. It restores the intercourse between the divided parts of the world.

In his death he goes beyond the friend, as Christ surpasses the mere ascetic who by renouncing the world merely removes himself from harm's way. What separates Georg from Christ is of course that which separates the tragic hero from Him—guilt. But what connects him with the savior is his sacrifice and its function in renewing the world. The cleaning woman's exclamation "Jesus!" as she sees Georg rushing past her, down the stairs, is both a cry to be expected under the circumstances within the conventions of realistic fiction and a strong hint at the universal implication of Georg's role. It is the son rushing to his self-sacrifice who is addressed by the name of the scapegoat savior. Georg shares the scapegoat function with all tragic heroes in the Dionysian view of tragedy, in which the individual, a separating factor, is sacrificed for the higher life of Dionysian unity.[24] Georg Bendemann's scapegoat function emerges more clearly if viewed in connection with the other stories—"The Stoker," "The Metamorphosis," and *In the Penal Colony*—to which Kafka saw "The Judgment" intimately linked (wanting to unite all four tales in two volumes, entitled *Sons* and *Punishments.*[25]) From Kafka's special perspective, Georg is a scapegoat figure as are all of his son figures. These protagonists are modeled on Kafka's view of himself as burdened with a sacrificial mission that precluded his participation in the life stream—marriage, procreation, family life. On the contrary, he has to sacrifice himself so that the happiness of families might prevail. One of his most revealing reflections expresses this view.

> He does not live for the sake of his personal life; he does not think for the sake of his personal thoughts. It seems to him that he lives and thinks under the compulsion of a family, which, it is true, is itself superabundant in life and thought, but for which he constitutes, in obedience to some law unknown to him, a formal necessity. (Kafka 1946, 269 f.)

It is against such a law that Georg had sinned by seeking to realize his independent self and for which he atones by his death.[26]

Yet Kafka was very concerned with guarding himself and his protagonists from making a special virtue of the sacrificial exclusion from the life stream. At the end of "The Judgment," he makes sure that no perversion of self-execution into a martyr's cult occurs. Before taking his plunge, Georg espies a passing bus and waits for its sound to drown out his splash. He insists on a death that will go unnoticed. In this total self-obliteration of the ego in any guise, including even that of martyrdom, Georg's perspective merges with his father's. Both perspectives coincide as Georg's death is presented as necessary. Both father and son seem to unite in judging the "innocent child" preferable to the adult ego that stands in opposition to its source in the struggle for self-assertion and power. It is therefore most consistent with the meaning of his punishment that Georg's last statement and thus his ultimate truth—his declaration of love for his parents—should be united in the same sentence with a death that will not divert attention from the unending "intercourse" of life. Love and genuine self-erasure are one. This seems to be the ultimate statement in "The Judgment." Uncontradicted by the rest of the text, it represents a kind of "truth" at which the works of Kafka's later periods never arrive.

NOTES

1. Paul Raabe's edition is the most reliable text of Kafka's fiction, apart from his novels. Despite the in many ways fine quality of the standard English translations of Kafka, they frequently fail to convey the literal accuracy of his texts. Since the literal wording is an indispensable key to the understanding and elucidation of Kafka's art, I use my own translations of his German wherever I quote him. Franz Kafka, *Sämtliche Erzählungen,* ed. Paul Raabe (Frankfurt am Main-Hamburg: Fischer Bücherei, 1970).

2. The story fragment "The Urban World," to which Kafka refers when he lists the associations occurring to him during his writing of "The Judgment," first introduces the father figure into his oeuvre. However, because of the unimportant and rather confused role that the friend figure plays in "The Urban World," discussion of this fragment would fit more properly into a study tracing the evolution of the father figure in Kafka's work. For an excellent analysis of the role of "The Urban World" in the evolution of Kafka's narrative technique, see Rolleston's *Kafka's Narrative Theater,* chap. 3.

3. Cf. Kate Flores: "The Judgment" (Flores and Swander 1958, 12). A very similar view of the split between the artistic side of Kafka, represented by the friend, and the "social" Kafka, represented by Georg, is held by Marson (1961).

4. Demmer (1973, 144 ff).

5. Binder (1975, 129.)

6. Politzer (1962, 49).

7. Elias Canetti, *Der andere Prozess: Kafkas Briefe an Felice* (Munich: Hanser, 1969).

8. Cf. Sokel (1964, 59). A year later Greenberg also referred to *Totem and Taboo* in *Terror of Art,* 56 f.

9. In a letter to Brod, Kafka sees himself as "a child" in comparison to his successful married friends who stand firmly planted in reality. Cf. Kafka (1958, 313).

10. Cf. Stern (1972, 121). Also included elsewhere in the present volume.

11. For Kafka's acquaintance with psychoanalytic thought, see Binder (1966, 92–114).

12. The sentence to which I refer is ambiguous because the third-person personal pronoun in it could refer to the father as well as to the friend. "As you thought just now that you had got him down, so far down that you could sit on him with your behind and he won't move, at that moment my fine son decided to get

married!" (Kafka 1970, 30). The father could have himself in mind here as Georg's presumed victim. With at least equal likelihood, however, he might be referring to the friend. His tirade, although it began with himself, switched, in its second sentence, to the friend. Two sentences earlier the father still talked of Georg's "false little notes to Petersburg." Furthermore, Georg himself seems to relate the father's harangue to the friend. In the paragraph following it, his thoughts are focused entirely on the friend. All this points to the friend as the "him" and "he" of the above-quoted sentence. The reader's inability to make a clear-cut decision for the friend or the father as the exclusive object of the sentence is in itself significant. The ambiguity of the text makes the partners in the "alliance" against Georg literally indistinguishable. I am grateful to Kate Flores for having pointed out this ambiguity.

13. Stern (1972, 122 f.).

14. In *Motiv und Gestaltung,* Binder (1966, 371), also sees two perspectives at work in "The Judgment," but in a way that differs radically from the interpretation attempted here. Binder sees a "neutral" perspective, in which the father is actually senile (which is indeed the opposite of our view), and Georg's "emotional" perspective, in which the father becomes a "vision of terror." His approach completely ignores the fact that the father's actions and pronouncements are presented by the narrator as "objective" facts, and are perceived as such by the reader. That is, in contrast to the friend's feelings, as surmised by Georg, the reader gets a direct, "objective" view of the father's terrifying height and vigor. Although we experience the father's rising through Georg's sensibilities, the narrator nevertheless compels us to assume that what Georg perceives is actually happening and is not merely the result of his interpretation. This is, of course, particularly true of the father's pronouncements.

15. The father's senility, equated with madness, is the key to the interpretation of "The Judgment" by Claude-Edmonde Magny (Flores 1946, 85–106). This interpretation is determined entirely by a perspective suggested to the reader by the protagonist's point of view. It therefore misses, as we shall see, the meaning of Kafka's story.

16. Cf. Kafka's letter to Max Brod of June 1921 (Kafka 1958, 336 f.), in which a very similar view of Westernized Jews is elaborated. Cf. also Seidler (1971, 188) and Steinberg (1962, 23–30).

17. J. P. Stern's (1972, 126) term.

18. Politzer (1962, 54) rightly sees Georg's move into his father's room as a move into the interior "of his own mind."

19. Cf. Politzer (1962, 55).

20. Cf. Greenberg (1968, 57).

21. See Sokel (1964), chaps. 18–20.

22. Seen also by Politzer (1962, 60), but not elaborated by him.

23. Brod (1960, 158).

24. See Sokel (1964, 71–76). Erich Heller (1975, 33–36) expounds a very similar view.

25. Cf. Kafka (1958, 116, 148 f.).

26. Stern (1972, 123), aptly calls this kind of "law" an "oxymoron," a "subjective law."

REFERENCES

Binder, Harmut. 1966. *Motiv und Gestaltung bei Franz Kafka* (Bonn: Bouvier), 125–35, 349–96.

———. 1975. *Kafka-Kommentar zu sämtlichen Erzählungen* (Munich: Winkler Verlag), 123–52.

Brod, Max. 1960. *Franz Kafka: A Biography*, 2d enlarged ed. (New York: Schocken Books).

Demmer, Jürgen. 1973. *Franz Kafka, der Dichter der Selbstreflexion. Ein Neuansatz zum Verstehen der Dichtung Kafkas, dargestellt an der Erzählung "Das Urteil"* (Munich: W. Fink).

Flores, Angel, ed. 1946. *The Kafka Problem* (New York: New Directions).

Flores, Angel, and Homer Swander, eds. 1958. *Franz Kafka Today* (Madison: University of Wisconsin Press).

Greenberg, Martin. 1968. *The Terror of Art: Kafka and Modern Literature* (New York: Basic Books, 1968), 47–68.

Heller, Erich. 1975. *Franz Kafka* (New York: Viking, 1975), 1–13, 27–28.

Heller, Erich, and Jürgen Born, eds. 1967. *Briefe an Felice und andere Korrespondenz aus der Verlobungszeit* (Frankfurt am Main: S. Fischer Lizenzausgabe von Schocken Books, New York).

Kafka, Franz. 1946. *Beschreibung eines Kampfes: Novellen, Skizzen, Aphorismen aus dem Nachlass. Gesammelte Schriften.* Vol. 5. Ed. Max Brod. New York: Schocken Books.

———. 1948. *Tagebücher, 1910–1923*, ed. Max Brod (New York: Schocken Books, 1948 and 1949).

———. 1958. *Briefe, 1902–1924*, ed. Max Brod (Frankfurt am Main: S. Fischer Lizenzausgabe von Schocken Books, New York).

———. 1970. *Sämtliche Erzählungen*, ed. Paul Raabe (Frankfurt am Main-Hamburg: Fischer Bücherei).

Marson, Erich L. 1961. "Franz Kafka's 'Das Urteil'." *AUMLA* (University of North Queensland), 16 (1961): 167–78.

Politzer, Heinz. 1962. *Franz Kafka: Parable and Paradox* (Ithaca, N.Y.: Cornell University Press, 1962), 53–65.

Seidler, Ingo. 1971. "Das Urteil': 'Freud natürlich?' Zum Problem der Multivalenz bei Kafka," in *Psychologie in der Literaturwissenschaft*, ed. Wolfgang Paulsen. (Heidelberg: L. Stiehm, 1971), 174–90.

Sokel, Walter H. 1964. *Franz Kafka: Tragik und Ironie* (Munich/Vienna: A. Langen/G. Müller), 44–76.

Steinberg, Erwin R. 1962. "The Judgment in Kafka's 'The Judgment.'" *MFS* 8(1) (1962): 23–30.

Stern, J. P. 1972. "Franz Kafka's 'Das Urteil': An Interpretation." *GQ* 45 (1972): 114–29.

10

FROM MARX TO MYTH

The Structure and Function of Self-Alienation in Kafka's "The Metamorphosis"

KAFKA'S UNIQUENESS as a narrative author lies, among other things, in the literalness with which the metaphors buried in linguistic usage come alive and are enacted in the scenes he presents. The punishing machine devised by the Old Commander in *In the Penal Colony,* for instance, engraves the law that the condemned have transgressed on their minds by imprinting it literally on their flesh. By the appellation "vermin," linguistic usage designates the lowest form of human self-contempt. Seeing himself as vermin, and being treated as such by his business and family, the traveling salesman Gregor Samsa literally turns into vermin.

Kafka's narratives enact not only the metaphors hidden in ordinary speech, but also ideas crucial in the history of thought. "The Metamorphosis" is a striking example. Gregor Samsa's transformation into vermin presents self-alienation in a literal way, not merely a customary metaphor become fictional fact. The traveling salesman wakes up one morning and cannot recognize himself. Seeing himself as a gigantic specimen of vermin, he finds himself in a fundamental sense estranged from himself. No manner more drastic could illustrate the alienation of a consciousness from its own being than Gregor Samsa's startled and startling awakening.

The idea of human self-alienation has played a crucial role in modern thought from German classical Idealism to Marxism and Existentialism. First encountered in the thought of Wilhelm von Humboldt, Schiller, Fichte, and Hegel, and subsequently in Feuerbach and Marx, this idea

From *The Literary Review* 26 (1983): 485–95.

always implies the individual's estrangement (*Entfremdung*) from his humanity or "human species being," i.e., from the individual's membership in the human species. The individual is estranged from himself insofar as he is alienated from his essential nature as a human being.

Rooted as he was in German Idealism and the tradition of German classical literature, the young Marx saw the essential nature of the human species residing in freely productive activity. Human species-being was for him the production of objects that were literally *Gegen-stände,* things that having issued from the labor of his hands and mind now face their producer as the objects of his world. Thus the human species is defined by world-creating or world-modifying activity. It is an activity that by virtue of its productive inventiveness humanizes nature. In order to be truly human, this praxis must be, at least partly, self-determined. Work must be engaged in for its own sake. It must have been chosen, partially at least, for its intrinsic pleasure. It must not merely be dictated by external need or the commands of others. In exact analogy to Immanuel Kant's corollary to the categorical imperative, which defines genuine morality, genuinely human labor for Marx must be at least partially its own end, its own freely chosen purpose, and not entirely "a means" for something else such as the satisfaction of extrinsic needs or the assurance of mere survival. To qualify as truly human, labor must always have an element of free choice. It must, at least partly, be its own reward and satisfaction. At any time it must be considered its own purpose, an end in itself.

This freedom of doing one's work for its own sake, for the joy it affords the worker, is the factor that, according to Marx, distinguishes human from animal productivity. Animals, Marx observes, "produce only under the compulsion of physical need. Man, on the other hand, produces even when he is free of physical need, and only in this freedom is he humanly creative. . . . Such production is his active species being. By virtue of it, nature itself appears as man's creation and his reality."[1] Only where work appears as its own reward are human beings truly human. Where it is imposed solely by economic necessity, the worker is not merely alienated from himself as an individual; he is estranged from his humanity. Marx's idea of human self-alienation is not restricted to factory work, but includes any kind of work in which an individual is engaged merely for the wage or income it brings him. The worker is dehumanized wherever his work fails to involve his creative urge and desire.

Here we have arrived at the prehistory of Gregor Samsa's metamorphosis, as the reader learns from Gregor's reminiscences of and meditations about his job as a traveling salesman. We learn that Gregor had been estranged from himself in his all-consuming work even before he finds himself literally estranged from his bodily being. Gregor had found his work unbearable. He had longed for nothing more passionately than to leave his job, after telling the head of his firm his true opinion of this job. Gregor's profound self-alienation corresponds, with uncanny precision, to Marx's definition of the "externalization" of work under capitalism:

> His work is *external* to the worker, i.e., it does not form part of his essential being so that instead of feeling well in his work, he feels unhappy, instead of developing his free physical and mental energy, he abuses his body and ruins his mind. (I, 564)

Gregor Samsa's professional activity has obviously been such purely instrumental work, external to himself, imposed upon him by the necessity of bailing out his bankrupt family, supporting them, and paying back his parents' debt to the boss of his firm. It is not only joyless and uncreative, it is totally determined by needs external to itself and Gregor. Freedom of creativeness—according to Marx the essence of truly human labor—finds an outlet in Samsa's life, prior to his metamorphosis, only in the carpentry in which he indulges during free evenings. Parenthetically we might recall that Kafka himself hated his bureaucrat's desk job because it served as a mere means to a purpose totally extrinsic to itself, namely a relatively short work day, and found by contrast genuine satisfaction in carpentering and gardening, activities chosen for their own sake, which, like writing, united creativeness with the satisfaction of inner needs.

Compared to accusations of his office work found in his autobiographical documents, Kafka's story, "The Metamorphosis," "systematizes," as it were, the Marxist factor, not by conscious design, of course, but by virtue of the astonishing parallelism in the point of view, particularly the presentation of self-alienation. Gregor's sole reason for enduring the hated position, the need to pay his parents' "debt" to his boss, drastically highlights the doubly extrinsic purpose of Gregor's work. For not only is his labor alien to his true desires, but its sole purpose, its fruit—the salary or commission that it affords him—does not even belong to him. Gregor's toil does not serve his own existence. It is not his own *Lebensmittel,* to use Marx's term—if left to himself, he would have quit long before—it belongs to and serves another.

This other is Gregor's father. He is the nonworking beneficiary and exploiter of Gregor's labor. The product of this labor is the money that Gregor brings home. This money belongs to the other who does not work himself, but enjoys and disposes of the fruits of Gregor's work: "the money which Gregor had brought home every month—he himself had kept only a few pennies to himself—had not been used up completely and had accrued to form a small *capital*" (E, 97; italics mine).[2] Gregor's father had expropriated the "surplus value" of Gregor's labor and formed with it his—to be sure, very modest—"capital." Gregor's relationship to his father thus represents an exact paradigm of the worker's exploitation by his capitalist employer, as described by Marx. The worker is alienated from the product of his labor because he has to yield it to the capitalist. The latter retains the lion's share for himself and returns to the worker only what the latter barely needs to survive. Through this despoiling of the fruits of his work the worker's existence becomes, in the words of Marx, "self-sacrifice and castigation" (I, 546): "In the last analysis, the extrinsic nature of his work is shown to the worker by the fact that his work is not his, but belongs to another. . . . It is the loss of his self" (I, 564 f.). Gregor's metamorphosis literally enacts this "loss of self." It makes drastically visible the self-estrangement that existed even before his metamorphosis.

It is the father's "capital" that leaves Gregor tied to his servitude and bondage, for as the narrator says, "with this *surplus money* [Gregor] could have paid back a much larger part of his father's debt to his boss and the day on which he could have freed himself from this job would have been much closer" (E, 97; italics mine).

The last-mentioned fact represents a point at which an entirely different interpretative dimension intersects the Marxist framework of self-alienation that we have so far considered by itself. Although we have by no means as yet exhausted the parallelism between the Marxist concept of self-alienation and the structure and function of Gregor Samsa's metamorphosis in Kafka's text, we might state at this point that Kafka's "The Metamorphosis" is by no means completely defined, if merely seen as the literal enactment of self-alienation. Even if we were to restrict ourselves to this aspect, the centrality of the concept of self-alienation in modern thought would demand additional interpretative frameworks from which to approach Kafka's text, such as psychoanalytic, existentialist, biographical, linguistic, and phenomenological systems of reference that all must needs play important parts in a relatively comprehensive interpretation of Kafka's richly referential narrative.

However, what we shall consider now is Kafka's "The Metamorphosis" as the telling of a myth, for the mythic dimension relates to the Marxist one the way a picture frame relates to the picture that it contains and transcends, at one and the same time. In order to recognize this relationship, we shall have to consider the mythos of "The Metamorphosis." I use the term "mythos" in the Aristotelian sense as the whole chain of fictive events in their chronological order as distinct from their narrated order.

The initial point of the mythos is not Gregor's transformation, but the business failure of Gregor's father five years before. This failure led to the contracting of the burdensome debt to the head of Gregor's firm. Thus the mythos begins with a family's cataclysmic fall into adversity through the fault of the father, more precisely the parents, since the text speaks of "die Schuld der Eltern" and only afterward of "die Schuld des Vaters." The German word *Schuld* signifies debt, guilt, and causative fault. This triple meaning is crucial to the understanding of Kafka's mythos. If understood in the sense of debt, the *Schuld* of Gregor's parents belongs to socioeconomic quotidian reality. If understood in the two other senses, *Schuld* belongs to a framework of moral and religious values. The text's repeated use of the singular *Schuld* in contrast to the more customary plural *Schulden* for debt provides a subliminally effective counterpoint to the obvious surface meaning of the word.

This subliminal allusion to guilt receives corroboration from the position of "die Schuld der Eltern" ("the guilt of the parents") at the initial point of the narrative mythos. This position creates a subtle analogy to the fall of mankind as told in Genesis. To be sure, this analogy amounts to the faintest of hints. However, we cannot and must not avoid noting the allusion if we take seriously Kafka's view of language as expressed in one of his aphorisms: "Language can only be used allusively for anything outside the sensory world."[3]

The son of these guilty parents—Gregor—has to assume their guilt and pay it off "by the sweat of his countenance" (to quote Genesis), by his self-consuming drudgery for his parents' creditor. In the allusive context established by the semantic ambiguity of *Schuld*, Gregor's profoundly alienated existence prior to his metamorphosis establishes the parallel to man's fate after the expulsion from Paradise. Like the children of Adam and Eve, Gregor through his sonship in the flesh has been condemned to a perennial debtor's existence. The two semantic realms of *Schuld*—debt and guilt—converge in the fateful consequence of the father's debt. With it, the father surrendered his family to a world in which the exploitation of man by man holds infernal sway. The world to which the father's failing has handed over his family is ruled by the principles of capitalist economics. In this world, the family ceases to be a family in the original and ideal sense of a community in which the bonds of blood—the *Blutkreis* to which Kafka in discussing "The Judgment" accords his highest respect—and natural affection prevail. Instead the family falls victim to the egotistical principle of *gegenseitige Übervorteilung* (mutual defrauding) in which Marx saw the governing principle of human life under capitalism.

Precisely because of his self-sacrifice in assuming his father's debt, Gregor rises to power as the breadwinner in his family and threatens to displace his father as the head of the household. This process reverses itself with Gregor's metamorphosis. Gregor's self-inflicted debasement entails his father's rejuvenation and return to power. These successive displacements—first the father's, then the son's—that find their parallel in Grete's ambiguous liberation through her brother's fall, have their contrastive complements in the parasitic exploitation of the winners by the losers. Before Gregor's metamorphosis, the father was the parasite. After the metamorphosis, the son assumes this role.

A world is shown in which the enjoyment of advantages by the one has to be purchased at the cost of the other. This is the world in a fallen state. Gregor's initial self-sacrifice through work whips up his pride in his ability to support his family in style. Those had been "happy times" when he had been able to "amaze and delight" his family by putting his hard-earned money on their table. But his self-surrender to his work causes a twofold alienation. Inwardly he remains estranged from his work because it is the kind of labor that cannot satisfy a human being. Outwardly his rise to power in the family overshadows the other members and results in their alienation from him. "A special warmth toward him was no longer forthcoming" (E, 98), so the text informs us. Long before his metamorphosis, Gregor and his family have lived coldly and incommunicatively side by side.

The metamorphosis reveals this alienation in its essence as the total dehumanization of man in which Marx saw the ultimate fate of man under capitalism. But it has another and ultimately more important function. Through it Gregor ceases to treat the *Schuld* of his parents as a debt that can be paid back by work, and assumes the *Schuld* in its deeper meaning. He no longer tries to pay back the *Schuld;* he incorporates it. With his incarnation he raises the narrative mythos from its socioeconomic to its mythic meaning.

That Gregor's metamorphosis literally incarnates guilt becomes apparent first of all by the fact that his immediate reaction to his transformation is a guilty conscience. He has missed the hour of his work and feels guilty for it. He feels guilty for having plunged his family into misfortune. He is ashamed. He seeks to hide, to make himself invisible. But even apart from all subjectively felt or morally accountable guilt, guilt becomes evident in him objectively. For his transformation into vermin entails the crassest form of parasitic exploitation, a perfect turning of the tables on his family. His metamorphosis compels them to work for him and in his place. Because of him they will henceforth be "overlooked and overtired" (E, 112), condemned to suffer the fate of "paupers." To be sure, his father's bankruptcy five years before had condemned Gregor to an exploited existence. But by his metamorphosis, Gregor himself turns into an archexploiter, the archetypal parasite that vermin represents. His very appearance as *ungeheueres Ungeziefer* is emblematic and flaunts a gigantic form of parasitism. Even as Gregor's subsequent daydream of declaring his love to his sister constitutes a gruesome parody of bourgeois-sentimental courtship, so his vermin existence as such embodies exploitation as the essence of human relations.

By embodying parasitism in his shape, Gregor objectifies the guilt of his entire society. This guilt had originally shown itself in his father when he secretly cheated his son and furtively put aside his son's earnings to form "a modest capital." Reversing their roles, the son now becomes exploitation in its most honest, clearly visible form. To use T. S. Eliot's term, most appropriate to Kafka's tale, Gregor becomes the "objective correlative" of the insight that exploitation is the original guilt of mankind. Gregor literally becomes what his father had committed in stealthily performed acts.

In the narrative mythos of Kafka's tale, the metamorphosis literally takes the place of the father's debt. The text mentions a debt only for the prehistory of "The Metamorphosis," as a flashback in Gregor's memory. In the action that the reader witnesses, the debt plays no role. The text never mentions it again. It seems that Gregor's *Schreckgestalt,* his new terrifying shape, which the first morning after his awakening had chased away the deputy of the firm, has thereby also canceled the parents' debt. In place of it, Gregor himself has become "the misfortune" of the Samsa family.

Later, the father wounds Gregor with an apple that rots and festers in Gregor's flesh. This apple functions not only as a renewed allusion to "the guilt of the first parents"; it also signifies the function of Gregor's metamorphosis as the literal incorporation of his father's guilt. Gregor, mortally hurt by the blind "rage" of his father, has obviously become his father's victim in the concluding section of the story. Yet this final violation of the son by the father only repeats in a transparent way Gregor's initial victimization. In the beginning, Gregor had to assume his father's debt and thus become its victim. At that time *Schuld* had been understood in the economic and juridical meaning of debt. By his metamorphosis Gregor incorporates this *Schuld* and transforms it from a legal-contractual concept into its full and profound meaning as the concretely visible form of alienated life. Parenthetically one might say that the *Schuld* the father bequeaths to the son is in the last analysis life itself. The "rotting apple in the flesh" not only causes but also embodies Gregor's protracted dying. This seems to suggest that the original "guilt of the parents" was the dubious "gift" of physical existence. This reading would connect "The Metamorphosis" with numerous other works by Kafka and with the spirit of his aphorisms.

In contrast to his father, Gregor does not incur guilt; he is guilt. His incarnation of guilt corresponds to Christ's incarnation of God in man, in one sense only. Like Christ, Gregor takes the cross upon himself to erase "the guilt of the parents." But in contrast to Christ, Gregor does not merely assume suffering for his fellow creatures; he also assumes their guilt. Since he has made guilt identical with himself, he must liberate the world, i.e., his family, from himself.

"The guilt of the parents" showed itself as indebtedness. It constituted capitulation to the world in its capitalist makeup. In strict consequence, economic determination inserts itself now into the myth as Kafka presents it. This insertion can be understood in sociocultural and, indeed, Marxist categories. The plot inserted into the mythic events depicts a classic case of the proletarianization of a petty-bourgeois household. The "modest capital" created by the father's exploitation of Gregor's work for the firm "sufficed . . . not at all to permit the family to live on its interests" (E, 97). In consequence the family loses its bourgeois status, its economic independence. Father Samsa remains the omnipotent potentate in his family. But in the world outside, he toils as a humble bank messenger. By the self-elimination of her brother as a human being, Grete rises to monopolistic eminence and privilege in her family. But in the outside world, she has to serve strangers as a poor sales girl. Gregor's mother is reduced to taking sewing and dress-making work home. In regard to the socioeconomic world of exploited labor, Gregor, by the horrible paradox that is his metamorphosis, is now the only "free" member of the family, the only one who does not have to labor and let himself be exploited by the world outside.

The family's proletarianization reaches its nadir when it has to yield the control over its household to the three lodgers. According to Marx, as capitalism increasingly absorbs all precapitalistic forms of human life, the contrast between natural and social existence becomes progressively more extreme. In Kafka's tale, the displacement of the "natural," traditional head of the family, the father, by the three strangers exemplifies the development described by Marx. The three lodgers assume the dominant place in the household merely by virtue of their paying power. Kafka's plot mimetically conforms to and expresses Marx's observation of the historic change from blood kinship to money as the determining element in all human relationships. "The Metamorphosis" shows how the basis of power, even within the "natural" unit of the family, slips from blood, age, and sex, the foundations of the father's dominance, to money, which makes the unrelated strangers the rulers of the family. The family forfeits its autonomy even within its own walls. Of course, even prior to this loss, the family's independence had been appearance only since the father's debt to Gregor's firm had handed it over to the tyranny of the business world, represented by the creditor's firm. The lodgers' invasion of the household and their assumption of absolute control over it thus, in Marx's words, only "brings to a head" (I, 578) what had been inherent in the family's enslavement to the capitalist world through the father's original guilt.

Since his metamorphosis, however, Gregor must assume the blame for this state of affairs. He alone now appears to be the cause of the whole "misfortune" of his family—unique as it is "in the entire circle of their relatives and acquaintances" (E, 112). He is guilty in a manner that lifts his "guilt" completely out of the sphere in which a socioeconomic interpretation could still be relevant. To be sure, in consequence of its economic impoverishment, the family disintegrates as a natural community. So far the analogy to Marx's world view holds. However, the limits of such an analogy are reached as soon as we realize that the ultimate cause of this proletarianization is a circumstance that transcends the observable laws of nature. In the midst of an environment that otherwise seems to be wholly determined by socioeconomic factors, Gregor's metamorphosis supplies the evidence of something inexplicable in, and therefore transcendent of, the terms of that *Weltbild.*

Mythic thinking also underlies Marx's view of history. Behind Marx's economic determinism one can glimpse the messianic martyr-savior's part played by the proletariat. In the world view of the young Marx especially, the proletariat suffers the fate and assumes the task of Christ. Today the proletariat is the scapegoat of humanity; tomorrow it will be its redeemer. So runs the Marxist myth. The proletariat will save the very society that has victimized it and committed the worst injustice against it. In his Preface to his "Critique of Hegel's *Philosophy of Law,*" Marx states that

> in order that *one single estate* may stand for the condition of the whole society, all the defects of that society must be concentrated in one . . . class; a particular estate must be the estate of general offense, must be the embodiment of all frustrations; one particular social class must be seen as the *notorious crime* of the whole society, so that liberation of this class will appear to be the universal self-liberation. (I, 501)

In the microscopic society of his petty-bourgeois household, Gregor Samsa plays the same role that the proletariat, in Marx's vision, performs in the macroscopic social and universal society of the bourgeois-capitalist system.

The analogy between Gregor and the proletariat becomes clearer when we realize that Gregor's metamorphosis is bound up with "guilt" in a twofold way. The "guilt of the parents" is embodied *in* him, but it is also perpetrated *on* him. Insofar as his vermin appearance is the incarnation of parasitic selfishness, their guilt is embodied in him. However, insofar as he serves as the butt of the injustice and cruelty of his family, insofar as he suffers their total neglect and withdrawal of love, their guilt is perpetrated on him. As the unrecognized member of his family, Gregor corresponds to that universal victim of the capitalist order—the proletariat.

Gregor also exercises its eschatological function as the liberator and savior of his society. The "notorious crime" of society diagnosed by Marx as the surrender of man to inhumanity is embodied in the hero of Kafka's tale much more literally even than in the hero of Marx's view of history.

Like the proletariat for Marx, Gregor bears in his family "radical chains." His existence, like the proletariat's, represents "the universal sorrows" of mankind. "No particular injustice," but "injustice as such" is committed against him. His very being, like that of the proletariat, proclaims "the total loss of humanity"—a loss that in his case manifests itself of course in its most literal meaning. Finally, like the proletariat in Marx's eschatological view of history, Gregor can regain his own humanity only by the liberation of his whole community.

However, in sharp contrast to Marx, the optimistic "synthesis" of self-liberation and liberation of all others is totally lacking in Kafka's world. Marx's proletariat redeems itself by redeeming mankind. In Kafka, liberation can be achieved only by the total sacrifice, the self-eradication of the scapegoat. Only by vanishing completely can Gregor save his family and himself.

While Marx's messianic view of the proletariat represents a secularized version of the Judaeo-Christian eschatology, the mythic dimension of Kafka's tale contradicts the latter. In the Christian version of the scapegoat myth, the savior's self-sacrifice is merely temporary. He arises again and takes the redeemed with him to eternal bliss. Kafka's myth follows the more primitive and universal "transference" myth that James George Frazer in *The Golden Bough* calls the myth of "the assassination of the god":

> The accumulated misfortunes and sins of the whole people are sometimes laid upon the dying god, who is supposed to bear them away for ever, leaving the people innocent and happy. . . . It is not necessary that the evil should be transferred from the culprit or sufferer to a person; it may equally well be transferred to an animal or a thing.[4]

In "The Metamorphosis," "the guilt of the parents" has been transferred to Gregor. He is the scapegoat on whom the refuse, the filth, the "sin" of the whole community is deposited. This transference appears in him not only physically and externally as when the *Unrat* of the whole apartment is thrown into his room. It also shows itself inwardly as the—temporary—reprehensible and shocking deterioration of Gregor's character makes clear.

What remains for Gregor to do is to recognize that it is his role and mission "to bear away forever . . . the accumulated misfortunes and sins" of his family by removing himself in whom they are incarnated. In this lies the inner meaning of his metamorphosis that his sister's words make clear to him. "His opinion that he must disappear was if anything even more decided than his sister's" (E, 125).

He literally carries out the "turning," the spatial "return . . . back into his room" (E, 124) that transposes "The Metamorphosis" from its economically determined foreground plot into the mythic frame from which it had issued. Hitherto intent on breaking out and returning to power, influence, love, and life, Gregor now withdraws forever into his room, into himself. He gives himself up to death by which he liberates not only the world from himself, but more importantly for Kafka, himself from the world.

The death of Gregor Samsa is self-imposed in the literal sense that it occurs only after the consent of the "hero." Gregor carries out the death sentence on himself that his sister, as the representative of the family and of life, has pronounced against him. He executes it by virtue of what can only be considered psychic power. He kills himself simply by his will—resembling in this respect Kleist's *Penthesilea.* His will is to obey the "law" that has chosen him for sacrifice so that his family can live free of *Schuld,* and the formulation of this will is immediately followed by its fulfillment—Gregor's death. It is a sacrificial death for the family of whom he thinks "with tenderness and love" (E, 125).

Kafka was satisfied with this death of his "hero," as his letter to Felice Bauer composed immediately after the writing of Gregor's death scene shows:

> Cry, Dearest, cry; now is the time for weeping! The hero of my little story died a short while ago. If it can console you, I shall tell you that he died quite peacefully and *reconciled* with all.[5]

The rhythm and the anaphoric structure of that first sentence resemble the lament for the "hero" of an epic of universal, at any rate of collective, significance. The "synthesis" expressed by the "consolation" of the third sentence is, in contrast to Marx's view of history, not the synthesis of fulfillment, but that of tragedy. Death as reconciliation implies not only the ancient idea of "atonement," but also the even more basic idea of the tragic as the sacrificial defeat of the individual in his ancient and eternal agon with the collective. This idea emerges as the "meaning" of the myth embedded in Kafka's story. The individual's extinction is balanced by his elevation and "eternalization" in the lament ("Now is the time for weeping") in which the intention of Kafka's "little story" appears to be summed up. Conversely, the sacrifice of the individual in whom "guilt" has become embodied allows the community to enter upon a new life and entertain "new dreams." At the conclusion of the narrative text, Gregor's parents had grown

> more quiet and half unconsciously exchanging glances of agreement, that it would soon be time to find a good husband for [Grete]. And it was like a confirmation of their *new dreams* and *good intentions* that at the last stop of their trip their daughter got up first and stretched her young body. (E, 130; italics mine)

No matter how cruel and illusory the "new dreams" for the life of the daughter, purchased by the carcass of the son, may appear to be, about Kafka's unqualifiedly affirmative evaluation of his "hero's" sacrificial death his letter to Felice leaves no doubt.

Kafka's definition of the writer's relationship to mankind applies to Gregor's role in the deliverance of his family:

> The writer is the scapegoat of humanity; he allows human beings to enjoy sin guiltlessly, almost guiltlessly.

In this sense, and in this sense alone, the mythos of "The Metamorphosis" describes a myth of literature. Gregor allows his family, as the writer allows humanity, to enjoy their guilt guiltlessly, which does *not* mean that he restores to them their innocence. They remain guilty, but they can now enjoy the fruits of this guilt without being held accountable. For the scapegoat who embodies their conscience makes them free of it.

NOTES

1. Karl Marx, *Frühe Schriften,* Erster Band, ed. Hans-Joachim Lieber and Peter Furth (Stuttgart: Cotta Verlag, 1962) [Karl Marx Ausgabe. Werke Schriften Briefe. Bd. I], 567. My translation. All further quotations from Marx are taken from this edition and translated by me. Volume (in roman numeral) and page are cited in parentheses in the text immediately following the quotation.

2. Franz Kafka, *Erzählungen und kleine Prosa,* Gesammelte Schriften, Bd. I, ed. Max Brod, 2d ed. (New York: Schocken Books, 1946), 97. My translation. All subsequent quotations from Kafka's "The Metamorphosis" are taken from this edition in my translation. Hereafter text quotations are cited with "E" followed by the page number.

3. Franz Kafka, *Hochzeitsvorbereitungen auf dem Lande und andere Prosa aus dem Nachlass,* Gesammelte Werke, ed. Max Brod (New York: Schocken Books, 1953), 45. My translation.

4. Sir James George Frazer, *The Golden Bough: A Study in Magic and Religion,* 3d ed., Part 6: The Scapegoat (New York: MacMillan, 1935), 1.

5. Franz Kafka, *Briefe an Felice und andere Korrespondenz aus der Verlobungszeit,* ed. Erich Heller and Jürgen Born (Frankfurt am Main: S. Fischer Lizenzausgabe von Schocken Books, New York, 1967), 160. My translation. Emphasis mine.

THE PROGRAM OF K.'S COURT

Oedipal and Existential Meanings of *The Trial*

THE CRUCIAL circumstance about K.'s trial is the fact that the charge against him is never specified. The existence of a guilt—some guilt—is assumed, but its nature is left undefined and remains unknown both to the protagonist and to the reader. The conclusion is often drawn that this kind of unspecified guilt corresponds to the theological concept of original sin. However, the doctrine of original sin holds everyone guilty; this does not seem to be the case with K.'s Court. The Court "arrests" only some persons, while many others remain free.[1] Manager and Deputy Manager of the bank where K. works, his landlady, Fräulein Bürstner, the manufacturer in chapter 7, K.'s uncle and girl cousin—they are all free of the accusation that has befallen only some characters in the work. Thus the analogy between K.'s guilt and original sin does not get us very far.

What else can unspecified guilt indicate? One possibility is that it implies the accused's guilt is his whole way of life at the time of his arrest. Such guilt cannot be specified because it is total. Unlike original sin, it is a particular kind of life, the one lived by K., that is equated with guilt. It is the existence of a representative bourgeois, atypical only on account of his extreme representativeness, most of whose relationships before his arrest are based on the cash nexus or on a superficial need for diversion. The little we can learn about the other defendants does not contradict the inference that K.'s type of existence is considered guilt.

If the guilt of the accused is his whole life, his punishment can only

From *On Kafka: Semi-Centenary Perspectives,* ed. Franz Kuna (New York: Barnes and Noble, 1976), 1–21, 184–85.

be death. This view is expressed by K.'s uncle when he says that having such a trial amounts to having lost it, and that in turn amounts to being erased. I would call this view the Oedipal view of the trial. In his most coherent attempt at an autobiography, the famous "Letter to His Father," Kafka presented his own life in terms closely corresponding to the Freudian Oedipus conflict. A father incomparably stronger than the son aroused infinite guilt in him and burdened him with the conviction that he lived a life totally unworthy, or nearly so, when judged in the light of his father's standards and example. No matter what Franz would or would not do, he was guilty: beginning with his totally inadequate body, his whole existence, next to his father's, was guilt. In Kafka's early tale, "The Judgment," a father condemns his son to die; in "The Metamorphosis" he mortally wounds him with an apple; in *Amerika* he brutally exiles him into a highly dangerous and uncertain fate. In *The Trial,* written two years after these works, the situation is abstracted from the family context, of which only remnants, such as K.'s uncle and mother, are left. The son has become the accused and the father has been generalized, depersonalized, and elevated into an accusing court. But the basic structure is the same as the one articulated in Kafka's "Letter to His Father" and the earlier family tales.[2]

The Oedipal nature of the court system seems to be concentrated with special force in the law student Berthold, in the third chapter of the novel. In the service of K.'s judge, Berthold acts out the classical pattern of the paternal antagonist's behavior in the Freudian drama of the so-called Oedipus complex. He tempts K. into aggression for the sake of the woman, the attendant's wife—whose marital status suggests not only a desirable sex object, but a mother figure as well—and then thwarts K.'s attempt to gain the woman for himself. K. has to give in to the Court member's superior strength, as the male child in Freud's Oedipus complex has to learn to do without his mother's sexual love and yield her to his father. *The Trial* gives us the impression throughout of a court enjoying sexual power and liberty while denying these to the accused. This tendency is enunciated by the prison chaplain when he warns K. particularly against seeking the help of woman, which, he suggests, is not "true help."

This Oedipal view of *The Trial* is consistent with the assumption of total guilt of the accused. For we find that the Court's apparent hostility towards K.'s sexual fulfillment is only part of a general hostility towards his worldly self. The adult ego of the modern bourgeois is to be broken, humbled, impoverished, made ready for death. In the very beginning, the warders frustrate K.'s desire for breakfast, take away his personal property, deny him a chair to sit on, and berate him for not showing sufficient deference to the man in authority, the Inspector. They point out to him that in the future he will not need his fine shirts. The Court has the warders thrashed later on, not for the theft of K.'s shirts, but because K. complained about it. The whipping is carried out in his presence. Thereby the Court makes sure that K. will suffer the disconcerting effects of his bourgeois insistence upon his property rights, and be given to understand that he has made too much of his property. He receives a similar lesson when, during the interrogation, he, so proud of his important position as a high official in a bank, is addressed as a house painter. When K. insists on his bourgeois status, laughter answers his boastful correction of the Court's "error." K. is carried along and moved to join in this gay irreverence toward his sense of status. These instances hint at the trial's purpose as an education towards the monastic virtues of poverty, chastity, and obedience, or humility, and beyond that, towards the obliteration of the self-confident ego that distinguishes rational bourgeois man. Seen from this aspect, *The Trial* is the culmination of a pattern running through Kafka's earlier stories of family conflicts and the picture of the penal colony as given by the Officer.

Yet the fact that the Court allows K. full freedom to continue his normal life seems to contradict this pattern. K. is not imprisoned. He is free to choose whether or not to heed the Court's summons, since, in the completed chapters, no sanctions are mentioned for disobeying the summons.[3] This freedom in fact strikes K. as inconsistent with the idea of his being arrested. For the defendant is thereby enabled to accept or to reject his trial, and not only once, but every time he is summoned to it. The trial is the accused's own consent to it and implies his tacit acceptance of an unspecified guilt. Here a very different view of K.'s trial seems to emerge.

And indeed, the inference that lies at the bottom of the Oedipal view—that K.'s guilt is his life—is not the only possible inference to be drawn from an accusation left unspecified. An undefined guilt may also imply that the accused has to discover what his guilt is. From this perspective, the arrest is the alerting of the accused, and his trial is the invitation to discover himself in his search for his guilt. "Not to show you what is wrong with you but that something is wrong with you," so runs one of Kafka's aphorisms that seems like a commentary on this view of guilt in K.'s trial.[4] Many details point to the structure of *The Trial* as a travelogue, an aborted voyage of discovery. It is no coincidence that the first member of the Court to appear to K. seems to be wearing traveling clothes, and that K., in pursuing his trial, continuously discovers unknown locales, unfamiliar districts, unsuspected circumstances, etc. According to this inference, the trial should be considered a process of exploration and questioning. The double meaning of the German title, *Der Prozess,* meaning both trial and process, would lend support to the view that the trial is, or should be, the process of the discovery of K.'s guilt.[5]

At one point, K. himself seems to approximate to this view of his trial, when he thinks of dismissing his lawyer and starting work on a plea by himself. His plea would recall and examine every one of his actions and experiences and try to illuminate it from all angles. This total self-examination he feels is necessary "because of his ignorance of the charge" (P, 154).[6] He would have to devote nights and Sundays and every available free moment to this labor. Here K. comes closer than anywhere else in the novel to the realization that his trial should be a process of self-confrontation. He also realizes that it would be endless. However, K. fails to understand that the reason for this unending nature of the process is not the amount of work required but the essence of self-confrontation itself. An unspecified accusation concerning an unknown guilt cannot be related to a particular fact or facts to be discovered by detective work. The unknown guilt in K.'s trial is identical with his being, not in the sense of original sin, but as a consequence of the silence of the Court as to what constitutes guilt. Whatever the accused might discover would still come up against this silence. In the face of it, any act or omission in one's entire existence might be guilt. If the defendant adjudges a particular act innocent, even if in good faith (which K. incidentally lacks), it might yet—who knows—contain aspects that the self-examining mind has overlooked or seen in an inadequate or incorrect light, and that might make his act guilty. Worse still, in the absence of any standard and definition of guilt and nonguilt, what might appear most innocent to the examiner might be precisely the root of his guilt if viewed from another perspective. It is not a matter of the impossibility of a good outcome for this process of self-examination, as has been maintained,[7] but rather of the impossibility of any outcome. The reason for this is not only the silence of the Court. Even if a dialogue with the Court were conceivable, there would still be no possible end to the process. For the self that is to be examined is living and continuous and constantly adds new acts and aspects to itself during the very process of self-evaluation. Only death can put an end to the process that is the trial.

K. furthermore overlooks the additional impossibility of self-discovery by merely cognitive and reflective self-examination. "Truth," said Kafka, "is indivisible, and therefore cannot know itself; he who desires to know it, must be a lie."[8] The same reservations Kafka harbored against the necessarily deceptive and fraudulent character of self-observation would apply to K.'s idea of a plea based upon a scrutinizing examination of his past acts.[9]

There is, however, built into K.'s trial a different route of self-discovery, namely self-revelation through action based upon choice. In a "procedure"[10] that leaves the accused freedom to heed the summons or not, he chooses his self, in the Kierkegaardian sense, as one who either accepts or rejects the accountability that his own hand has called for. (We remember that it is K. who, ringing his bell for his breakfast, has made the warder Franz appear before him. Literally and unconsciously, he calls for his own arrest.) That his trial is a true choice by K. becomes clear when he receives a phone call at his office, telling him to appear at the Court for his interrogation the following Sunday. But for that Sunday he also has an enticing invitation from the Deputy Manager of his bank, to spend the day on his yacht. When K. prefers the Court's summons to the Deputy Manager's invitation, he clearly makes a choice that can be called existential. He deliberately puts his trial above his pleasure and social advantage, thereby establishing a pattern that he will follow henceforth. By this choice K. defines his true self.

The obvious policy of the Court is to allow K. to reveal himself by this freedom to choose. This existential policy differs markedly from the Oedipal strategy of breaking the self and its will. It tends to make K. the free arbiter of his fate. There is, within the Court system itself, a conflict between the two views of the trial. This conflict is explicitly stated by the law student Bertold who severely criticizes the examining judge for allowing K. "to run around so free." He calls it a "mistake," about which he had complained to the judge. "Between the interrogations at least, [K.] should have been held captive in his room" (P, 74). The student's view of K.'s trial conforms to the Oedipal pattern of Kafka's earlier story, "The Metamorphosis," in which Gregor's family keeps him prisoner in his room. The student would make confinement the policy towards the arrested. He would not seek K.'s free commitment, but his captivity, the repression of his ego, the reduction of his vital capacities, a harsh and severe education towards inwardness, and ultimately a preparation for the grave. The student's policy would conform to the treatment accorded to the prisoners in *In the Penal Colony,* in that golden age of the Old Commander's rule that the Officer so nostalgically evokes. The plot of *In the Penal Colony* shows the decline and breakdown of this older system. Begun shortly before and continued after *In the Penal Colony, The Trial* presents the older system, as desired by the student, countermanded and superseded by the judge's new policy of physical freedom for the accused, which changes the whole concept of the trial from an Oedipal to an existential intent. For the student, the new policy, as represented by the judge, is "incomprehensible."

We are dealing, in *The Trial,* with two contrasting layers of intention, which explains a good deal of the particular obscurity and ambiguity of this novel, and which is extreme even for Kafka's opus. This duality conforms to Kafka's development, which makes *The Trial,* like *In the Penal Colony,* a work of transition and evolution from the harsh Oedipal law of the family tales of 1912 to the ironic existential mode of his late phase, as represented by *The Castle,* "A Hunger Artist" and "Investigations of a Dog." *The Trial* shows a primitive layer, expressed by the Lower Court organs—the warders and the student—advocating physical coercion, being contravened by the higher and official law of the Court, enunciated and practiced by the Inspector and the Examining Judge, which insists on the accused's freedom to commit himself to his trial. In composing *The Trial* Kafka made the Oedipal law of "The Metamorphosis" and the penal machine be literally superseded by the new law of *The Trial* as a series of existential decisions. The structure of self-alienation is very similar to that of "The Metamorphosis," but the difference is even more significant. In "The Metamorphosis" Gregor is physically forced into his alienation before the action starts. Extremely limited options remain to him. But in *The Trial,* the Inspector expressly states that the arrest only serves the function of "informing" Josef K. of his condition and seeing "how he has received it" (P, 24), leaving him the freedom to continue his previous life, and to neglect his trial or to concentrate on it, as he chooses. This difference in intent makes for a difference in form between the two works. The fatalistic realism of "The Metamorphosis" in which the initial event inexorably determines the outcome, in a tight plot, gives way, in *The Trial,* to a loose sequence of scenes reminiscent of old morality plays. In these the protagonist has to choose between several options. *The Trial* is not, like Gregor Samsa's metamorphosis, a determining condition from the start. It is a series of challenges. The protagonist's reactions to or evasions of them determine the structure. This structure corresponds to the existential policy of the Court.

The Inspector tells K. that his sole task was to inform him that he is arrested and to see how he has taken it. In this statement two factors can be distinguished: (1) The arresting power merely brings K.'s condition to his consciousness, and (2) it observes his reaction to this new awareness. The Court functions as K.'s observer, and one meaning of his trial is his being challenged to reveal himself to an audience as well as to himself. This audience is the Court, and we the readers are an extension of K.'s Court—a point that we shall take up later. This meaning of the trial makes for the theatrical and dramatic structure of the novel. It is not for nothing that the two executioners remind K. of actors. K. literally stands on a stage, on a raised platform, holding forth for an audience, which, as he finds out later, is the Court, with a demagogic speech full of rhetorical flourishes. Even where an actual stage is absent, K. moves about on an invisible stage because his interplay with the other characters is so structured that it constantly exhibits him but not the other "players." The function of all the other characters is very pointedly that of prompters. The "interrogation" to which the Court summons him looks as if designed to give K. the chance to react and act and to show by his behavior who he is. We are reminded of the *theatrum mundi* structure: the Court is in the role of God, i.e., spectator and judge in one; K., or everyman, is the actor, and the various locales of K.'s city are the stage that represents human existence. As in *Everyman* there is a single real actor with all other figures fulfilling subordinate functions in *his* plot. The use of the initial K. in place of a real name points up his kinship with abstract figures of morality plays.

Yet K. is far from being an abstract everyman, "a man without qualities." He is a very definite type of person with definite qualities that we come to recognize through his confrontations with the Court organs and related characters. For instance, when the warders deny K. his breakfast (which they eat themselves) and then offer to fetch him "a more modest one" from the café across the street, K. ignores the offer because he does not want to owe anything to them and because the apple he eats in defiance is surely better than anything they could get from "that filthy café" (P, 17). His reaction and thinking reveal his aggressive defiance and his snobbish-bourgeois contempt of the cheap and low-class place. His general arrogance, in both thought and behavior, towards the warders, the lowly bank clerks, the Court itself, and many other figures encountered, consistently repeats and reinforces this initial impression throughout the novel.

However, even though we are able to infer from K.'s mental, emotional, and behavioral reactions a certain type of character with definite qualities, these are not the issue, as they would be in a psychological novel in which exposé of character is the main purpose, or in a social-realistic novel in which exposure of a social type is the raison d'être of the work. K.'s qualities are merely instrumental in revealing him by his reactions to situations presented by his trial. Each of these situations could call forth several possible reactions. The action (or more frequently inaction) chosen by K. in preference to alternatives is what matters.

A good example is his initial reaction to the arrest itself. It occurs to K. that he might attempt to walk out of the door against his warders' "advice"—significantly they only "advise" and do not command him—and that such a resolute action might perhaps be the simplest solution to his predicament. But he decides against risking it, because he is afraid that in that event the warders might perhaps grab him, after all, and knock him down, in which case he would lose "all the superiority which now he was still able to keep vis-à-vis them" (P, 16). Thus he decides to return to his room and let the natural course of events take care of things. The function of the door points, of course, to the close parallelism between K. and the man from the country in the prison chaplain's parable to which we shall soon turn. What strikes the reader in this and many other instances is the function of the trial as a series of challenges compelling K. to adopt one or the other course of behavior and thus to show himself, or rather to show how he chooses the self he is.

This presupposes that he is being presented with situations that seem to show him something, although the meaning that is shown is never explained. The subordinate Court members first supply him with hints, advice, warnings, bits of information. By summoning him to the slums, the Court shows K. a type of setting that had been unknown to his bourgeois middle-class existence. By failing to issue a further summons to him, and by being absent when K. comes the second time, after he had announced that he would never come to the Court again, he is being notified that his words are taken seriously. The whipping of the warders in a junk room of his bank gives him the same message. Because K. had complained about their thieving and blackmailing, the warders are being punished. The Court puts on a grim show for him that drives home the seriousness and effectiveness of all words, attitudes, and "principles." K. claims he had not intended the warders' punishment, since he was only concerned with "a principle." The Court teaches him a lesson in consistency between opinion and action that might be seen as a demonstration of the essence of morality. It teaches him responsibility. For by his charges against them, K. has assumed a responsibility for the warders, a responsibility that is expressed in drastic and physical terms. K. is made to witness and to feel the sufferings that he, or rather his "principles," have caused, and he is made to feel that his "principles" cannot be separated from his self. At the same time, he is literally being called upon to act, and by the very same persons who had responded to his own unconscious call in the first place. By the kind of action he will now take in answer to his fellow men's desperate appeals, he will show himself, disclose his being.

The two aspects of the arrest, as defined by the Inspector, unite in this twofold show. A performance staged for K. shows him the consequences of words and opinions. At the same time, his victims, beseeching him to liberate them from the plight that he has caused, make him the chief player in the show staged for him. Their torment is the cue that K. has to take one way or another. He simply cannot help but reveal himself to the Court, to the reader, and above all to himself, a revelation, to be sure, that his consciousness does not pick up.

That the existential emphasis on personal responsibility is consistent Court policy is also shown by K.'s lawyer, Huld. Huld informs K. that the Court does not recognize counsel for the defendant, and bars lawyers from all official proceedings. The judges' hilariously contemptuous treatment of lawyers reflects this complete lack of official standing and function. In K.'s kind of trial, the defendant must face his Court in radical aloneness. In advanced stages of a trial, K. is told, the defendant even vanishes from sight.[11]

However, while admitting that lawyers have no official standing whatsoever in the Court, Huld argues strongly for their crucial importance to the defendant. This contradiction is much more than self-serving double-talk; it is part of the fundamental contradiction between two opposed views of the nature and purpose of the trial. If the trial is interpreted as the challenge of arriving at one's self-determination, counsel is irrelevant and even vitiating. But if the trial is seen as a defensive struggle against an external foe, counsel is essential, and to do without it would, as Huld warns K., entail the gravest peril to the defendant.

Titorelli reveals, with even greater clarity, this juxtaposition of the existential and the Oedipal view of the trial. Titorelli makes it clear to K. that real acquittal can never be obtained through helpers, but must be based solely upon the defendant's innocence. Innocence is an inner certainty that is not in need of external confirmation. Where innocence is involved, acquittal flows naturally from it, and judges cannot be influenced. But real acquittals lie outside experience. They are rumored from ancient legends and no proof exists of their attainability. In fact, holding out for real acquittal is an enormous risk precisely because of the Oedipal nature of the Lower Court, which is the only one accessible to empirical experience. For Titorelli the actual Court—in contrast to the unknown and unknowable Highest Court, which alone has the power to acquit—has the appearance of a merciless Oedipal power of horrifyingly wrathful divinity. Like the penal colony under the Old Commander, the known Court takes guilt for granted in any accused. Never can it be dissuaded from its conviction of guilt. "If I paint all the judges in a row here on a canvas," says Titorelli to K., "and you'll defend yourself before this canvas, you will be more successful than if you stand before the real Court" (P, 180). Faced with such a court, the dream of gaining real acquittal can only be a wish for suicide or else an overwhelmingly strong and venturesome faith of the self in itself. Like the entrance into the law, in the legend of the priest, it can only be the kind of faith that would bear out Kafka's dictum, "Believing means: to liberate the indestructible in oneself, or better: to liberate oneself, or still better: to be indestructible, or better: to be."[12] K.'s way of going about his trial, therefore, appears ironic from Titorelli's perspective, because K. says he is innocent and yet searches for helpers in his trial.

Titorelli's comments on the Court show the same contradiction in its program as is revealed by the lawyer's intimations. Titorelli admits the possibility of a defendant's innocence and complete acquittal. This possibility conflicts flagrantly with the guilty verdict for every accused that Titorelli assumes with certainty on the basis of his own and all known experience with the Court. However, if the trial is interpreted as a choice between one's faith regardless of consequences, and precautions for one's survival, the contradiction falls away. For then the defendant is free to commit himself or not to commit himself to his faith in himself.[13] In these terms innocence appears as a resolve. It is a choice of being—of being innocent. Such a choice of the self precludes, of course, the usefulness of any helpers.

When K. considers dismissing his lawyer and making his plea by himself, he seems to be veering towards such a course. He decides never to admit guilt under any circumstances. Yet this is only an apparent convergence between K.'s plan and the Court's program. For his refusal to admit guilt would not be at all the same as the innocence of which Titorelli speaks. Refusal to admit guilt would be a device, a strategy in a struggle with the Court; unlike innocence it would not be a commitment to be.

However, according to Titorelli, innocence and real acquittal are legendary exceptions to the rule of human reality. For the real, i.e., the regular case, Titorelli recommends two other courses—ostensible acquittal and indefinite procrastination. The assumptions on which these two possibilities rest are diametrically opposed to the assumptions of innocence. For them guilt or innocence is not the issue. In relation to these options, the trial is conceived as an attack upon the accused against which he has to protect himself for his survival. Therefore, helpers, compromises, and subterfuges are necessary as a matter of course.

Thus there issue from Titorelli two mutually contradictory concepts of the trial—the trial as self-choosing and the trial as self-defense. One is concerned with being, the other with surviving. The former is the existential, the latter the Oedipal view.

While the existential interpretation always pertains to official and explicit Court policy, ascribed to the unseen High Court, the Oedipal view is based upon the weaknesses and limitations of the lower judges. According to Titorelli's advice, the existential possibility, real acquittal, can issue only from the Highest Court, while the subterfuges of ostensible acquittal and procrastination exist by virtue of the corruptibility of the Lower Court members. In all instances, the existential meaning of the trial relates to the genuine and pure essence of the Court whereas deviations and corruptions on the lower levels support the pattern of an Oedipal struggle.

This by no means invalidates the reality and seriousness of the Oedipal aspect of the trial. The trial operates on two levels at once, and both are necessary to an understanding of it. The existential aspect of Court policy as described by the lawyer can, for instance, easily be interpreted as an extreme of Oedipal intimidation. The defendant is to be isolated and deprived of all human fellowship and comfort in order to be more quickly destroyed. The text certainly allows for such a reading.

This coexistence of two opposed levels of meaning, however, intensifies the protagonist's necessity to choose between different interpretations of his situation. Interpretation must precede choice as choice must precede action. Interpretation is a careful weighing of the various meanings implied in a situation. One of these the protagonist has to choose in order to act. Thus his reading of his situation must be the antecedent of his acting on it. K.'s whole trial, from the moment of his awakening, is a single challenge to him to read, and interpret, and then to act. K.'s arresting warder, Willem, reads a book when K. first sees him. This sign seems to tell K. that he is asked to read. Both warders and the Inspector explicitly admonish K. to listen more and to talk less. They ask him to concentrate and to reflect; they advise him not to jump to hasty conclusions and warn him that great efforts are in store for him. All that points to the fact that he will be asked to find the meaning of his trial by himself. It is in the same vein when we hear Frau Grubach refer to K.'s arrest as "something learned . . . which does not have to be understood" (P, 30), i.e., for which there does not seem to exist a meaning prepared for the accused. Huld by implication, and Titorelli explicitly, make clear to K. that it is he who has to choose what meaning he will give to his trial by choosing a course of action from the several possibilities outlined to him. Basically the choice boils down to one of two interpretations—the existential and the Oedipal—the choice of treating his trial as a commitment to self-exploration or as a struggle in self-defense. Both are possible and both are applicable according to Titorelli. The main point is the choice itself. Its urgency cannot be overlooked in Titorelli's insistent admonitions to K. to make his choice soon. Regardless of what it will be, the choice itself must not be deferred.

This necessity to choose culminates in the necessity to interpret with which the prison chaplain confronts K. It is no accident that the trial culminates in a parable to which the listener, K., seems to be called upon to supply the key and make the application to his own case. The legend of the doorkeeper who stands before the law abstracts the challenge that the trial itself represents.

The priest tells K. the legend of the doorkeeper as an illustration of K.'s delusion in regard to the Court. This delusion is explicitly stated in the text of the parable. At the end of his life, the man from the country asks why no one else has come to ask for the entrance, although everyone strives to enter the law. The doorkeeper answers that this entrance was destined for this man alone. The man's delusion consisted in the belief that the entrance into the law is something universal.

This delusion is implicit in the parable from the beginning. It is so strong that it easily escapes the reader because it is built into the man's perspective, which the reader, like K., tends to share. The delusion is implied in the man's initial reaction to finding the doorkeeper blocking his way. The text says the man has "not expected such difficulties," for he assumes "that the law is supposed to be accessible at any time" (P, 256). The man, in other words, has come with the expectation that entrance into the law is an automatic right available to everyone and at all times. To be sure, he does ask for permission to enter, but assumes that the permission will be a formality.

The doorkeeper says that he cannot allow the man to enter "now." The word is crucial because it is intimately tied to the man's expectation that the law would be open at any time. The doorkeeper's "not now" proves that this expectation is the man's primary illusion. The implication in his answer is this: At the moment of his asking for permission the man is not allowed to enter. Left open is the possibility that he might be able to enter if and when he does not ask for permission. This implication becomes explicit almost immediately. The doorkeeper suddenly steps aside and laughingly invites the man to go in despite his prohibition. Now "the door," the text tells us, "stands open as always." That is, no physical force whatsoever prevents the man from going in. The doorkeeper underlines the man's freedom by his jocular invitation. To be sure, in the same breath, he warns him of the frightening appearance of further doorkeepers inside.

Now there is nothing in the man's way except his fear. It is not the doorkeeper, but the man's fear that keeps him from entering. His desire for the law is great, but his fear is greater. To enter would involve a grave risk. The man decides not to take this risk. Intimidated by the doorkeeper's words and looks, he prefers to wait for permission. And this permission never comes.

The timing is a decisive key to the understanding of the parable. Entrance into the law is possible only at a definite, unique moment, which the man allows to pass by unused. The unique moment is linked to the unique individual for whom alone this entrance is destined. Uniqueness of moment and uniqueness of person are united in the free decision that is necessary to enter the law. No one else can make the man's entrance possible since it is *his* alone, and the one single moment for it must be seized by him who is to enter. If the doorkeeper were to grant the entrance, it would not be the man's entrance. It would be a gift bestowed on him by another or it would be a general right belonging to anyone and everyone. Furthermore, the entrance can truly belong to the man alone only if it results from his own free decision. Given the absolutely individual nature of the entrance, the man must lose it from the moment he fails to choose it. We are reminded of Kierkegaard's *Fear and Trembling* in which the individual's relation to the Absolute—in terms of Kafka's parable "the law," i.e., that which everyone strives for—can only be individual, i.e., completely and utterly unique.

The function of the doorkeeper as a figure of denial is necessary for the existential meaning of the parable. The obstacle is essential to the quest. Significantly the text does not begin with the man, but with the doorkeeper standing in front of the entrance.[14] If there were no doorkeeper, the entrance would be a simple wish fulfillment. Only by overcoming difficult resistances can the entrance become the individual's entrance. For that, the naysaying authority is necessary. This explains the priest's later remark that one does not have to accept everything the doorkeeper says as true, but only as necessary. Whether there really are such horrible doorkeepers inside the law, i.e., the truth, is impossible to ascertain. However, the fear aroused by them is necessary to make the entrance a true decision.

With his challenge to the man to try the entrance in the face of possibly terrifying odds, the doorkeeper imposes the existential meaning of the parable.[15] For he burdens the man with the necessity of making a decision that will determine his further existence. His choice will reveal what he is. Like Heidegger's *Dasein,* Sartre's *réalité humaine,* and Kierkegaard's eternal self, the man before the law creates himself by his choice. He is free to put his passion for the law above his life, which he would risk if the inner doorkeepers were really what the doorkeeper says they are. But at the same time, he is also free to place his life above the law and wait. In fact, he would even be free to leave his quest altogether and go home. Thus the doorkeeper makes the man choose himself before our very eyes. And the man, carefully deliberating, does make his choice. Among his three possible existences he chooses himself as one who rejects his freedom and waits for the permission of another. He has chosen himself for all his life as a dependent and supplicant and thereby literally cheated himself of his true existence—his authentic, or self-determined, life.

The man from the country is K.'s mirror image. K. too has decided to seek his law, i.e., his trial, by choosing the Court over the yacht. But, like the man from the country, he then refuses to accept the paradox of the self-determined entrance. He wants the Court, *his* doorkeeper, to relieve him of his own self-discovery and hand him his acquittal, or else take the blame for murdering him. Listening to the parable, K. mistakes the Kierkegaardian paradox of a law of freedom for an authority figure's dirty trick. He takes an Oedipal view of the doorkeeper, as he does of his trial. The doorkeeper appears to him as an oppressive deceiver, withholding and denying the man's right to enter. K. completely ignores the intent of the law, the uniquely personal nature of the entrance into this law, even though the parable itself had explained it to him.

Thus the doorkeeper legend illustrates K.'s delusion in regard to the Court. K. views his trial as an unjust attack by illegitimate power figures. He misunderstands the fact that the trial is his own choice, in which acquittal cannot come from another, even as the doorkeeper cannot give the man an entrance that belongs to the man alone. K. experiences his trial as a fight inflicted upon him by a vicious antagonist, and therefore he looks for aid. Although he does not go as far as Block or the man from the country in enslaving himself to helpers, he cannot see his way without them, either. The parable "Before the Law," like the degrading spectacle staged by K.'s lawyer and Merchant Block, illustrates the priest's warning to him, "You are looking too hard for the help of others. . . . Don't you realize that it is not the true help?" (P, 253). But K. fails to connect the priest's clear warning with the legend that illustrates it. Otherwise he would be able to see that it is not the doorkeeper's malice, but the man's fearful dependence that cheats him of his entrance into the law.

It is K.'s Oedipal perspective that blocks his understanding of both the parable and his own trial. He sees the Court as a gang of corrupt lechers who, if a woman is shown to them, "would overrun the bench and the defendant to get there in time" (P, 253). The image drastically conveys the Oedipal sense of the trial in which a feeble defendant is literally victimized by the sex drive of his judges. This view seems to appal the priest, as though it were not only blasphemous, but a most dangerous misapprehension. He shouts at K., "Can't you see two steps ahead?" (P, 254). Yet, even though the priest seems to consider it a fatal blindness, K.'s experiences in the novel do not contradict his Oedipal view. The priest himself contributes to the Oedipal atmosphere of *The Trial* when he singles out the help of women as a particularly illusory form of help. Here we come up once more against the two meanings of the trial as, on the one hand, an Oedipal assault upon the defendant's male adulthood and ego and, on the other, an existential challenge to choose and define oneself. K. himself has to find his own interpretation as the man has to find his own entrance into the law.

Hermeneutics, or the art of choosing the appropriate understanding of a text, and the trial, or the process of choosing the appropriate reaction to one's condition, are forms of one another. This explains the crucial importance of the priest's observation on hermeneutics in his discussion with K., "I only show you the current opinions," he says to K. "You must not pay too much attention to opinions. The text is unchangeable and its interpretations are often only expressions of despair over that fact" (P, 260). In the context of the parable, this remark is not an absolute discouragement of the hermeneutic attempt, as it is usually interpreted, but the opposite, a forceful suggestion of the necessity to find one's own interpretation. In his discussion of the legend, the priest behaves like a careful New Critic, restraining a hasty student from identifying the text's meaning with the protagonist's point of view. He always seeks to bring K. back to the text and points out the need to be faithful to the literal wording.

Furthermore, although he shows all sorts of interpretations, he never offers his own, or any definitive one. K. himself has to find *his* interpretation, just as the man from the country has to find *his* entrance into the law. Text and doorkeeper parallel each other. The unchangeable text stubbornly retains its ambiguities and withholds its meaning, functioning like the doorkeeper who withholds permission.

As we have seen, interpretation is the necessary first step in the process of deciding on a course of action. The parable tells of a man who has to interpret the doorkeeper's words and gestures. He has to weigh one meaning—the invitation to go in—against another that contradicts it. To which should he give preference? He has to choose his interpretation before he can decide his action. He has to choose between his own desire for entrance and his fear of the possible consequences. In fact, there is no way for the man to discover the true meaning of the doorkeeper prior to his own action. Only by attempting the entrance can the man find out the truth or falsehood of the doorkeeper's statements and the truth about the law. Before he can understand doorkeeper and law, the man must reveal himself by his choice of action.

As K. is the reader of the legend, the Court is the reader of K. As we have seen, K.'s arrest, so the Inspector informs him, amounts only to his being made aware of the condition of being arrested and to show the Court how he will take it. Kafka wrote K.'s story from the vantage point of the Court. He made himself the reader of the situation in which his character, on whom he bestowed his own initial, finds himself. The first member of the Court who comes to "arrest" K. bears Kafka's own first name, Franz.[16] Franz, or the Court, is Kafka's writing and recording self, arresting, inspecting, and seeking to read Kafka's other—his living—self, K., truncated and reduced to the ignominious condition of life, which forces us to choose between equally essential but mutually contradictory courses of action. In his letters to his fiancée, Felice Bauer, which shortly preceded *The Trial,* Kafka had constantly shown his awareness of the overwhelming need for decision and his inability to arrive at any.[17] Now, in writing about K.'s trial, he arrests himself for close inspection of the possibilities given to him. It is significant, in this context, that the man who presides over K.'s arrest carries the title of "Inspector" or "Supervisor," "*Aufseher,*" in the original German. In the designation of his function, the word "to see" is built in. It attests to the universality of Kafka's metaphoric language, and therefore its subliminal power, that the metaphoric meaning, which carries the action, applies even to the translation.

The Trial is a self-confrontation not only on account of Kafka's recorded self-identification with K.[18] Kafka himself shared the Oedipal perspective, which finds its most cogent formulation in his famous "Letter to His

Father." In it he traces his all-pervasive guilt feelings and the wretchedness of his whole life directly back to his father's disastrous influence upon him. Given his own sensitive and vulnerable character, next to and under the overpowering and uncomprehending vitality of his father, the former had to become deformed, short of being totally crushed. To be sure, Kafka absolves his father of all intentional guilt and malice, but instead invokes an inexorable necessity, a tragic fate, condemning both himself and his father to interminable sufferings from and through each other. Until the "correction" at the end of the letter, which Kafka puts into his father's mouth, his letter appears to be the document of a strict determinist. It could have come from the pen of a refined writer of the naturalist school. The tormented relationship between father and son depicted in it resembles a marriage portrayed by Strindberg in his naturalistic phase. It reflects the mental climate of late nineteenth-century positivism in which Freud also had his intellectual roots. The determinism of the letter shows itself linguistically in such phrases as "you *had to have* such effects on me," "*I could not* according to my nature . . . ," "my feeling *stems from your* influence."[19] In this very important document, Kafka blames heredity (his being a mixture of the paternal Kafka and the maternal Löwy line) and early environment for his predicaments, and raises circumstance to the level of fate. There is hardly any room here for free self-determination through choice and act, only a modicum of resigned peace to be gained from insight into one's situation. In terms of existential thought, Kafka's "Letter to His Father" is a prime example of what Sartre calls "bad faith," with which we deny our freedom by making nature, fate, situation, circumstances, and the Other bear the responsibility for our being. At the end of *The Trial,* it is Josef K. who echoes Kafka's own determinism, as expressed not only in his "Letter to His Father," but in a more subtle and less systematic form throughout his diaries and the letters to Felice. K., having recognized that it would be his inner duty to seize the knife and kill himself, finds that he lacks the strength for the act. For his lack of strength he blames someone else.

> He could not completely prove himself adequate to his task; he could not relieve the authorities of all their work; the responsibility for this ultimate failure bore he who had denied him the remnant of strength needed for that. (P, 271)

This leaves it unclear who is to bear responsibility for K.'s failure to live up to his own expectations—whether the Supreme Judge, or his father and progenitor, or God who created him. But in any case, it is not he himself who bears responsibility. He claims by implication that he could not have acted in any other way than he did. Here Josef K. adumbrates the same deterministic view that his author exhibits five years later in his autobiographical document.

Subsequently K. is slaughtered "like a dog" rather than allowed to die like a man, and it looks as if the shame of this will survive him. There are several meanings contained in this ending.[20] But one of them surely refers to the fact that K. is condemned to such a degrading inhuman death by his own evasion of the self-determined end that he has shirked against his own explicit understanding. Seen together with Kafka's "Letter to His Father," *The Trial* represents a confrontation between Kafka's own deterministic perspective, assumed by him from time to time, and the possibility of a faith transcending the conditioning of human existence, which he also envisaged. But that this confrontation was also a judgment of the Oedipal by the existential perspective is shown by this aphorism written three years after *The Trial:* "There was a time when I did not understand why I received no answer to my question; today I do not understand how I could ever have believed that I could ask. But, of course, I did not believe, I only asked."[21]

Beyond K., and beyond his creator, the Court reaches out to the parable's reader—ourselves. Like the man before the door, the reader assumes that a definitive entrance into the law, or into the text, is to be offered by the proper authority, and he or she assumes that this entrance is general and relatively easy to obtain—one and the same door for every seeker, one and the same meaning for every reader. But the text resists the attempt at unambiguous understanding. The events depicted and the statements perceived remain contradictory. K.'s preliminary interrogation takes place in Fräulein Bürstner's room. Is the meaning of this to punish K. for his desire for the girl? Or is it the opposite, a signal drawing him to a more personal form of eros, which his weekly visits to Elsa have drowned in routine? There is no answer given, only the unchangeably ambiguous text. But the open question challenges us, as it challenges K. There does not seem a way to meaning except by a choice entailing the risk of error. K.'s guilt remains impenetrable because the only access to it is interpretation, which is risk, instead of revelation, which gives certainty.

NOTES

1. Cf. Wilhelm Emrich, *Franz Kafka* (Bonn: Athenäum, 1958), 260.
2. For a detailed discussion of the Oedipal structure of *The Trial,* I should like to refer the reader to my book, *Franz Kafka: Tragik und Ironie* (Munich-Vienna: Langen-Müller, 1964), chaps. 7 and 8.
3. The exception is the fragmentary chapter, "Zu Elsa."

4. Max Brod, ed., *Hochzeitsvorbereitungen auf dem Lande und andere Prosa aus dem Nachlass* (New York: Schocken Books, 1953), 115. All translations from Kafka in this essay are my own.

5. Cf. also Emrich's view, *Franz Kafka,* 265, that the purpose of the trial is K.'s taking issue with himself and coming to understand himself.

6. Quotations from *The Trial* are taken, in my own translations, from Max Brod, ed., *Der Prozess,* Roman, 5th ed. (New York: Schocken Books, 1946), which will be referred to in the text as P.

7. Cf. Ingeborg Henel, "Die Türhüterlegende und ihre Bedeutung für Kafkas 'Prozess,'" *Deutsche Vierteljahrsschrift für Literaturwissenschaft und Geistesgeschichte,* Vol. 38 (1964): 61. Although I disagree with Ingeborn Henel's formulation on this point, the pioneering contribution of her article should be emphasized.

8. Brod, *Hochzeitsvorbereitungen,* 48.

9. Beda Allemann's analysis of the novel ("Kafka: Der Prozess," in *Der deutsche Roman,* ed. Benno von Wiese (Düsseldorf: Bagel, 1963), Vol. 2, 234–90, assumes that the plea cannot conform to K.'s real (and impossible) task of justifying his existence "fundamentally" because it would "only contain a justification after the fact," which is futile for the problem of his trial. However, if K.'s task is to discover his guilt, the impossibility of the plea is based on the necessary self-deception and duplicity involved in the attempt to justify all his past actions in retrospect. Allemann's assertion that the Court is not at all interested in K.'s plea is of course unprovable. It is based upon the analogy between the Deputy Manager and the Court that lacks persuasiveness because the Deputy Manager is the character at the opposite pole of K.'s trial, as K.'s choice of the Court over the Deputy Manager's invitation shows.

10. In addition to "*Prozess,*" the word "*Verfahren*" ("procedure") is used to designate K.'s trial.

11. Cf. Emrich's view, *Franz Kafka,* 281, that Kafka by his treatment of the lawyer and Leni expressed his own rigorous rejection of the idea of help from another.

12. Brod, *Hochzeitsvorbereitungen,* 89.

13. Cf. also Emrich, *Franz Kafka,* 261.

14. This circumstance has been pointed out by Heinz Politzer, *Franz Kafka: Parable and Paradox* (Ithaca, N.Y.: Cornell University Press, 1962), 177.

15. Although Ingeborg Henel specifically states that the doorkeeper by his very existence points to the entrance at the same time as he forbids it, she curiously fails to mention the passage in which he does so explicitly. Emrich does point out that the doorkeeper invites the man to enter, but he draws from this fact a conclusion very different from the one pointed out here. For Emrich the contradiction between prohibition and invitation indicates the dichotomy between "official" and "private person" present in all of Kafka's bureaucrats (*Franz Kafka,* 268). According to Emrich, the officials want to break out of the rigidly determined order of their service into a "freer" existence. In contrast to Emrich, I hold that Kafka's restriction of the narrative perspective to the protagonist compels us to consider only the function

their characters possess for the protagonist. Their own "wishes" are inaccessible to us, as they are to K.

16. Cf. Michel Carrouges, *Kafka versus Kafka,* trans. Emmett Parker (University: University of Alabama Press, 1968), 39. The original version *Kafka contre Kafka* appeared in Paris (Librairie Plon, 1962). Carrouges refers here to an article by Michel Cournot (*L'Arche,* No. 23) who suggests that the use of the name Franz for the arresting warder points to Kafka's participation in the carrying out of K.'s arrest.

17. Cf. Franz Kafka, *Briefe an Felice und Andere Korrespondenz aus dem Nachlass,* ed. Erich Heller and Jürgen Born (Frankfurt am Main: S. Fischer Lizenzausgabe von Schocken Books, New York, 1967), 535, 546, 511. See also p. 289, where the ability to be decisive is ascribed to Felice, but by implication found wanting in the writer himself.

18. Brod, ed., *Hochzeitsvorbereitungen,* 196, and Max Brod, ed., *Briefe, 1902–1924* (New York: Schocken Books, 1958), 195.

19. Brod, ed., *Hochzeitsvorbereitungen,* 166 f.

20. The multivalence of the ending is very well discussed by Politzer, *Franz Kafka: Parable and Paradox,* 217.

21. Brod, ed., *Hochzeitsvorbereitungen,* 43.

12

THE THREE ENDINGS OF JOSEF K. AND THE ROLE OF ART IN *THE TRIAL*

As with the tip of an iceberg, the visible part of *The Trial* is borne by a submerged part of repressed alternate possibilities in which Kafka's real intentions concerning K. are revealed with relative clarity. This is especially true of the two alternative endings of Josef K.'s life, respectively his trial, which K. dreams. Neither dream was admitted into the novel. One was published separately, in *A Country Doctor* under the title "A Dream"; the other, which concluded the chapter "The House," was crossed out by Kafka and suppressed altogether. Comparisons of these dream endings with Josef K.'s end in the novel will make *The Trial* appear as something like the negative of K.'s dreams. The nature of these dreams as well as the fact of their excision shed an important light not only on the truncated text of the novel itself, a fragment despite its ending, but on Kafka's total oeuvre as it presented itself at this exact midpoint in his career as a writer.[1]

The parallels between Josef K.'s execution in *The Trial* and his death in "A Dream" are very strong. In both cases an inner "duty" seems to compel K. to his death. In K.'s waking life, it is the Court, through its executioners, that brings this "inner law" to K.'s consciousness; in his dream, it is an artist. In the novel, he realizes "that it would have been his duty to seize the knife, as it traveled from hand to hand above him, and plunge it into himself" (Kafka 1946b, 271).[2] In "A Dream," two men, who correspond to the two executioners in the novel, hold a gravestone in the air and as soon as K. appears, thrust it into the ground so perfectly

---

From *The Kafka Debate: New Perspectives for Our Time*, ed. Angel Flores (New York: Gordian Press, 1977), 335–53.

that it stands "as if cemented there" (Kafka 1948a, 171). But from behind the executioners a third man emerges "whom K. immediately recognizes as an artist." At once the artist sets to work inscribing on the gravestone with "golden letters" issuing "from an ordinary pencil . . . here lies." But something impedes him; he cannot continue his work; "he let the pencil sink and . . . turned towards K." K. feels miserable. The artist's frustration grieves him; he cries and sobs into his hands. The artist tries to go on with his work, but the former luster of the golden letters fades and is gone. With great effort, he manages to write a capital J—Josef K.'s first initial—but then loses his patience and stomps on the grave mound. "At long last K. understood him" (Kafka 1948a, 172). With his bare hands, he rapidly digs his own grave and sinks into it. While K. is

> received by the impenetrable depths, his name on high was racing with mighty flourishes across the stone.
>
> Enchanted by this view, he woke up. (Kafka 1970, 147)

In K.'s dream the artist assumes the role of the Court in making K. aware of his destiny. In both death is seen as a duty, a personal law that both times K. seeks to obey. In both works, K. while alive is felt to be an obstacle to someone else's progress. In "A Dream" this is transparent. In *The Trial* it is expressed with extreme indirection and subtlety. When on his second Sunday in the Court K. forays into the attic where the offices of the Court are located, he feels sickened by the close air. "The girl" who is a member of the Court bureaucracy points out to him that he cannot stay because he would "disturb the intercourse (or traffic)" and "K. asked with his glances what intercourse (or traffic)" he was disturbing (Kafka 1946b, 86). The German word used by Kafka in this passage is "Verkehr," which can mean both "traffic" and "intercourse," and thus includes not only the spatial and commercial, but also the sexual aspect of interaction among human beings. We find here an obvious echo of the concluding words of "The Judgment"—the "unending *Verkehr*" that coincides with and outlasts Georg Bendemann's self-removal from life. His death brings back infinite life to the bridge that had seemed lifeless when he had been alive. We are likewise reminded of Gregor Samsa's self-removal from his family, which, as the last scene of the story makes abundantly clear, is only now enabled to reenter that stream of procreative life that Gregor's existence had seemed to dam up and inhibit. The "severely" beautiful girl of the Court is coupled with a male figure, the Court usher who had let K. into the Court offices. The pair confronts him, "looking at him" in such a way "as if in the next minute some great metamorphosis would have to happen to him which they did not want to miss" (Kafka 1946b, 85). The standard English translation uses the word "transformation" (Kafka 1957, 83), instead of "metamorphosis" for the German word "Verwandlung," which has both meanings. Thereby it obscures Kafka's important verbal reference to his earlier work "Die Verwandlung" ("The Metamorphosis") that only consistent employment of the same English equivalent for Kafka's term is able to convey. In addition to the allusion in the term "metamorphosis," a subtle connection between Gregor Samsa's fate and the Court offices of *The Trial* is established.

In *The Trial,* that totally excluding and absolutely alienating phenomenon, the metamorphosis, remains a metaphor even as K.'s inhuman degradation at the end is restricted to the simile "like a dog." Yet, from the vantage point of the last chapter, the banishment from the human race implied by the narrator's use of the term "metamorphosis," even though restricted to the metamorphic, sheds light on the important parallelism of structure between the novella of 1912 and the novel of 1914. In "The Metamorphosis," Grete makes Gregor understand that he has no place among the living and that had he been human, he would have vanished long before by his own free will. In the last chapter of *The Trial,* Fräulein Bürstner, or a woman resembling her, convinces K. of "the worthlessness of his resistance" (Kafka 1946b, 268) to his executioners. From then on he himself leads the way to his death. In both works, the female figure, articulate or symbolic voice of the power system that, at the same time, represents life itself, enlightens the protagonist about his fate. She teaches him that for him self-destruction is the only self-fulfillment.

In K.'s dream, his existence also forms an obstacle, but not to "intercourse." His life blocks the progress and fulfillment of the artist's work. The artist in "A Dream" performs the work of "the hammer" that, Kafka felt, had "to smash [him] to bits" before the onrushing flood of his visions could be "liberated" (Kafka 1948b, 321). The threefold division of labor in "A Dream"—between the artist, K., and K.'s name—reflects the structural relationships within Kafka's masochistic and sacrificial poetics. The artist corresponds to the murderous demand of literature for the sacrifice of life. K. corresponds to the living self that is to be sacrificed to literature. The glorious characters of K.'s name on his grave symbolize the visionary work of Kafka's "dreamlike inner life." In the period between "The Metamorphosis" and *The Trial,* the beneficiary of Kafka's scapegoat figure changed from the family to literature. For the "liberation" of his "dreamlike inner life" (Kafka 1948b, 420), Kafka had, shortly before he began *The Trial,* renounced his engagement. His empirical life was to be a sacrifice on the altar of his work. Even in the midst of his courtship of Felice, more than a year before he began *The Trial,* Kafka had indicated the necessity of this self-immolation. In a diary entry of June 21, 1913, he writes:

> This monstrous world which I have in my head. But how to liberate myself and how to free it without being torn apart. And yet [it is] a thousand times better to be torn apart than to keep it locked or buried in myself. For that purpose I live on earth; that is utterly clear to me. (Kafka 1948b, 306)

Like the penal apparatus of *In the Penal Colony,* the artist of "A Dream" embodies the mission of "literature" as a fatal duty and at the same time as a redemption that raises the self to a bliss greater than any happiness ordinary life can offer. Both apparatus and artist are "writers," one writing the sentence of punishment into the prisoner's flesh, the other immortalizing K.'s name high above the body that sinks into oblivion.

This diary entry of December 26, 1914, close in time to the actual composition of "A Dream," stands in an even closer thematic relationship to Kafka's visionary short tale. His redemption, Kafka says here, will come not by literature, but by death.

> Do I complain in these pages [of his diary] in order to find redemption in them? From this notebook it [redemption] will not issue; it will come when I am in bed and it will turn me on my back so that I shall be lying beautiful and light and bluish-white; no other redemption will ever come. (Kafka 1948b, 452)

Comparing this remarkable diary entry with the description of K.'s dying in "A Dream," one is struck by the almost identical wording of the passages. K. sinks into his grave "turned onto his back by a gentle current" (Kafka 1970, 147). The beauty, lightness, and bluish-white appearance, with which Kafka visualizes his own corpse, conveys an analogous feeling of supreme contentment, and indeed delivery, as that which animates K.'s dreamed death. Both death scenes are related to and take the place of literature.

Dying is seen by Kafka as the parallel road to writing, but one that leads further and more effectively to the common goal—redemption. Seen in this context, the artist is not only the embodiment of the writing self that kills and sacrifices the living self for the sake of literature, but he also continues the line of Kafka's Oedipal father figures who, from Old Bendemann to the two old executioners of *The Trial,* cause or demand the protagonist's death as the fulfillment of a "special law." Impatiently stomping the grave mound and chasing K. down into his grave, the artist particularly resembles the archetypal Mr. Samsa, stomping, hissing, and chasing his son into his room that is to become his grave. The artist too shows that the protagonist's "duty" lies in erasing himself from the living. At the same time, however, this artist-executioner of "the dream" reveals the remarkable transformation that Kafka's Oedipal power figure undergoes in the period of *The Trial* and *In the Penal Colony.* For K., as for the Officer of *In the Penal*

Colony, death ceases to be a punishment or even a sacrifice and becomes a treasured end in itself. With this the Oedipal father figure changes from the protagonist's master to his instrument. He frankly serves the latter's experience of delivery.

The close parallel between K.'s dream and the Officer's yearning in *In the Penal Colony* is immediately apparent. K.'s "enchantment" is the experience of "being written" even as the Officer's coveted goal is the experience, and not the discovery, of the "sentence" that is to be engraved in his flesh. However, "A Dream" goes beyond *In the Penal Colony* in making the punitive agency subservient to the self. Although the Officer's goal is utilization of punishment as the instrumentality for pleasure, the content of his experience is still to be the reception of the "law" into his flesh. Although this law in his case is self-given and self-administered, it still is separate from his self. The Officer searches for the aggrandizement of self by the experience of something distinct from and higher than the self, by the experience of "a law" that forms part of a power structure or penal system external to the self, a creation of the quasi-divine father figure of the Old Commander. Josef K., however, experiences no "law," no "sentence," other than the glory of his name. His ecstasy derives from knowing himself abstracted into his pure sign, his essence, his name. By virtue of this distillation he is allowed to shine with a splendor that his mere empirical self could never hope to attain. The transformation of life into literature, i.e., the change of the living self into its sign, gives such joy that death is more of a prize to be seized than a price to be paid.

Josef K. in the novel is closely linked to Josef K. in the dream. It is for his name, his good repute, that K. consents to die at the end of *The Trial.* The admonition that Fräulein Bürstner's shape conveys to him is partly the condemnation of his will to live, of his ardent possessiveness with which as if "with twenty hands" he had wanted "to snatch at the world . . . and not for a very laudable motive either" (Kafka 1946b, 282). But his wish to leave a good name behind seems to be even more important to K.

> [A]m I to show now that not even a year's trial has been able to teach me anything? Am I to exit as a slow learner? Should they be able to say of me after I am gone that at the beginning of my trial I wanted to finish it and at its end to start it all over again? I don't want people to be able to say that of me afterwards. (Kafka 1946b, 269)

Thus K.'s acquiescence to his execution is only for the smaller part an acceptance of guilt and atonement. For the greater part it is self-regard for the survival of his image. This is a version—greatly subdued to be sure—of those intimations of immortality that the "gilded" letters of his name evoke in K.'s dream. In both cases the self is to be freed from the sullying admixtures and demeaning ambiguities of life. It is to be perpetuated in its desired essence, as a purified image or beautified form—we remember the "mighty flourishes" that K.'s name has become—for others to remember and to behold.

Although explicitly stated only in the last chapter, implicitly this tendency is inherent in K.'s whole struggle for the Court's recognition of his "innocence," and it thus supplies the key to the subliminal drift of the work. In Josef K.'s behavior toward his trial, two basic tendencies are discernible once his initial pretense of disregarding and belittling it is seen through. One is to provoke the Court into punishing and destroying him; the other is to force the Court to recognize him at his own evaluation, as "guiltless." In the later chapters of *The Trial,* K. holds on tenaciously to his claim for a supreme prize—real and definitive acquittal. It makes him ignore and, tacitly or overtly, reject the possibilities for survival by procrastination that Huld and Titorelli seem to offer to him. Against their counsel, K. holds out for an existence justified and confirmed by the highest authority in his ken.

K.'s behavior in his trial parallels the rushing motion and overpowering "pull" that in his dream carry him swiftly toward his grave. In his dream, K. "glided along" on the paths of the cemetery, "as if on a rushing stream" (Kafka 1948a, 170), and when he arrives at the grave mound, "the path went rushing on under his shifting foot" so that "he tottered and fell on his knees just in front of the grave mound" (Kafka 1948a, 171). This rushing movement toward an imminent and abrupt ending also characterizes K.'s actions in his trial. K. rushes toward a verdict. From its very inception, he seeks a quick end of his trial. Even at his arrest, he obliges the demands of the warders for a black jacket because he is determined to do anything that might "accelerate the matter" (Kafka 1946b, 18). He heeds the telephone summons of the Court in order to put an end to his trial once and for all. "This first interrogation must also be the last" (Kafka 1957, 40). Later he is dissatisfied with Huld because of the lawyer's slow interminable pace, and decides to dismiss him because he "could not tolerate obstacles in his trial which were perhaps caused by his own lawyer" (Kafka 1946b, 153). He fails to accept, or even consider, Titorelli's counsels because they would either lead, as in Ostensible Acquittal, to a repetition of the trial, or to its indefinite procrastination, in Titorelli's other course. The lawyer calls K. "impatient" (Kafka 1946b, 223) and his counsel exactly parallels Titorelli's. He advises seeking every means to postpone judgment and warns of rushing precipitously toward it. His old client Block is the obvious example for K. to learn the patience and concomitant humility that the ability to wait over protracted periods of time expresses. Titorelli generalizes Huld's advice into systems of dodging definitive judgments, and in contrast to the lawyer actually gives K. cogent logical arguments why dodging is essential for survival. For any verdict known to experience is a verdict of guilty. Thus both Titorelli and Huld adumbrate the position of the doorkeeper who, in the parable, withholds permission to enter the law. By rejecting such counsel, K. rejects waiting as a condition of existence and insists on rushing toward his judgment.

Georg Bendemann in "The Judgment" also rushes to carry out the judgment against him. In contrast to "The Judgment," however, the verdict is never pronounced in *The Trial*. It is merely executed. The only voice coming anywhere near articulating a judgment, in the sense of supplying a reason for execution, is K.'s own. From the very beginning of his arrest, K.'s inner tendency is to arrive at a verdict that no one gives him and that he finally gives himself.

There is a third ending of K.'s trial that Kafka later discarded, but that also exerts a powerful subliminal influence upon the novel. In the fragmentary chapter "The House," K. muses on the possibility of persuading Titorelli to lead him to "the office . . . from where the first denunciation in his case had been issued" (Kafka 1946b, 290). Reaching the house, K. undergoes a glorious "metamorphosis" (Kafka 1946b, 294); the word "Verwandlung" strikingly refers to Kafka's earlier tale of punishment and sacrifice. But this "metamorphosis" is the complete opposite of Gregor Samsa's. It is a miraculous elevation from "the low life he had led until then" into a radiant, ecstatic condition. "The light that had until now come in from behind, changed and suddenly streamed in dazzlingly from the front. K. looked up, Titorelli nodded at him and turned him around. . . . K. was wearing a new long and dark garment, it was pleasantly warm and heavy. [He] knew what had happened to him, but he was so happy that he did not yet want to admit it to himself. In the corner of a corridor, on one wall of which great windows were opened, he found his former clothes in a pile" (Kafka 1946b, 295).

This turning around of K., the 180-degree shift of the source of light, and the change of K.'s garments—all translate into event the metaphors contained in such concepts as "transfiguration" (in which "metamorphosis" receives a solely positive meaning), "regeneration," "rebirth." The idea of "rebirth" enacted in these happenings of K.'s reverie clearly links the "House" chapter to the fragmentary "Mother" chapter.[3] In both, K. thinks of returning to an origin—in the "Mother" chapter to the origin of his life, in the "House" chapter to the origin of his trial. But in the "Mother" chapter, K. realizes that any hope for delivery placed in this return must be futile; in the "House" reverie, on the other hand, return brings salvation. Unlike Georg Bendemann, Josef K. does not reach a merely symbolic reconciliation with his accuser and judge, but a literal one. He does not atone, he is redeemed.

It is not difficult to see in K.'s reverie a transparent aspect of Kafka's personal myth, the eternal dream of reconciliation with and justification by the parental power to which he owed his life together with his lifelong sense of guilt. But here this dream merges with its opposite, Raban's dream of narcissistic omnipotence through total withdrawal from all "engagement" in human life. The artist, Titorelli, becomes the doorkeeper who, in contrast to the doorkeeper in the priest's parable, does lead into the law that is the place, the *locus amoenus,* where justification and liberation are one. The artist is the guide for K.'s return trip to his accuser. In K.'s waking life, Titorelli tells him that the only cases of real acquittal are reported in ancient legends. Thus acquittal appears as a return to a remote and nonremembered past, a past of myth and legend rather than of recorded memory. In waking life, not even Titorelli is able to offer an approach to that redeeming past that seems such a close parallel, indeed a variant, of the entrance into the law. But in reverie and dream the artist can be used to effect it. Titorelli's dream service goes even beyond the artist's in "A Dream." In "A Dream" K. has to pay for his transfiguration with his life. Titorelli, however, demands no price at all for the transfiguration procured by him for K.

Titorelli, we remember, turns K. around and the light that had hitherto been behind now shines at him in front. So blatantly does Kafka show that K.'s trial is the negative of K.'s dream of redemption. What looks negative to K.'s waking mind—arrest, accusation, judgment, punishment, Court—is turned around in his dreams and transformed into the instrument of bliss.

Even by such an apparently minor feature as the use of the image of water does Kafka point to that reversal of evaluation.[4] In K.'s waking life, which is his trial, only the negative side of the image of water—with its roots in an early childhood memory[5]—is allowed to appear. In the third chapter of *The Trial,* K.'s condition in the Court offices is compared to "seasickness" (Kafka 1946b, 91), the same malady that in "Description of a Struggle" conveys the disorientation of the protagonists in the face of the utter incapacity of words to cope with the objects they are supposed to designate. The incommensurability between human consciousness, as organized in language, and the being of things outside this consciousness is repeated in the utter incompatibility between K.'s breathing and the air of the Court. Not until he gets outside the Court offices can he breathe freely and normally and "at once regain all his forces" (Kafka 1946b, 91), while now conversely the Court employees, "accustomed as they were to the air of the bureaus, felt ill in the relatively fresh air" coming in through the open door (Kafka 1946b, 92). Still inside the Court offices, K. "felt he was on a ship rolling in heavy seas" (Kafka 1957, 89). With the same metaphor to seasickness or nausea—the etymological root of nausea is "ship sickness" (*malum navis*)—Sartre more than twenty years after *The Trial* described man's unsettling exposure to the existence of things that is forever alien and impervious to human consciousness. In Kafka, as in Sartre, seasickness ("nausea") conveys the bewilderment, helplessness, and terror of the human self suddenly confronted with a world that utterly transcends any hope for comprehensibility, familiarity, and protection.[6] We remember from another of Kafka's early works, "The Stoker," that it is the sea, the liquid element in its largest extent, that gives rise to the profound anxiety that K.'s seasickness, like the Fat Man's and the Praying Man's of his earliest work, expresses.

> A movement without end, a restlessness transmitted from the restless element to helpless human beings and their works! (Kafka 1946a, 17)

And like Georg Bendemann, Josef K. looks down upon a river on his way to his execution.

But in K.'s dream the function of water is reversed. A powerful current sweeps K. toward fulfillment, washing away all obstacles and freeing him from gravity. When Titorelli leads him to the dream Court, their effortless rise and descent on the stairs is compared to the "easy" course of "a light boat in water" (Kafka 1946b, 294). And in "A Dream," as we have already seen, the simile of "rushing water" (Kafka 1970, 141) describes the rapid movement of the pathways that carry K. toward his predestined grave, and as he sinks down into the depths of the earth, it is again a "current"—"gentle" this time—that turns him on his back so that he can look up as "his name up there swept with mighty flourishes across the stone" (Kafka 1970, 147). The image of current or flow has evolved from the fearsome threatening force of an avenging and menacing power into the vehicle of the self's aggrandizement and transfiguration. In his waking state, Josef K. still experiences the Court, and with it the image of water, in its earlier threatening guise; but in his dream, authority cannot resist the flow of inspiration in which all obstacles are overcome. In both dreams the artist is the conveyor to transfiguration. Titorelli transforms the Court, at K.'s behest, from an accusing to a redeeming authority. In K.'s reverie, Kafka portrayed Titorelli as the artist who could lead the self back to that accusatory father figure from whom both guilt and existence issued. Art might effectuate the plea that would transform the accusation into acceptance. K.'s reverie of Titorelli represents a utopian contrast to Kafka's own view of his writing expressed in the "Letter to His Father." There he describes it as a "purposefully drawn-out farewell" (Kafka 1953, 203). But through the dream figure of Titorelli, art brings about not departure, but arrival.

Even though K. excised this dream from *The Trial,* its undertow can be detected in his insistence on "real and definite acquittal." In the guise of the Court's affirmation of his innocence, K. looks for redemption. The headlong rushing toward his verdict, typical of the time structure of K.'s behavior in the trial, receives its full meaning only from the excised dreams.

But the fact of their excision is perhaps even more important for understanding Kafka's full intent in *The Trial.* In this respect, the figure of the painter Titorelli plays a crucial role. In Titorelli's contradictory attitudes, Kafka presents the contrast between art as dream, wish fulfillment, and vision, and art as demythologizing self-preservation.

In K.'s actual encounter with the painter, in the seventh chapter of *The Trial,* Titorelli warns him that real acquittals occur in legends only and are unknown to experience. That is, existence appears justified only in myth. Proofs of real acquittals do not exist, even as the proofs of revealed religion are contained only in documents that the secularist mind declares to be myth. Sensory experience cannot verify them. Titorelli consigns the reports of real acquittals either to faith or to art. He calls them "beautiful," a fine subject matter for paintings. Nor should they be ignored; "they probably do contain a certain truth" (Kafka 1946b, 186). But the only place in which this "truth" manifests itself is myth. That is, the ancient legends of real acquittal represent the refuge of a possible symbolic significance. Like a "realist," Titorelli establishes or accepts a cynical dichotomy between what should be and what is, between the "law" as idea and empirical reality. Experience and the law are "two different things" that should not be "confused" (Kafka 1946b, 185).

> In the law . . . we are told of course that the innocent is acquitted, but, on the other hand, we are likewise told there that judges cannot be influenced. But from my experience I have learned exactly the reverse. I don't know of any real acquittal, but of many cases of pull. (Kafka 1946b, 185)

He who wants to survive must not permit the theoretical hope for acquittal, the ideal portrayed by art and legend, in other words, "the law," to mislead him. Guided only by empirical experience he must lower his sights, stick to observation, and renounce the expectation of final answers. He should not overestimate the judges. In fact, he should hold them in low esteem, realize their weaknesses, vanities, venalities, and play on their unlawful but all too human character. Above all, he must make the supreme sacrifice and renounce all desire for the unknown and unknowable Highest Court, which alone can grant real acquittal. The Highest Court

> is totally inaccessible for you, for me and for all of us. What things look like there, we don't know and incidentally, don't want to know. (Kafka 1946b, 190)

As there is no salvation and no justification for human existence, without God, neither is there real acquittal without the Highest Court. However, it is only the renunciation of this hope that permits the trial to stay within the limits that make survival in it possible by virtue of the indefinite postponement of a verdict of guilty, which is the only kind of verdict known.

Here the difference between Titorelli's advice and the hope by which Block and the man from the country are reduced to canine existence should be pointed out. Block and the man from the country allow themselves to be degraded because they never cease to hope for acquittal, respectively for the entrance into the law. This hope they share with K., even though they are willing to wait for its fulfillment indefinitely, while he is not. But Titorelli counsels the abandonment of all hope for anyone relying on experience. Only by absolutely believing in his innocence, contrary to all evidence gathered from experience, could K. hope for real acquittal. As I have pointed out elsewhere, Titorelli's radical equation of innocence with faith contrary to reason makes his advice identical with the meaning of the priest's parable "Before the Law," in which the only possibility for the man's entrance is the enormous risk of walking through the gate despite the prohibition by the doorkeeper and his horrifying information about the interior of the law. Titorelli's counsel, however, differs from the priest's legend by its point of emphasis. The legend emphasizes the risk attendant upon faith, while Titorelli stresses keeping out of the law in order to survive. He thus anticipates the point of view of the ape in Kafka's parable "A Report to an Academy." The price that the ape has to pay for a relatively acceptable "way out" of the disaster that has overtaken him is the renunciation of all hope for true freedom. As the ape by his renunciation helps himself out of his cage, Titorelli offers Josef K. a "way out" (in two versions) of the invisible cage of his "arrest" and trial. As in the case of the ape, Titorelli also shows that true freedom, i.e., real acquittal, lies buried in legends of a past as inaccessible to the accused as is the native jungle to the ape. In contrast to these spokesmen of Kafka's middle period, 1914–1917, the heroes of the family tales of 1912, Georg Bendemann, Karl Rossmann, and Gregor Samsa, never yielded the hope for an actual return to or a symbolic reconciliation with the source of their misfortune and existence.

Titorelli shows the so-called "truth" of myth and art to be useless for survival. If survival is to be the central concern, Titorelli presents a picture of human existence that corresponds in essentials to the world view of the modern secularist, as an examination of the time structure built into his proposed "ways out" will show. The time structure of Ostensible Acquittal corresponds to the scientific view of "truth" as verifiable hypothesis. Ostensible Acquittal is distinct from real acquittal by its totally provisional nature. After he has been ostensibly acquitted, the accused must live in constant expectation of a new arrest. He must be extremely wary and utilize whatever changes might take place among the judges. His "efforts for his second acquittal must be adjusted to altered circumstances and generally be as vigorous as those before the first acquittal" (Kafka 1946b, 192). A complete lack of ultimate certainty, security, and freedom characterizes life under Ostensible Acquittal. No state of final harmony can ever be hoped for. Since no acquittal is definitive, the cycle of re-arrests and ever-renewed efforts for new acquittals must go on *ad infinitum*. It can end only arbitrarily with exhaustion or natural death. Life under Ostensible Acquittal reflects the world view of modern scientific secularism, which knows no ultimate finality and certainty, no definitive answers, no ultimate solutions, no permanent goal, and above all no justification of human existence, and whose sole Absolute is survival. It accepts the alternation of unpredictable contingency—the ever-possible arbitrariness of new arrest—and predictable repetition—ever-new trials with ever-repeated ostensible acquittals. This alternation requires of the accused an ever-ready alertness, patience, infinite flexibility, and preparedness for the utilization of sudden possibilities. It also resembles that "Eternal Return" in which Nietzsche saw the cause of the spiritual nausea of modern man and, at the same time, the greatest challenge to strong stomachs and vigorous spirits.

The second avenue for survival, Indefinite Postponement, keeps the trial going at its initial stage, and seeks to prevent its ever coming to a termination. For any termination would seem to be condemnation. The accused and his helper must bend all their efforts toward assuring the permanent procrastination of the trial. The trial has to stay confined to its lowest stages. The means are constant observation of the lowest judges and never-tiring attempts to humor and influence them. The accused must never "lose the trial out of sight" (Kafka 1946b, 193). Indefinite Postponement functions analogously to the man's waiting before the door. The lowest judges take the Doorkeeper's place. They have to be cajoled, flattered, and influenced, but for a reason exactly opposite to the one that moves the man from the country to bribe his doorkeeper. The judges are to be made to prevent, not to facilitate, the entrance into the law. The method consists in trivializing the trial, in substituting the semblance of a trial for its reality,

> turning the trial around and around in the tiny circle to which it has been artificially contracted. . . . everything [is] only apparent; the interrogations, for instance, are quite brief, if one has no time or inclination to go for once, he is permitted to excuse himself. . . . it is mainly a matter of reporting to one's judge from time to time just to remind him that one is an accused. (Kafka 1946b, 194)

One goes through the motions of a trial, but these motions are meaningless. They are not to achieve results, except the single one of not coming to any fruition. Meaninglessness is their sole meaning. Indefinite Postponement reads like a parable of modern religion as exemplified by the Judaism of Kafka's father, religion reduced to a social ritual serving the maintenance of one's standing in the community. Postponement likewise postulates the absence of a teleological development; it refuses to view existence as history.

The difference between the two approaches to survival is only one of emphasis. In Ostensible Acquittal, it lies on effort and concentration; in Postponement the stress lies on observation and on mollifying the power that has arrested and continuously threatens one. Both are alike in shutting out any assumption of a final word in one's trial and thus a meaning in one's life beyond survival. Both courses are the exact denial of what Titorelli can accomplish in K.'s excised dream.

The fact that Titorelli is an artist is of greatest significance. In him, and through him, Kafka presents two diametrically opposed views of art that he later juxtaposes more clearly and definitively in the two artist stories of "A Report to an Academy" and "A Hunger Artist." One is the mimetic or realistic, the other the inspirational and redemptive view of art. In the former the artist counsels the self's survival through the faculties of observation, concentrated effort, and deliberate resistance to the "pull" of self-destructive yearning for an empirically impossible redemption. In the other, the artist speaks of the "beauty" of transcending the fetters of empirical experience, or in Kafka's words, of assaulting "the last frontier of earthly life" (Kafka 1948b, 553). The existential poetics that Kafka built into his fiction is more clearly apparent in his subsequent *A Country Doctor* and *A Hunger Artist* volumes. The two aspects of Titorelli, for instance, are beautifully repeated by the juxtaposition of the opening and the closing stories of *A Country Doctor*. The nostalgia of the lawyer, Bucephalus, who in former times had been Alexander the Great's battle horse, for his master's transcendental heroism finds itself repudiated, at the end of the volume, by the ape's resigned exchange of absolute freedom, "freedom on all sides," for a modest "way out" assuring physical survival. The two aspects of Titorelli form an earlier version of this juxtaposition of two contrasting views of existence.

Titorelli says he painted pictures inspired by the beauty of the ancient legends that tell of real acquittals; but he never shows them. What he does show instead, and imposes upon his visitor, are pictures that express the utter monotony of a world from which any hope for change and development has been banished.[7] These are the heathscapes that Titorelli himself admits "are rejected" by "some people . . . because they appear too gloomy" (Kafka 1946b, 197). As a startled K. perceives, they are not just similar to each other, they are "the one utterly identical heathscape" (Kafka 1946b, 197). Titorelli's actual art then is the precise expression of that artificially maintained monotony that survival through Postponement represents. However, both methods of avoiding an authentic verdict have to do with a certain type of artistic endeavor. As we have noted, both methods are based on close observation and concentrated effort. They depend upon the correct estimate of observed reality. They thus resemble the view of art as "mimesis," as the reproduction of external reality observed with the physical eye, from which the mental eye, imagination, is not only absent, but with which it would interfere.[8] Thus Titorelli represents two views of the function of art. One is to recapture the beauty of fulfilled hope contained in myth; the other is to show the somber monotony of existence as Indefinite Postponement and eternal recurrence. But K. is allowed only to see the latter. The idealizing task of art is reserved for his dreams, which are excised from the novel.

The elimination of K.'s dreams from his story leaves only the gloom to which, according to Titorelli, he is particularly drawn. The ecstatic hope alive in his dreams is absent from the narrative text that describes his fate. Hope is a "negative presence" in the novel. It exists there only by virtue of K.'s rejections of those courses of action that would preclude continuous hope for justification and redemption that inspires his dreams. Kafka is careful to bar the dreams themselves. The exclusion of the dreams has two structural consequences for the novel, both of which help explain Kafka's intent in *The Trial.* One effect is to unmask the mythologizing nature of art and to strengthen its demythologizing function. The other is to make K. still more opaque and not to allow him that transparency that his dreams give him.

In *The Trial* art is shown as myth-creating. We see the pictures of judges in Huld's office and in Titorelli's studio and learn about their genesis. In the lawyer's office we see a picture of a judge as a powerful figure about to utter a verdict. Art suggests that meaningfulness that K. himself expects from his trial. The painted judge mirrors his own impatience and craving for judgment. The dynamism that informs his dreams is reflected in the savagely tense dynamic posture that the artist has given to the judge.

> The unusual fact [about this picture] was that this judge was not seated there in calm and dignity but . . . as if he were about to spring up the next moment with a violent and perhaps indignant twist in order to say something decisive or even to pronounce the verdict. (Kafka 1946b, 131)

Art presents the judge in an elevated position and godlike majesty "seated on a high throne," strikingly gilded. At the same time, it debases the accused, "who was to be imagined at the foot of the high stairs" only "the highest of which covered with a yellow carpet could still be glimpsed in the picture" (Kafka 1946b, 131). The lowly wretchedness of the defendant, who is not even worthy to be included in the representation, only heightens the glory and grandeur of the authority figure. On the portrait in Titorelli's studio, the maleness of the judge is emphasized by his beard and bushy brows. He is about to rise threateningly from his throne. In his entourage a female figure of justice, consort and ally of the godlike judge, has wings on her feet, which heightens the dynamism of the picture. The judge has the figure of justice painted as the goddess of victory and of the hunt, showing the infallibility of the justice administered by his Court as well as the merciless and violent power with which the Court rules the defendants.

Art heightens the power of the Court by tending to overwhelm and humble the defendant. It serves a ferocious and despotic power. While it may give meaning to the defendant's life, threatening him with a quick terminal point of his trial, this meaning is terrible. It is inimical to human freedom, dignity, and life. As in his description of the penal system of *In the Penal Colony*, Kafka presents here an aspect of his own art as far as it tends to deify the father figure and thus helps to strengthen arbitrary and irrational authority in general. Günther Anders has seen this tendency as Kafka's primary one.[9] But it would be a misunderstanding of his method to equate such a perspective with the total intent of Kafka's work. For the function of art in assisting the hold of a wrathful authority over the longing hearts of men is precisely what he exposes to our understanding. By having Titorelli explain that the portrait of the judge is not true to life, but on the contrary the obedient execution of the judge's instructions for having himself magnified into a mythic image, which has nothing to do with his real appearance, Kafka unmasks the role of art as the servant of tyranny. Art is shown as the creator of myth in the service of power.[10] The painter does not portray fact, but invents according to the judge's guidelines that aim at giving an elevated, untrue image of him. Together with K., the reader too observes art literally manufacturing myth in its pejorative meaning. Repeating the processes of traditional religious art, Titorelli adds a kind of halo around the judge's head.[11]

> K. watched as under the quivering points of the crayons a reddish shadow was beginning to form adjoining the judge's head and passed out beyond its radiating toward the edge of the picture. Gradually this play of shadings surrounded the head like an ornament or a high distinction. (Kafka 1946b, 177)

Titorelli demonstrates to K. and to the reader an art inventive rather than mimetic, raising reality and transforming it into myth. He shows the appearance of the mythic significance of power as the product of the studio, a fraud serving a petty tyrant's vanity. In and by the very process of being shown as myth-making, art acts as supreme debunker and demythifier. It reveals the semblance of the halo surrounding power figures as artifice, "public relations" and propaganda—basically as plain swindle. Leni in particular teaches K. this lesson. The judge's picture, which K. discovers through her, shows a man of imposing height; but as she informs K., in actuality the judge is "almost tiny." He "had himself elongated to a great height on the picture, because he is insanely vain as they are all here" (Kafka 1946b, 132).

By putting on the halo, Titorelli is shown as doing two opposite things at one and the same time. He mythologizes and by the very act of visibly mythologizing, he deflates. The novel repeats what the artist shown in it does. It creates the giant Oedipal father figure of the Court, gives it daemonic and quasi-divine appearance, but simultaneously unmasks and deflates what it creates. Neither the mythologizing nor the demythologizing aspect in the writing of the novel provides its exclusive interpretation. As I have tried to show elsewhere, K.'s trial cannot be comprehended by any single interpretation because of the contradictory programs built into it. The fact, for instance, that we gain no knowledge of the Highest Court shrouds it in such an aura of mystery that the idea of the Godhead is inevitably suggested to the reader. However, when we see how the suggestion is literally added by the artist's touches, the novel counteracts its own mythologizing tendency and calls its "bluff." Yet the absence of any explanation of the Court's indubitable power over the minds of men and women counterbalances in turn the demythologizing achieved by showing art at work. Since, however, it is only one mind to whose thoughts we are privy, namely K.'s, the constant alternation between a mythologized and demythologized Court depends on the ambivalence to be found in K.

It is K.'s perceptions and conduct that make the double process of inflating and deflating of the Court come into being for the reader. K. consistently maintains a double perspective on the Court and on authority in general. On the one hand, he sees it in a deflating satirical light. On the other, as he lets his longing for the verdict come to the fore, he mythologizes the Court. In this way, the excised dreams radiate into and suffuse the novel. K.'s wish to enter the Court world, to penetrate it, to be accepted in it is openly voiced by him in the "House" chapter. In implicit form, however, this wish lives in *The Trial* from the beginning. In his very first encounter with the Court, through its warders, K. reveals his desire "somehow to sneak into the warders' thoughts, turning them to his advantage or taking up a residence there" (Kafka 1946b, 15). This adumbrates in precise terms his later emphatic thought of joining the Court through Titorelli.

> Even then there was a possibility of salvation; all he had to do was to slip into the ranks of those people; even if they had on account of their low position or for other causes not been able to help him, in his trial, they could accept and cover him, indeed they could not refuse to serve him in this way, particularly not Titorelli whose close acquaintance and benefactor he had become. (Kafka 1946b, 291)

In the third chapter, when K. penetrates the Court offices at the suggestion of the usher, he seems to do so reluctantly and merely, as he says, to prove to himself again how "repugnant" the Court is; but his body rushes up the stairs faster than the usher. While his consciousness resists the Court and pretends lack of interest, his action belies it. His body affirms K.'s desire for the Court, which his consciousness does not want to admit. The body adumbrates the dream. In the dream of Titorelli, K. will fly up stairs leading toward the Court; then body and consciousness will be attuned to each other, the self will be one, and therefore transparent.

Kafka makes sure that the contrast between waking life and dream reflects more than K.'s own division between conscious resistance and unadmitted desire for the Court. The narrator insists on employing the demythologizing technique in presenting Court reality. In his dream, K. flies effortlessly up the stairs toward his transfiguration, but K.'s entrance into the real Court offices looks like the caricature of such wish fulfillment. The narrator shows us that as soon as K. opens the door to the attic, he would have almost fallen flat on his face because there was one more step behind the door. In his mind, he reproaches the Court for its lack of consideration. In the contradictory perspectives of reality and dream, not only K.'s but his creator's ambivalence is clearly seen. However, by excising the dreams Kafka shifted the weights of the scales quite decisively toward the demythologizing side. The dreams are the most powerful instances of mythologizing. They show the self's apotheosis through its union with, or its submission to, authority. By taking out the dreams, Kafka leaves in the novel only the negative aspect of this relationship to authority and death, the "shame" without the glory. What the dreams show as positive, actualized, and fulfilled appears in the novel in negative form, as K.'s "no" to a life not owed to the Court.

The Trial is so structured, however, that both dreams, although invisible in the novel, exert a powerful pull on K., which constitutes the greatest peril to his life. This pull is shown in the novel as K.'s proclivity toward self-destruction, on the one hand, and as his tenacious struggle for a saving verdict, on the other. The intimate interplay of both these tendencies with each other and with K.'s stubbornly cultivated show of independence and rationality constitute his behavior in *The Trial.* Kafka leaves no doubt as to K.'s awareness of the danger that the realm of dreams poses to him.

At the beginning of his trial, he tells Frau Grubach that the arrest could never have happened to him in the bank because there he is "prepared"; there he is in possession of "presence of mind." Such things as the arrest can take place only in one's bedroom, soon after waking up, when one is, as K. complains, "so ill-prepared" (Kafka 1946b, 31). K. sees survival as the difficult achievement of constant alertness and preparedness against the realm of sleep and dream that, as he mentions in a crossed-out passage, are "conditions entirely different from waking life."

> An infinite presence of mind [*Schlagfertigkeit,* which literally means "readiness to strike back"] is needed when one wakes up, so that one can grasp at once everything that had been let go the night before, and make sure that everything is on the same spot where it had been left. That's why the moment of waking up is the most risky in the whole day; once it is behind you, without your having been carried away from your place, you can be quite confident for the rest of the day. (Kafka 1946b, 304)

Here K. himself is aware of that imperative need for concentrated watchfulness and ever-ready observation that Titorelli's schemes of survival demand. Kafka crossed out this passage that would have given K. too great an awareness for a character conceived as self-deceiving and driven.[12] Yet, he left no doubt as to the close connection between K.'s trial and the submerged continent of the self—sleep and dream.[13] The most decisive proof of this is, of course, the placing of the arrest in the protagonist's bed and its coinciding with his waking up from his night's sleep. K. is indeed frequently conscious of his need to be more observant and alert. He is apprehensive about his increasingly frequent lapses of attentiveness and preparedness. He repeats Georg Bendemann's self-admonition "to observe everything exactly" (Kafka 1970, 30), and like his predecessor is incapable of following his own advice. Like Uncle Jacob in *Amerika,* he sees the highly organized life of modern economic man as the ego's most promising defense against the inner and outer forces that threaten individuated existence. In his bank, K. says, he is so much better protected.

> Outside line phone and office phone stand on my desk; clients and clerks come and go all the time, but above all there I am constantly in the firmly coherent context of work and consequently possess presence of mind. There I would actually enjoy confronting such an intrusion. (Kafka 1946b, 31)

But any distraction and loosening of attention weakens the defensive organization of the ego, and sleeping and dreaming are of course the worst offenders. As for Gregor Samsa, the couch or sofa (*Kanapee*), seat of daydreaming and distracted flow of thoughts, becomes for Josef K. the locus symptomatic for his increasing defenselessness and deterioration.

In Kafka's universe, self-preservation requires the same single-minded resolve as the entrance into the law. K. says to Frau Grubach that if he had resolutely walked past the warders into her kitchen, "ruthlessly oblivious of anyone stepping into his way," he could have "stifled" the trial in its inception (Kafka 1946b, 31). But K. is as unable to walk out through the door and reach his landlady's kitchen, safety zone of *l'homme moyen sensuel,* as the man from the country is unable to walk in through the door and penetrate the realm of spiritual fulfillment called the law.[14] In Josef K., Kafka presented a figure in whom the will to live as economic man, secularized and self-reliant, is not strong enough to prevail over the twin lures of self-transcendence and justified existence, but too strong to permit what Leni calls "the confession" (Kafka 1946b, 132) of these needs.

By his excisions Kafka can be seen deliberately depriving K. and his reader of experiencing that fascination which the movement away from life holds for the author. Thus *The Trial* repeats the central experience of *In the Penal Colony.* It withholds confirmation. Pursuing the analogy further, we see Josef K. uniting in himself the functions distributed over Officer and Explorer in *In the Penal Colony.* K. has to observe in his own dying that meaninglessness of death which horrifies the Explorer in surveying the features of the "murdered" Officer. The excision of K.'s dreams parallels the self-refutation of the ingenious apparatus that, according to the Officer, produces transfiguration through slow capital punishment.

The opaqueness with which the novel ends reflects more than its protagonist's negativity derived from ambivalence. Like the breakdown of the Old Commander's creation, it demythologizes Kafka's myth of redemptive dying. If K. dies in a darkness that is never lifted from his trial, if he dies in a shame that results from total inability to discern any unambiguous reason for action, Kafka prevents the mythologizing element of his art from having the last word. The death of a dog robs not only K., but also the Court of all glamor. The butcher knife, in place of the artist's transfiguring pencil, deflates death as well as the authority that metes it out.

When K. comes to the cathedral, he expects to show an Italian the art treasures of his native city. Instead of the art lover, however, he meets the prison chaplain who, before telling him the legend of the doorkeeper, commands K. to put aside his guide book to the art treasures as "unimportant." In terms of the legend, K.'s dreams show a doorkeeper who leads to fulfillment. This obliging doorkeeper is the artist who works with the "rushing waters" of inspiration. By eliminating the dreams and substituting for them a legend with a most nonobliging doorkeeper, Kafka diminishes not only hope invested in mediators, but also in the inspirational art that two years before had carried him through his composition of "The Judgment" and that had celebrated death and contentment, and finally death and transfiguration. Like its contemporary *In the Penal Colony, The Trial* represents a thrust against the myth-making tendency of Kafka's own art. To be sure, he still published "A Dream" and united it with the doorkeeper legend in *A Country Doctor.* But by entitling it "A Dream," he provided a warning label against mistaking self-fulfillment through dying and death for the representation of any, even a fictional, reality.

NOTES

1. The connection between the end of *The Trial* and Josef K.'s endings in "A Dream" and in "The House" fragment has been pointed out by Emrich (1958, 296 f.). Emrich views "A Dream" and "The House" as two alternate possibilities for ending the novel. Cf. also Politzer (1962, 213). Franz Kuna (1974, 113) points indirectly to the connection, as he sees in K.'s arrest not a disaster but the possibility of happiness.

2. Since the literal wording of Kafka's *Der Prozess* is an indispensable key to the understanding and elucidation of Kafka's art, I frequently use my own translation of his German, particularly where the standard English version deviates from the literal meaning of Kafka's German in such a way as to obscure the subtle allusions and double or multiple meanings contained in the words he uses.

3. Cf. also Binder (1975, 182).

4. Politzer (1962, 213) connects the water imagery used in K.'s visit to the Court offices with the "House" chapter, as he also links the artist in "A Dream" to Titorelli.

5. J. P. Stern (1977) rightly points out the crucial importance that an early childhood memory assumed for Kafka, according to "Letter to His Father." In the childhood incident, water is linked to the child's frightful experience of his father's punitive wrath.

6. Cf. also Greenberg (1968, 137).

7. Cf. Emrich (1958, 29). Emrich points out that the absence of individual nuances among the pictures perfectly reflects the world view of one who, like Titorelli, has "seen through the inescapable determinism of all earthly affairs."

8. Michel Dentan (1961, 145 f.) sees in the heathscape a satire of art.

9. Anders (1951, passim).

10. Emrich (1958, 287) underlines the banality of the judges "in actuality," from which, however, the artist extracts "the actual essence, the function and significance of the office of judge which remains invisible in everyday life." Rooted in an idealistic German "classical-romantic" view of art, Emrich fails to note the function of art in *The Trial* as a mythologizing, propagandistic enhancement of power.

11. Cf. also Politzer (1956, 210).

12. Cf. also Allemann (1963, 245).

13. Greenberg (1968, 122) has seen the connection between the Court and "the dream dimension that is at a tangent to K.'s workaday existence."

14. For this function of the doors in the novel, see also Frey (1965, 17 and 148 f.).

BIBLIOGRAPHY

Allemann, Beda. 1963. "Kafka. Der Prozess." In *Der deutsche Roman vom Barock bis zur Gegenwart. Struktur und Geschichte*, ed. Benno von Wiese. Vol. 2, 234–90. Dusseldorf: Bagel.

Anders, Günther. 1951. *Franz Kafka. Pro und Contra. Die-Prozess Unterlagen.* Munich: C. H. Beck.

Binder, Hartmut. 1975. *Kafka Kommentar zu sämtlichen Erzählungen.* Munich: Winkler.

Dentan, Michel. 1961. *Humour et création litteraire dans l'oeuvre de Kafka.* Geneva: Droz.

Emrich, Wilhelm. 1958. *Franz Kafka.* Bonn: Athenäum.

Frey, Gesine. 1965. *Der Raum und die Figuren in Franz Kafka's Roman "Der Prozess."* Marburg: N. G. Elwert.

Greenberg, Martin. 1968. *The Terror of Art: Kafka and Modern Literature.* New York: Basic Books.

Kafka, Franz. 1946a. *Amerika*, trans. Edwin Muir. Norfolk, Conn.: New Directions.

———. 1946b. *Der Prozess.* Roman, ed. Max Brod. New York: Schocken Books.

———. 1948a. *The Penal Colony: Stories and Short Pieces*, trans. Willa and Edwin Muir. New York: Schocken Books.

———. 1948b. *Tagebücher, 1910–1923*, ed. Max Brod. New York: Schocken Books, 1948 and 1949.

———. 1953. *Hochzeitsvorbereitungen auf dem Lande und andere Prosa aus dem Nachlass*, ed. Max Brod. New York: Schocken Books.

———. 1957. *The Trial*, trans. Willa and Edwin Muir. Definitive edition. New York: Knopf.

———. 1970. *Sämtliche Erzählungen*, ed. Paul Raabe. Frankfurt am Main: Fischer Bücherei.

Kuna, Franz. 1974. *Franz Kafka: Literature as Corrective Punishment.* Bloomington and London: Indiana University Press and Elek.

Politzer, Heinz. 1962. *Franz Kafka: Parable and Paradox.* Ithaca, N.Y.: Cornell University Press.

Stern, Joseph Peter. 1977. "Guilt and the Feeling of Guilt." In *The Problem of "The Judgment": Eleven Approaches to Kafka's Story*, ed. Angel Flores, 114–31. New York: Gordian Press.

13

IDENTITY AND THE INDIVIDUAL, OR PAST AND PRESENT

Franz Kafka's "A Report to an Academy" in a Psychoanalytic and a Sociohistorical Context

KAFKA'S "A Report to an Academy" beautifully shows the close connectedness of a Freudian reading with a historical, sociopolitical one. In that respect, it represents a fictional analogue to Horkheimer and Adorno's *The Dialectic of Enlightenment* by bringing to light the full meaning of the Freudian notion of the Ego when it is understood in its relationship to the bourgeois individual of Enlightenment and capitalism. A psychoanalytic reading that does not bring out the—in the broadest sense—political dimension of the link between Kafka and Freud cannot do justice to the richly historical dimension of the "former ape's" report to the Academy. Western colonial imperialism—of which the marauding "hunting expedition" of the "firm" of Hagenbeck, an obviously capitalist enterprise, is a typical example—marks a radical rupture in its victims' lives. As for many other victims of Western colonial imperialism, Rotpeter's subjugation has overturned his existence and cut it into two halves, only tenuously connected with each other.

There are, immediately upon his capture, two threads connecting the temporal halves of his existence before and after capture—an inner and an external one. The former is his memory, the latter is his body, his physical life. In the radically new situation into which he finds himself thrown upon

This essay, in its present form, is published here for the first time. A greatly abridged version appeared in German in *Moderne Identitäten. Studien zur Moderne,* ed. Alice Bolterauer and Dietmar Goltschnigg, 212–24. Vienna: Passagen Verlag, 1999.

waking up in the cage, his memories of his previous life have become totally useless. His experiences as a "free ape" have lost all bearing upon and cannot help guide him in his unprecedented situation. His past has ceased to have any relevance. "I had had so many ways out before and now none at all" ("Ich hatte doch so viele Auswege bisher gehabt und nun keinen mehr.") (Kafka 1994, 304). If there is to be a "way out," it will have to be totally different from any in the past. There is no example for what he faces.

His memories are not merely useless; they have turned dangerous. For they hold out the temptation of a return to the past that is impossible and, if attempted, might easily be fatal. A conflict has emerged between internal and external continuity in the ape's existence. Memory has become a threat to survival. The continuity of the inner self has turned perilous to the continuation of life. That enduring of the past that is identity threatens to foreclose the organism's future. Incarcerated in his stiflingly narrow cage, the ape desperately needs a "way out" in order to live.

> I had no way out, but had to procure one, for without it I could not live. Crushed forever against that box wall—I would inevitably have croaked.

> Ich hatte keinen Ausweg, musste mir ihn aber verschaffen, denn ohne ihn konnte ich nicht leben. Immer an dieser Kistenwand—ich wäre unweigerlich verrckt. (Kafka 1994, 304)

However, as long as the ape remains tied to his past, his family and species, his identity, he is bound to his cage. For, "at Hagenbeck's apes belong at the box wall" ("Aber Affen gehören bei Hagenbeck an die Kistenwand"). External force has dictated that his species identity must doom him to permanent imprisonment, and thus to early death. His past has become his cage and his executioner. His self-preservation demands the renunciation of his identity: "thus I ceased to be an ape" ("also hörte ich auf, Affe zu sein"). This, as he calls it, "clear beautiful train of thought" ("klarer, schöner Gedankengang") marks an epochal event—the emancipation of the individual from its inherited, collective identity, its "essence" (Kafka 1994, 304). Rotpeter's self-preservation at the cost of his species identity depends, in exact conformity with the Freudian view of the ego's emergence, upon the collaboration of two factors—the organism's narcissistic concern for the body as a separate individual entity and its attunement and adaptation to external reality.

For Freud, the ego develops in opposition to memory that encapsulates and preserves past experience. In his early "Project for a Scientific Psychology," Freud introduces a sharp dichotomy between memory, the repository of the organism's past, and perception, which is turned toward and attuned to its present surroundings. Being both outward- and present-directed, accurate perception is vital to the individual's survival. It is the origin of both the ego and rational thinking. With the organism's orientation in its present situation, which perception makes possible, the emotional hold or "cathexis" of memory may become distracting and is "not to be carried beyond certain amounts" (Freud 1966, 326). A potential conflict arises between the incipient ego, which, building on perception, is to safeguard the individual's survival, and the organism's remembrance. While memory is freighted with emotion, perception works in the service of quick adaptation to the ever-changing circumstances of the current environment. Its task is to take cognizance of the present, which is also the presence of whatever surrounds the organism and what it encounters at any given moment. Spatial presence and temporal present merge into one. Emotions invested in remembered but no longer present scenes divert the individual's attention from the urgent tasks at hand. Memory evokes a "hallucinatory reality" that might easily interfere with the essential needs of life. Thus the system of perception has to guard against and, to a certain extent, inhibit memory. Descending from perception, the ego has to carry on that task.

The ego's fundamental opposition to fixation on the past characterizes Freud's ego concept throughout his work. In his posthumously published *Outline of Psychoanalysis,* Freud still defines the ego as being determined mainly by "what it has itself experienced, by what has been accidental and current" ("das selbst Erlebte, also Akzidentelle und Aktuelle") (Freud 1991, 69). The ego is concerned with current and recent experience rather than the distant past. It serves the life of the individual rather than that of the species. Reality for the ego is the here and now, the circumstances confronting and affecting the individual in its immediate present.

That turn to the present, to perception and to observation of his new environment, marks the ape's attitude as the initial shock of his trauma, which makes him cling to his past for consolation, yields to the urgent need to deal with his unbearable situation. If he is to find succor in his wretched present, he has to turn his attention to it and not lose himself in dreams of his past. He has to struggle against the lure of memory and inhibit the impulse to return to the past regardless of the impossibility of such an undertaking. Instead he has to begin to survey the scene surrounding his cage and to espy a "way out" consistent with it. His awakening interest in the world of his captors is the sign of his will to live.

As we have mentioned, the ego for Freud has two sources. One is perception. The other is concern for the body, the need of self-preservation. "The ego," says Freud, "is first and foremost a bodily ego" (Freud 1961, 26). What gives rise to the ego as an agency separate from the instinctual and libidinal part of the psyche, later called the Id, is the will to preserve the body. Thus one source of the ego lies in narcissism in its basic nature as channeling of libidinal energy or "love" toward the individual's body. In this original and fundamental form, "narcissism . . . would not be a perversion, but the libidinal complement to the egoism of self-preservation, a measure of which may justifiably be attributed to every living creature" (Freud 1957, 73). The instinct or drive for self-preservation is universal, and the psychic organ entrusted with it is the ego. Thus while one side of the ego is outward-directed, the other side is self-directed. It is solicitous concern for the body, its welfare, its comfort, its safety, and, above all, its continued existence. The first side is a function serving the second. The ego develops as the organism's need to pay close attention to the external world precisely in order to safeguard the body's survival and prosperity to which the instincts and desires of the Id pay no heed. "For the ego, perception plays the part which in the id falls to instinct" (Freud 1961, 25).

The contrast between instinct and perception, the starting point and foundation of consciousness and rational thought, has not only a spatial dimension—instinct being built into the organism while perception mediates with the outside world—but also a temporal one. Instinct is always bound to the past. It directs the organism to repeat again and again the behavior it has always followed. It is inherited from the generic past that precedes the individual. Instincts for Freud are, therefore, always "conservative," indeed reactionary, since they always seek to regain a previous state of affairs. Thus they quite consistently culminate in the death drive that Freud sees inherent in all organic matter as its wish to return to its origin in the inorganic. The system of perception, on the other hand, which serves the individual's self-preservation through observation and adaptation to an ever-changing external reality, compels the organism to adopt at times new and unprecedented behavior. Thus the reality principle is also the motor of progress. It is life-enhancing.

The life that the ego's reality principle safeguards and advances is the life of the individual. The ego is concerned with the survival of the body as a discrete, separate entity, independent of its family and species. The ego's province is the ontogenetic sphere, the sphere of individual existence, rather than the phylogenetic, the life of the species that is transmitted through eros. Individuation, the individual organism's fundamental drive to maintain and assert itself, is for Freud the only means that life possesses to counteract and delay the triumph of the death drive.

> [T]he instincts of self-preservation, of self-assertion and of mastery . . . are component instincts whose function it is to assure that the organism shall follow its own path to death, and to ward off any possible ways of returning to inorganic existence other than those which are immanent in the organism

> itself. . . . What we are left with is the fact that the organism wishes to die in its own fashion. (Freud 1955, 39)

The confluence of the instinct of self-preservation with the "reality principle," a confluence that explains the Freudian notion of the ego, illuminates Rotpeter's narrative of his mimetic adaptation to an alien species. He insists on surviving as an individual, even at the price of his "natural," his species identity, and he does so by adopting the "reality principle," by literally turning around and changing his outlook. He ceases to be riveted to the back of the cage, behind which he imagines his native jungle, and starts to look outward, into the present surrounding his cage. He begins to search, no longer for a way back to his origin, but for a "way out" of his prison, even though it leads into the realm of his jailers. His absolute will to live compels his concentrated attention to the external presence that he finds just outside the bars that keep him immobilized.

What Rotpeter calls a "way out" marks the turn to the present necessary to individuated life. The present is the temporal aspect of the presence of the new reality that surrounds him. It is a sociopolitical reality formed by his captors and jailers, hitherto instinctively shunned by him. However, life, life as an individual organism, desperately needs a fruitful connection with external reality, no matter how distasteful to one's instinct and "nature." The ape's natural, instinctive, and spontaneous reaction to his capture had, of course, been to recoil from the new world outside his prison and turn backward and inward toward his lost freedom. However, in the situation imposed on him by the power structure of human society, natural instinct would condemn him to die either sooner or later, sooner by a doomed attempt to flee, later by languishing in a cage too cramped to permit survival. His self-preservation demands the "unnatural," the renunciation of his nature. Propelling him forward out of his cage, it will eventually also lift him upward on the evolutionary scale. Rotpeter's story exemplifies Freud's theory of development. Only contingent intervention by external forces that block the instinctive and "natural" ways can, according to Freud, lead to ascent toward a new and higher form of life.

> [T]he phenomena of organic development must be attributed to external disturbing and diverting influences. The elementary living entity would from its very beginning have had no wish to change; if conditions remained the same, it would do no more than constantly repeat the same course of life. (Freud 1955, 32)

Freud's statement could be a description of the motivating circumstances of Rotpeter's development into a humanlike being that is forced upon him solely by "external, disturbing and diverting influences," and not by any inner drive.

Rotpeter sharply contrasts the lifesaving way out of the cage with freedom, "freedom on all sides." He is at pains to make sure that we do not confuse his way out with freedom:

> I am afraid it will not be exactly understood what I mean by "way out." I use that term in its most common and fullest sense. On purpose I do not say freedom. I do not mean that great feeling of freedom on all sides. Perhaps I had known it as an ape and I have met human beings who yearn for it. But as for myself, I asked for freedom neither then nor now.
>
> Ich habe Angst, dass man nicht genau versteht, was ich unter Ausweg verstehe. Ich gebrauche das Wort in seinem gewöhnlichsten und vollsten Sinn. Ich sage absichtlich nicht Freiheit. Ich meine nicht dieses grosse Gefühl der Freiheit nach allen Seiten. Als Affe kannte ich es vielleicht und ich habe Menschen kennen gelent, die sich danach sehnen. Was mich aber anlangt, verlangte ich Freiheit weder damals noch heute. (Kafka 1994, 304)

To understand the significance of Rotpeter's "way out" we should examine the notion of freedom from which he is so intent on distinguishing it. In temporal terms, freedom for him lies in the past. He might perhaps have known it when he had still been nothing else but an ape. He refers to his being an ape as being "free," while calling his becoming human a "yoke" (Kafka 1994, 299). In spatial terms, freedom is situated in a remote distance, immeasurably far beyond the ship that is now carrying him toward Europe, beyond the ocean that stretches between his present captivity and his lost home. Freedom belongs to apedom. Human beings can only long for it, but if they try to attain it, as circus artistes and acrobats, for instance, the pathetic futility of such attempts merely arouses the laughter of apes. Human civilization precludes freedom.

By its great remoteness from the captured ape's present, freedom assumes the aspect of a transcendent Beyond. It has become unreachable to empirical reality. The former ape calls human pretensions at freedom a "mockery of holy Nature" ("Verspottung der heiligen Natur") (Kafka 1994, 305). The adjectival attribute, "holy," alludes to that naturalized version of Christian transcendence associated with Rousseauan Romanticism. "Freedom on all sides" suggests the Infinite, the Absolute, an unbounded unrestricted totality. From the perspective of civilization, however, into which Rotpeter has fallen, it has become synonymous with death. It is an illusion inimical to life, one against which, as we shall see in greater detail, the individual has to be on his guard.

In contrast to absolute freedom, the relative freedom of the "way out" fastens on the immediate present of the lived moment and the immediate presence of the reality in which the subject happens to find himself. Unlike absolute freedom, it is not a way back into memory, but a way out into the world as perceived by the senses. Initially this is a hostile reality, the source of Rotpeter's misery. However, in seeking a way out, he has to accept this reality, monstrously difficult as this seems to his natural instincts, because it is the only one that offers a way out of his cage. The way out into that world demands a colossal sacrifice of dreamed and remembered pleasure and a submission to great unpleasure. However, this unpleasure alone can save him from the infinitely greater unpleasure of slowly dying in the cage. It is an exchange, a payment with a smaller unpleasure for escape from an incomparably greater one.

Very different from freedom, the way out leads into a very limited space, circumscribed by the limits of the ship. Surrounded by the vast ocean, it is a small area, also a kind of cage, but one promising a greatly enlarged room for free movement than the cage in which Rotpeter squats. This difference in degree is enough to amount to one in kind, to a true liberation. Measured against the total impotence of existence in the cramped cage, the scope of movement, the degree of independence and power that the way out will eventually attain for Rotpeter is so considerable that it must be called essential.

In temporal terms, the way out leads forward through the present into the future. Present and future, in fact, are united in it as means are to the end. The present turns into an instrument employed toward the future.

Rotpeter's way out comes about through his looking out, his observing and familiarizing himself with the society of his captors. Preceding and making that possible is his abandonment of his initial hostility. Instead of withdrawing from them, he begins to observe his prison guards and finds: "They are good people, after all" ("Es sind gute Menschen, trotz allem.") (Kafka 1994, 305). This new evaluation of his jailers is decisive to his outward turn, his acceptance and eventual utilization of external reality for the sake of self-preservation and -advancement. Looking out of the cage becomes the preparation for stepping out of it. The sentence following Rotpeter's declaration that finding a way out of his cage is a necessity for his survival sums up his realization of the power structure prevailing at Hagenbeck's: "at Hagenbeck's apes belong at the box wall" ("Affen gehören bei Hagenbeck an die Kistenwand") (Kafka 1994, 304). This insight is the result of the ape's looking out, of his observations, which have made him familiar with the layout and the arrangements of the power structure on the ship. The ape's understanding of these results from deductions drawn from close and thorough observation. As in Freud's theory, rational thought follows from the application of the reality principle, its fastening on sense data and their utilization for and through action. Concentration on external reality leads the ape to reasoning adaptation to it. "But at Hagenbeck's apes belong at the box wall—well, so I stopped being an ape. A clear beautiful train of thought" ("Aber Affen gehören bei Hagenbeck an die Kistenwand—nun, so hörte ich auf, Affe zu sein. Ein klarer, schöner Gedankengang") (Kafka 1994, 304). Through adjustment to it, the ape is ready to use reality for the ego's survival in the only way left to it by the prevailing discriminatory power system on board ship—his decision to cease to belong to the disempowered group. We are confronted with a literally fantastic opportunism, a radical submission to reality.

At the same time, the ape's surrender of his species identity is also the birth of the pure unaffiliated individual, an epochal event, which can be regarded as a potentially liberating emancipation of the greatest magnitude. The conflict between the notions of identity and individual emerges here with a particular clarity.

Identity, in this context, is membership in a collective. It is super- and transindividual. The ape possesses his identity through being an ape, offspring and member of an extended family, group, or species—the latter constituting the biological equivalent of what, in ethnographic and sociological terms, would be called ethnicity. Ceasing to be an ape before becoming human—and we must remember, Rotpeter will never be fully human, for he will always retain body, appearance, and sexual behavior of an ape—is to be nothing but a pure, unique individual, abstracted from all group affiliation, cut off from origin, nature, and "being" or "essence," an uprooted, atomized, and, by that very same token, liberated individual, coming as close as conceivable to the concept of the individual as the ultimate unit of society in classical-liberal political thought. To gain a way out into freedom of movement, the ape has to turn himself into a mere individual, unattached to defining and confining heredity, free of identity grounded in the past, and thus utterly open to unprecedented development in the future. Abject adaptation to social reality and its power structure paradoxically entails unparalleled liberation from the fetters of "essential being" or "nature." Yielding identity implies overcoming of stigmatizing essentialism. It is his past that, in the social order in which Rotpeter has been awakened, keeps him caged. In principle, he is already liberated from the cage the moment he stops being an ape and becomes nothing but a "free," i.e., generically unfettered, individual. It is his identity, the superindividual part of his being, that stifles him and threatens his survival. What looks like total surrender to the flagrant injustice and cruelty of social reality emerges, from another perspective, as emancipation from all suprapersonal bonds holding the individual captive to its origin and descent.

The ape's renunciation of his species identity in exchange for liberation from his cage can, in Freudian terms, be read as a narcissism essential to the individual's maturing. The transference of libidinal energy from persons in the child's family—normally his/her mother—to the self leads to sublimation. By way of a rhetorical question, Freud suggests the possibility that "all sublimation . . . [may] take place through the mediation of the ego, which begins by changing sexual object-libido into narcissistic libido" (Freud 1961, 30). Shifting of libidinal attachment from the bosom of the family to the self is for Freud the indispensable condition of the individual's higher development. The price paid by libidinal renunciation will purchase the individual's advance. Narcissism liberates from the retarding tyranny of libidinal desire within the family by rechanneling it toward achievements of the ego. First and foremost, it leads the individual's emancipatory separation, his "weaning," from the mother or mother substitute, toward the formation of a separate independent person.

If we substitute for mother family and species, the "troop" of apes in the midst of which "sinful" shots had felled Rotpeter and separated him forever from the source of his being, his decision to cease to be an ape corresponds precisely to that transfer of libido from the family to the self by which, according to Freud, "the egoism of self-preservation" (Freud 1957, 70) brings about the cultural development Freud calls sublimation. Renouncing his species identity and concentrating on his individual salvation, Rotpeter will advance to a—in evolutionary terms—higher form of life. His self-education into a creature with the mental abilities of a human being depends on his inner abandonment of his family—species being an extension of family. He must sunder the libidinal bonds to the "troop" of apes from which he had sprung, which had sheltered and enwrapped him in the past, and become a solitary, unattached ego in order to free himself from his imprisonment. The original violent separation from his extended family had been his first, his external individuation. Making him a solitary prisoner, it had set him apart and made him an isolated individual. Significantly his remembered consciousness begins with his "awakening" in his prison. There the self that is now writing the memoir was born. But that first, purely external—physical and spatial—individuation has to be completed by a second, a conscious, deliberate, internalized individuation that starts with his turning away from the inner bonds that still attach him to his species and yielding up his fellowship with the "troop" by deciding to stop being one of it. The imperialist social order of Western mankind works upon and through its victim's "egotistical" determination to preserve and improve his life. It forces upon him the severance of his umbilical cord. It is a necessity imposed upon him from without, but one to which he then freely consents. As a "free ape I submitted to this yoke" (Kafka 1994, 299).

Freeing himself from his bonds to his family and origin will set him on the road of freeing himself also from his utter dependence on his jailers. The way out of the cage will allow him not only to survive, but also to support himself by his own efforts and contributions rather than being fed in his cage like an infant or a pet. It will set him on the way to life as an independent self-supporting adult.

That Rotpeter's renunciation of the identity received through his species can be read as liberation receives strong evidence from the context of Kafka's biography. In a letter to Felice, Kafka, as Gerhard Neumann has pointed out, refers to himself as the "ape of my parents" (Neumann 1975, 182 f.), and, in another letter, he refers to his family with the same word, "Rudel" (Kafka 1967, 129), used by his simian protagonist for the "troop" of apes in which he had lived when he was captured. Kafka's use of a term normally reserved for groups of animals is one instance of many that make it clear that, for all his strong emotional ties to his family and his warm esteem of family life in general, Kafka also considered his inability to free himself from his family's powerful hold on him a lifelong prison sentence. His protracted inability, until the final year of his life, to tear himself loose from his family and live away from them as a freelance writer, served as the basis for his worst self-accusations. In such a context, Rotpeter's choice must appear as a desirable alternative, a "way out" into an adulthood his creator seemed unable to attain for himself. What "sinful" bullets, combined with a robust urge to survive, enabled Kafka's simian hero to achieve remained denied to his author. They made him into what Kafka yearned for but could not achieve for himself—an artist able to support himself by his art. Of course, it is a humorous, ironic treatment of an "ideal," filled, as everything in Kafka, with profound ambivalence. Yet, on an intertextual reading of "A Report" and Kafka's life-documents, his identity-shedding protagonist appears more of a "hero" than a "heel," because in him individual self-realization wins out over tribal dependence. The social reality in which the captured ape has to live presents itself as one of glaring self-contradiction. On the one hand, it is a society of horrendous cruelty, injustice, and inequality. Yet, on the other, it is one that holds open literally unprecedented opportunity for the individual willing to free himself from his past. What one might call the psycho-politics of the Freudian concept of the ego, its links to the sociocultural context in which it appears, has been explored in Horkheimer and Adorno's *The Dialectic of Enlightenment.* That work exposes the close interconnectedness of the psychological concept of the ego with the Baconian-Lockean Enlightenment, the free market economy of capitalism, and the political notion of the autonomous individual underlying the classical theory of modern democracy. "A Report to an Academy" is its analogue in narrative fiction. In it, "healthy" narcissism and the reality principle, which together comprise the ego, operate in a social setting that has the earmarks of Western bourgeois society and help to illuminate its ethos.

The interplay of psychological and sociopolitical elements in Kafka's text can best be seen at that decisive point in the ape's narrative at which his turn toward the world of his captors crystallized into the thought of becoming like them and thereby to be set free eventually. It comes as the culmination of the ape's studious observation of the human beings around him. By making observation the enabling condition for liberation, the ape implicitly uses Francis Bacon's formula for regaining paradise through applying the scientific method. Expelled from Eden, helpless in the face of an all-powerful, indifferent or hostile, and ever-threatening reality, mankind, victimized like Rotpeter, has to learn to observe its foe assiduously, to study nature, so as eventually to learn to outwit, utilize, and conquer her for its own advancement and salvation. If we substitute for man's natural Rotpeter's human environment, we can easily conclude that the course Rotpeter follows must be called Baconian. He observes and studies human beings continuously and makes discoveries about them that will lead to his liberation.

The most crucial observation he makes pertains to human freedom from assault by arbitrary force. He notes that humans go about "unmolested" ("unbehelligt"). With this observation, "an exalted goal dawned on [him]" ("Ein hohes Ziel dämmerte mir auf"). Human beings appear to be free. If he were to become like them, if he were to become human, he, too, would be free. The sociopolitical setting, the state of the human society that engenders in the ape such "seemingly impossible fulfillments" ("scheinbar unmögliche Erfüllungen") (Kafka 1994, 307) is of decisive importance to the ape's metamorphosis. It is a society that seems to guarantee its members freedom of movement.

Freedom on the human scale, to be sure, is quite different from "freedom on all sides." It is not absolute freedom. What signifies it is a privative syllable, "un,"—"*un*molested" ("*un*behelligt"). It is freedom from rather than freedom to, freedom from arbitrary assault, protection from the kind of aggressive power that had overturned Rotpeter's life. "Unmolested" points toward existence under the rule of law, a civil society with legal protection and constitutional guarantees of all individuals' rights—above all, the fundamental right of equal protection against aggression by superior might. It signifies a state in which the basic aspect of liberal government holds sway. The text makes the crucial role of the individual as the foundation of this human society quite apparent. It lies in a textual detail that, read out of context, seems rather puzzling and can be easily overlooked. Immediately prior to his observation that humans go about "unmolested," it seems to the ape "as if [these human beings] were only one" ("als wäre es nur einer"); and in the following sentence, in referring to human beings as "unmolested," he commingles singular and plural: "So *this* human being *or these* human beings were walking about unmolested" ("Dieser Mensch oder diese Menschen gingen also unbehelligt.") (Kafka 1994, 307; emphasis mine).

Every individual's freedom from "molestation" by superior power makes all human beings equal, and thus one, in the ape's sight. They are all like one insofar as each is equally free. Their equality gives them the appearance of uniform likeness: "forever the same faces, forever the same movements" ("immer die gleichen Gesichter, immer die gleichen Bewegungen") (Kafka 1994, 307). This notion of the individual is bound up not only with freedom, but also with equality to the point of likeness. The individual, in this context, does not express individuality, but equality of status and condition. While individuality betokens difference, uniqueness, each individual's inviolability under the law stresses a sameness of status that partakes of uniformity. Individual uniqueness is not what the individualism of modern capitalism and democracy envisage. They aim for the opposite—the uniform equality of all individuals as consumers and as citizens. It is not the fact that each individual is different from all others and unique that concerns the Declaration of Independence, but that all are presumed to be created equal. It is this equality of protectedness of all individuals that the ape espies as characterizing human life around him. When he resolves to join human beings in order to gain release from his cage, his "exalted goal" will not be freedom, but equality of treatment. He strives to become like human beings not because he likes them—"In themselves there was about those human beings nothing that especially appealed to me" ("Nun war an diesen Menschen an sich nichts, was mich sehr verlockte") (Kafka 1994, 307 f.), he avers—but because he aspires to share in their common security from aggression.

Rotpeter's aspiration to join the human species will entail a further extension, a heightening and intensification of the ego's Baconian reality principle—observation. It will compel him to advance from mere passive watching of his captors to active imitation. His attempts to mimick them decisively strengthen the interaction between him and them, resulting in his education in the ways of humanity and finally his liberation from the cage. Considering this sequence we realize that a purely Freudian approach, limiting itself to the psychology of the individual, will not suffice to do full justice to Kafka's text. Because of the essential part played, in Rotpeter's way out of the cage by the sociopolitical example of equal and protected freedom for the members of human society, consideration of the Freudian notion of the ego has to expand to include its social and political foundations and implications. The attraction freedom from assault exerts on the captured ape is essential to his project of assimilation to the human species, and it also leads to the broad sociohistorical context of Kafka's text.

The geographically closest social context pertains, to be sure, not to freedom, but to the colonial imperialism of Kafka's Europe. Hagenbeck, a famous concern in Wilhelminian Germany, has marauded in colonial Africa. Its result has been the ape's capture and brutal incarceration. A native of Africa has been enslaved and is being exported to Europe as a captive, subject to barbarously inhumane treatment. The face of mankind presented to the African is European imperialist capitalism in its most unmitigated, its German-Wilhelminian form. However, if the next element in the narrative plot is kept in mind—the attraction that the sight of freedom and equality among his captors exert on their exotic prisoner—a very different frame of reference emerges. It is the context of the liberal-bourgeois democracy of Western society in general and the United States in particular. Thus "A Report" demonstrates the extreme two-sidedness that modern Western humanity presented to its victims in the rest of the world. Hated and resented as the source of unspeakable misery, dislocation, deracination, and heartbreak, on one side, it showed, on the other, the beacon of individual rights, equal security from aggression, and limitless opportunity for the future of an individual capable of gaining admission into it.

All countries of the West showed that dual face to the world of the twentieth century, but none more so than the United States of America, scene of Kafka's novel, *Der Verschollene* (*Amerika*). Some aspects of the intertextual relationship between Kafka's novel and the ape's report I have tried to show elsewhere (Sokel 1964, chap. 20). Here I want to single out analogies between the historical myth of "the land of unlimited opportunity," as America was called in Kafka's Europe, and the "exalted goal" of assimilation to humanity that the discovery of "unmolested" freedom among human beings inspired in Rotpeter. His liberation from the cage can come about only through successful mimicking of those fortunate beings who already own the riches of liberty and equality. Those are, of course, not granted to all creatures; they are restricted to the individuals of a single group. The society of the "unmolested" excludes outsiders. However, in Rotpeter's view, the privileged group will extend its privilege to outsiders on condition of their successful assimilation to those who already enjoy the insiders' enviable status. This severely restricted nature of freedom is part of the brutal and forbidding face that the West, in its Imperialist aspect, shows to the rest of creation. It relegates those with the wrong, the victims', identity to the "box wall" of prison. However, in both stories—Kafka's "Report" and Western history—Western humanity also offers another face, at least potentially, to its victims: the prospect of equal freedom extended to those who, shedding their identity, are able to assimilate to the victors. On first sight, such a reading bears close resemblance to one that sees Kafka's text as an allegory of Jewish assimilationism and conversion.

In such a reading, Rotpeter's renunciation of his species identity appears as morally shabby opportunism and ultimately futile self-betrayal. However, what speaks against a Jewish-assimilationist reading of Rotpeter's "Report" is not only the obvious discrepancy between Jews as "the people of the Book" and a transcendent God's chosen people being fundamentally set aside from nature with which simian existence is associated in "A Report." Even more importantly, a Jewish-assimilationist reading of Kafka's story ignores an essential dimension of its sociopolitical aspect—the pull of attraction that the promise of the equality of freedom has for its hero. After all, equal freedom and security of all individuals from arbitrary power were not prime characteristics of European cultures that sought to exclude Jews from their midst. Rather, the vision of "undisturbed" freedom of the individual shone forth from liberal societies, above all the American, instilling hope in the downtrodden, but aspiring immigrants on the ships that were taking them to a new world. It was the hope of an unprecedented experiment, which a leap across the space between species certainly suggests, with which the news of a life of equal and protected freedom of all individuals inspired the immigrant as it does the ape in Kafka's story.

At the core of Rotpeter's vision of his freed future, as at the core of the poor immigrant's hope of a liberated life in the New World, lies the absence of predestinating essentialism, the racist's conviction that an individual's past and descent might forever bar him or her from entering the charmed circle of the privileged. The lack of preordained, unalterable exclusion connects Rotpeter's with the American immigrant's dream. If capable of acquiring the language and behavior of the dominant group, any individual can become free and prosper. Any immigrant can become an American even as, in the ape's assumption subsequently verified by events, any creature can become human provided the necessary "effort" (Kafka 1994, 312) and ability are marshaled and tenaciously applied. It never occurs to the ape that the human community might deny him acceptance merely because of his descent and origin.

The human response to Rotpeter's learning effort will prove him correct. His past and species, his "essence," his race, will not be held against him. On the contrary, the "civilized world" (Kafka 1994, 301) will shower him with admiration and affection, and not only after he has mastered his mutation of species being. From the very beginning, his captors evince an interest in him. They gather around his cage, seek to stimulate him, are curious about his responses (Kafka 1994, 306). Very soon they evolve from jailers into teachers. His "racial" heredity is not an obstacle, but quite the opposite. It is precisely because he is an ape, member of an alien species, showing an eager willingness to become human, that humans appreciate, encourage, and love him—a love he feels "like a kiss on my entire sweat-dripping body" ("wie einen Kuss auf meinem ganzen schweisstriefenden Körper") (Kafka 1994, 311). What counts is not his biologically inherited native identity, his past, but his effort at and achievement of change. In the attitude human beings adopt toward him effort and achievement take the place of nature, species or "race," as determining identity.

Effort and achievement are bound to the individual, and it is solely as an individual that humans value and cherish Rotpeter. What distinguishes him from other apes and makes him an individual—his ambition unique among apes, his "exalted goal," and his extraordinary effort to actualize it—is the standard by which human beings judge, enthusiastically accept, and richly reward him. What liberates and catapults him to eminence in human society is his demonstration of the colossal range of individual capability, his role as the initiator and performer of a bold and unique experiment, "hitherto unrepeated on earth" ("sich bisher auf der Erde nicht wiederholt hat") (Kafka 1994, 312).

Yet, his old apish identity plays a vital role in his success. For Rotpeter is celebrated and beloved not only because he has aspired to and succeeded in ceasing to be an ape and becoming human, but also because he has done so as the ape he has remained in his bodily appearance and biological makeup, a fact borne out by his sexual behavior "in the manner of apes" ("nach Affenart") (Kafka 1994, 313). His entire phenomenal success would not have been possible if he had not been an ape to begin with and continued to be one all the time. It is precisely because he is an ape succeeding so well in *aping* humans that he is the beneficiary of applause and "scarcely surpassable successes" ("kaum mehr zu steigernde Erfolge") (Kafka 1994, 313). Thus his apish identity constitutes a crucial element in the human reception of his project. It bears testimony to the liberal openness of human society and its unprejudiced appreciation of achievement by the Other. Rotpeter's success depends on his dual identity—as an ape and as a human being. If he were only human and had never been an ape, there would, of course, have been no special achievement in his acquiring "the average education of a European" ("die Durchschnittsbildung eines Europäers") (Kafka 1994, 312), and he would be an ordinary and obscure person, and certainly not the celebrity he has become as an ape. However, if he had remained nothing but an ape, he would, had he survived at all, be an animal in a cage. His identity as a world-famous individual lies in the union of ape and human being, in the simultaneity of two identities—one original and one acquired.

However, this duality is not a static coexistence of identities, but a process, a continuous, dynamic interaction, and the performance that is its result. His identity is a work in progress as well as a finished product. It is creating and creation in one. Rotpeter has, at the time of writing his report, created himself by an enormous and unprecedented "effort" ("Anstrengung") (Kafka 1994, 312). This work, however, is never really completed. In every performance on stage of the variety shows, and indeed in every act of his social life among human beings, he recreates himself, reiterating and varying his original self-creation of an ape attempting to be human. For Rotpeter, identity is performance. It is not a static essence, a given, but a constantly reenacted self-representation.

Rotpeter is literally a self-made man. Insofar as he is a man, a human being, he has made himself, with the help of humans, to be sure, but still basically on his own, "at bottom alone" ("im Grunde allein") (Kafka 1994, 299). As a self-made man he corresponds, as an enacted metaphor, to the classical American myth. The myth implies the triumph of the individual over his circumstances, or the victory of present and future over the past. No inherited nature, no anterior group membership, prevents the individual from making himself, given sufficient daring and ingenuity.

The self-made man bears a very close relationship to the Freudian notion of the ego, according to which the ego succeeds, not only by adapting the organism to its surrounding reality, but likewise by changing reality, making it conform to the advantage of the individual. Rotpeter not only changes himself, but in the process influences his surroundings, inducing human society to accept him as a free and honored member. The story of the ego, as exemplified by Rotpeter, is like the myth of the self-made man a triumph of the individual over his inherited collective identity and thus over the past in which the latter is rooted. In terms of the "ecstasies of time," to use Heidegger's term, or the tenses of existence, Rotpeter's biography begins, exactly as the myth of the self-made man, in a terrifyingly underprivileged past. An overwhelmingly strong will, coupled with extraordinary cleverness and ironclad concentration on the goal, enables the individual to free himself from this past, and accomplish a dizzying ascent into a present totally unlike it. What is the self of the self-made man? It is the achievement that transformed a wretched past into a glorious present. It is the work itself of fashioning a new self.

This has a close bearing on the genre, the generic form, of "A Report." Rotpeter's report is not an autobiography in the traditional sense. It does not narrate a life. Instead it describes the making of a self, the educational process that has resulted in Rotpeter's finding himself as what and where he is now. It dwells on his overcoming of his original identity that had kept him in the cage, and his finding a way out by remaking himself into a new being. His report is "to show the guiding line on which a former ape invaded the human world and established himself there" ("es soll die Richtlinie zeigen, auf welcher ein gewesener Affe in die Menschenwelt eingedrungen ist und sich dort festgesetzt hat") (Kafka 1994, 300). His report is an immigrant's story, describing an outsider's maneuvering in wresting for himself a firm place in the insiders' society.

His livelihood and standing as an entertainer, however, depend, as mentioned, on his forever repeating the process of his formation. Each time the "former ape" steps onto the stage, he has to prove himself there. His act has to be a confirmation of his ability to maintain his human status. What his public pays to see is his sliding from the apish creature his physical appearance presents to them into the manners and behavior of "a European with an average education." In each performance he repeats the metamorphosis from ape to human being. It is this ever-renewed transformation taking place in their sight that thrills each of his audiences anew. Put in temporal terms, each of his stage performances shows the past changing into the present, or, putting it perhaps more accurately, it shows the present, as the presence of an ape's body, ascending into a future in which the physical ape will meet his public as a socialized human being.

Rotpeter's "being" can perhaps best be defined, in Jean-Paul Sartre's terms, as a lack of being. Rotpeter is what he is not and is not what he is. He is not the human being his mimetic behavior pretends to be, since he performs it in and with the body of an ape. Neither, however, is he identical with his ape's body, since his behavior is that of a human being. Thus his "being" is lack of being. No unitary, positively definable identity defines him. His "identity" is not a condition or a substance. It resides in his achievement.

His achievement, however, is founded on the ejection of his past to a point at which he lost the inner continuity of his being. "This achievement," he confesses, "would have been impossible if I had wished to hold on stubbornly to my origin, to the memories of my youth" ("Diese Leistung wäre unmöglich gewesen, wenn ich eigensinnig hätte an meinem Ursprung, an den Erinnerungen der Jugend festhalten wollen."). The Academy requests a report on his "äffisches Vorleben," his existence as an ape prior to his capture (Kafka 1994, 299). Rotpeter, however, cannot meet this request. In order to enter and succeed in the new, the human world, he had to forget his memories of the old one.

A significant gap between the assumptions of the Academy and the reality of Rotpeter's life becomes starkly evident at this initial point of Rotpeter's text. The "Exalted Gentlemen of the Academy" ("Hohe Herren von der Akademie") (Kafka 1994, 299), whose request for a report Rotpeter answers, view life with assumptions contradicted by Rotpeter's experience. The traumatic violation and overturning of his existence, caused by the rapacity and aggressive incursion of Western imperialist society, has wrought a radical discontinuity in his life. As we have seen, it forced him to abandon the continuity of his inner life, since it allowed him to save his physical life only by radically altering it. The "Exalted Gentlemen of the Academy," however, ignore the brutal side of their culture, entertaining a scientific and profoundly liberal interest in all life no matter how alien to their own. The ethos of objective science, of knowledge for its own sake, the open-minded, liberal curiosity of the Enlightenment combines in them with a belief in the permanent continuity of the self. They overlook the fundamental dislocations brought about by the colonial imperialism that is the other face of the liberal civilization that has founded and sponsored learned societies like their own.

The "Exalted Gentlemen of the Academy" represent the classical modernism of the nineteenth and early twentieth century also on account of what might be termed their historicism. Their desire to learn about Rotpeter's "prior life as an ape" expresses an interest in the past for its own sake. They wish to understand the past historically, i.e., from the past's own perspective, and, from pure thirst for knowledge, seek to share in it. Their desire presupposes a faith in the unfractured continuity and persistence of memory, and, with it, the unbroken identity of the self. That faith too makes the exalted academicians typical representatives of classical modernity.

Rotpeter's inability to meet their request shows that the assumptions of classical modernity no longer hold. His experience reflects a world-historical change from classical modernism to what might be described as postmodernism. The expansive capitalism and colonial imperialism of the West—the hunting expedition that captured our hero has been sent to Africa by the "firm" of Hagenbeck, a business enterprise—have produced a world in which the past has become irrelevant, and holding on to it tenaciously has grown incompatible with a tolerable life. In its capitalist-colonialist aspect, modernity has brought about a radical rupture, a total discontinuity in the life of its individual victims as in the general course of history. The same modernity that is represented by the Academy's search for pure knowledge has brought forth the world-penetrating and -subjugating social order that subjects all regions and all creatures to its sway. To it Kafka's simian hero owes his enslavement, but also his subsequent "whipped-on evolution" ("vorwärts gepeitschte Entwicklung") (Kafka 1994, 299) to a humanoid being. Rotpeter's "whipped on evolution" forms a part of the "whipped-on development" (the German word "Entwicklung," used by Kafka, denotes both "evolution" and "development") of economy and technology whipped forward by capitalism as it spread across the globe. "Simian nature raced, somersaulting, out of me and away" ("Die Affennatur raste, sich überkugelnd, aus mir hinaus und weg") (Kafka 1994, 311 f.), the ape recounts, and adds that, springing over into his teacher, it turned him insane. But this "furiously somersaulting"—the

German word "rasen" signifies both "to race" and "to rave,"—expulsion of apish nature reflects, in terms of the historical context, the breathlessly advancing expulsion of nature as a whole by the onslaught of a ravingly forward-racing humanity. Both expulsions of nature, on the individual as well as on the global scale, aim for the utterly new, the unparalleled, the hitherto unimaginable, for efforts, achievements, and sensations that, like the humanization of an ape, have never yet been seen on earth.

In such a world, holding on to the past and one's inherited identity has, as we have seen, become a form of the death instinct. In close analogy to the ape's death-threatening longing to return to his origin, the death instinct in Freud's *Beyond the Pleasure Principle* is life's striving to return to its distant past in inorganic nature. Similarly, in *The Dialectic of Enlightenment,* Horkheimer and Adorno interpret the deathly temptation that the sirens' songs hold for Odysseus and his sailors as the pull of the past, life according to instinct, the dreamed-of unconscious unity of the organism with surrounding nature. Like Odysseus, the caged ape has to resist the sirens' call of his past in order to save his life by finding a way out of his deadly cage. Instrumental reason, which thinks in terms of the future, of possible harm and advantage, has to take the place of instinct that, according to Freud, is embedded in a past transmitted from the collective life of preceding generations. Rotpeter's initially disastrous encounter with the colonialist-capitalist West necessitates his concentration of all his psychic energies upon his liberation from the cage in a way that would save his physical being. Compelled by this strenuous concentration, his "memories more and more shut themselves to me" ("verschlossen sich mir die Erinnerungen immer mehr" (Kafka 1994, 299). Thus he can no longer be what the Academy wants him to be—a historian of his whole life. His life has been torn apart and fallen into two absolutely separate halves. It has lost all inner coherence. Rotpeter has become irredeemably alienated from his own past existence. His utterly vanished memory shows that the violent incursion by the modern West has irrevocably destroyed the inner unity of its victims' lives.

This fragmentariness of Rotpeter's existence bears a close connection to the contingency of his victimization. That it had been only Rotpeter who had been hit by the shots of the hunting expedition and torn away forever from his group had been due to pure chance. There was no inner necessity, no special predestined meaning, no fate involved. This enormous revolution in an existence had been nothing but a fluke, a mere contingent accident.

Richard Rorty, frequently considered the voice of postmodernism in American philosophy, sees in contingency the most practicable key to the description and understanding of the world. What Rorty calls "contingency" comes close to that lack of "grand narratives" viewed by Jean-

Francois Lyotard as most characteristic of the age he calls "the postmodern condition." Postmodern society, according to Lyotard, no longer has "grands recits" (Lyotard 1979, 63), grand narratives that pretend to give unity and meaningful coherence to a culture. Rotpeter's life that can no longer be recounted as a whole, as a unity, constitutes, in terms of an individual's biography, an analogue to the disappearance of a "grand narrative" in society as a whole.

Connecting Rorty with Lyotard, we might say that history as a series of chance occurrences, without a causally determined, linear coherence and unitary direction, has ceased to be a narratable story, a "history" in the original sense with which the French word "histoire" and the German word "Geschichte" still indicate the intimate link of history to narrative. Seen from a postmodern perspective, history lacks a mythos in the Aristotelian sense of a causally transparent and, therefore, explicable and interpretable sequence of events that makes any entity—whether a culture, a society, or an individual life—representable in narrative terms. It is this nondetectability of any connection between events and their antecedent "reasons" that establishes the analogy between postmodern "history" and Rotpeter's life. Rotpeter's fateful capture took place without any reason that had to do with him. He finds no understandable cause of a fate that has torn him away from his fellow apes. "Why that?" ("Warum das?") he asks himself and, by implication, his readers, and finds no reason. "Tear open the flesh between your toes, you will not find the reason. Press your back against the bar of your cage until it almost cuts you in two, you will not find the reason" ("Kratz dir das Fleisch zwischen den Fusszehen auf, du wirst den Grund nicht finden. Drück dich hinten gegen die Gitterstange, bis sie dich fast zweiteilt, du wirst den Grund nicht finden.") (Kafka 1994, 304). Even as the bar of his cage would cut him in two, if he were to persist in his search for a reason of his punishment, so his violation and capture have actually cut the course of his life into two parts. The German word "Grund" signifies both explanatory cause or reason and the ground on which something or someone is enabled to stand and rest. Thus the text alludes both to the lack of a meaningful rational explanation of Rotpeter's fate and to the absence of a ground that would support his existence on a bedrock of meaning. This groundlessness of his fate makes his past and the experiences in it literally meaningless, lacking any interpretable sense. His past is inapplicable, and a stubborn clinging to it fatal. Sine his past that has formed him now condemns him to death, only the future can perhaps save him. His past's desertion of him forces him to create himself anew.

Rotpeter's self-staged metamorphosis corresponds to the second fundamental principle of Rorty's postmodern anthropology, the "self-fashioning" of the individual that issues from the contingency of his/her existence.

Rotpeter cannot tell the story of his past life, but he is able to report on a specific strategy pursued by him in response to a special situation in his life. He can deliver the description, not of a whole life, but of a unique "achievement," an experiment performed by him as an "artist" ("Künstler") (Kafka 1994, 310) whose creation is himself.

However, what enables the individual's self-creation is a society that permits and even encourages it. According to Rorty, the enabling of self-creation is the distinguishing mark of a society ruled by the principles of liberal democracy. Rotpeter's achievement likewise depends on the society around him. As we have already seen, the very thought of recreating himself as a human being would have never occurred to him without his witnessing the undisturbed freedom of movement human beings seemed to enjoy, and the success of his experiment would not have been possible without the constant energetic encouragement and assistance by the same humanity that had originally taken his freedom from him. Rotpeter relates that it was the emotional attitude he learned from human beings that formed the precondition of his way out from the cage. "Today I see clearly: without the greatest inner calm I would have never been able to escape. . . . That calm, however, I surely owed to the people on board ship" ("Heute sehe ich klar: ohne grösste innere Ruhe hätte ich nie entkommen können. . . . Die Ruhe wiederum aber verdankte ich wohl den Leuten vom Schiff.") (Kafka 1994, 305). The individual does not fashion himself alone; society is his co-creator. Rotpeter's jailers become his teachers. Without their good will, their active aid, their solidarity with *his* will, his project could never have been begun, and it certainly could not have been carried out to its triumphal conclusion. By the essential role society plays in it, the idea of individual self-creation in postmodern thinking and in Kafka's story differs from its precursors in Nietzsche and existentialist thought. Although at bottom a lonely road, self-creation also requires the collaboration of many individuals. In Rotpeter's words, it was "accompanied in stretches by excellent people, advice, applause and orchestral music" ("streckenweise begleitet von vortrefflichen Menschen, Ratschlägen, Beifall und Orchestralmusik"), even though "at bottom alone" ("aber im Grunde allein") (Kafka 1994, 299). It is an "achievement" that somehow always takes place on stage, in a public space, as interaction between the individual and a society that meets his effort halfway. Rotpeter benefits from and utilizes the liberalism that represents the other, the—in a double sense—"human" face of Western society. It is a society that shows its solidarity with the struggling alien who seeks to refashion himself in its image.

"Solidarity" is the third noun in the programmatic title of Richard Rorty's key text of postmodern philosophy, *Contingency, Irony, and Solidarity*. For Rorty, solidarity is the opposite of cruelty. Solidarity defines cultural—and not merely political—liberalism. Human solidarity with it is essential also to Rotpeter's project. About the sailor who was his first, untiringly helping teacher, Rotpeter says that "he was not angry with me, he understood that we fought on the same side against apish nature" ("er war mir nicht böse, er sah ein, dass wir auf der gleichen Seite gegen die Affennatur kämpften") (Kafka 1994, 310)—an example of liberal solidarity building bridges over the chasm separating not merely races, but species.

However, a profound irony underlies the idea of the individual's self-creation, and, in this context, let us recall that "irony" is the middle member of Rorty's liberal-postmodern triad. The freedom to create oneself offered by modern Western society has narrow limits. It is by no means "freedom on all sides," but merely a "way out," freedom profoundly relativized and restricted. Self-creation remains limited to a single model that it has to imitate—Western mankind's way of life. The former ape acquires something specific, in geographic-cultural terms, and rather narrowly defined—an "average *European* education" ("die Durchschnittsbildung eines Europäers"). The new self that he has created for himself is his ability to master "average European" behavior and conventions. There was no other choice if he wished to escape his cage and *live*. He was forced to assume "that freedom was not a choice" ("dass nicht die Freiheit zu wählen war") (Kafka 1994, 312; italics mine). Rotpeter could not recreate himself as just anything, but only as something desired and appreciated by the society that had imprisoned him. Thus self-creation can have no other goal but conformity with a prevailing form of life. The ape is free to create himself in its image, but not free to conceive and project a self according to his own deepest wish. He does not even possess the liberty of postmodern architecture of choosing one of many models of the past at the disposal of the present. He can, and must, adapt himself to one single model—Western society of the twentieth century.

In that sense, Kafka's little text helps to uncover fallacies and boundaries of contemporary, postmodern thinking. Dissenting from Lyotard, "A Report" shows that, in a global frame, there can indeed be found one "grand narrative," one single overarching historical tendency—the Westernization of the world that also means its final subjection to the dominion of man. Against Rorty's idea of free self-creation, Kafka's text makes clear that the individual's "freedom" to create himself is nothing other than successful adaptation to the world-dominating culture that has uprooted one. It is not true freedom, "freedom on all sides," which it would be if it offered the possibility of forming the self according to an infinite variety of norms and patterns. However, it is a "way out," infinitely preferable to existence in the cage of colonial imperialism that preceded it.

Through this doubleness of the evaluating perspective that is built into Kafka's text, it makes us see, in the world it depicts, conformity and liberation as interchangeable. With that "A Report to an Academy" exhibits an astounding, paradigmatic relevance to a century that has advanced from the colonialist imperialism of its beginning via the liberal "capitalism with a human face" of its middle to the global uniformity at its end.

BIBLIOGRAPHY

Kafka, Franz. 1967. *Briefe an Felice und andere Korrespondenz aus der Verlobungszeit.* Ed. Erich Heller and Jürgen Born, with an Introduction by Erich Heller. Frankfurt am Main: S. Fischer Lizenzausgabe von Schocken Books, New York.

———. 1994. *Drucke zu Lebzeiten.* Ed. Wolf Kittler, Hans Gerd Koch, and Gerhard Neumann. Frankfurt am Main: S. Fischer Lizenzausgabe von Schocken Books, New York. Translations from the German text are my own.

Freud, Sigmund. 1955. *Beyond the Pleasure Principle,* in *The Standard Edition of the Complete Psychological Works of Sigmund Freud.* Translated from the German under the general editorship of James Strachey in collaboration with Anna Freud. Assisted by Alix Strachey and Alan Tyson. Vol. 17 (1920–1922): *Beyond the Pleasure Principle: Group Psychology and Other Works,* 7–64. London: Hogarth Press and the Institute of Psychoanalysis.

———. 1957. "On Narcissism: An Introduction," in *The Standard Edition of the Complete Psychological Works of Sigmund Freud.* Translated from the German under the general editorship of James Strachey in collaboration with Anna Freud. Assisted by Alix Strachey and Alan Tyson. Vol. 14 (1914–1916): *On the History of the Psychoanalytic Movement: Papers on Metapsychology and Other Works,* 73–102. London: Hogarth Press and the Institute of Psychoanalysis.

———. 1961. *The Ego and the Id,* in *The Standard Edition of the Complete Psychological Works of Sigmund Freud.* Translated from the German under the general editorship of James Strachey in collaboration with Anna Freud. Assisted by Alix Strachey and Alan Tyson. Vol. 19 (1923–1925): *The Ego and the Id and Other Works,* 12–66. London: Hogarth Press and the Institute of Psychoanalysis.

———. 1966. "Project for a Scientific Psychology," in *The Standard Edition of the Complete Psychological Works of Sigmund Freud.* Translated from the German under the general editorship of James Strachey in collaboration with Anna Freud. Assisted by Alix Strachey and Alan Tyson. Vol. 1 (1886–1899): *Pre-Psycho-Analytic Publications and Unpublished Drafts,* 295–397. London: Hogarth Press and the Institute of Psychoanalysis.

———. 1991. "Abriss der Psychoanalyse." In *Gesammelte Werke: chronologisch geordnet,* ed. Anna Freud in collaboration with Marie Bonaparte. Vol. 17, 63–183. Frankfurt am Main: S. Fischer, 1991–1998.

Horkheimer, Max, and Theodor W. Adorno. 1947. *The Dialectic of Enlightenment*. Trans. by John Cumming. New York: Herder and Herder, 1972. (Original version Amsterdam: Querido, 1947; (c) 1944).

Lyotard, Jean-Francois. 1979. *La condition postmoderne: rapport sur le savoir*. Paris: Editions de Minuit. (English version: *The Postmodern Condition: A Report on Knowledge*. Translated from the French by Geoff Bennington and Brian Massumi. Foreword by Frederic Jameson. Theory and History of Literature. Vol. 10. Minneapolis: University of Minnesota Press, 1984. The reference here is on p. 37).

Neumann, Gerhard. 1975. "'Ein Bericht für eine Akademie.' Erwägungen zum 'Mimesis'-Charakter Kafkascher Texte." *Deutsche Vierteljahrsschrift für Literaturwissenschaft und Geistesgeschichte* 49 (1975): 66–83.

Rorty, Richard. 1989. *Contingency, Irony, and Solidarity*. Cambridge: Cambridge University Press.

Sokel, Walter H. 1964. *Franz Kafka: Tragik und Ironie: Zur Struktur seiner Kunst*. Munich-Vienna: Albert Langen, Georg Müller, 1964.

BETWEEN GNOSTICISM AND JEHOVAH

The Dilemma in Kafka's Religious Attitude

KAFKA WAS certainly not religious in a conventional dogmatic sense. One of his few statements about God, for instance, suggests that belief in a personal God may be the cover under which man's faith in something indestructible in himself is concealed—a view that resembles Feuerbach's humanism rather than theistic religion. Kafka views his lack of religion as symptomatic of his historical situation: "I have not been led into life like Kierkegaard by the already heavily drooping hand of Christianity and I have not, like the Zionists, still caught the last corner of the Jewish prayer shawl that is flying away. I am end or beginning" (Kafka 1953, 121).

The great religions of the Western world themselves appear from this perspective as historical phenomena, not as absolute truths. Kafka mocks religion where, as in the case of his father's remnants of Judaism, it has been reduced to social convention and meaningless ritual. He found the obligatory visits to the synagogue of his childhood an occasion for boredom relieved by the comedy of the spectacle (Kafka 1953, 197–98). Hugo Bergmann, Kafka's friend from his school days, attests to Kafka's inclination toward atheism and recalls that his own faith was threatened by Kafka's arguments against the existence of God (Bergmann 1972, 742)—arguments that Kafka himself also remembers in his diary. His strong and growing interest in Judaism, ever since the profound encounter with the Warsaw Yiddish Theater group in Prague in 1911, seems often more

From *South Atlantic Review* 50 (1985): 3–22. This essay was delivered as a lecture at the 1983 SAMLA Convention on 29 October. All translations from Kafka's works are my own.

ethnically, morally, and existentially motivated rather than religious, a concern with rootedness in a communal way of life rather than with God.[1]

Nevertheless, if we take the term "religion" in a broader and deeper sense, then Kafka's very criticism of the conventionalized remnants of religion is in itself a sign of deep religious involvement. He took religion too seriously to have been satisfied with its involuntary self-mockery that the so-called "Yom Kippur Jews" of his social milieu represented. Similar to Kierkegaard, in this respect, Kafka would rather have no religion than its caricature.

The *religious* nature of Kafka's thinking and sensibility becomes clear if we look at one dominant explanation of the etymology of the word "religion." According to this etymology, the Latin word *religio* originally signified a holding or a tying back, a restraint or a bond, and denoted a sense of absolute obligation and dependence. In Kafka's case, such *religio* manifests itself as his sense of living under absolute laws that obligated him in his deepest being but remained incomprehensible to his rational understanding. The following aphorism articulates this sense of personal duty to an unknown superpersonal power:

> He does not live because of his personal life; he does not think because of his personal thoughts. It seems to him as though he were living and thinking under the compulsion of a family which in its own right, to be sure, had superabundance of life and thought, but for which he, according to a law unknown to him, represents a formal necessity. Because of that unknown family and those unknown laws, he cannot be released. (Kafka 1946, 283)

Kafka's basic *religio* is a sense of responsibility to an unknown collectivity.

What complicates this case enormously is the duality of Kafka's laws. Kafka confronts not one law, but two, each absolute in its demand. These two absolutes stand in radical opposition to each other. Compliance with one violates the other, so that guilt is inescapable. If *religio* means "bond" or "bind," then one can speak in Kafka's case of a "double bind" in the most literal sense (Bateson et al. 1956, 251–64). This double bind works on all levels—psychological, ethical, metaphysical, salvational. Kafka describes someone who is bound around the neck by two chains that are fastened at opposite points, one on earth, the other in heaven:

> Now, when he desires to move down toward earth, the necklace of heaven strangles him, and when he desires [to raise himself toward] heaven, the earthly chain strangles him. And yet he possesses all possibilities and feels them; indeed, he refuses to attribute the whole dilemma to a mistake at the original chaining. (Kafka 1953, 46–47)

It would be misleading to see this double bind in terms of a conflict merely between the religious and the worldly dimensions of the self. For the earthly chain has itself the force of *religio*. It constitutes an absolute law for Kafka that contradicts the other absolute that Kafka locates in heaven. In documents from Kafka's life this double bind manifests itself as a conflict between two ways of life that are also absolute moral responsibilities for him. To bring it down to its essential character, the contradiction that rends him asunder inheres in the Judeo-Christian tradition from its beginnings. It derives from God's contradictory position to the world and the moral double bind that follows from it. Let us then begin from the beginning, the Book of Genesis, which had a particular significance for Kafka.

This paradox within the God of Genesis lies in His double nature. He is a god of immanence, creator and ruler of the universe. But He is also a god of transcendence, who stands outside His world, unrecognized by it, an unknown God to all except a select few of His creatures. He is a stranger to a world that He Himself has made. He reenters this world only by making the Covenant with a special individual, Abraham, and his descendants.

I propose to call the moment of God's utmost estrangement from His world, prior to the Covenant with Abraham, the proto-Gnostic phase or aspect of God. For, at this moment in Genesis, between the Tower of Babel and Abraham, a possibility of religious thought emerges that will eventually lead to Christianity and culminate in Gnosticism. In Gnosticism, the transcendent strain of Judaism was to unite with Greek and Iranian dualisms at the beginning of our era. The Gnostic hypostatized one side of the Jewish paradox and eliminated the other. God for the Gnostic is pure transcendence. He dwelled forever beyond this world, an eternal stranger to it, and is neither its creator nor its ruler. The cosmos is the handiwork of inferior beings, of a jealous demiurge called Jehovah, of petty gods or demons, or else it is a delusion, the result of a fall, the self-estrangement of God from Himself. To those who are smitten by the inkling of true divinity, this physical universe is a huge prison. They turn away from this world, while condemned to live in it, and strain toward another life, a life unlike anything known here. Followers of an Alien God, they are sharers of a hidden knowledge, and therefore called Gnostics or "the knowing ones."

Judaism itself was preserved from developing its Gnostic potential by the idea of the Covenant. With Jehovah's pact with Abraham and Abraham's descendants a countermovement to pure transcendence sets in, from which Judaism proper results. Judaism is a synthesis between the Edenic or immanent aspect of God and His transcendent or proto-Gnostic aspect. Even after the Covenant, God remains outside His creation. He is not domiciled in nature; He is not immanent in His cosmos. Yet, in another sense, he does dwell in it potentially, by virtue of His covenant with His chosen people. In and through the stream of generations of the Hebrew people, God lives toward a future in which the world will be entirely His again. This confluence of immanent and transcendent phase constitutes the properly Judaic concept of God.

This paradox that resides in the Judaic God entails a moral *aporia*, an ethical double bind, for the individual Jew. God's demand and expectation confronts the Jew with the same paradox that, as Kierkegaard saw, characterizes the existence of Abraham. To heed the call of God, the natural man, Abram, had to become the new man, Abraham. Abraham had to abandon his native home, his family, his natural world, and move toward a strange land to live as a stranger. He was to move in the Gnostic direction, out of and away from the familiar world. By the same token, however, he had to move back into this world, reconnect with nature, found a family, establish a home, fill the world with his seed. Following in Abraham's footsteps, the Jew, partner of a transcendent God, is to stand apart from the natural world of the gentiles. At the same time, he is to do God's bidding by means of nature. Procreating by the flesh, he is to serve and fulfill a promise of spirit.

The paradox within Judaism was fought out to an extraordinary degree of intensity in Kafka's life and work. Salvation lay for Kafka in two opposite directions—continuity of and apartness from earthly life. The continuity of past and future was for him, as an early dialogue in his diary makes clear, a circle of time in which the self is sheltered as long as it can stay within it (Kafka 1948, 17–24). This feeling of the saving power of continuity received concrete content in the overwhelming impact that the Yiddish Theater exerted on him. Yiddish culture revealed to him the warmth and inner wealth on which a collective life, drawing sustenance from roots in the remote past, could thrive. In this continuous, ethnic-spiritual identity, Judaic religion revealed itself to Kafka in its most basic and archetypal form. What Kafka longed for, but found lacking in his own family, was revealed to him in the encounter with the extended family of Jewish people who seemed to live in still-unbroken connection with their distant origin. His diary of 1911 and 1912 shows Kafka elated and fascinated by the discovery of this "circle of blood"—his term for the continuity between father and son (Kafka 1948, 296). But as a thoroughly estranged Western Jew, he found it impossible to enter the circle himself.

The only way in which, at least at this time, he could conform to the Judaic law was to marry and to found a family of his own. "A man without a wife is not human," he quoted the Talmud in his diary (Kafka 1948, 174). The Talmudic inveighing against bachelorhood and childlessness merely confirmed Kafka's own original guilt toward life, which he felt he had incurred because of his natural tendency toward solitude and separateness that the demands of his writing reinforced. The relationship to Felice, which lasted for five years, led to two engagements and played an enormous role for his work, followed almost immediately upon the experience of the Yiddish Theater. Felice represented a test case for Kafka. His "judgment" that here was *his* challenge was made the first time he met her (Kafka 1948, 285). It was a "judgment" on the fundamental question: Can I connect with Judaism on its deepest level and take my place, as a Jew must, in the chain of generations which bind the Jew in partnership to his God, who is a God of life and its promise on earth? But the overwhelming power of Kafka's Gnostic sensibility proved to be the decisive obstacle to fulfilling Jehovah's commandment, at least at this point in his life.

Kafka seemed to have been familiar with Gnostic thought both directly and indirectly. According to Klaus Wagenbach's list of the volumes of Kafka's personal library, he owned Walter Köhler's book entitled *Gnosticism,* and he also seemed to be very interested in Jewish religion at the time of Jesus in which the origins of important strains of Gnosticism have to be looked for (Wagenbach 1958, 262–63). Gnosticism was, as the recent discoveries of Nag Hammadi have shown, in essential respects an outgrowth of Judaic origin (Rudolph 1977, 36–38). The Gnostics formed an important part of the reception that the Old Testament found in late Hellenistic and Roman times. The Holy Book of Judaism served as a point of reference, a background against which the Gnostics were able to highlight their deviations (Rudolph 1977, 79, 81, 102, 111–112, 140, 148). Even their antagonism reveals their indebtedness. Gnosticism, in turn, left a lasting imprint on the Judaism from which it had sprung. As Gershom Scholem has shown, strong echoes of Gnosticism are found in the *Kabbalah* and other sources of Jewish mysticism (Scholem 1961, 35, 49–50, 260–77). "Gnostic myth, and not history, provided the extra strength that Jewish memory needed for Jewry to survive its latest catastrophe" (Bloom 1983b, 23–24). These words of Harold Bloom do not refer to the holocaust, but to the expulsion of the Jews from Spain at the beginning of the modern era, and to the consequences of this event for the development of the *Kabbalah* in Palestine.

This close connection between Gnosticism and important trends within Judaism is of the greatest importance for understanding the Gnostic strain in Kafka.[2] Kafka's strong interest in the sources of the Jewish past, his growing preoccupation with the *Kabbalah* and Jewish mysticism, reinforced the Gnostic sensibility and predisposition that had been deeply implanted in his outlook and character long before he became acquainted with direct and indirect sources of Gnostic thought.[3] Much more decisive than external "influences," however, are the kinship and parallelism in patterns of interpreting life and the world that link Kafka to Gnosticism from the beginning of his writing, and long before we can detect any evidence of his acquaintance with the historic phenomenon of Gnosticism. We are faced here with a case analogous to the astounding parallelism prevailing between the narrative structure of Kafka's fiction and Freud's theory of human life (Sokel 1980, 145–58).

To be sure, Kafka's close relationship to Gnostic thinking is not a unique case in our century. We can speak of a powerful revival of Gnostic sensibility in the twentieth century, after Gnosticism had become a subject of historical scholarship that made its doctrines available to the broader public. For in Gnosticism of the Hellenistic and Roman world, the modern phenomenon of alienation first appeared in human history. This explains the intense appeal of Gnostic ideas to our time. Hans Jonas in his book, *The Gnostic Religion,* has pointed out striking analogies between Gnostic and existential thought. Any study of the revival of Gnostic ideas would have to include August Strindberg, Otto Weininger, C. G. Jung, Hermann Hesse (Quispel 1975, 241–58), Oskar Kokoschka, Hans Henny Jahnn, Antonin Artaud, Robert Musil, and above all, Franz Kafka. (Harold Bloom [1983a] has found Gnosticism even in Norman Mailer's *Ancient Evenings.*)

Kafka's exceptionally developed Gnostic sensibility resided in two factors: In his writing, and in his ingrained abhorrence not only of sexuality—"coitus" was, he said, "the punishment of the happiness of being together"—but of all reminders of the material and sensory nature of human beings. Very much in the Gnostic vein, Kafka perceived life as imprisonment, and death as liberation. The wish to die was for him the dawn of a "knowledge" that corresponded exactly to the meaning that the Gnostics gave to the term (Rudolph 1977, 126, 130–31). It is the kind of knowledge that sees through the illusion that earthly, corporeal, individuated life represents:

> A first sign of beginning knowledge is the wish to die. This life seems unbearable, another life unattainable. One is no longer ashamed of wanting to die; one asks to be taken out of the old prison cell which one hates and to be brought to a new one which one will learn to hate. But in this wish there also glimmers a remnant of faith that during the transport the Lord will perchance pass by, look at the prisoner and say: "This one you shall not lock up again." (Kafka 1953, 40)

This aphorism of Kafka's reproduces the exact structure of a particular sect of Gnostic religion. Marcion preached that an Alien God has gratuitously taken pity on the poor prisoners in Jehovah's cosmic jail and sent Christ into this world to liberate those who would heed His call of pure compassion (von Harnack 1924; Jonas 1963, 137–45). To be sure, in Kafka, liberation is not knowledge, Gnosis, but only belief in a perhaps remote possibility. Knowledge in Kafka's case is purely negative. Knowledge sees the worthlessness of this life and the unattainability of any other.

Yet in contrast to Schopenhauerian pessimism,[4] there is in Kafka frequently the supposition or conjecture of another world, another life, or at least another standpoint from which the thoroughly distressing picture that earthly life presents might appear quite different:

> Viewed by earthly clouded eyes, we are in the situation of railroad passengers who have suffered an accident in a tunnel at a spot where one can no longer see the light from the entrance, while the light from the exit is so faint that the eyes of the passengers must make a constant effort and yet constantly lose sight of it; and, to top it all, neither entrance nor exit are certain.[5] (Kafka 1953, 73)

Implied is the possibility that an unclouded, unearthly, and therefore truer vision would see the light, and know that a world exists outside the tunnel. From such a well-nigh Platonic perspective it would appear that

> Only down here is suffering suffering. This is not to be understood as an assertion that those who suffer here shall be raised elsewhere on account of their sufferings, but only in the sense that what is called suffering in this world is bliss in another world, without undergoing any change and merely freed from its opposite. (Kafka 1953, 51)

Kafka's dualism is one of two diametrically opposed ways of being and experiencing, which frequently seems to hide behind the more traditional dualistic image of two worlds.[6]

The origin of this dualism and the positing of a higher and truer world or state of being than the one known to the earthly eye seems to lie in Kafka's perception and experience of writing. In an interview with the theosophist Rudolf Steiner in 1911, which Kafka recorded in his diary, Kafka asserts to have experienced in literature "states (not many) which in my opinion are very close to the clairvoyant states described by you [Dr. Steiner] . . . in which I felt not only at my own limits, but at the frontiers of the human altogether" (Kafka 1948, 57). Kafka describes his writing, or rather his experiences of writing, frequently in terms customarily reserved for religion. It would exceed the limits of this essay to show the religious nature of the language with which Kafka depicted everything pertaining to his writing. Part of Kafka's poetics provides a fine example of what Hegel calls "the Religion of Art" (Hegel 1952, 490–520). To be sure, Hegel had the Greeks in mind when he coined the term, while Kafka's concern with writing represents what I should like to call, in the terms of the dichotomy of styles that Erich Auerbach (1957) develops in *Mimesis,* the "Hebrew" variant of *Kunstreligion.* Auerbach's distinction between the mimetic, visual relationship of the Homeric style to physical reality and the auditory hearkening posture with which the Biblical style refers to man's relationship to an invisible, inward reality is extremely relevant to Kafka. The Hebrew God manifests Himself not by images, but by the voice, and by the call. The call from beyond the world is also a fundamental theme of Gnosticism; it is the call that awakens us (Rudolph 1977, 137). Kafka, in whose work the call is a fundamental structural principle as well as a primary theme, obviously conforms to Auerbach's biblical type (Sokel 1978, 37–38). The exclusiveness with which literature fills Kafka and requires him to live in its service provides striking analogies to the demands God made on Abraham. Kafka, too, feels commanded to estrange himself from his family and indeed from all worldly concerns—his job, women, friends, and so on—in order to devote himself to an absolute task that fills him as completely as God wants His chosen ones to be filled by Him.

But, while alienating him completely from the world that he knows, writing opens another world to him. This strange unknown world dwells in his depths. It is inchoate, immaterial, indescribable. Only writing provides an approach to it, which, however, must remain mere allusion and the barest of hints.[7] Kafka is able to say of it only *that* it is, that it dwells inside him, urging to be revealed. For this task of revelation he must sacrifice his life. It is a task that, in its absoluteness, can only be described as holy. He feels that for the "uncertain liberation" of this inner world, a hammer might be needed that would smash *him* to pieces (Kafka 1948, 321). His destruction would then be the birth of the "enormous world . . . in [his] head" (Kafka 1948, 306). In a sense, Kafka stands in relation to his writing as Abraham and Isaac combined stand in relation to God. The sacrifice that *his* divinity (literature) demands of *its* "Abraham," Kafka, is his own life: "The enormous world which I have in my head. But how to release myself and how to release it without being torn to pieces. But rather be torn to pieces a thousand times than to hold it back in me or to bury it. For this task I exist; that is completely clear to me" (Kafka 1948, 306).

What distinguished Kafka's *Kunstreligion* from the aestheticism fashionable in his youth was this religious dimension. Kafka's religion of literature was service in the cause of a world, strange and yet more real, deeper, truer, purer, more alive than anything experienced in empirical existence.

In the meditations and the aphorisms of his *Oktavhefte* of 1917–1918, Kafka transformed the deep and inner world of his writing experience into a realm more akin to the higher world of traditional dualistic religion and metaphysics. A religion of art became an art of religious and metaphysical thinking that, far from constituting a system, must, in keeping with the tradition of the aphorism from Lichtenberg to Nietzsche and Karl Kraus, be seen as a series of stabs into, or momentary flashing points of contact with, a truth that can never be grasped, let alone formulated, in its totality.[8]

"Truth is indivisible. It therefore cannot know itself. He who claims to know it must be a lie" (Kafka 1953, 48).

In such an approach to truth, contradictions are essential. Thought that harbors contradictions comes closer to the infinite truth than the attempt to systematize neatly, and resolve or eliminate contradiction. Given the infinite discrepancy between the individual mind and the totality that is truth, any appearance of consistency is a symptom of what Kafka calls the cardinal sin of man, impatience—"a premature discontinuation of the methodical, an apparent fencing in of an apparent subject matter" (Kafka 1953, 39). The meditations and aphorisms of the *Oktavhefte* in which Kafka's religious thought is most overtly expressed still belong to art, not to discursive reasoning. They are a different genre in the same body of writing to which his narrative fiction belongs.

The step from the religion of writing to the Gnostic dualism of the meditations and aphorisms can be followed in the way in which the absolute demand made by literature tends to strengthen Kafka's natural disposition to experience the world as a prison, a place of intolerable confinement, frustration, disruption, and estrangement.[9] The constant interruptions with which family, profession, and human relationships in general frustrate his writing, stealing precious moments from what should have been a perennial task, the noises of the world that interfered with concentration, and above all the conflict between the need to write and the long hours of office duty force a duality upon his life, dividing it between the true life away from the world and the false one within it. This divided self is the background for the emergence of a dualistic world view.

In the "Meditations," Kafka projects dualism into the heart of the Judeo-Christian tradition. His retelling of the story of Eden and the Fall is a reinterpretation of the Edenic myth from a dualistic, Gnostic perspective. For Kafka changes the expulsion from Paradise from a temporal event to a spatial separation. He posits the possibility of the continued existence of Paradise, and of our own continued residence in it, even while we live banished from it in the world:

> The expulsion from paradise is in its main portion eternal: That is, the expulsion from paradise is final; life in the world is unavoidable; but the eternity of the event (or expressed in temporal terms, the eternal repetition of the event) makes it possible nonetheless, not only that we might be living permanently in paradise, but that we actually are continuing to live there, regardless of whether we are aware of it here or not. (Kafka 1953, 46)

Thus two worlds, or rather two forms of being, exist side by side. One is paradisiacal, the other is earthly. This duality is not merely one of two worlds or two distinct states of being. It resides in each of us as a split between our earthly and our heavenly nature, as beautifully expressed in this aphorism about the duality of love: "Sensuous love deludes us about heavenly love; it would be incapable of doing this by itself; but since it contains the element of heavenly love unconsciously within itself, it is able to do it" (Kafka 1953, 48). Every one of us is a citizen of two universes. We live in Paradise and in the fallen world simultaneously. But, exactly as in Gnosticism, this knowledge may be, and usually is, hidden from man so that he lives unaware of his true nature and residence. The recognition that our sensuous existence is a state of self-alienation is precisely what *Gnosis* means.

Such a dualistic anthropology is the means by which Kafka is able to universalize his double bind. The double bind appears in the "Meditations" as every human being's dual citizenship in a heavenly and an earthly world. Man's fall is the fall into the split existence. If man had stayed in Paradise, he would have remained unified and one with himself. This unity is what Kafka calls life.

The world view expressed in Kafka's "Octave Notebooks" of the Zürau period becomes most precisely analogous to the thinking of Gnosticism through the fact that, in both, the apparent dualism reveals itself as ultimate monism (Rudolph 1977, 65). In his Zürau writings, Kafka attempted an "experiment." Here, for once, he attempted to overcome the dualism in his own existence. During his whole life he had suffered the emotional and spiritual strangulation that two equally powerful but contradictory demands performed on him. He tried to free himself from the double bind of the two chains by resolutely giving sole allegiance to the one anchored in heaven. He did not succeed. The earthly absolute pulled him back; the strangulation persisted. However, the attempt of breaking loose toward the heavenly pole left us the unique genre in his oeuvre, the Gnostic meditations of the Zürau period.

In them, Kafka, like the Gnostics, assigned absolute primacy to the spiritual world over the sensory one: "There is nothing but a spiritual world; what we call the sensory world is the evil in the spiritual one" (Kafka 1953, 44). In the light of this aphorism, no reading of Kafka that seeks to view him as a Manichaean can be convincing (Heller 1959, 223). For while Manichaeism sees two autonomous principles—light and darkness, spirit and matter, good and evil—engaged in mortal combat, Kafka, in this aphorism, views the one as lodged in the other. Of all forms of Gnosticism, the Valentinian or Syro-Egyptian variety possesses the greatest relevance for Kafka. For in it, evil emerges within the good and the material world is the delusion of spirit. For the Valentinian Gnosis, the material universe is the result of the fall of divinity into self-estrangement. The main difference between this type of Gnosis and Judeo-Christian religion lies in the radically different view of the relationship between Creation and the Fall. According to Valentinian Gnosis, our world owes its being not to the free, beneficent act of God, but to His seduction that embroiled Him in matter. It is not the Fall of man, but the Fall of God that forms the point of origin of the historical world. In the words of Hans Jonas, it is

> the distinguishing principle of the [Syro-Egyptian] type [of Gnosis] . . . to place the origin of darkness, and thereby of the dualistic rift of being, *within* the godhead itself, and thus to develop the divine tragedy, the necessity of salvation arising from it, and the dynamics of this salvation itself, as wholly a sequence of inner-divine events. Radically understood, this principle involves the task of deriving not only such spiritual facts as passion, ignorance, and evil but the very nature of *matter* in its contrariety to the spirit from the prime spiritual source: its very existence is to be accounted for in terms of the divine history itself. (Jonas 1963, 174)

The history of the cosmos is understood as a "defection" of God from Himself, as His self-fragmentation and exile into the world of corporeal individuation, and as a gradual remembering and return to Himself through the process of seeing through and recognizing the material world for what it is: the self-estrangement of divine reality, the "error and failure" of the Godhead, the evil lodged within Him (Jonas 1963, 175; Rudolph 1977, 93, 132–133).

Kafka's special interest, as that of the Gnostics, was devoted to the Book of Genesis and in it to Paradise and the Fall. Many of his aphorisms concern themselves with these parts of the Judaic narrative. However, the above-quoted aphorism about the sensory world being the evil in the spiritual one points to a fall totally different from the sin of Adam and Eve as described in Genesis. Kafka's aphorism identifies the creation of our sensory world with evil. That which has made our world is the evil that inheres in spirit. The Fall thus appears conditioned by the divine itself. Finding evil in the bosom of the spiritual itself, Kafka stands infinitely closer to Gnosticism than to the Bible. His aphorism hints at a fall much more radical than the mere act of disobedience of the ancestral pair of mankind. What Kafka shares with Gnosticism, and what separates both from Genesis is the view of evil as self-estrangement rather than rebellion. Evil, and with it the cosmos, is the self-defection of the divine.

It is this view of divine self-betrayal that moves Kafka so uncannily close to Gnosticism. For what predisposes him toward this particular Gnostic perspective is not only the split in the self between two contradictory demands, each of absolute validity, but also the radical division in the source of the law, the split in the father figures, power figures, and God figures of his life and work.

This split appears in its clearest form where the father figure first emerges in Kafka's work—in the early fragment, "Urban World," of February 1911. There a father heaps violent abuse upon his son, Oskar. The son rejects his father's accusations indignantly. His protest culminates in this exclamation in which we can see an important seed of Kafka's Gnostic attitude: "This is not my father who speaks to me in this way. Since noon something has changed you or you are an alien whom I meet in my father's room for the first time. My real father—he would have had to embrace me" (Kafka 1948, 49). In this distinction between a "real" or true father who is absent, and a false and "alien" father who is present, resides a dualistic structure that closely corresponds to the Gnostic concept of divinity. To be sure, here it still appears in the biographical-psychological framework of the realist convention of fiction, and it receives biographical corroboration from Kafka's "Letter to His Father." Kafka discerns a very similar incongruity in his own father, who, Kafka claims, never adhered to the commandments he himself had laid down:

> When I was a child everything you commanded was practically a commandment from Heaven for me. I never forgot it. It remained the most important means for judging the world and especially for judging you; and there you were found wanting utterly. . . . You, the immeasurably important lawgiver, did not adhere to the commandments you yourself had imposed on me. (Kafka 1953, 172–73)

Kafka's language alludes to the close connection, typical of him, between the autobiographical-psychological and the religious sphere. His metaphors import heaven and the decalogue into the family dining room of his childhood. The "jokes" about his father, exchanged between Kafka and his sister Ottla, he calls "jokes of the kind one spreads about gods and kings" (Kafka 1953, 81). His mythologizing of his father points toward a dualism that also inheres in the Gnostic concept of the divine.

If there is anything all Gnostic sects and religions hold in common, it is the doctrine of the two Gods, the true God and the false one, or the upper and the lower, the pure and the fallen aspect of divinity. The heavenly commandment of Kafka's father corresponds to the true and supreme God of the Gnostics. Kafka sees this heavenly commandment as an absolute that makes it possible for him to judge his actual father's failure to live up to himself and his own law. We find here a close analogy to the Gnostic division of divinity into a true and supreme spirit of pure luminosity, whom some Gnostic texts call "the Father," and into the inferior powers that have made this world of imperfection and rule over it. The Gnostic is enabled to judge and reject the inadequacy of cosmic reality because he possesses the knowledge, the *Gnosis,* of the true "father," who is the substance of light and spirit, and the absolute measuring yard for all else. Thus we find in Kafka's view of the paternal figure of his life and in the Gnostic concept of divinity a closely paralleled structure of contradiction between essence and actuality. The actuality of this life flies in the face of what the "essence" or the law, the heavenly commandment of the true "father," make their creature, respectively their son, expect. The Gnostic imagination holds divine perfection contradicted and mocked by the way things are. Instead of attributing the discrepancy, in the manner of the mainstream Judeo-Christian tradition, to human sin and the Fall of man, the Gnostic separates the two aspects of God—perfection and power—and distributes them over two radically different gods or groups of divine beings. Kafka's image of his father and the Gnostic idea of divinity have this in common: In both cases the power that rules the actual world is false or has fallen away from itself, while that which is true has become remote from and ineffectual in actual life.

This Gnostic duality can be demonstrated in all the father figures as well as those of power and authority in Kafka's works and constitutes an essential feature of it. Three years before the aphorisms of the Zürau period, Kafka gave one of the most memorable poetic formulations to it in the doorkeeper parable "Before the Law," which he inserted into his novel, *The Trial.* The law, the highest goal of human yearning, corresponds to the supreme divinity that the Gnostics call "the father" and equate with the substance of light. This connection can be seen in Kafka's parable in "the radiance that streams inextinguishably from the door of the Law." The doorkeeper of Kafka's parable, on the other hand, stands in a direct line of descent from his archetype whom we first encounter in Gnostic texts,[10] and then, under the strong influence of Gnostic sources, in Jewish Merkaba mysticism (Politzer 1962, 182–83). He belongs to the so-called Archontes or Aeons, or "Powers" that have created the sensory world and keep it enslaved. They block man's access to his true home and destination. If man wishes to reach the true God, he must see through the works of the powers and doorkeepers, and overcome them.

The Gnostic duality of law and doorkeeper becomes in Kafka's aphorisms and meditations of the Zürau period an aporia of the divine. On the one hand, God is here identical with the "spiritual world" to which man's essence, the indestructible core in him, also belongs. Thus God is essentially identical with the core of man. On the other hand, Kafka speaks of God's "raging against the human family." Obviously, Kafka's idea of God in the aphorisms is not unitary, and the strange contradiction in it closely corresponds to Gnostic dualism.

In the Coptic-Gnostic text, "Treatise without a Title," man's expulsion from Paradise is caused by the jealous "powers" of the cosmos who feel threatened by Adam. They wish to keep him from the tree of life because his eating from it would make him immortal and thus equal to them.[11] Analogously Kafka says about the Fall: "Why do we lament original sin [*Sündenfall*]? We have not been driven out of Paradise because of it, but because of the tree of life so that we should not eat of it" (Kafka 1953, 99). Like the Gnostics, Kafka, in this aphorism, pronounces man free of guilt for his loss of Paradise. Not because of his sin did man lose Paradise, but because he was to be kept from the tree of life. The implication is that God begrudges man eternal life. He keeps man from life as the doorkeeper in the parable keeps the man from the country from entering the law. As in Gnosticism, man appears here as a guiltless victim of a power that is intent on keeping its monopoly.

Both Kafka and the Gnostic text derive their heterodox interpretation of the Fall directly from Genesis. God drives Adam from Paradise with this argument: "Behold the man is become as one of us, to know good and evil; and now, lest he put forth his hand, and take also of the tree of life, and eat, and live for ever: Therefore the Lord God sent him forth from the garden of Eden, to till the ground from whence he was taken" (Gen. 3:22).

The Gnostics cannot reconcile their exalted idea of true divinity with such petty jealousy and fear of rivalry. Therefore they divorce the true and highest God from Jehovah's behavior and motivation and attribute these to lower divinities, the "Archontes" or "powers." In fact, the Gnostics interpret man's expulsion from Paradise as a hostile act of the cosmic "powers" against the true God. The true God stands on man's side and encourages him to acquire knowledge.

Kafka's dualism appears as a duality in God Himself. God's true nature may be infinitely good; however, He has bad moods. In a conversation that was recorded by Max Brod, Kafka said that "our world is only a bad mood of God, a bad day of his" (Benjamin 1969, 116). He continued, that there is "plenty of hope, an infinite amount of hope—but not for us." From the context of this conversation, it appears that Kafka's dualism is not essentially different from that of the Gnostics of whom Brod was immediately reminded. To be sure, Kafka denies that his view of the world as one of the "nihilistic thoughts, the suicidal thoughts that come into God's head" was to be equated with the "Gnostic view of life" in which God is "the evil demiurge" and "the world [is] his Fall." Kafka denies the permanence of God's fall and emphasizes the temporary character of His self-defection. There is "infinite hope" for God, who will pass again from His bad to His good mood. However, from the human perspective, the result is as dismal as though God had permanently fallen. There is no hope "for us," no hope for this temporal universe that, as an emanation of

God's self-destructiveness, can never free itself from that evil which forms its essence. In the finite time that is our cosmos, God's destructive and self-hating side is all we get to know.

As for the Gnostics, there exists for Kafka another God who is completely different from the tyrant who rages against the human family. This God is not a ruler. He is no doorkeeper, no power figure excluding man from entering his sphere. He is the indestructible in man himself, man's real God, who is one with man as Oskar, the hero of Kafka's early fragment, "Urban World," thinks himself to be one with his "real" father whom he cannot recognize in his accuser.

The essential identity between God and man, which connects Valentinian Gnosticism[12] with Hegelian philosophy, also forms the best base from which to approach this aspect of Kafka's idea of God as it appears in the Octave notebooks: "We are separated from God on two sides. The fall separates us from Him; the tree of life separates Him from us" (Kafka 1953, 101). But the life that separates God from us is also in us. Kafka makes it very clear that this God is not a superhuman person different from man's essence: "Man cannot live without a permanent trust in something indestructible in himself. But both the indestructible and his trust in it may be permanently hidden from him. One of the ways by which this concealment is expressed is belief in a personal God" (Kafka 1953, 44). Belief in a personal God is man's blindness to the indestructible in himself. We cannot think of this God as an individual, even as we cannot think of the indestructible within man as identical with the individual soul: "The indestructible is one; it is each single human being and, at the same time, it is common to all men; from it follows the uniquely inseparable connectedness of human beings" (Kafka 1953, 47).

Kafka's thought seems to suggest a startling resemblance to the atheistic anthropology of the Hegelian Ludwig Feuerbach. Faith in a personal God masks our true belief in the unity and divinity of mankind. But such an equation of Kafka with Feuerbach would distort Kafka's thought. For Kafka's faith in the indestructible is not the faith of left Hegelian humanism in the unique value of mankind's "species being." Rather, it is trust in man's participation in that eternity which is the indestructible, and in that indivisibility which Kafka calls "truth." Again the analogy with Gnosticism may help us to understand Kafka's thought. According to Valentinian Gnosticism, God's self-estrangement fragmented Him into innumerable individual sparks of spirit or "pneuma." These "pneumatic" sparks are imprisoned in the visible walls of the flesh of human beings and the invisible walls that enclose and isolate each psyche. But the imprisoned sparks of pneuma hidden in human beings are fallen particles of God, literally one with Him, and thus with each other. They are scattered, isolated fragments of the unitary and divine substance. To recognize them in ourselves is to recognize our own indestructible essence and, at the same time, to discover the essential oneness of all spiritual life.

Like Valentinian Gnosticism, Kafka believes in the fundamental oneness of spiritual existence. Such a faith differs radically from the Biblical belief in the personhood of God and the creatureliness of man. Biblical faith sees man and God as different from each other as the creature is different from its creator. There cannot be identity between God and man; there can only be bonds relating separate individuals to each other through obedience, partnership, judgment, love. Kafka, like Valentinian Gnosticism, by contrast, sees the multiplicity of the sensory world not as the fruit of creativeness, but as the result of delusion. Individuated existence follows the self-estrangement of original unity. Individual man is "the failure" of the divine.

The idea of divine self-estrangement explains the contradiction in Kafka's concept of God. God in His fallen state, God divided from His own law and essence, appears as the anxious and arbitrary ruler who, like an Oedipal father, fears man as his rival and cuts him off from eternal life. But God, in His true being, *is* this eternal life. He is the indestructible unity that embraces man, in which man is one with God. These two aspects of God seem so radically different that nothing appears to be able to reconcile them.

So far I have dealt with only one side of a dichotomy. Next to Gnostic Dualism, there is in Kafka an equally, or perhaps even more profound and powerful component of something much closer to traditional Judaism—something corresponding to the "earthly chain" of the literal "double bind" with which we began our discussion. At no time, not even in the "Meditations" of the Zürau period, in which Kafka's Gnostic sensibility seems to assume absolute ascendancy, is Jehovah's demand on the earthly, historical, ethnic, and ethical existence of the individual Jew completely absent. What connects Kafka with traditional Judaism is also that which, in important respects, sets him apart from Gnosticism. In two factors above all can we see a fundamentally anti-Gnostic, traditionally Judaic side of Kafka: in his radical devaluation of knowledge—*Erkenntnis* or *Gnosis*—that causes him to interpret the Fall in some aphorisms in a much more traditional manner than in the aphorisms we have discussed here; and in his conviction that action alone can realize and indeed redeem knowledge. In other words, *Gnosis* or the cognitive is for Kafka subordinate to the practical, moral, and existential dimension of man. Space does not permit elaboration of these distinctions here; such an elaboration must be postponed for subsequent exploration.

NOTES

1. For the most detailed treatment of Kafka's encounter with the Warsaw Yiddish Theater, see Beck (1971).

2. On the Jewish foundations of Gnosticism, see particularly Wilson (1964), esp. 71–75 and 123; see also Quispel (1953, 195–97). The discoveries of the Coptic-Gnostic texts at Nag Hammadi are of supreme importance for the illumination of the indebtedness of Gnosticism to Judaism. See Rudolph (1977, 40–57). Because of the rich documentary yield of these excavations, "the part played by Jewish tradition and ideas in the genesis of gnosticism . . . can be shown even more clearly and persuasively [than before]" (Rudolph 1977, 157).

3. See the important and informative study by Hoffmann (1975), who investigates the influence of Jewish mysticism on Kafka's aphorisms and arrives at many illuminating results. However, he ignores the fact that the closeness of Kafka's writings to Jewish mysticism lies in precisely those areas where Jewish mysticism in turn is profoundly marked by Gnostic thought. Hoffmann's neglect of this connection results in his underestimation of the continuity and consistency in Kafka's work and thought that, apart from all influence, Kafka's extreme predisposition toward the Gnostic cast of mind establishes.

4. Foulkes (1967) as well as Kurz (1980) emphasize a nihilistically or existentially interpreted pessimism in Kafka, and tend to neglect his dualistic cast of thought.

5. For this perspectivist dualism, to be sure, no equivalent can be found in Gnosticism.

6. The only parallel in Gnosticism to Kafka's experimental dualism can be found in the view held by many Gnostics of an unbridgeable gulf between themselves, "the knowing ones," and the masses who are incapable of ever perceiving the truth. See Wilson (1964, 132–33). On the spiritual elitism of the Gnostics, see also Rudolph (1977, 63).

7. See Kafka's extremely important aphorism on allusion as the sole way in which language is able to refer to "anything outside the sensory world" (Kafka 1953, 45).

8. See the excellent dissertation by Gray (1981).

9. Hoffmann (1975), 116, sees "a break in Kafka's existence with the onset of his tuberculosis" and divides Kafka's writing into an earlier phase, in which he sees a "justification of existence," and a subsequent phase that he calls "meditation on ultimate things." However, such a division contradicts the powerful diachronic unity of Kafka's entire oeuvre. An examination of Kafka's Gnostic predisposition makes this unity most apparent.

10. See *Origenis contra Celsum libri octo,* quoted by Rudolph (1977, 186).

11. See *Nag Hammadi Codex* II, S, quoted by Rudolph (1977, 117).

12. See Jonas (1963, 123–24), in regard to the Mandaeans, and pp. 174–75 in regard to the Valentinians. See also Rudolph (1977, 165).

WORKS CITED

Auerbach, Erich. 1957. *Mimesis: The Representation of Reality in Western Literature.* 1946. Trans. Willard Trask. New York: Doubleday Anchor Book.

Bateson, Gregory, et al. 1956. "Toward a Theory of Schizophrenia." *Behavioral Science* 1(4): 251–64.

Beck, Evelyn Torton. 1971. *Kafka and the Yiddish Theater: Its Impact on His Work.* Madison: University of Wisconsin Press.

Benjamin, Walter. 1969. *Illuminations.* Ed. and introd. Hannah Arendt, trans. Harry Zohn. New York: Schocken Books.

Bergmann, Samuel Hugo. 1972. "Erinnerungen an Franz Kafka." *Universitas* 27(7): 739–50.

Bloom, Harold. 1983a. Review of *Ancient Evenings,* by Norman Mailer. *New York Review of Books* (28 April 1983): 3–6.

———. 1983b. Review of *Zhakor: Jewish History and Jewish Memory,* by Yosef Hayim Yerushalmi. *New York Review of Books* (17 February 1983): 23–24.

Foulkes, A. P. 1967. *The Reluctant Pessimist: A Study of Franz Kafka.* The Hague: Mouton.

Gray, Richard Terrence. 1981. "Aphorism and Metaphorism: The Aphoristic Tradition and the Aphorisms of Franz Kafka." Diss., University of Virginia.

von Harnack, Adolph. 1924. *Marcion: Das Evangelium vom fremden Gott. Neue Studien zu Marcion.* Leipzig: Hinrichs.

Hegel, Georg Wilhelm Friedrich. 1952. "Die Kunst-Religion." *Phänomenologie des Geistes.* Ed. Johannes Hoffmeister. 6th ed. Berlin: Meiner, 490–520.

Heller, Erich. 1959. *The Disinherited Mind.* Cleveland: Meridian Books, World Publishing.

Hoffmann, Werner. 1975. *Kafkas Aphorismen.* Bern: Francke.

Jonas, Hans. 1963. "Epilogue. Gnosticism, Existentialism, and Nihilism." *The Gnostic Religion: The Message of the Alien God and the Beginnings of Christianity.* 2nd ed. Boston: Beacon Press.

Kafka, Franz. 1946. *Beschreibung eines Kampfes: Novellen, Skizzen, Aphorismen aus dem Nachlass. Gesammelte Schriften.* Vol. 5. Ed. Max Brod. New York: Schocken Books.

———. 1948. *Tagebücher, 1910–1923.* Gesammelte Werke. Ed. Max Brod. New York: Schocken Books, 1948 and 1949.

———. 1953. *Hochzeitsvorbereitungen auf dem Lande und andere Prosa aud dem Nachlass.* Gesammelte Werke. Ed. Max Brod. New York: Schocken Books.

Kurz, Gerhard. 1980. *Traum-Schrecken: Kafkas literarische Existenzanalyse.* Stuttgart: Metzler.

Politzer, Heinz. 1962. *Franz Kafka: Parable and Paradox.* Ithaca, N.Y.: Cornell University Press.

Quispel, Gilles. 1953. "Der gnostische Anthropos und die jüdische Tradition." *Eranos Jahrbuch* 22 (1953): 195–234.

———. 1975. "Hesse, Jung und die Gnosis: Die 'Septem sermones ad mortuos' und 'Basilides,'" in Publications de l'Institut historique et archeologique néerlandais de Stamboul 34.2. Istambul: Nederlands historisch-archaeologisch Instituut te Istambul, 1975, 2: 241–58. (First published in *Gnostic Studies,* 1970.)

Rudolph, Kurt. 1977. *Die Gnosis: Wesen und Geschichte einer spätantiken Religion.* Göttingen: Vandenhoeck & Ruprecht.

Scholem, Gershom. 1961. *Major Trends in Jewish Mysticism.* New York: Schocken Books.

Sokel, Walter H. 1978. "Kafka's Poetics of the Inner Self." *Modern Austrian Literature* 11 (3–4): 37–58.

———. 1980. "Freud and the Magic of Kafka's Writing." *The World of Franz Kafka.* Ed. J. P. Stern. London: Weidenfeld & Nicholson, 145–58.

Wagenbach, Klaus. 1958. *Franz Kafka: Eine Biographie seiner Jugend, 1883–1912.* Bern: Francke.

Wilson, R. McLachlan. 1964. *The Gnostic Problem: A Study of the Relations between Hellenistic Judaism and the Gnostic Heresy.* 1958. London: Mowbray.

15

FREEDOM AND AUTHORITY IN THE FICTION OF FRANZ KAFKA

KAFKA'S REPRESENTATIONS of the theme of freedom and authority make him appear to be both a master of subversion, a champion of the individual's protest and revolt, and, at the same time, one of the most subtle and consummate eulogists absolute power has found in modern literature. The ambivalence of Kafka's writing shows not only in his protagonists' conflicting attitudes toward the power figures that always function as their antagonists. It is also evident in the division, within the authority figures, of two aspects—one despotic and malevolent, the other godlike and benign.

Let me begin with Kafka's autobiographical document, his "Letter to His Father," which he wrote at the age of thirty-six, but never dared to give to his father himself. It becomes obvious to any reader of the letter that the father depicted in it represents more than Kafka's empirical father. He appears as the principle of arbitrary power incarnate. The son indicts not only his father's injustice, the imperious commands that he substituted for education, his utter disrespect for the autonomous personality of his child; he also indicts the capricious, self-righteous arbitrariness with which his father treated the world. In his father, Kafka analyzes and condemns despotism.

Yet, Kafka reserves his worst accusation for his father's transgressions of his own rules. Kafka defends an adored father against one who besmirched his own exalted image. There was a time, Kafka writes, when his father's utterances had been like "Heaven's commandments" (Kafka 1953, 172)

This essay, in its present form, is published here for the first time. Translations from Kafka are my own.

for his son. His father seemed to dwell in a realm of purity that no earthly filth could reach. The son's most shattering experience was to see his father break his own "heavenly" law and sully the empyrean purity that was his proper realm. It was inconsistency, self-contradiction, that degraded the image of the father for his son.

Preoccupation with the self-contradiction in authority is indeed paradigmatic for Kafka's work. It attacks actual authority from the vantage point of the notion of ideal authority. Ideal authority is the true original essence of authority comparable to the father of Kafka's letter as he appeared before his fall into self-contradiction. This true or essential father commands respect so absolute that it is beyond questioning and reproach. What Kafka and his protagonists question, accuse, satirize, and rebel against are deviations from and caricatures of this "heavenly" image of authority. The target of attack is authority found wanting in terms of what it should be ideally. This division of authority into pure and impure echoes the Gnostic division between a Godhead of pure light and grace and daemonic aberrations nd defections from Him among whom the demiurge of our universe must be counted.

The division within authority, a fundamental structural-thematic principle of Kafka's writing, reflects the split within the protagonists' attitude—loving, worshiping, submissive, on the one hand, and, on the other, critical, aggressive, and rebellious.

Kafka's early narrative fragment, "Urban World," found in his diary of February 1911, represents the earliest and most schematically explicit illustration of this division. Oskar, the protagonist from whose point of view the story is narrated, has to endure an unexpectedly vicious verbal assault by his father. He counterattacks with the assertion that this father who is berating him is not his real, his true father. His true father "would have had to embrace me" (Kafka 1990b, 156). Either his true father has been metamorphosed or else this abusive tyrant facing him now is a total stranger who has assumed his father's guise.

We encounter here, in its archetypal form, the split so characteristic of Kafka's representation of authority figures. The protagonist retains loyalty to a "real," i.e., actually ideal, authority that, projected into the past, embodies the original or "true" nature of authority. His faith in that form of authority allows the protagonist to rebel against and reject the actual authority figure that confronts him. This split finds an analogy in the division underlying Freud's notion of "the uncanny." In the experience of the uncanny, the father image splits into the "real" father who is kind, good, benevolent, and an evil threatening figure who is, in a sinister way, associated with the real father. (This model of "the uncanny" is exemplified for Freud in E. T. A. Hoffmann's story, "Der Sandmann." In Hoffmann's story, it is the father's nefarious business partner who exerts a destructive influence on the hero's real father.) According to Freud, the evil figure embodies the castrating father of the male child's Oedipal fantasy, while the "real" father corresponds to the father image produced by the child's socialization and maturing, which leads to his identification with his father. Yet, where the archaic menacing aspect of the father is not overcome, but merely repressed, its resurfacing, the "return of the repressed," transforms him into a figure of the uncanny. The child's consciousness cannot bear to face the persistence of the dread aspect of a father whom he loves. The hostile father image must, therefore, return in an unrecognizable disguise. However, through the estranged appearance, the all-too-familiar but long-repressed fear of the Oedipal father is felt once more. The uncanny is the lurking menace making the canny, the homey and familiar, dreadfully strange.

In Kafka's "Urban World," Oskar's statement proclaims this alienation in literal terms. A stranger or a strange form has usurped his real father's appearance. "Urban World" not only anticipates, to an amazing degree, Freud's theory of the uncanny, published eight years after Kafka's fragment was written, it actually produces, at this point in the story, an uncanny effect in the reader. Kafka was to develop this aspect of "Urban World" in his subsequent story, "The Judgment." In the earlier version, the uncanny is still limited to a single moment in the narrative and lacks the full literary effect of estrangement that Kafka was to use with such mastery in his subsequent text, which he called the work of his "breakthrough." Here, however, we shall concentrate on the motif of the literally twofold authority figure in Kafka's writing. In it, the problematic relationship between the urge for freedom and the need for authority reveals itself as an essential aspect of Kafka's work and its development.

As we have seen, the protagonist of "Urban World" refuses submission to his actual father when the latter fails to conform to the remembered image of his real or true father. Henceforth, I will use the term "true" in referring to the wished-for aspect of the father or authority figure and the term "actual" for its visible manifestations. "True," in this sense, comes close to the meaning of "ideal" but includes likewise the connotation of "essential" or "authentic," proper, that is, to the referent's original nature or being. Oskar's invocation of his "true" father enables him to refuse recognition to the actual father who accuses him.

The device of splitting the father thus functions as a perfect device for representing an ambiguous relationship and situation. On the one hand, it allows the son to revolt. On the other, it prevents a true emancipation from the idea of patriarchal authority. The son remains enslaved to his desire for the father. This desire appears as the name or idea of "father" from which the tyrannical actual father figure cannot help but benefit. The ideal father becomes internalized. He becomes part of the Kafkan protagonist's attitude toward authority. Kafka's protagonist looks beyond the ugly and oppressive manifestations of authority toward an ideal contrast for which he yearns and that he projects into a distant aboriginal past.

A particularly clear stage of the development of this paradigm is *The Trial* of 1914/1915. The most puzzling feature of *The Trial* is the protagonist Josef K.'s inconsistency toward the Court, the enigmatic authority, that has "arrested" him without, in any way, restricting his freedom of movement. As the citizen of a modern state ruled by codified laws, he protests the illegality of the Court's procedure against him. Yet, in his behavior and his actions, he submits to the jurisdiction of this nonlegal authority. He obeys the proceedings it has instituted against him, fights for his acquittal by an agency he has not recognized as legitimate, and ultimately bows to the death sentence it executes on him. His defiance aims only at the Lower Court organs. It stops at the so-called High Court. However, the Lower Court, corresponding to the actual father in "Urban World," is the sole authority in evidence. The High Court never appears. The Court painter Titorelli, who seems so knowledgeable about and intimate with the Court functionaries, knows nothing about a High Court and ventures his opinion that one would not wish to know it. This unknown or even unknowable High Court, which resembles Kant's thing-in-itself, is actually mentioned first by Josef K. himself, without any prior external suggestion that such an invisible authority actually exists. Thus it seems that the High Court might be a projection of the defendant's wish for an aspect of the authority accusing him that would nullify the accusation and transform it into a justification and exculpation of his existence. Although he claims to despise the actual manifestations of the Court, he subjects himself to them by virtue of his hope for rehabilitative acquittal by an authority that, according to Titorelli, has never been known to acquit anyone except in ancient legends. Combating the authority that he meets, K. stays steadfastly loyal to its idea or ideal, craving for and strenuously seeking its verdict of exoneration. However, the answer to his quest is the executioner's knife thrust into his breast the very moment he raises his arms pleadingly toward a distant figure who, he thinks, might be a member of that High Court he has never seen. This coupling of K.'s execution with his gesture of appeal to an unknown, perhaps only imagined authority suggests that it is K.'s self-subjection to authority *per se* that kills him. He dies "like a dog" (Kafka 1990a, 312), deprived of the dignity resistance might have given him.

The parable "Before the Law," which highlights the problem of K.'s trial in metaphoric-parabolic form, presents an analogous relationship between two forms of authority, one palpable but negative, the other desired but inaccessible. Desire to enter the law fills the man from the country who has arrived at its gate. However, a doorkeeper in front of it withholds permission, at least, as he says, for the time being. Henceforth the man wastes his entire life waiting for an entrance he is never granted, even though, as he is told in his dying moment, this entrance had been reserved for him alone. The law sought by him stays forever beyond his grasp. Its sole tangible manifestation is the very obstacle that denies it to him. In this paradox, the irony of the desire for authority expresses itself. The longing for an ideal, quasi-divine authority—the law—that promises to give meaning and fulfillment to a human life enslaves the quester to an actual authority that frustrates, oppresses, and deprives his life of meaning. One has to agree, however, with the priest, who, after telling Josef K. the parable, denies that the doorkeeper is to blame for the man's predicament. The doorkeeper, the priest avers, never deceives the man. It is, one would have to add, the man's own assumption of an identity between entrance into the law and freedom that deceives him. The law in fact does not seem compatible with the individual's right to follow his or her pursuit of happiness that a liberal-democratic state guarantees to the citizen. By placing a doorkeeper at its entrance, the law reveals itself as an authority that bars such guaranteed free indulgence of desire. In the precincts of this law, freedom is possible only in one of two ways: as rebellion or as renunciation. As the doorkeeper points out to him, the man is free to enter in defiance of the doorkeeper's prohibition. However, such freedom would entail possible deadly risks, for, as the doorkeeper warns him, the man from the country would encounter further and much more horrifying doorkeepers beyond this first gate, the sight of whom even the first doorkeeper finds unendurable. Taking advantage of the doorkeeper's physical yielding of the entrance to the law, while flouting his "official" prohibition, would thus amount to a frightfully dangerous and quite possibly, or even probably, fatal gamble. Neither protagonist nor reader is in any position either to verify or to disprove the doorkeeper's assertions about the interior of the law. They could discover the truth only if the man dared to violate the doorkeeper's "official" prohibition. In any case, "freedom" to enter this law amounts to breaking it.

The man's other possibility of realizing freedom would be his renunciation of desire for the law. He would have to recognize that he can achieve a risk-free independence from the doorkeeper only by freeing himself from the spell of the law itself. In this second instance, freedom would not, as in the first, rest on a radical divorce between law and doorkeeper—the dual face authority shows to the man. Instead it would be a rejection of authority altogether, in both its forms. Emancipation from the doorkeeper would necessitate overcoming the fascination exerted by the law itself.

In his next phase of creative productivity, the period of the volume *A Country Doctor* (1917), Kafka took a big step toward clarifying further the connection between the actual and the ideal aspect of authority. In "An Imperial Message," the bifurcation of authority appears in its most gnostic form. The emperor, on his deathbed, sends a message "to you, the individual, the wretched subject, the tiny shadow that has fled from the imperial sun into the most remote distance" (Kafka 1994, 280). Despite the messenger's speed, the message will never reach "you." The appurtenances of imperial authority—the throngs of dignitaries surrounding the emperor's bed, the countless multitudes crowding the stairways and courtyards of the palace, the enormous expanse of the capital city filled with teeming mobs—they all prevent the messenger from ever reaching the "open field" that stretches between the imperial capital and the emperor's subject. No doubt the emperor—figure of true authority—has the desire to reveal himself, to communicate with his subject. He bears good will toward the individual. The emperor corresponds to a High Court that would answer K.'s longing, summon him, deem him worthy of its attention, and acquit him of guilt. However, in a close parallel to the doorkeeper legend, the intermediaries who constitute the actuality of authority block all contact between it and the individual. "Before the Law" and "An Imperial Message" have an almost identical structure with reversed directions. In the former, the individual is kept from attaining access to "true" authority, the goal of his desire, while in the latter, the message from true authority cannot reach the individual. In either case, the result is the same. Like the father whom Oskar calls his "real" father, the emperor has the desired disposition. A proper father figure, he is mindful of his subject and solicitous toward him. He is concerned, well-intentioned, generous, and thoughtful. However, his palpable actuality, the manifestation of his being emperor, makes his goodness ineffectual and unreal. To be sure, the multitudes surrounding him and the huge expanse of his palace and city are not part of the emperor's person; they belong essentially to the authority, the office, he personifies. But one cannot imagine an emperor without a court, without throngs of dignitaries, without a teeming capital enclosing him. For the practical and existential being of the individual subject, the emperor's good will cannot be actualized. His setting deprives the emperor of any possible effect upon his worshiper whom his message never reaches and who can only "dream of it," "seated by [his] window . . . when evening comes" (Kafka 1994, 282). The figure of "true" authority is reduced to unreality, to a purely subjective existence in the subject. The individual is left alone. He is free. But his freedom is worthless to him as long as he strains for authority, even though the latter cannot reveal itself to him.

The fragment "The Great Wall of China," of which "An Imperial Message" forms a part, juxtaposes idealized authority and negative power figure in the remote Emperor of China and the nomadic tribes invading the empire from the North. The narrator tells us that his native province is equidistant from the Northern tribes and from Peking—the seat of imperial power. The people in his region, he writes, would desire nothing more than feeling the emperor's touch. In his embrace, they would gladly pass away. However, enormous distances keep them from any possibility of ever experiencing such a consummation of their lives. The same distances, however, likewise protect them from the murderous raids of the Northern tribes. Freedom from their assault, freedom from enslavement and death, is theirs, but at the price of never attaining ecstatic fulfillment in the presence of their revered emperor. Whether as object of dread or of adoration, power, in the narrator's China, kills the individual it touches.

For the lucky inhabitants of such sheltered remoteness, both poles of power have lost their existential urgency. The menacing ferocity of the nomads and the idealized person of the emperor have both turned into myth, into literature, the subjects of tales of instruction, edification, and entertainment. No one in the narrator's latitudes has ever caught sight of the Northern savages. They have turned into children's bogeymen, figures of pedagogic fables to keep naughty children in line. The emperors in turn have ceased to be part of history. In the narrator's remote provinces, one does not know which emperor, or even which dynasty, rules at the moment. The timelessness of myth has absorbed imperial existence. The grim reality of the Oedipal authority figures, from "Urban World" to *The Trial,* is gone from Kafka's China, but a simultaneous process of attenuation has removed the longed-for "true" authority figure, the emperor, even further away from actual life than the dream to which he had been reduced in "An Imperial Message." In the main narrative of "The Great Wall of China," the emperor has become a mere holiday diversion—escapist literature frivolously interrupting the serious business of everyday life. And yet, at the same time, having ceased to be the subjects' obsession, the emperor, as the subject of literature and myth, has become the content and inspiration of that festive relaxation from which workaday life receives strength and sustenance for its renewal.

The people, the narrator tells us, lack the strength of imagination to raise the emperor from the misty abode of mythic timelessness into the present and presence of reality. It is, however, according to the narrator, precisely this weakness of the imagination that grants the people the freedom to pursue the happiness that ordinary life may hold. Indeed it is this "weakness" that enables them to be a people: "precisely this weakness seems to be one of the most important means of unifying our people; indeed, if one may dare to go so far to use this expression, it is, as it were, the very ground of our lives." And to reproach the people of being content with a merely mythical authority instead of a real one is tantamount to "shaking, not our conscience, but, what is far worse, our legs" (Kafka 1946, 82). Independence is the foundation of the soundness and well-being of empirical existence. With this concluding thought of his meditations, the narrator appears to justify paying any price for the good fortune of being left alone. Obsession with the aura of quasi-heavenly authority is not compatible with the individual's empirical life and welfare. The craving for it can be satisfied, to a degree, in myth and literature, but mundane existence flourishes best if free of the actual touch by such authority. Being eternally deprived of the father figure of its dreams is, by the same token, the people's protection and guarantee of survival. Absence of the emperor shields them from an embrace in which they would perish.

Yet, Kafka's narrator does not restrict himself to such a counsel of resigned self-sufficiency. While he demotes imperial authority to an unreal status, he raises an alternative authority to quasi-divine power and effectiveness. This parallel authority is the leadership of the momentous collective project of the building of the Great Wall. The leadership takes the place left vacant by the emperor as the real authority over Kafka's China. It is infinitely effective, wise, and everlasting. It possesses the attributes of divinity. Its plans and motivations are mysterious, beyond ordinary human ken, the subject of mere speculation and theorizing on the people's part. Yet it is made clear that this authority gives meaning to each individual's life insofar as he contributes to the overarching national project—the erection of the Great Wall. The leadership provides to each subject's life that superpersonal significance the emperor can no longer give. The building of the Great Wall in small, easily surveyable sections, capable of completion in a limited number of years, gives to each worker in the innumerable building teams a clear sense of individual accomplishment and fulfillment that lasts a lifetime. The leadership provides the Chinese people with a cause and purpose that links all provinces and unifies countless generations. It makes every fellow worker a brother for whom one is building "a wall of protection, and who would render lifelong thanks for it with all he had and did. Unity! Unity! Breast to breast, a round dance of the people, blood, no longer imprisoned in the paltry circulation of the individual body, but sweetly rolling on and yet ever returning through infinite China" (Kafka 1946, 70).

During the Nazi period, the perceptive critic Günther Anders pointed to this passage, among others, in accusing Kafka of allowing himself to be interpreted in a politically irrationalist, even "proto-Fascist" vein (Anders 1951, 28, 34). One cannot claim that Anders's accusation lacks all pertinence. However, we must likewise be aware that it applies at best to one extreme pole of Kafka's profoundly ambiguous world. The reproach overlooks the conjunction, we have shown, of the narrator's glorification of total national unification under a quasi-divine leadership with his laying bare the incompatibility of real omnipotent authority, as personified in the emperor, with individual and communal happiness and even survival.

Anders's charge of Kafka's crypto-totalitarianism loses still more credibility if we consider another tale dealing with the emperor/nomads dichotomy, which Kafka published under the title "Ein altes Blatt" ("An Ancient Page" or "An Old Manuscript"). In this text, the narrator's criticism targets the true or "ideal" authority figure, the emperor himself. The imperial administration, we are told, seems to have neglected the defenses of the empire and thus opened the floodgates to the nomadic hordes who have thus become the actual power in the realm. From the window of his palace, the emperor watches, without intervening, their savage doings. "Ideal" authority has forsaken and betrayed the people who have trusted it to protect them. The people will have to get rid of the nomads by their own effort. However, this hour of emancipation is not welcomed. The narrator, a member of the people, calls it "a misunderstanding . . . by which we shall perish" (Kafka 1994, 267). Kafka's spokesmen abhor autonomy. However, it is imposed upon them, against their will, when revered authority reveals itself as strangely callous or impotent.

What is most remarkable about "An Old Manuscript," in the context of our theme, is the emergence, for the first time in Kafka's work, of an explicit causal link between the two opposed aspects of authority. The narrator clearly shows that the benign aspect of power indeed entails the brutal one. It was the emperor's palace, he relates, that has attracted the nomads. It has been the reason they have invaded. Ideal authority, on which the people have always depended, is the very source from which ferocious power derives.

At the beginning of his late period, Kafka takes the exploration of this relationship further, in the parable "The Problem of Our Laws" (literally, "On the Question of the Laws"). The narrator, speaking again as the spokesman and consciousness of a community, as in so many texts of Kafka's middle and late period, points to two different kinds of authority ruling the commonwealth. One is the true authority, the ancient venerable laws; the other is the actual authority of the nobles who interpret the laws. The laws themselves are not known to the people who are governed by them. They are a secret kept by the interpreting nobility. True authority is inaccessible to the people. All they get to know is actual authority, that is, the nobles. The narrator calls this ignorance of and separation from their true authority a perpetual torment for the people. Its real cause is not their lack of self-government, but the inaccessibility of the authority that supposedly rules them. However, the narrator avers, the people do not hate the nobility for keeping knowledge of the laws from them. Instead, they hate themselves for not yet having been deemed worthy of receiving their revelation. They look forward to a future day when that will come to pass. Then the nobility will disappear. The tormenting distinction between true and actual authority—between the laws and their interpreters—will vanish. True and actual authority will be identical. Thus the people's maturing does not imply freedom to choose their own laws, but only the right to know the laws that are said to rule them. Here the authoritarian-religious character of the narrator's community becomes evident. Their "torment" is not the democrats' sense of frustration at having to obey laws that others have made for them without their consent. Their torment is more like the religious believer's anguish at being separated from God. They yearn for the happiness of coming face to face with the power whose absolute rule they cherish and adore.

However, there exists among the people a small group who deny the existence of the ancient laws. According to them, the laws are simply the will of the nobles. Actual authority is all there is, and no true authority hides behind it. This minority thus disputes the distinction that we have seen as a constant in Kafka's work. The minority stands in radical opposition to the eschatological expectation of the majority. For the minority, unified authority will not be achieved by the ultimate revelation of its "truth." For them, unity of authority has always already existed in the actuality of authority in those who practically wield power. Authority that is "true," but not actually evident, has never existed and never can exist. The position of the minority is one of extreme nominalism or antimetaphysical scepticism. In epistemological terms it corresponds to positivism, in theological terms to atheism. For them, one might say, God is nothing but the words of His priests. Yet, even they are far from being secular democrats. They, too, endorse the rule of the nobility. They merely insist that despotism should be openly and honestly acknowledged. For them no law exists outside the power that interprets and executes it.

The party that sees the caprice of the nobles as the sole source of law corresponds not only to the school of Positive Law, but also to modern theories of textuality. While the majority of the people assume that laws exist independently of their interpreters, the minority maintains that the only actualization a text can attain is its interpretation. A text does not exist completely independent of its readers. It needs the reader in order to be realized. The distinction between textual meaning arrived at by acts of interpretation and a meaning in itself, that is, a "true" or "correct" meaning independent of readers and interpreters, is for them as untenable as is, for empiricist philosophers, Kant's distinction between phenomena and the thing-in-itself from which phenomena supposedly issue. The minority party has, as it were, seen through Kafka's device of splitting the authority figure in two. However, it does not draw the conclusion that the modern reader would be likely to expect. It does not demand the abolition of the nobility and the establishment of self-government by the people. No one in the community of Kafka's narrator desires an overthrow of the nobles. An interpreter of literature—literally, an "interpreter of writing" or of "scripture," ("*Schriftgelehrter*")—in the text, sums up the reason: "The sole visible, indubitable law imposed upon us is the nobility, and we should deprive ourselves of that *single* law we have?" (Kafka 1946, 92; italics mine). What is assumed is an ineradicable desire for authority, for law imposed upon the people by a revered source, a source beyond themselves. Such authority, they hold, gives to their lives the only meaning and significance they have. To paraphrase Nietzsche's dictum in *The Genealogy of Morals,* Kafka's people prefer an authority that is specious to no authority at all. However, the fact of introducing the minority party's view at all does suggest to the reader that "true" or ideal authority is not a reality, but a need of the subject. It is the need to look for a meaning of life beyond oneself. If the people could only free themselves of this need—the reader might conclude—they would be free not only of a self-delusion, but of oppression by the nobles as well. External force does not withhold autonomy. It is the people who deny it to themselves. In that sense, the function of the text can be considered enlightening and emancipatory. It allows the reader to examine the opinions advanced in it and submit them to critical analysis. The reader is enabled to reflect upon the connection between submission to despotism and the search for a meaning of life supplied from outside the individual. The reader can choose whether she or he wishes to identify with any of the views expressed in the text or distance oneself from all. What the text does is allow the reader to see through and evaluate those views. The ultimate consequence of the split in Kafka's representation of authority is the reader's choice among alternative interpretations.

This becomes most clearly evident in the treatment that the theme of authority receives in Kafka's last novel, *The Castle.* Two Castle officials with nearly like-sounding names, Sordini and Sortini, represent two opposite faces of authority in the novel. Their names are in fact so similar that K. confuses them—a hint at the interchangeability of the two sides of authority that seem, on the surface, diametrically opposed.

Sordini is the official who, K. is told, several years prior to K.'s arrival had been in charge of the task of getting a land surveyor appointed. He had committed all his indefatigable and inexhaustible energies to that project. It is, of course, K.'s most ardent desire, and apparently also his desperate need, to get himself appointed land surveyor by the Castle. In Sordini, authority would thus have offered the protagonist a likely, or at least possible, fulfillment of his quest and given meaning to his life. Sordini would have been his redemption. Through him, authority acts as the individual wishes it to act. Sordini corresponds to the "true" father of "Urban World," the High Court of *The Trial,* the emperor of the China stories.

In Sordini's near-namesake, Sortini, authority appears in its most shockingly offensive and despotic guise. In an obscenely worded letter, Sortini, we are told, demanded that the beautiful Amalia, a girl of the village, give herself to him without delay. He asserts the time-honored right of all Castle officials. The women of the village simply must surrender to their desire. In Sortini, we meet that total disregard of the individual subject's rights, dignity, and humanity of which Kafka's actual authority figures always tend to make themselves guilty.

The striking resemblance and near-identity of the two names suggests a hidden identity of the benevolent and the revolting face of authority. In the novel, they are indeed two manifestations of the same power—the Castle. Benevolence and tyranny are both integral parts of it, and the one cannot appear without the other.

The close parallelism between the two bureaucrats also shows itself in the ineffectuality they have in common. Sordini is not able to get the land surveyor post approved, and Sortini, after Amalia tears up his letter defiantly and scorns his command, does not try to enforce it, but fades from the scene. Power seems to be in need of cooperation by its victims. If, as in Amalia's case, such cooperation is withheld, power turns powerless. Amalia receives no punishment for her assertion of autonomy. It is solely her family's dread of retribution by the Castle that makes them abject supplicants. They plead for a forgiveness they can never obtain because, as the Castle informs them, there is nothing to forgive. Thus while Amalia shows that she is free, her family's story shows that an overwhelming inner need for consideration by authority enslaves us to it.

K.'s case is the obverse of Amalia's. It shows that the desired, ideal face of authority fails to be effective in actuality. The actual face the Castle shows K. is eternal frustration of his quest. K., in close analogy to Amalia's family, endows authority with the power it has over him. It is K.'s insistence on being installed as the land surveyor that produces the Castle's power to deny it. His utter dependence on the authority of the Castle for the confirmation of his being what he claims to be, in a sense, *creates* the Castle as the content and substance that is to fill the void he is. Like the people, as interpreted by the "*Schriftgelehrter*" in "The Problem of Our Laws," K. chooses external authority to give meaning to his life. K.'s need for authority brings about its split into two opposed aspects. Authority is true when it seems to promise what he needs and seeks, and it is false when it denies it to him. His identity that he pursues can come to him only as a gift from the Castle. He has made the Castle the sole agency that can justify his existence.

Amalia, by contrast, has no need of such a gift. Unlike K., she is not a stranger. She was born into and has always been a member of the community in which she lives. She wants nothing from the Castle. Therefore, one is tempted to say about this most Proustian of Kafka's works, the Castle wants something from her, and desire makes it a potential aggressor and violator. For Amalia authority does not have an ideal face, since, far from desiring anything from it, she has only to defend and assert herself against its attack. In consequence, she, in contrast to K. and almost all of Kafka's other protagonists, does not see authority as dual, as split between ideal and actual, benign and wicked. She encounters it as unitary, as purely actual, bare of any ideal aspect, rapaciously desiring to dominate its subject. Power wants to take possession of her and, therefore, it needs her, the subject, and not, as is usual in Kafka, the other way around. Since it is authority that wants and needs *her,* she is enabled to disdain it and uphold her integrity. Her lack of the need for confirmation and approval by external power makes her invulnerable to it.

The writer of *The Castle* presents the reader with two contrasting alternatives of dealing with authority. One is Amalia's way, the other K.'s. Even though her family cannot match and live up to her courage, Amalia herself remains unbowed and inviolate. In her combat with the Castle, she emerges as the victor. K., on the other hand, who enslaves himself to his claim and tries all tricks to have himself accepted by the Castle, runs up against an unyielding wall and fails to get a single step nearer to his goal. The huge fragment that finds no terminating point reflects the time dimension of frustration.

The writer of *The Castle* does not take sides. He endows Amalia, in her self-sufficiency, with a degree of arrogant sterility that detracts somewhat from the reader's admiration of her brave integrity. At the same time, he gives K. a persistence, an unwavering determination, a resourcefulness, a readiness to sacrifice, and a willingness to learn and modify his tactics, with which we cannot help but sympathize and even come to admire. In this balancing of emotional effects emanating from two characters, each admirable and each objectionable for opposite reasons, Kafka's ambivalence toward the themes of freedom and authority decisively contributes to the huge emotional span of his work. This work accommodates two of our most fundamental, but mutually exclusive desires—our craving for separateness and self-determination, and our longing to find ourselves embraced and confirmed by a parentlike power that we place above and beyond ourselves.

BIBLIOGRAPHY

Anders, Günther. 1951. *Kafka. Pro und Contra. Die Prozess-Unterlagen*. Munich: C. H. Beck.

Kafka, Franz. 1946. *Beschreibung eines Kampfes. Novellen, Skizzen, Aphorismen aus dem Nachlass. Gesammelte Schriften*. Ed. Max Brod. Vol. 5, 2d ed. New York: Schocken Books.

———. 1953. *Hochzeitsvorbereitungen auf dem Lande und andere Prosa aus dem Nachlass*. Gesammelte Werke. Ed. Max Brod. New York: Schocken Books.

———. 1990a. *Der Prozess*. Ed. Malcolm Pasley. Frankfurt am Main: S. Fischer Lizenzausgabe von Schocken Books, New York.

———. 1990b. *Tagebücher*. Ed. Hans-Gerd Koch, Michael Müller, and Malcolm Pasley. Frankfurt am Main: S. Fischer Lizenzausgabe von Schocken Books, New York. (First edition Berlin, 1935.)

———. 1994. *Drucke zu Lebzeiten*. Ed. Wolf Kittler, Hans-Gerd Koch, and Gerhard Neumann. Frankfurt am Main: S. Fischer Lizenzausgabe von Schocken Books, New York.

OTHER ESSAYS ON KAFKA BY WALTER H. SOKEL

"Kafka's *Metamorphosis:* Rebellion and Punishment," in *Monatshefte: A Journal Devoted to the Study of German Language and Literature* 47(4) (1956): 203–14.

"Kafka als Expressionist. Zur Wiederkehr seines Geburtstags am 3. Juni 1963," in *Forum: Österreichische Monatsblätter für kulturelle Freiheit* 10(114) (1963): 288–90, 363–65.

"Kafka und Sartres Existenzphilosophie," in *Arcadia: Zeitschrift für Vergleichende Literaturwissenschaft* 5(3) (1970): 262–77.

"Franz Kafka as a Jew," in *Publications of the Leo-Baeck Institute: Year Book* 18 (1973): 233–38.

"Zwischen Drohung und Errettung. Zur Funktion Amerikas in Kafkas Roman 'Der Verschollene'," in *Amerika in der deutschen Literatur: Neue Welt—Nordamerika—USA.* Wolfgang Paulsen zum 65. Geburtstag. Ed. Sigrid Bauschinger, Horst Denkler, and Wilfried Malsch. Stuttgart: Reclam, 1975, 246–71.

"Kafka's Law and Its Renunciation. A Comparison of the Function of the Law in 'Before the Law' and 'The New Advocate'," in *Probleme der Komparatistik und Interpretation.* Festschrift für Andre von Gronicka zum 65. Geburtstag am 25.5.1977. Ed. Walter H. Sokel, Albert A. Kipa, and Hans Ternes. Bonn: Bouvier, 1978, 193–215.

"Frozen Sea and River of Narration: The Poetics behind Kafka's 'Breakthrough'," in *Newsletter of the Kafka Society of America* 7(1) (1983): 71–79, and in *New Literary History: A Journal of Theory and Interpretation* 17(2) (1986): 351–63.

"Two Views of 'Minority' Literature: Deleuze, Kafka, and the German-Jewish Enclave of Prague," in *Council on National Literatures, Quarterly World Report* 6(1–2) (1983): 5–8.

"Kafkas 'Der Prozess': Ironie, Deutungszwang, Scham und Spiel," in *Etudes Germaniques* 39(2) (1984): 175–93, and in *Deutsche Romane des 20. Jahrhunderts. Neue Interpretationen.* Ed. Paul Michael Lützeler. Königstein/Ts.: Athenäum, 1983, 110–27.

"The Wolfman and the Castle," in *Journal of the Kafka Society of America* 12(1–2) (1988): 64–68.

"Franz Kafka," in *European Writers: The Twentieth Century.* Ed. George Stade. Vol. 9. New York: Scribner's Sons, 1989, pp. 1151–79.

"Kafka and Modernism," in *Approaches to Teaching Kafka's Short Fiction.* Ed. Richard T. Gray. Vol. 51, *Approaches to Teaching World Literature.* New York: Modern Language Association of America, 1995, 21–34.

"Schuldig oder subversiv? Zur Schuldproblematik bei Kafka," in *Das Schuldproblem bei Franz Kafka. Kafka-Symposium 1993, Klosterneuburg.* Ed. Wolfgang Kraus and Norbert Winkler. Vol. 6, *Schriftenreihe der Franz-Kafka Gesellschaft.* Vienna-Cologne: Böhlau, 1995, 1–11.

"Kafka and the Twentieth Century: Its Discourses in His Work," in *Journal of the Kafka Society of America* 19(1/2) (1997): 4–8.

INDEX

Books in the Kritik: German Literary Theory and Cultural Studies Series

Walter Benjamin: An Intellectual Biography, by Bernd Witte, translated by James Rolleston, 1991

The Violent Eye: Ernst Jünger's Visions and Revisions on the European Right, by Marcus Paul Bullock, 1991

Fatherland: Novalis, Freud, and the Discipline of Romance, by Kenneth S. Calhoon, 1992

Metaphors of Knowledge: Language and Thought in Mauthner's Critique, by Elizabeth Bredeck, 1992

Laocoon's Body and the Aesthetics of Pain: Winckelmann, Lessing, Herder, Moritz, Goethe, by Simon Richter, 1992

The Critical Turn: Studies in Kant, Herder, Wittgenstein, and Contemporary Theory, by Michael Morton, 1993

Reading After Foucault: Institutions, Disciplines, and Technologies of Self in Germany, 1750–1830, edited by Robert S. Leventhal, 1994

Bettina Brentano-von Arnim: Gender and Politics, edited by Elke P. Frederiksen and Katherine R. Goodman, 1995

Absent Mothers and Orphaned Fathers: Narcissism and Abjection in Lessing's Aesthetic and Dramatic Production, by Susan E. Gustafson, 1995

Identity or History? Marcus Herz and the End of the Enlightenment, by Martin L. Davies, 1995

Languages of Visuality: Crossings between Science, Art, Politics, and Literature, edited by Beate Allert, 1996

Resisting Bodies: The Negotiation of Female Agency in Twentieth-Century Women's Fiction, by Helga Druxes, 1996

Locating the Romantic Subject: Novalis with Winnicott, by Gail M. Newman, 1997

Embodying Ambiguity: Androgyny and Aesthetics from Winckelmann to Keller, by Catriona MacLeod, 1997

The Freudian Calling: Early Viennese Psychoanalysis and the Pursuit of Cultural Science, by Louis Rose, 1998

By the Rivers of Babylon: Heinrich Heine's Late Songs and Reflections, by Roger F. Cook, 1998

Reconstituting the Body Politic: Enlightenment, Public Culture, and the Invention of Aesthetic Autonomy, by Jonathan M. Hess, 1999

The School of Days: Heinrich von Kleist and the Traumas of Education, by Nancy Nobile, 1999

Walter Benjamin and the Corpus of Autobiography, by Gerhard Richter, 2000

Heads or Tails: The Poetics of Money, by Jochen Hörisch, translated by Amy Horning Marschall, 2000

Dialectics of the Will: Freedom, Power, and Understanding in Modern French and German Thought, by John H. Smith, 2000

The Bonds of Labor: German Journeys to the Working World, 1890–1990, by Carol Poore, 2000

Schiller's Wound: The Theater of Trauma from Crisis to Commodity, by Stephanie Hammer, 2001

Goethe as Woman: The Undoing of Literature, by Benjamin Bennett, 2001

Peripheral Visions: The Hidden Stages of Weimar Cinema, edited by Kenneth S. Calhoon, 2001

Narrating Community after Kant, by Karin Schutjer, 2001

The Myth of Power and the Self: Essays on Franz Kafka, by Walter Sokel, 2001